Beyond WikiLeaks

Beyond WikiLeaks

Implications for the Future of Communications, Journalism and Society

Edited by

Benedetta Brevini
*Lecturer in Media Policy, Department of Journalism,
City University, London, UK*

Arne Hintz
*Lecturer, School of Journalism, Media and
Cultural Studies, Cardiff University, UK*

Patrick McCurdy
*Assistant Professor, Department of Communication,
University of Ottawa, Canada*

First published 2013 by
PALGRAVE MACMILLAN

Palgrave Macmillan in the UK is an imprint of Macmillan Publishers Limited,
registered in England, company number 785998, of Houndmills,
Basingstoke, Hampshire RG21 6XS.

Palgrave Macmillan in the US is a division of St Martin's Press LLC,
175 Fifth Avenue, New York, NY 10010.

Palgrave Macmillan is the global academic imprint of the above companies
and has companies and representatives throughout the world.

Palgrave® and Macmillan® are registered trademarks in the United States,
the United Kingdom, Europe and other countries

ISBN: 978–1–137–27572–1 hardback
ISBN: 978–1–137–27573–8 paperback

This book is printed on paper suitable for recycling and made from fully
managed and sustained forest sources. Logging, pulping and manufacturing
processes are expected to conform to the environmental regulations of the
country of origin.

A catalogue record for this book is available from the British Library.

A catalog record for this book is available from the Library of Congress.

10 9 8 7 6 5 4 3 2 1
22 21 20 19 18 17 16 15 14 13

Printed and bound in Great Britain by
CPI Antony Rowe, Chippenham and Eastbourne

This book is dedicated to freedom of speech advocates around the world

Contents

List of Tables

List of Figures

Foreword

Birgitta Jónsdóttir

Nothing is more powerful than an idea whose time has come.

– Victor Hugo

My first encounters with people from WikiLeaks occurred on December 1, 2009. Julian Assange and Daniel Domscheit-Berg were speaking at the same event as I. The event was hosted by the Icelandic Digital Freedom Society. WikiLeaks had become known in Iceland a few months earlier for leaking a loan book from Kaupthing, a large failed Icelandic international bank. The country was just waking up from its financial crash in 2008 that, for many, brought to bear the realization that everything we had put our trust in had failed us; academia, media, our regulatory bodies, parliament and heads of state.

When the Icelandic state broadcaster RUV was about to run a story based on the Kaupthing leak, the bank's resolution committee sought to have the loan book removed from the Internet and managed to secure a temporary injunction against its publication by RUV. The RUV news anchor, however, was so outraged at the gag order that instead of complying with it, he told his viewers about it and recommended that they go and investigate the loan book at the WikiLeaks website.

The leaked document provided a snapshot of Kaupthing's loans at a critical moment just before the bank failed. Confidential loan details in the document exposed the risks the failed bank and its largest customers were taking just weeks before the 2008 Icelandic financial meltdown. Alongside each loan, the leaked presentation provided a brief assessment of the risk tied to the loans and relations with many of the customers. A senior director from the bank sent WikiLeaks threatening letters that demanded that the site would take the leak down. Yet the WikiLeaks lawyer replied defiantly:

No. We will not assist the remains of Kaupthing, or its clients, to hide its dirty laundry from the global community. Attempts by Kaupthing or its agents to discover the source of the document in question may be a criminal violation of both Belgium source protection laws and the Swedish Constitution.

The heart of the talk by the WikiLeaks duo Daniel and Julian at the event we shared was not so much about WikiLeaks but an idea – an idea that impressed me to such a degree that I approached them later that day with a simple suggestion: "Let's do it." The idea had first been introduced to the same conference a year earlier by John Perry Barlow, a cyberlibertarian political activist and the co-founder of the Electronic Frontier Foundation (EFF). Julian and Daniel had developed the idea based on their own hands-on experience in relation to keeping information online, no matter what, and to protect their sources. The concept was to make Iceland a safe haven for online freedoms, including freedom of information, expression, and speech, based on the reality of the digital transformation. A transparency haven; a reverse tax haven.

If there was something Icelanders learned from the crisis, it was that the culture of secrecy is destructive and that we need more transparency and accountability. We needed a strong shield and encouragement for whistle-blowers and sources in order to be sure that a similar disaster never occurs again. And thus on Iceland's independence day, December 1, 2009, the journey began to develop new standards for freedom of expression and to counterstrike at the erosion of the very fundamental freedoms of a healthy democracy. We set into motion a team of experts within the legal scope of online freedoms, with the task of going on a mission searching for the best functioning laws from around the world, and we discussed our vision with parliamentarians and members of all parties. On June 16, 2010 the Icelandic Parliament unanimously passed the proposal for an Icelandic Modern Media Initiative (IMMI), tasking the government to introduce a new legislative regime consisting of source protection, whistle-blower protection, limits to prior restraint and libel, process protection, protection of historical records, and an ultra-modern Freedom of Information Act. The various components of the proposal are currently being written into law by a special committee appointed by the minister in charge.

During the time when we were preparing and researching the groundwork for IMMI, I worked closely with Julian Assange on a daily basis. In February 2010 he showed me something in a cafe facing the Icelandic Parliament that would change my life forever. It was a video shot from the cockpit of an American helicopter, showing people being gunned down by that very helicopter in Iraq. It was so shocking to watch that even hardened investigative journalists would shed tears while being exposed to it for the first time. Thus begun my participation in one of WikiLeaks' projects that became known as *Collateral Murder*, a project that would etch WikiLeaks into the historical records on a global scale.

I put my name to it as a co-producer and helped to realize its release with maximum exposure. I felt it was of utmost importance that the video showing war crimes in Iraq in such a stark way would be brought into the public domain, in the naïve hope that it might help end the war.

The video showed, among other horrific scenes, the killing of Reuters employee Saeed Chmagh, and of Iraqi citizens trying to get him to a hospital, including a man driving his children to school who had stopped his van in order to bring the wounded man out of the killing fields of New Baghdad. Despite the obvious war crimes exposed in this leak, no one has been held accountable. Instead, the US government has prosecuted those who have exposed the information, particularly alleged whistle-blower Bradley Manning, and most of us who put our names to the release of the video are a subject of investigation by the WikiLeaks Task Force (better known as WTF) and a grand jury in the United States.

The American government demanded access to my personal Twitter messages, my IP numbers, and various other personal data in a desperate attempt to criminalize everyone who volunteered for WikiLeaks in 2009/2010. Not only was Twitter forced to hand over my personal data, but so were three other companies which the courts are refusing to reveal to me. I have, in my battle to protect my personal data, been represented by lawyers from two amazing American organizations, the EFF and ACLU (American Civil Liberties Union). The unfortunate result of this battle is that we have lost at every level of the court system, effectively legalizing it for the federal government to probe anyone's data that floats in the data clouds above American territory. The court ruling suggests that we, the people who use the Internet, do not have permission to watch our own backs but have to rely on social media companies to look after us. It is clear that it might not always be within the scope, interest or even abilities of such companies to do so.

Just a few days before writing this foreword, military documents obtained through a Freedom of Information Act request and posted online by WikiLeaks suggest that the US government has designated WikiLeaks and its founder Julian Assange as "enemies of the state" – the same legal category as Al Qaeda and other foreign military adversaries. It is not clear if I, for example, as a former volunteer for WikiLeaks and vocal supporter, am now a formal "Enemy of the State." What of other people or volunteers in a similar position?

However, the conflict around WikiLeaks is much more than a conflict between people, or between an institution and a group of activists. As the Icelandic case has demonstrated, it is about the use of technology

for social change, democratic progress, and globally connected communication – and about restrictions to all these. On a tiny island in the
North Atlantic Ocean with only 300,000 souls, and speaking an ancient
language that no one but we understand, these opportunities seem
particularly vivid. For me, discovering the Internet in 1995 transformed
creative and intellectual claustrophobia into international connections
and opened up a new planet of possibilities, free, wild, and untamable.
A poem I wrote in 1996 included the words:

> The countries of the world
> are merging
> borders falling
> cultures crossing
>
> Through the void
> of cyberspace
> earth is shrinking
> sense for distance changing
>
> One race
> emerging
>
> Floating through space
> virtually real
>
> I feel home
> in every corner of the world
>
> Expressions
> through symbols
> we can all understand

Imagine what your ideal free world would be. A blueprint for how we
could interact, collaborate, share and trade freely beyond race, class,
social status, faith, borders. Now imagine if this world already exists.
The online world of the Internet employs many features that we would
like to see in the offline world, and this is why we fight to keep it free
from the walls that politicians and corporations have erected. But this
world is under attack. The industrialization of the Internet is in full
swing as those in power begin to put the same reigns and harnesses on
it as are in place in the real world. Our freedoms online are eroding and

melting at the same alarming rate as the permafrost and the ancient glaciers. There is no time to lose. We must understand what is at stake.

We would be sailing obliviously at even greater speed into the eradication of online freedoms, had the icebreaker WikiLeaks not challenged our indifference and silence. WikiLeaks gave the words "freedom of information, expression, and the press," "whistle-blowers," and "source protection" new meaning, new understanding, and a new life in the digitalized reality.

The Internet has allowed us to understand that the world is increasingly globalized, financially and economically, as well as in terms of pollution and food. Through facilitating the coordination and sharing of information and collective efforts, the Internet has also provided us with a repertoire of tools to fight the lords of the offline world. As more people gain access and develop the skills to leverage the capacities of the Internet to push for positive social change, the ability to transform the offline world grows. People have come to understand that the all-embracing offline systems are old and rusty self-serving mechanisms of the global and local power elite. With the acts of WikiLeaks and its sources, the world became not only more informed, but also more inspired to rise up against these forces.

One of this book's key themes is activism. The Internet has allegedly given us the tools to empower ourselves in the real world, with knowledge beyond the cultural conditioning we acquire within our own culture. The Internet has given us the tools to work together beyond traditional borders, and it has allowed us to create windows into the real world that reach far beyond our cultural beliefs about other countries. However, this world beyond borders is now under serious threat, a threat that is growing at an alarming rate. Those who hold the reins of power in our world have discovered that the Internet needs to be tamed, like the rest of the world, and brought under their control – to be industrialized in the same manner that other media have been brought under control by industry and the state. Yet, as these untouchables try to hide their secrets for the chosen few, those secrets keep spilling out in a whirlwind of letters in every digital corner of the world. They sweep through the streets of Iraq, Afghanistan, Egypt, Tunisia, Greece, China, Iceland, Spain, Iran, and the United States. They fan the fires of a hope that believes in the free spirit within the wilderness of the Internet.

The Internet has given people access to information that should remain in the public domain; yet it is a trending policy within the belly of the all-embracing system to make everything secret by default. It is time to reverse this tendency and create a consensus about the process of keeping secrets. Transparency and open access to information are the only real pressures on governments to remain true democracies. If you don't have freedom of information and expression, you are not living in a democracy; rather it is ruled by dictatorship with many heads.

As the media discourse has focused on the personalities of WikiLeaks, attention has been diverted from the historical significance of the leaks. Instead, if we allow ourselves to step away from the persons, we can see that the broader achievement of WikiLeaks was to put freedom of information on the agenda, all over the world, and make whistle-blowing a viable option in the fight against criminal behaviour in the public, military, and private sectors.

More than focusing on the plight of the organization WikiLeaks, this book serves as a reminder that there is a world beyond. This world includes, for example, one very brave individual who will have served 1001 days and nights in military prison before he will face trial: Bradley Manning. Many see his harsh treatment – he was kept on suicide watch for nearly a year – as a signal to other whistle-blowers to not blow the whistle if they witness a crime. The US Administration is on a witch-hunt mission against whistle-blowers. No other president has gone after as many whistle-blowers as Obama. He claimed that Manning was guilty when the latter had not even stood trial, making a mockery of any expectations of a fair trial. My parliamentary group nominated Manning for a Nobel Peace Prize in 2012 and will do so again in 2013. I firmly believe that blowing the whistle on war crimes is not a crime but a call of duty. Manning's alleged contribution has reached to every corner of the world, the real impact of which will never been fully understood or known.

Many feel that mainstream media have failed them and are turning to alternative media sources. Personally, I am shocked by the lack of courage shown by American media in relation to WikiLeaks. Shocked because WikiLeaks simply acted as the "safe box" in cyberspace that received the brown envelope from the source and handed it over to the media. Shocked by the ignorance of the media, for it is obvious to me that if WikiLeaks or the people behind it will be taken down, it will be harder for other media to stand on firm ground when under attack for publishing leaked material from whistle-blowers and secret sources.

To be sure, the WikiLeaks age has also ushered in an age where corporations and specialized law firms are using a litany of libel laws, super injunctions, prior restraints, gag orders, and out-of-court settlements to attack and gag journalists, writers, publishers, and the rest of the media. Important stories have vanished from the public domain, altering the historical record and denying the public the opportunity to be informed about the activities of the most influential corporations and politicians in our world. These modern-day book burnings occur daily. Through lawmaking and creative resistance we must do everything in our power to stop them.

The evolution and transformation of our democracies depends on an informed public having access to the information that should remain and be brought into the public domain. WikiLeaks set the tone; now it is up to each and every one of us to use the information provided and to help create safe passage for more to come, be it from local sources or from services such as WikiLeaks. This includes creating a legal environment that supports and safeguards the freedoms we hold dear as the pillars for healthy democracies. If we manage to legalize freedom of information, expression, and speech to such a degree that transparency of the state is the norm we won't need websites like WikiLeaks.

I left WikiLeaks a while ago for various reasons. I might not agree with how it has developed, but its significance remains the same. We need many more leak sites until we have real laws in place that protect content, whistle-blowers, sources, and journalists. The culture of free flow of information is still strong online, and every attempt to block, hinder, or erase information is met with increased creativity. Yet those of us who care for freedom of information have to step up our quest to remove the gags, tear down the firewalls, and dissolve the invisible filters.

Our flagship known as WikiLeaks might be dented, for the walls to pass have been great and mighty as it took on some of the most powerful giants in our world. But WikiLeaks did not sink and has thus shown the rest of the world that the story of David and Goliath is not a myth but reality. Aptitude, speed, and resilience are trademarks of this new culture. This book will bring you closer to understanding how and why WikiLeaks became legend and how it has changed our world. Within it are words by some of the people that have shown they have a comprehensive understanding of why WikiLeaks is important and why it will remain important during these extraordinary times – times in our human history when nothing is what it seems and when the people of this world have started to understand that this century belongs to us, the people. Information is the true power. WikiLeaks provided us with this understanding.

Reykjavík, Iceland
October 2012

Acknowledgements

We would like to thank the International Association for Media and Communication Research (IAMCR) for opening up an initial space for a conversation about WikiLeaks at its July 2011 conference in Istanbul. We would also like to thank our colleagues for their support and feedback on the project. Of course, the book would not be possible without the chapters from our contributors, and we would like to thank them for delivering quality pieces within such tight deadlines. Further, we would like to thank our families and friends for their love and support throughout this project, and their patience during the absences and long hours spent away from home, or hidden inside our homes, working to complete this. Finally, we wish to acknowledge the enormous efforts by numerous activists – who are sometimes named and known, but most often unnamed and unknown – towards creating projects such as WikiLeaks, and thereby expanding information sources, challenging gatekeepers, and creating the processes that we as academics observe and analyse. Thank you to Pamela Campagna and Katie Raso for their efforts to help us find a suitable cover design.

Notes on Contributors

Stuart Allan is Professor of Journalism in the Media School, Bournemouth University, United Kingdom, where he is also the director of the Centre for Journalism and Communication Research. He has published widely on a range of topics, including the emergence and development of news on the Internet, the online reporting of crisis, conflict and war, science journalism (special interest in nanotechnology), and citizen journalism. He is currently conducting a research study examining the use of digital imagery in news reporting during times of crisis. His most recent book, *Citizen Witnessing*, will be published in 2013 by Polity.

Julian Assange is the editor-in-chief of WikiLeaks. He has made public speeches and participated in conferences in many parts of the world to speak about media freedom, investigative journalism, and censorship issues. He has received a number of awards and nominations, including the 2009 Amnesty International Media Award for publishing material about extrajudicial killings in Kenya and Readers' Choice for *Time* Magazine's 2010 Person of the Year.

David Banisar is Senior Legal Counsel for Article 19: Global Campaign for Free Expression (http://www.article19.org/), a London-based human rights group. He has worked in the field of information policy for over 20 years and is considered a leading expert on the right to information, freedom of expression, media policy, whistle-blowing, communications security, and privacy. Previously he was the director of the FOI Project at Privacy International, a non-resident fellow at the Center for Internet and Society at Stanford Law School, a research fellow at the Harvard Information Infrastructure Project at Kennedy School of Government, Harvard University, and a visiting research fellow at the School of Law, University of Leeds. He was a co-founder and policy director of the Electronic Privacy Information Center in Washington, DC.

Yochai Benkler is the Berkman Professor of Entrepreneurial Legal Studies at Harvard, and faculty co-director of the Berkman Center for Internet and Society. Since the 1990s he has played a part in characterizing the role of information commons and decentralized collaboration in innovation, information production, and freedom in the networked economy and society. His books include *The Wealth of Networks: How Social Production Transforms Markets and Freedom* (2006), which won academic awards from the American Political Science Association, the American Sociological Association, and the McGannon award for social and ethical relevance in communications. His work is socially engaged, winning him the Electronic Frontier Foundation's Pioneer Award for 2007, Public Knowledge's IP3 Award in 2006, and the Ford Foundation Visionaries Award in 2011. *The Wealth of Networks* is also anchored in the realities of markets, and has been cited as "perhaps the best work yet about the fast moving, enthusiast-driven Internet" by the *Financial Times* and named best business book about the future in 2006 by *Strategy + Business*. His most recent book is *The Penguin and the Leviathan: How Cooperation Triumphs over Self-Interest.*

Benedetta Brevini is Lecturer in Media policy and Journalism in the Department of Journalism of City University, London. Her research addresses a range of current issues in international media policy and the political economy of online media. Her work has appeared in international publications such as *European Journal of Communication, Interaction: Studies in Communication and Culture, Westminster Papers in Communication and Culture,* and *Political Communication (Polcom).* Benedetta holds a PhD from the University of Westminster, a master's in Communication Policy and Regulation from the London School of Economics, and an LLM from the University of Modena. Her book *Public Service Broadcasting Online: A Comparative European Policy Study of PSB 2.0* will be published in 2013. Before joining academia, she worked as a journalist in Milan, New York, and London and she currently writes for the *Guardian's* "Comment is free."

Gabriella (Biella) Coleman is the Wolfe Chair in Scientific and Technological Literacy in the Art History and Communication Studies Department at McGill University. Trained as an anthropologist, she examines the ethics of online collaboration/institutions as well as the role of the law and digital media in sustaining various forms of political activism. Her first book, *Coding Freedom: The Aesthetics and Ethics of Hacking* (2013), was published by Princeton University Press. She is currently working on a new book on Anonymous and digital activism. As the most renowned international expert on the cyber-activist network Anonymous, she has appeared in the media and as conference speaker worldwide.

Hopeton S. Dunn is Professor of Communications Policy and Digital Media at the University of the West Indies in Jamaica. Professor Dunn is the Director of the University's Caribbean Institute of Media and Communication (CARIMAC) and of the Mona ICT Policy Centre. He is the chairman of the Broadcasting Commission of Jamaica and a former secretary general of the International Association for Media and Communication Research (IAMCR).

Chris Elliott is the *Guardian's* readers' editor. Elliott joined the *Sunday Telegraph* in 1983 as a reporter before becoming its home affairs correspondent in 1985. He went on to work as a reporter and then chief reporter for the *Sunday Correspondent* and then as an assistant news editor at *The Times*. Chris joined the *Guardian* news desk in 1995, and progressed to the roles of executive editor in 1998 and then managing editor in 2000.

Francesca Fanucci is a lawyer in International and EU Law with a focus on freedom of expression, access to information and media pluralism. She is currently Senior Associate at Free Expression Associates (www. foeassociates.com) and consultant for the Open Society Foundations. She has previously been an associate at Global Partners & Associates, as well as a project manager and Latin America programme coordinator for ARTICLE 19. She has been a legal analyst and researcher in corporate law for global and European public affairs consultancies in Europe (United Kingdom, Belgium, Italy), North and West Africa (Egypt, Cameroon), North America (United States) and South America (Argentina, Chile, Ecuador, Peru, Venezuela).

Amy Goodman is the host and executive producer of *Democracy Now!*, a national daily independent award-winning news program airing on over 1,000 public television and radio stations worldwide. *Time* Magazine named *Democracy Now!* its "Pick of the Podcasts," along with NBC's *Meet the Press*. Goodman is the first journalist to receive the Right Livelihood Award, widely known as the "Alternative Nobel Prize," for "developing an innovative model of truly independent grassroots political journalism that brings to millions of people the alternative voices that are often excluded by the mainstream media."

Arne Hintz is Lecturer at the School of Journalism, Media and Cultural Studies at Cardiff University, United Kingdom. He was previously a Research Fellow at McGill University, Montreal, and Program Director of the Center for Media and Communication Studies at Central European University in Budapest. His research connects communication policy, media activism, citizen media, and technological change. He is Chair of the Community Communication Section, and Vice-Chair of the Global Media Policy Working Group, of the International Association for Media and Communication Research (IAMCR). He has a practical background as journalist, media activist, and communication rights advocate. His publications include *Civil Society Media and Global Governance* (2009).

Birgitta Jónsdóttir is a member of the Icelandic Parliament for the Movement and chairperson of the International Modern Media Institute. She has worked as a volunteer for various organizations including WikiLeaks, Saving Iceland, and Friends of Tibet in Iceland. She carries on being an activist in Parliament, a Poet and a Pirate. She organized Iceland's first online broadcast in 1996, was the first female Icelandic web developer and has worked as a publisher in cyberspace for Beyond Borders.

Geert Lovink is a Dutch-Australian media theorist, Internet critic and author of *Zero Comments* (2007) and *Networks Without a Cause* (2012). Since 2004 he has been a research professor ("lector") at the School for Communication and Media Design (CMDA), Amsterdam University of Applied Sciences (HvA), where he is the founding director of the Institute of Network Cultures (www.networkcultures.org). His institute organizes conferences, publications, and related research networks on topics such as the projects Video Vortex on online video, Society of the Query on search, urban screens, Critical Point of View on Wikipedia and Unlike Us on alternatives in social media. He also teaches in the new media master's program at Media studies, University of Amsterdam, and is media theory professor at the European Graduate School (www.egs.edu).

Lisa Lynch is Assistant Professor of Journalism at Concordia University. Her research is situated at the intersection between culture, technology, and political change. As part of this work, she has been researching and presenting on WikiLeaks since early 2008. Her article "We're going to crack the world open: WikiLeaks and the future of investigative reporting" (*Journalism Practice*, 4.3) was one of the first academic articles on WikiLeaks and explored the relationship of the media to the site at a moment when Assange and his project were still unknown to many journalists.

Patrick McCurdy is Assistant Professor in the Department of Communication at the University of Ottawa, Canada. He is interested in the representation of politically contentious issues and correlating actions of political actors in an age of media saturation. Patrick holds a PhD from the London School of Economics and Political Science (LSE), awarded in

2009. His thesis focused on how radical social movement actors think about and interact with media at the site of protest. It was selected as one of the LSE History of Thought Theses that showcase theses deemed as having contributed to the development of thought at the LSE. Patrick's work has been published in several peer reviewed journals such as the *International Journal of Communication* and *Critical Discourse Studies*. His co-edited book *Mediation and Social Movements* was published by Intellect in 2012; his new co-authored book, "Protest Camps," will be published by Zed in 2013. He can be found on Twitter at @pmmcc.

Stefania Milan is Assistant Professor of Data Journalism at the Department of Communication and Information Sciences, Tilburg University, the Netherlands. She is also a fellow at the Citizen Lab, Munk School of Global Affairs, University of Toronto. Stefania holds a PhD in Political and Social Sciences from the European University Institute. Her research focuses on the interplay between technology and society, with an emphasis on social movements, radical Internet activism, and the politics of code. Stefania taught communications governance, digital technologies, and digital research methods at the University of Lucerne, Switzerland, and at the Central European University, Hungary. Her co-authored textbook *Media/Society* was published by Sage in 2010. Her new book on social movements and technology will be published by Palgrave Macmillan in 2013.

Graham Murdock is Professor of Culture and Economy at the Department of Social Sciences at Loughborough University, Professor of Sociology at the University of Auckland, and Adjunct Professor at the Graduate School of Business at Curtin University. His work in the critical political economy of culture and communications has played a leading role in developing contemporary perspectives in the field. He has held the Bonnier Chair at the University of Stockholm and the Teaching Chair at the Free University of Brussels and has been a Visiting Professor at the Universities of California, Mexico City, Leuven, and Bergen, where he taught for a decade. His work is available in 19 languages. Major collections of his essays have recently appeared in Poland and South Korea. His recent books include (as co-author) *The GM Debate: Risk, Politics and Public Engagement* (2007), and (as co-editor) *Digital Dynamics: Engagements and Disconnections* (2010), *The Idea of the Public Sphere* (2010), and *The Blackwell Handbook of Political Economy of Communication* (2011).

Patrice Riemens is a geographer and currently political adviser of the Waag Society in Amsterdam and board member of the Antenna

Foundation in Nijmegen (NL). As propagator of Open Knowledge and Free Software, he has been involved as "FLOSSopher" (a "philosopher" of the Free/Libre and Open Source Software movements) for the Tactical Technology Collective. He is also member of the Dutch hackers collective Hippies from Hell.

Chindu Sreedharan is Lecturer in Journalism and Communication, and the programme coordinator for MA International Journalism at the Media School, Bournemouth University, United Kingdom. Formerly a journalist, he holds a PhD in conflict journalism – specifically, on the reportage of the Kashmir crisis in Indian and Pakistani newspapers. His research interests include media coverage of crisis situations, peace journalism, and social media. He blogs at http://www.chindu.net and is on Twitter as @chindu.

Ibrahim Saleh is Convenor of Political Communication and senior lecturer at the Centre for Film and Media Studies, University of Cape Town, South Africa, a Fulbright scholar, a senior media expert on the Middle East and North Africa (MENA), editor of global media journal, African Edition and co-editor of *Journal of Applied Journalism and Media Studies*. Saleh's research includes monographs and anthologies with most of his research in indexed publications. Saleh's third book was published in 2006: *Prior to the Eruption of the Grapes of Wrath in the Middle East: The Necessity of Communicating Instead of Clashing*. Saleh has received several international prizes such as the Carnegie Research Award (2010), Fulbright Certificate of Merit (2009), the World Association of Public Opinion Research (WAPOR) in 2007, and the Arab-US Association for Communication Educators (AUSACE) in 2005 and 2006. Saleh chairs the Journalism Research and Education Section of the International Association for Media and Communication Research (IAMCR).

Einar Thorsen is Senior Lecturer in Journalism and Communication, and the programme coordinator for MA International Journalism and New Media at the Media School, Bournemouth University, United Kingdom. His work is concerned with citizen involvement in online journalism, particularly during crisis and conflicts, and in response to political and environmental change. He conducted research on *BBC News Online* during the 2005 and 2010 United Kingdom General Elections, analysing news sources and opportunities for citizens to contribute to public discourse and democratic life. He co-edited *Citizen Journalism: Global Perspectives* (2009) and has published research on BBC

News Online, Wikinews and WikiLeaks. His website is http://journal-ismstudies.info/, and he is on Twitter as @einarthorsen.

Dwayne Winseck is Professor at the School of Journalism and Communication, with a cross-appointment to the Institute of Political Economy, Carleton University, Ottawa, Canada. His research focuses on the political economies and history of communication and media, surveillance and national security, democracy and globalization. He is a columnist for the Globe and Mail, and maintains a highly-regarded blog, Mediamorphis (dwmw.wordpress.com). His book (co-authored with Robert Pike), *Communication and Empire: Media, Markets and Globalization, 1860–1930* (2007), was awarded the Canadian Communication Association's book-of-the-year prize in 2008. He is also co-editor, with Dal Yong Jin, of *Political Economies of the Media: the Transformation of the Global Media Industries* (2011). He can be found on Twitter as @mediamorphis.

Jillian C. York is Director for International Freedom of Expression at the Electronic Frontier Foundation (EFF). She specializes in free-speech issues in the Arab world, and is also particularly interested the effects of corporate intermediaries on freedom of expression and anonymity, as well as the disruptive power of global online activism. Prior to joining EFF, Jillian spent three years at Harvard's Berkman Center for Internet & Society, where she worked on several projects, including the OpenNet Initiative. Jillian writes regularly about free expression and activism for a variety of publications, including *Al Jazeera, PBS MediaShift*, and the *Guardian*. She can frequently be found blogging or tweeting, as @jilliancyork.

Slavoj Žižek is a senior researcher at the Institute of Sociology, University of Ljubljana, Slovenia, and a visiting professor at a number of American universities (Columbia, Princeton, New School for Social Research, New York University, University of Michigan). He obtained his PhD in philosophy in Ljubljana, studying psychoanalysis. He also studied at the University of Paris. Žižek is a cultural critic and philosopher who is internationally known for his innovative interpretations of Jacques Lacan. He is admired as a true "manic excessive" and has been called the "Elvis Presley" of philosophy. He is author of *The Indivisible Remainder, The Sublime Object of Ideology, The Metastases of Enjoyment, Looking Awry: Jacques Lacan through Popular Culture, The Plague of Fantasies,* and *The Ticklish Subject*.

Introduction

Benedetta Brevini, Arne Hintz, and Patrick McCurdy

We live in fascinating times. Technological, social, and political changes have created new opportunities for people to communicate and exchange information; participatory culture continues to expand in many shapes and forms, from Wikipedia to participatory political practices; and campaigns for transparency and openness are challenging established administrative routines. Yet, while such changes create opportunities for some, they pose challenges for others, many of which strike at the very heart of traditional power relations and structures. Although the extent to which the rise of the network society has altered relations is debatable, the fact that societal changes are afoot is undeniable. The rise and legacy of the online transparency and whistle-blowing website WikiLeaks offers a lens through which we can try and understand such changes. As WikiLeaks' release of classified information becomes a historical moment and its repercussions become gradually clearer, it is useful to start reflecting on the broader implications of WikiLeaks' practices and actions. What lesson does it represent for journalism, policy making, transparency activism, and social change? How does it help us identify transformations in these fields? What are the responsibilities, the consequences, and the changes brought by the freeing of an unprecedented amount of information?

To embark on this reflection, *Beyond WikiLeaks* has brought together a select group of international authors. The book's contributors include renowned scholars in the field of media and communications, international experts on key areas affected by WikiLeaks, and "insiders" who were directly involved with WikiLeaks or its media partners. Their contributions range from shorter pieces, recounting practical experiences and focusing on specific aspects of the WikiLeaks story, to longer, elaborate academic analyses of the broader social, political, and communicative subjects that WikiLeaks touches upon.

1

The chapters discuss a variety of such issues, from changes in journalism to new developments in online activism, from questions of political economy to trends in policy, and from the representation of whistle-blowing to its social and political effects in places like the Middle East. Together, these themes, as well as the variety of practical and theoretical approaches taken by the authors, enable us to explore the richness and wideness of the consequences of the WikiLeaks saga.

A history of WikiLeaks

WikiLeaks was founded in 2006 as an online platform for whistle-blowers and for publishing information that is censored by public authorities and private actors. Its goal has been to harness the speed, interactivity, and global reach of the Internet to provide a fast and secure mechanism to anonymously submit information, and to make that information accessible to a global audience. In its first few years of existence, WikiLeaks electronically published a range of documents of varying significance that had mixed media impact. Revelations included secret Scientology texts; a report documenting extensive corruption by the family of former Kenyan President Daniel Arap Moi; proof that British company Trafigura had been illegally dumping toxic waste in Côte d'Ivoire (a story that the British media became legally barred from reporting); the financial dealings of Icelandic banks that led to the collapse of the country's economy (here, too, local media had been banned by court order from reporting on the issue); the private e-mails of then US Republican vice presidential candidate Sarah Palin; member lists of a British right–wing party; the Internet filter lists of several countries; and many other disclosures of information previously hidden from the public eye. In hindsight, these releases, which occurred between 2006 and 2009, stand as a warm-up for the torrent of information WikiLeaks was to unleash in 2010, a year that would establish WikiLeaks as a household name and see its founder lambasted by some as a traitor and high-tech terrorist and celebrated by others as a hero and leading transparency activist.

On April 5, 2010, WikiLeaks published a video online that it evocatively titled *Collateral Murder*, an edited version of a classified US army video taken from an American Apache helicopter. The video is of a controversial 2007 US Baghdad air strike that resulted in the deaths of Iraqi civilians along with two Reuters employees. On July 25 – now in collaboration with established media organizations the *New York Times,* the *Guardian* and *Der Spiegel* – WikiLeaks published the Afghan War Logs, and on October 22 it released the Iraq War Logs, altogether almost 500,000 documents and field reports that provided an unprecedented and comprehensive account of the two wars and revealed thousands of unreported deaths, including many US army killings of civilians. Finally, on November 28, WikiLeaks and its partner newspapers began publishing select US diplomatic cables in what became known as Cablegate. Taken from a pool of over 250,000 cables, the dispatches offered a fascinating perspective on international diplomacy. They revealed many backroom deals among governments, and between governments and companies; US spy practices on UN officials; cover-ups of military air strikes; and numerous cases of government corruption, for example in Middle Eastern and North African (MENA) countries, where the revelations fuelled the growing anger amongst populations at their national elites. Nine months after the first releases by partner newspapers, WikiLeaks made the full tranche of cables available on its website. It has since published other material, such as the Guantánamo Bay Files, information about the digital surveillance industry (Spyfiles) and e-mails from political figures and companies tied to Syria (Syria Files). However, in the wake of Cablegate, WikiLeaks operations became increasingly hampered by government investigations of its staff (particularly investigations of founder and editor-in-chief Julian Assange), internal strife, and extralegal economic blockades that have choked WikiLeaks' access to financial resources. WikiLeaks has seen an onslaught of attacks from both public and private actors, sustained attempts to shut down its operations, and even calls for Julian Assange's assassination.

Analysing WikiLeaks

A growing number of publications have emerged in the wake of the Cablegate releases and have described the organization, the major releases of 2010/2011, or have focused on specific aspects of WikiLeaks' activities. These include the first post-Cablegate book *The Age of WikiLeaks* by journalist Greg Mitchell, whose blog was one of the prime information sources on all things Cablegate during the most intense period of releases (Mitchell, 2011); *Inside WikiLeaks,* by disgruntled former member Daniel Domscheit-Berg, who gave a personal account of his time as Julian Assange's colleague (Domscheit-Berg, 2011); and the accounts by WikiLeaks' former media partners from the *Guardian* and the *New York Times* (Leigh and Harding, 2011; Star and Keller, 2011). Rosen (2010) has reflected on the emergence of the "stateless news organization," while others have written about how WikiLeaks might "lead us to mobilise ourselves to bring about a different functioning of power" (Žižek, 2011). Other authors have highlighted the organization's devotion to transparency and justice (Sifry, 2011), and have analysed its contribution to the evolution of news-making and journalism (Beckett and Ball, 2012).

Beyond the information that it has published, WikiLeaks has received significant attention for its peculiar characteristics, its ethics, organizational practices, and personalities. Rooted in hacktivism and in ethics of radical transparency, exploiting technological expertise and opportunities, and carrying the "wiki" concept of open publishing and collaborative work in its name, WikiLeaks connects with both an alternative countercultural and a digital citizen media model, similar to Indymedia, which had introduced easy participatory content production (what later came to be called "Web 2.0") at the turn of the millennium.

Beyond WikiLeaks

Beyond WikiLeaks provides a platform to discuss the richness and wideness of the consequences of the WikiLeaks narrative. Chapters 1–5 reflect on WikiLeaks' relationship to journalism and on what the WikiLeaks case suggests about the challenges and opportunities that established and emerging media organizations face at this historic juncture. Chapters 6–10 are concerned more explicitly with the effect of the WikiLeaks model on dominant articulations of power in contemporary societies, and they investigate how WikiLeaks challenges the current balance between openness and secrecy in domestic and international politics. Authors of these chapters question the policy implications of the formal and informal pressures and mechanisms deployed by governments to control information, and they suggest which policy environment we should promote to safeguard freedom of information and the communicative rights of citizens.

Finally, Chapters 11–15 examine whether WikiLeaks has ushered in a new generation of social movements and online activism. What type of media activism can be seen to have emerged in the wake of WikiLeaks activities? Are we witnessing new forms of engagement, new organizational models, and new repertoires of action, or is WikiLeaks-induced activism just an extension of the potential of Web-based resources to existing mobilization modes? Following the characterization of social change activism in the WikiLeaks age, authors also discuss a concrete instance of political change – the Arab Spring – and explore WikiLeaks' role in this historic uprising. The book closes with a conversation between Slovenian philosopher Slavoj Žižek – labelled by the *National Review* as "the most dangerous political philosopher in the West" – and Julian Assange, editor-in-chief of WikiLeaks. The book thereby gives the last word to the person who has been at the centre of the WikiLeaks saga and to a prominent observer and commentator, and we listen to how they expand and deepen the discussion of the impact of WikiLeaks on journalism, activism, politics, and society.

The chapters

The book opens with Yochai Benkler's provocative thesis on the rise of the networked fourth estate. Benkler outlines the downward economic spiral of the traditional news industry. Yet, while traditional models and identities of journalism are in jeopardy, WikiLeaks, Benkler argues, signals the rise of a networked fourth estate. Stemming from a collection of broad trends within the networked public sphere, this new web of media interactions combines elements of the traditional news media with new forces in media production to create a new model of watchdog journalism. At the same time the chapter also makes clear that from Benkler's perspective, the rise of the networked fourth estate has not been met with open arms by the traditional news media, as it poses a direct threat to established journalistic identities.

In "Following the Money: WikiLeaks and the Political Economy of Disclosure," Benedetta Brevini and Graham Murdock explore questions of the political economy and the sustainability of those parts of the networked fourth estate that include platforms like WikiLeaks. The analysis focuses on the costs incurred in sustaining radical platforms for disclosure, in terms of funds and economic support, but also in terms of "general intellect" – the people and the skills invested in it. By taking the WikiLeaks narrative as a starting point, the analysis also reflects on the curtailing effect on Net freedom of the combination of corporate and "national" interests.

Lisa Lynch, one of the first academic observers of WikiLeaks and a commentator on its journalistic and activist practices, brings us back to WikiLeaks' troubled interactions with established media. Lynch expands her focus beyond the initial restricted set of WikiLeaks' media partners in the United States and Europe to examine the broader range of media organizations that have collaborated with WikiLeaks in its later stages. In "The Leak Heard Around the World? Cablegate in the Evolving Global Mediascape," she discusses what she calls the second and third stage of WikiLeaks' media collaborations; investigates the different reactions to the Cablegate releases by journalists around the globe; explores common features of journalism as a global practice, as well as the legal, commercial, and institutional challenges to the idea of a global mediascape; and she reflects critically on the overall strategy of WikiLeaks to collaborate with large mainstream media.

Changing the perspective from academic observer to media practitioner, Chris Elliott reflects on the choices that WikiLeaks' British media partner, the *Guardian,* had to make concerning WikiLeaks documents, in the chapter "WikiLeaks and the Public Interest Dilemma: A View from Inside the Media." What is the right balance to strike between the public interest and national security priorities? In his powerful discussion from inside the newspaper, Elliott examines the moral case for publishing and how journalists at the *Guardian* assessed and addressed the risk for those on the ground.

Hopeton Dunn concludes this series of chapters on WikiLeaks' role in the media ecology of a network age on a conciliatory note. In "Something Old, Something New...: WikiLeaks, Newspapers, and Conjoint Approaches to Political Exposure," he discusses the relationship among WikiLeaks and other emerging new media platforms and their traditional media counterparts. Even though WikiLeaks undoubtedly challenged and disrupted existing tenets of "proper" journalism, Dunn emphasizes traditional journalism's prime role as filling an emerging gap in the media's information retrieval and news presentation in the context of communication convergence and an activist global public, and foresees a productive cohabitation of traditional and new information providers.

The chapter by Einar Thorsen, Chindu Sreedharan, and Stuart Allan, "WikiLeaks and Whistle-blowing: The Framing of Bradley Manning," shifts from a focus on WikiLeaks to Private First Class (PFC) Bradley Manning, the US soldier accused of providing classified documents to WikiLeaks. The chapter is divided into two core components. Part one outlines the complex history of the term whistleblowing and offers a working definition. This is followed by a brief account of how PFC Manning allegedly acquired and passed on the sensitive military material to WikiLeaks. The second part of the chapter presents a content analysis of the online news framing of Bradley Manning in the ensuing reportage and commentary published on the websites of the *Guardian* (guardian.co.uk), the *New York Times* (nytimes.com), and *Der Spiegel* (spiegel.de/international). Based on their analysis, the authors argue that despite the reportedly staunch US political rhetoric against Bradley Manning, he has largely been framed as a whistle-blower and often is the recipient of sympathetic media coverage whereas a "villain" framing of Manning was noticeably subdued – almost to the point of absence – in the coverage analysed.

Patrick McCurdy expands and deepens the discussion on whistle-blowing in his chapter "From the Pentagon Papers to Cablegate: How the Network Society Has Changed Leaking." He is interested in how WikiLeaks and its release of a cache of US classified information is representative of broader transformations in the potential and practice of leaking. To make his argument, McCurdy contrasts the case of Daniel Ellsberg and the 1971 leaking of the Pentagon Papers with that of PFC Bradley Manning. Through a detailed examination of the similarities and differences between the leakers and the practice of leaking in both cases, the chapter outlines how the rise of the network society has democratized the practice of leaking and positioned digital information and its networked flows as a source of "risk."

McCurdy's broader framework of societal change is picked up by Arne Hintz as he shifts the discussion to the new opportunities, challenges, and changing policy environments for freedom of expression, in his chapter "Dimensions of Modern Freedom of Expression: WikiLeaks, Policy Hacking, and Digital Freedoms." He asks what the WikiLeaks experience can tell us about current practices of censorship and other restrictions, and thus about the potential cornerstones for protecting future expression rights, or limiting them. He argues that several dimensions have to be considered in this discussion, including information control, access to infrastructure, surveillance, critical resources, and physical violence. He provides examples both for government-led restrictions and for civil-society–based policy campaigns that challenge those, and he thereby provides a broader perspective on the current (and likely future) contestations on freedom of expression.

Dwayne Winseck complements this analysis by focusing on the role of commercial Internet services in his chapter "Weak Links and WikiLeaks: How Control of Critical Internet Resources and Social Media Companies' Business Models Undermine the Networked Free Press." He builds on Benkler's concept of the networked fourth estate, presented in Chapter 1, to examine the role of the social media site Twitter in the WikiLeaks saga. Twitter, Winseck argues, is noteworthy for its tough legal battles, which sought to avoid turning over subscriber account information of prominent WikiLeaks volunteers to the U.S. Department of Justice. By focussing on the "Twitter – WikiLeaks" connection, Winseck raises questions around Internet users' communication rights, the role and reach of commercial entities that control critical Internet resources and the use of social media sites by journalists to access sources, share information, and generally to create and circulate the news.

In "WikiLeaks, Secrecy, and Freedom of Information: The Case of the United Kingdom," David Banisar and Francesca Fanucci investigate the difficult balance between secrecy and openness in contemporary democracies by focusing on the UK experience. What would have happened if Cablegate had occurred the United Kingdom? The chapter essay takes the WikiLeaks case as a starting point to analyze the main legal provisions that would apply in the United Kingdom, should a similar phenomenon take place. It outlines the potential challenges faced by the UK judges as well as the legislator in addressing a WikiLeaks-like saga, given its scale and impact well outside the national borders.

After the previous chapters have discussed policy-related aspects and the roles of state and private actors in influencing freedom of expression, Stefania Milan introduces the next theme as she explores some of the transformations to social and political activism in the age of WikiLeaks. In her chapter "WikiLeaks, Anonymous, and the Exercise of Individuality: Protesting in the Cloud," she applies the tools and concepts of social movement studies to understand the changing organizational forms, practices, and identities of both online and offline activism, using contemporary examples such as the Anonymous network and the Occupy protests of 2011. Focusing on the role of individual networked action and on practices of technology use, and tracing historic dynamics in these fields, she proposes the concept of "cloud protesting" to explain the characteristics of new forms of activism.

Gabriella Coleman then closes in on one of these instances, and undoubtedly the most prominent form of online activism coinciding with the WikiLeaks saga, in her chapter "Anonymous and the Politics of Leaking." A loose network of geeks and hacktivists, Anonymous has applied action repertoires such as distributed denial of service (DDoS) attacks against, for example, enemies of WikiLeaks; has conducted its own leaks releases; and has put fear into governmental and business actors no less than WikiLeaks itself has done. Coleman, who has observed Anonymous closely since its beginnings, discusses the network's history, its focus on frivolous action (the "lulz"), its politics and ethics, and thereby characterizes new forms of online activism.

Changing the perspective from the practices to both the agendas and outcomes of online activism, Jillian York reflects on the impact of WikiLeaks on political developments towards transparency and, particularly, the political change in the Middle East and North Africa

(MENA). In her contribution, "The Internet and Transparency Beyond WikiLeaks," York notes that WikiLeaks' release of diplomatic cables coincided with the first sparks of protest leading to the Arab Spring, which created a unique moment for existing freedom of information and expression movements to thrive. As a result, she argues, the zeitgeist in the Arab world is now bending toward transparency and openness.

Ibrahim Saleh expands on the discussion of WikiLeaks' impact in the Middle East and North Africa. In his piece "WikiLeaks and the Arab Spring: Twists and Turns of Media, Culture, and Power," Saleh situates WikiLeaks in the context of the political and media situation in the region and the technological change and opportunities of new social media. Tracing specific leaks that exposed government agendas and corruption, and discussing them in relation to established political and journalistic practices, he suggests that the leaks had a significant role in redefining the power of information processing and making new information available, and thus were a significant factor in fuelling discontent in the region.

Geert Lovink and Patrice Riemens start rounding up the book with their both critical and prophetic "Twelve Theses on WikiLeaks." Originally written at the height of WikiLeaks' notoriety in late 2010, the polemical theses are intended to stir and spark debate on what the WikiLeaks saga reveals about the state of society. WikiLeaks, the authors argue, is the product of decline – the decline of the US empire and of investigative journalism. Yet WikiLeaks is also the product of growth; growth in technology and of information and communication technologies (ICTs) specifically. The theses include a somewhat prophetic warning that flags the dangers of the "the self-inflicted celebrity cult of Julian Assange" and the fatal limits of WikiLeaks as a single-person organization.

Yet despite this note of caution, this book would not be complete without hearing from the man who has been at the centre of WikiLeaks and its controversies, editor-in-chief Julian Assange, and without considering his perspectives on the long-term implications of the organization he founded. The collection of chapters thus ends with an edited transcript of a public conversation between Assange and philosopher Slavoj Žižek in London in July 2011, moderated by journalist Amy Goodman.

Towards the beyond

The impetus for *Beyond WikiLeaks* was born out of two special sessions on WikiLeaks held at the annual conference of the International Association for Media and Communication Research (IAMCR) in Istanbul in July

2011. In the wake of the Cablegate saga, the sessions included several of the authors in this book, including Lisa Lynch, Gabriella Coleman, Hopeton Dunn, Ibrahim Saleh, Stefania Milan, Benedetta Brevini, Patrick McCurdy, and Arne Hintz, and other renowned academics such as John Downing and Sandra Braman. Our motivation was to provide a space for academic exchange on the long-term implications of WikiLeaks and to understand how the world will be different once the dust of Cablegate has settled. This book provides further steps in this quest and hopefully serves to open up this discussion to a broader audience.

References

Beckett, C. and Ball, J. (2012). *WikiLeaks: News in the Networked Era.* Cambridge: Polity Press
Domscheit-Berg, D. (2011). *Inside WikiLeaks: My Time with Julian Assange at the World's Most Dangerous Website.* London: Random House
Leigh, D. and Harding, L. (2011). *WikiLeaks: Inside Julian Assange's War on Secrecy.* London: Guardian Books
Mitchell, G. (2011). *The Age of WikiLeaks: From Collateral Murder to Cablegate (and Beyond).* New York: Sinclair Books
Rosen, J. (2010). The Afghanistan War Logs Released By WikiLeaks, The World's First Stateless News Organization. *Pressthink*, July 26, 2010
Sifry, M. (2011). *WikiLeaks and the Age of Transparency.* New York: OR Books
Star, A. and Keller, B. (2011). *Open Secrets: WikiLeaks, War and American Diplomacy.* New York: Grove Press
Žižek, S. (2011). Good Manners in the Age of WikiLeaks. *London Review of Books,* Jan 2011

1
WikiLeaks and the Networked Fourth Estate

Yochai Benkler

This chapter explores how the WikiLeaks case intersects with larger trends in the news industry. It begins by describing the economic challenges faced by traditional media and the emerging pattern of what I call the "networked fourth estate." This new media landscape will likely combine elements of the traditional news media with new forces in media production. "Professionalism" and "responsibility" can be found on both sides of the divide, as can unprofessionalism and irresponsibility. The traditional news industry's treatment of WikiLeaks throughout this episode can best be seen as an effort by older media to preserve their own identity against the perceived threat posed by the new networked model. As a practical result, the traditional media in the United States effectively collaborated with parts of the Administration in painting WikiLeaks and Assange in terms that made them more susceptible to both extralegal and legal attack. More systematically, this chapter argues that the new, relatively more socially and politically vulnerable members of the networked fourth estate are needlessly being put at risk by the more established outlets' efforts to denigrate the journalistic identity of the new kids on the block to preserve their own identity.

The crisis of the mass-mediated fourth estate

The American press – traditionally termed the "fourth estate" – is in the midst of a profound transformation whose roots are in the mid-1980s, but whose rate, intensity, and direction have changed in the past decade (Benkler, 2006, chapters 6–7). The first element of this transformation includes changes internal to the mass media – increasing competition for both newspapers and television channels and the resulting lower rents to spend on newsrooms, as well as fragmented markets that have led to new strategies for differentiation. The second element, nevertheless, was the adoption of the Internet since the mid-1990s. The critical change introduced by the networks was decentralized information production, including both news and opinion, and the new opportunities for models based on neither market funding nor state funding to play a new and significant role in the production of the public sphere (chapters 2–4 and 7).

Over the course of the twentieth century within the United States, local newspapers became local monopoly businesses. By 1984, the average market share of the top newspaper in small towns was close to 95 percent, and in medium-sized cities it was just over 93 percent. By 2006, the market share of the largest newspapers in such towns was over 97 percent. The absence of competition, in turn, sustained unusually high newspaper advertising rates, which then helped subsidize the cost of running newsrooms. However this practice began to change just before the emergence of the Internet with the rise of print and electronic advertising channels and the dispersal of advertising dollars (Benkler, 2006, chapters 2–4 and 7). This dispersion of attention and increase in competition meant that there were more outlets – not all of them having news – which consumers could go to. Changes within the industrial organization of American mass media led to disinvestment in newsrooms, audience fragmentation, and the emergence of right-wing media that used polarization as a differentiation strategy.

At the same time, the Internet rapidly shifted from being primarily a research and education platform to being a core element of our communications and information environment. The defining characteristic of the Net was the decentralization of physical and human capital (Benkler, 2006, chapters 2–4). In 1999, acute observers of the digital economy saw Encarta as the primary threat to *Britannica* in the encyclopaedia market (Shapiro and Varian, 1999, pp. 19–27). It was impossible to imagine that a radically decentralized, non-proprietary project in which no one was paid to write or edit, and that in principle anyone could edit, would compete with the major encyclopedias. And yet, 10 years later, *Wikipedia* was one of the top six or seven sites on the Net, while Encarta had closed its doors. Peer production and other forms of commons-based, non-market production became a stable and important component of the information production system. Just as open-source software became an important complement to and substitute for some proprietary software models, and just as things from photography (Flickr.com, 2011) to travel came to be based on peer production and on social production more generally, so too has news reporting changed. If the First Gulf War was the moment of the 24-hour news channel and CNN, the Iranian reform movement of 2009 was the moment of the amateur video reportage, as videos taken by non-professional journalists were uploaded to YouTube, and from there became the only significant source of video footage of the demonstrations available to the major international news outlets. Most recently, the Tunisian revolt was in part aided by amateur videos of demonstrations, uploaded to a Facebook page of an activist, Lotfi Hajji, and then retransmitted around the Arab world by Al Jazeera (Worth and Kirkpatrick, 2011, p. A1), and video taken by protesters was mixed with that taken by professional journalists to depict the revolt in Egypt. But the networked public sphere is constructed of much more, and more diverse, organizational forms than ad hoc bursts of fully decentralized activity.

The emerging networked fourth estate: Elements of the networked public sphere

As of the end of the first decade of the twenty-first century, it seems that the networked public sphere is constructed of several intersecting models of production, whose operations to some extent complement and to some extent compete with each other. Understanding the WikiLeaks events requires first understanding six broad trends in the construction of the networked fourth estate

1. Traditional mass media

One central component is composed of the core players of the mass media environment, who now have a global reach, and have also begun to incorporate decentralized elements within their own model. CNN, the *New York Times*, NBC News and MSNBC News, the *Wall Street Journal*, Fox News, the *Washington Post* and the *Los Angeles Times,* as well as the UK-based BBC and the *Guardian,* are among the top-ranked news sites on the Internet (Alexa, 2012). The *Guardian's* editor-in-chief has claimed to have at least 36 million readers a month, by comparison to the paper's daily circulation of about 283,000 (Reid and Teixeira, 2012). These major players are, in turn, complemented by the online presence of smaller traditional media platforms and sources from other countries, often accessed by readers through Yahoo and Google News, both among the top news sites in the world. The WikiLeaks case demonstrates how central these large, global online news organizational players are, but it also shows how hard it is for any one of them to control access to the news. One of Assange's strategically significant moves was to harness these global mass media to his cause by providing them with enough exclusivity in their respective national markets and therefore economic benefits, and enough competition in the global network to make sure that none of them could, if they so chose, bury the story. The global nature of the platform and the market made this strategy by a small player with a significant scoop both powerful and hard to suppress.

2. Mass media aggregation sites

We are seeing the emergence of other models of organization, which were either absent or weaker in the traditional mass media environment. Remaining for a moment within the sites visible enough to make major Internet rankings lists, the Huffington Post,[1] a commercial online collaborative blog, is more visible in the United States than any other news outlet except for the BBC, CNN, and the *New York Times*[2] (Alexa, 2012). There are, of course, other smaller scale commercial sites that operate on advertising, like the Drudge Report, Pajamas Media (now PJ Media), or Talking Points Memo. These form a second element in the networked public sphere.

3. Professional-journalism-focused nonprofits

A third model that is emerging to take advantage of the relatively low cost of news production and distribution is the nonprofit sector. Here, I do not mean the volunteer, radically decentralized peer production model, but rather the ability of more traditionally organized nonprofits to leverage their capabilities in an environment where the costs of doing business are sufficiently lower than they were in the print and television era. These new players can sustain effective newsrooms staffed with people who, like academic faculties, are willing to sacrifice some of the bottom line in exchange for the freedom to pursue their professional values. One example is Pro Publica, a foundation-supported model for an otherwise classic-style professional newsroom. A similar approach underlies the journalistic award-winning local reporting work of the Center for Independent Media, founded in 2006 and renamed in 2010 the American Independent News Network. This organization funds a network of local independent nonprofit media in several US states. A related model is the construction of university-based centers that can specialize in traditional media roles. A perfect example of this is Factcheck.org, based in the Annenberg Public Policy Center at the University of Pennsylvania, which plays a crucial watchdog role in checking the veracity of claims made by political figures and organizations.

4. Nonprofit organization with peer production

Combining standard nonprofit models with peer production also allows other organizations to achieve significant results in the public sphere. An excellent example is offered by the Sunlight Foundation, which supports both new laws that require government data to be put online and the development of web-based platforms that allow people to look at these data and explore government actions that are relevant to them. As WikiLeaks did before the events of 2010/11, the Sunlight Foundation focuses on making the raw data available for the many networked eyes to read. Unlike WikiLeaks, its emphasis is on legal and formal release of government data, the construction of technical platforms to lower the cost of analysis, and enabling distributed individuals with diverse motivational profiles to apply collaborative practices to analyse the data. These new experiences of peer production complement other forms of participatory nonprofit media, such as the alternative press, community radio, and online alternative media such as Indymedia. In many parts of the world, collaborative media practices on older platforms, particularly community radio, are expanding and are challenging established commercial and public-service media (Downing, 2011).

5. Party press culture

Alongside the professionals based in large-scale global media, small-scale commercial media, high-end national and local nonprofit media outlets, and other non-media nonprofits, we also see the emergence of a new party press culture. Over 10,000 Daily Kos contributors have strong political beliefs, and they are looking to express them and to search for information that will help their cause. So do the contributors to Town Hall on the right, although the left wing of the blogosphere uses large collaborative sites at this point in history more than the right (Benkler and Shaw, 2010). Digging up the dirt on your opponent's corruption, political ambition, and contestation is a powerful motivator, and the platforms are available to allow thousands of volunteers to work together, with the leadership and support of a tiny paid staff (paid, again, through advertising to this engaged community, or through mobilized donations, or both).

6. The individual

Finally, although less individually prominent and much more decentralized, individuals play an absolutely critical role in this new information ecosystem. First, there is the *sheer presence of millions of individuals with the ability to witness and communicate what they witnessed over systems that are woven into the normal fabric of networked life.* This is the story of the Iranian reform videos, the Tunisian and Egyptian revolutions and it is, of course, the story of much more mundane political reporting such as covering then Republican presidential contender John McCain's singing "Bomb Iran" to the tune of the Beach Boys' 1965 hit song "Barbra Ann" during a 2007 campaign stop in Murrell Infelt, South Carolina. Second, there is the *distributed force of observation and critical commentary,* as we saw in the exposure of error in a September 8, 2004, *60 Minutes* story that was critical of President George W. Bush's Texas Air National Guard service record. Claims quickly emerged challenging the authenticity of the memos that the story was based on. Twelve days after the original story aired, CBS issued a retraction and Dan Rather issued a public apology saying he was no longer "confident" in the documents (Murphy, 2009).

Third, there are the *experts.* For instance, academic economists like Brad DeLong, on the left, and Tyler Cowen, on the right, played a much greater role in debates over the stimulus and bailout than they could have a mere decade ago. Collaborative websites by academics, like Balkinization or Crooked Timber, provide academics with much larger distribution platforms on which to communicate, expanding the scope and depth of analysis available to policy makers and opinion makers.

WikiLeaks must be understood in the context of these trends that form the backbone of the networked fourth estate. Like the Sunlight Foundation and similar transparency-focused organizations, WikiLeaks is a nonprofit focused on bringing to light direct, documentary evidence about government behaviour so that many others, professional and otherwise, can analyze the evidence and search for instances that justify public criticism. Like the emerging party presses, it acts out of political conviction. And like so many other projects on the Net, it uses a combination of volunteerism, global presence, and decentralized action to achieve its results. As such, WikiLeaks presents an integral part of the networked fourth estate – no less than the protesters who shoot videos on the streets of Teheran, Tunis, or Cairo and upload them to the Web, or the bloggers who exposed the Rather/CBS story. Whatever one thinks about the particular actions of WikiLeaks in the particular instance of the release of the embassy cables, the kind of organization and the kind of effort to bring to light actual internal government documents bearing on questions of great public import is the networked version of the *Pentagon Papers* and of Roosevelt's Man with the Muck Rake.

Media tensions and crisis in the networked fourth estate

In 2009–2010 the state of mass media news reporting, in particular of newspapers, and the financial future of these organizations became a matter of substantial public debate. The US Senate held hearings on the future of journalism (AFP, 2009), and the Federal Trade Commission launched a series of public workshops under the title "How Will Journalism Survive the Internet?" (FTC Staff, 2009). Multiple media ran stories trying to understand the future of journalism. Examples include the *New Republic*'s thoughtful cover on the end of the age of newspapers (Starr, 2009) and NPR's *On the Media* careful exploration of sense of crisis (2010).

The flipside of the media crisis debate has been the critique of new networked forms of the press, primarily the concern that the Internet and the blogosphere provide misinformation, while the traditional media are necessary to provide reliable investigative reporting. However, as we will see below, being part of the mass media is no guarantee of high-quality and effective journalism; nor is being an online outlet a guarantee of falsehood and echo-chamber effects. What we can see, instead, is a much more complex interaction between the traditional and networked components of the fourth estate, and the distribution of high- and low-quality journalism on both sides of that divide. Understanding this fact, as well as the dynamic that seems to lead serious writers on the traditional side to discount it, provides important insight into the ways in which the WikiLeaks case, in turn, has been perceived.

On November 17, 2010 the *New York Times* published an op-ed by Thomas Friedman, "Too Good to Check," whose opening beautifully explains the whole:

> On Nov. 4, Anderson Cooper did the country a favor. He expertly deconstructed on his CNN show the bogus rumor that President Obama's trip to Asia would cost $200 million a day. This was an important "story." It underscored just how far ahead of his time Mark Twain was when he said a century before the Internet, "A lie can travel halfway around the world while the truth is putting on its shoes." But it also showed that there is an antidote to malicious journalism – and that's good journalism. In case you missed it, a story circulated around the Web on the eve of President Obama's trip that it would cost U.S. taxpayers $200 million a day ... (2010a, p. A33)

The quote appears to tell the whole of the story. The villain is "the Internet," which enables the lie travelling half way around the world – in this case, from India to the US public sphere – where it circulates around "the Web." The hero is the expert journalist in an established news outlet, who exposes the lie, airs his exposé on a mass media outlet, and thereby administers the antidote.

There is only one problem with this story: it wasn't quite so. The initial source of the $200 million a day story was an established media outlet: the Press Trust of India; it was primarily followed by the right-wing mass media in the United States, with one blogger playing an important importation role. "The Internet," on the other hand, was actually the first place where investigative journalism occurred to debunk the falsehood. Let us explore this case study in more detail:

At 11:25 am EST on November 2, 2010, New Delhi Television[3] posted a story with the byline of the Press Trust of India, India's equivalent of the AP and Reuters, entitled "US to spend $200 mn a day on Obama's Mumbai visit." This story was linked to within the next two hours by the Drudge Report (2010), Michelle Malkin's site at 1:53 pm (Powers, 2010), as well as three other lower-visibility right-wing blogs (Dailypaul. com; Lamecherry.com; katablog.com). Rush Limbaugh repeated it on his radio show (2010) and it also appeared in the British *Daily Mail* (White, 2010) and on *Fox News* (The Media Desk, 2010). By the end of November 2, a story had been created by some of India's most respected news outlets, imported to the United States by two highly visible right-wing blogs, and then repeated and amplified by two major right-wing mass media outlets – Fox News and Rush Limbaugh. Limbaugh's story actually revived and combines the new $200 million meme with an earlier one: claiming that the president was taking 40 airplanes.

On November 3, the right-wing mass media propagation continued. Fox Business News' program *Follow the Money* created a whole segment, repeating the claim with vivid images and the tag "The Obamas: The New American Royalty?" (Bolling broadcasted on MMTV, 2010), and that same evening, Fox hosted a panel discussion on the issue. A few hours later Representative Michelle Bachman repeated the accusation in an interview on CNN's *Anderson Cooper 360* (Cooper, 2010); the interview that ultimately led Cooper to investigate and refute the claim 24 hours later on his November 4 show. But that refutation, the one to which Friedman paid such high respects, was by no means the first. On November 3, Factcheck.org provided a clear breakdown of the source and flow of the story (2010). Mediamatters.org posted a long story in the afternoon of November 3, providing a similar flow and debunking of the story (Pavlus, 2010), as did Snopes.com (2010). By the end of November 3, only Internet-based reporting was doing the "good journalism" work; the only established media working the story were either purposefully repeating the misstatement – in the case of *Fox News* – or were being used by right-wing politicians to propagate the slander, as in Bachman's interview on Cooper's show.

By November 4, the tide of the story was turning, and an increasing number of blogs and mainstream outlets were picking up the White House and Pentagon denials. Over the course of that day, the MediaCloud database identified 13 blog posts within the political blogosphere that continued to support and propagate the story, and 14 blog posts that pointed to the critique and refutations of the story.

In the mainstream, *USA Today*, the *Washington Post*, the *Wall Street Journal*, and the *Kansas City Star* all had various versions of the refutation in their web-based versions. At 10 pm that night, Anderson Cooper aired a long segment that specifically emphasized the vacuity of the sources, and the central role that the right-wing conservatives – Limbaugh, Beck, Don Imus, and Michael Savage – played in repeating and amplifying the lie (Cooper, 2010). It was indeed a good piece of journalism. Its story captured the right tone of how the story emerged, why it was unreliable, and who repeated the lie. Cooper then went to his "data board" and explained how the $200 million dollar could not possibly be true, given what we know from public sources about the daily cost of the war in Afghanistan and what we know based on an old GAO (the US Government Accountability Office) report about the costs of Bill Clinton's Africa trip in 1999 (GAO, 1999). All these facts had already been reported over 24 hours earlier by Factcheck.org. Still, Cooper played an enormously important role in giving voice and amplifying Factcheck's excellent research and thus this demonstrates the continued importance of mass media outlets in reaching very large audiences. Nonetheless, the story is emphatically not one where "the Internet" spread lies and professional journalism combatted them.

The story of these three days in November 2010 offers some insight into the emerging structure of the global, networked fourth estate. It identifies a more complex relationship than simply either "good professionals vs. bad amateurs" or "pure-hearted net-based journalists vs. a corrupt mainstream media." It reveals a networked alternative to the more traditional models of media checks and balances. Here, publication by an Indian outlet was globally visible; "the Internet," or rather one entrepreneurial right-wing blogger, moved that information quickly, and the network and its relationship to mass media created and elevated the memes. But the networked environment also included nonprofit academic and professional groups (Factcheck.org; Mediamatters), as well as a small commercial professional publisher (Snopes), all of whom were able to check the reporting and criticize it. And the Net included over two dozen sites that sifted through the original and the refutation. The mass media, in turn, took both the false and the correct story lines, and in each case amplified them to their respective audiences.

Mass media anxiety and the networked fourth estate

The concern that the incumbent news industry has exhibited in the past several years over the emerging competitors in the networked information environment, played out in the way Friedman ascribed the blame for the $200 million a day story, was also on display in the way that American newspapers dealt with WikiLeaks after the release of the embassy cables. This anxiety has two practical consequences. The first is that the kind of cooperative venture that WikiLeaks entered into with the major newspapers was clearly difficult to manage. The cultural divide between established media players and the scrappy networked organizations that make up important parts of the networked fourth estate makes working together difficult, as the published reports from the media partners in this enterprise clearly reveal.

The second practical consequence is that, in seeking to preserve their uniqueness and identity, the traditional media are painting their networked counterparts into a corner that exposes them to greater risk of legal and extralegal attack. While the way in which the traditional media respond to, and frame, WikiLeaks or other actors in the networked fourth estate does not matter a great deal from a constitutional *law* perspective (Benkler, 2010), it does have a significant effect on what is politically and socially feasible for a democratic government to do. The more that newspapermen, in their effort to preserve their own identity, vilify and segregate the individuals and nontraditional components of the networked fourth estate, the more they put those elements at risk of suppression and attack through both legal and extralegal systems.

A difficult relationship

Two major pieces in the *New York Times* exemplify the effort to assert the identity of the traditional media as highly professional, well-organized, and responsible by denigrating the networked alternative. The first was a Tom Friedman op-ed piece published on December 14, 2010. In it Friedman wrote:

The world system is currently being challenged by two new forces: a rising superpower, called China, and a rising collection of super-empowered individuals, as represented by the WikiLeakers, among others. What globalization, technological integration and the general flattening of the world have done is to *superempower* individuals to such a degree that they can actually challenge any hierarchy – from a global bank to a nation state – as *individuals*. (2010b, p. A31)

He explains:

As for the superempowered individuals – some are constructive, some are destructive. I read many WikiLeaks and learned some useful things. But their release also raises some troubling questions. I don't want to live in a country where they throw whistle-blowers in jail. That's China. But I also don't want to live in a country where any individual feels entitled to just dump out all the internal communications of a government or a bank in a way that undermines the ability to have private, confidential communications that are vital to the functioning of any society. That's anarchy. (p. A31)

As a factual matter, "a country where they throw whistleblowers in jail" is, in fact, the United States (Greenwald, 2010). "They," read "we Americans," have been keeping Bradley Manning, the only whistle-blower involved in this case, in solitary confinement since his arrest in 2010. But the important insight from this op-ed is the expressed fear of anarchy and the fear that the decentralized network, with its capacity to empower *individuals* to challenge their governments or global banks, is not democracy, but anarchy. The fact that the individual in question did not in fact "dump out all the internal communications of a government," but rather partnered with major traditional news outlets, including the *New York Times*, is eliminated from the op-ed. By mischaracterizing what WikiLeaks in fact did and labelling those imagined actions "anarchy," Friedman is able to paint it as the dangerous "other," just like China. A decentralized, open network is a dangerous threat to what he concludes is the only thing standing between us and either anarchy or authoritarianism: "a strong America" (Friedman, 2010b, p. A31).

More revealing yet is an 8,000-word essay by *New York Times*'s executive editor Bill Keller in a *New York Times Magazine* cover story on January 26, 2011 (p. MM32). Parts of the essay, particularly around its middle, seem intended to emphasize and legitimate the fourth estate function of the *Times* itself against critics who argue that the *Times* should not have published the materials.

But any close reading of the essay makes crystal clear that a central purpose it serves is to separate WikiLeaks from the *Times*, and to emphasize the *Times's* professionalism, care, and organizational rationality while denigrating the contribution and reliability of WikiLeaks. Immediately in the first paragraph Keller refers to "an organization called WikiLeaks, a secretive cadre of antisecrecy vigilantes" (Keller, 2011, p. MM32). A few paragraphs later, Keller then criticizes WikiLeaks' effort of releasing the edited version of the *Collateral Murder* video, writing: "In its zeal to make the video a work of antiwar propaganda, WikiLeaks also released a version that didn't call attention to an Iraqi who was toting a rocket-propelled grenade and packaged the manipulated version under the tendentious rubric 'Collateral Murder'" (p. MM32). Keller ignored the fact that the opening slide of the edited footage had pointed to this possibility, and the fact that a side-by-side comparison of the two versions suggests that none of the critical elements of the event, for either side's position, was edited out. At a different point, Keller implies, without pointing to any evidence, that WikiLeaks volunteers hacked into the *Times's* computers during a rocky period of the relationship (p. MM32).[4]

Keller peppers the essay with a range of what reads more like gratuitous name-calling than substantive criticism. In the first paragraph, he introduces Assange as "an eccentric former computer hacker of Australian birth and no fixed residence" (Keller, 2011, p. MM32). He frames Assange by describing the impressions of the first *Times* reporter who met him: "Assange slouched into The *Guardian* office, a day late. ...' He was alert but disheveled, like a bag lady walking in off the street, wearing a dingy, light-colored sport coat and cargo pants, dirty white shirt, beat-up sneakers and filthy white socks that collapsed around his ankles. He smelled as if he hadn't bathed in days" (p. MM32). A few paragraphs later, Keller recounts, "Schmitt told me that for all Assange's bombast and dark conspiracy theories, he had a bit of Peter Pan in him. One night, when they were all walking down the street after dinner, Assange suddenly started skipping ahead of the group. Schmitt and Goetz stared, speechless. Then, just as suddenly, Assange stopped, got back in step with them and returned to the conversation he had interrupted" (p. MM32). By comparison, the *Guardian*, which had as difficult and stormy relationship with Assange as did the *Times*, introduced Assange in its editor's equivalent of Keller's overview essay very differently: "Unnoticed by most of the world, Julian Assange was developing into a most interesting and unusual pioneer in using digital technologies to challenge corrupt and authoritarian states" (Rusbridger, 2011). As *Der Spiegel* put it in reporting on Keller's essay, "For some time now, Julian Assange has been sparring with *New York Times* Executive Editor Bill Keller. Assange claims the paper didn't publish the material in its entirety and made too many concessions to the White House before going to print. Now, Keller is fighting back" (Rosenbach and Stark, 2010).[5]

These kinds of jabs make it difficult to separate personal animosity from structural and systemic concerns. Nonetheless, it is possible to observe a clear core theme: asserting a categorical distinction between the *New York Times* as an institution and organizational form and the decentralized, networked form represented by WikiLeaks. Keller says, "We regarded Assange throughout as a source, not as a partner or collaborator" (2011, p. MM32). Even when asserting that First Amendment values require that WikiLeaks not be suppressed, Keller prefaces by restating: "I do not regard Assange as a partner, and I would hesitate to describe what WikiLeaks does as journalism" (p. MM32). By contrast, the *Guardian* frames its own account of its relationship quite differently: "The fruit of Davies' eager pursuit of Assange would result in an extraordinary, if sometimes strained, partnership between a mainstream newspaper and WikiLeaks: a new model of co-operation aimed at publishing the world's biggest leak" (Leigh and Harding, 2011). It is certainly possible that the difference in framing reflects jurisdictional susceptibility and the advice of counsel: the *Times* may be trying to preempt possible co-conspirator charges against it, should the Department of Justice decide to proceed against Assange and WikiLeaks on such a theory. It seems more likely, however, that the difference reflects the *Guardian's* strategic embrace of the networked models of journalism and the *Times's* trepidation towards the model.

The professional/reliable vs. unprofessional/unreliable dichotomy is repeated throughout Keller's essay in more context-specific instances. At one point he describes a certain problem the *Times* reporters had with displaying the data. "Assange, slipping naturally into the role of office geek, explained that they had hit the limits of Excel" (Keller, 2011, p. MM32). By contrast to Assange, who was merely "the office geek," Keller later describes the challenge of organizing the data and explains how, "With help from two of The Times's best computer minds [the lead reporters] figured out how to assemble the material into a conveniently searchable and secure database" (p. MM32). When discussing the redaction efforts, Keller writes:

> Guided by reporters with extensive experience in the field, we redacted the names of ordinary citizens, local officials, activists, academics and others who had spoken to American soldiers or diplomats. We edited out any details that might reveal ongoing intelligence-gathering operations, military tactics or locations of material that could be used to fashion terrorist weapons. (p. MM32)

Keller does recognize WikiLeaks' efforts to avoid harming innocents and anonymize names, but he raises doubts "[w]hether WikiLeaks' 'harm minimization' is adequate, and whether it will continue ... " (p. MM32). When writing about responsible journalism, Keller again focuses on differentiating between the traditional media participants in the disclosure, and the networked elements, this time explicitly using WikiLeaks as an anchor for denigrating the networked fourth estate more generally.

> [W]e felt an enormous moral and ethical obligation to use the material responsibly. *While we assumed we had little or no ability to influence what WikiLeaks did, let alone what would happen once this material was loosed in the echo chamber of the blogosphere,* that did not free us from the need to exercise care in our own journalism. (Keller, 2011, p. MM32, italics added)

The essay was written two months after the initial release of documents. Keller by this point knew full well that WikiLeaks in fact did not release materials irresponsibly. Nor did anyone else in what he calls "the echo chamber of the blogosphere." The assertion of difference does not reflect an actual difference in kind relative to what was disclosed by one or another of the traditional media players. Instead, the aside largely seems to express the *Times's* own anxieties about WikiLeaks and the more general genre that it represents for Keller.

This sense of self appears to have been complemented and reinforced by the Obama Administration. Comparing the Obama Administration's response to that of the Bush Administration's response to the NSA (National Security Agency) eavesdropping story, Keller recounts:

> [T]he Obama administration's reaction was different. It was, for the most part, sober and professional. The Obama White House, while strongly condemning WikiLeaks for making the documents public, did not seek an injunction to halt publication. There was no Oval Office lecture. On the contrary, in our discussions before publication

of our articles, White House officials, while challenging some of the conclusions we drew from the material, thanked us for handling the documents with care. (2011, MM32)

This basic story line repeats itself in the *Der Spiegel* recounting. In describing their meetings with the Administration, Rosenbach and Stark state quite clearly that "the official fury of the US government was directed at the presumed source, Bradley Manning, and, most of all, WikiLeaks. The government was not interested in quarrelling with the media organizations involved" (2011). It appears as though the Administration either really did not fear disclosure, as long as it was by organizations it felt were within its comfort zone, or was using the distinction and relative social-cultural weakness of WikiLeaks to keep the established media players at the table and, perhaps, more cooperative with the Administration's needs.

Vulnerabilities of the networked fourth estate

It is in the descriptions from both the *Times* and *Der Spiegel* of their relationships with the US Administration that we see a danger to the networked fourth estate in the mixing of the press's anxiety over its identity and its anxiety of reporting on the press itself. As one observes the multisystem nature of the attacks on WikiLeaks, as well as its defences, it becomes obvious that law is but one dimension in this multidimensional system of freedom and constraint. Law is largely on the side of WikiLeaks, no less so than it is on the side of the *New York Times or Der Spiegel* (Benkler, 2010). Law, however, is not the only operative dimension. The social-political framing of the situation, alongside the potential constraints the government feels on its legal chances and political implications of attempting to prosecute, as well as the possibility of using various extralegal avenues (2010), have a real effect on how vulnerable an entity is. As Keller writes:

As one of my colleagues asks: If Assange were an understated professorial type rather than a character from a missing Stieg Larsson novel, and if WikiLeaks were not suffused with such glib antipathy toward the United States, would the reaction to the leaks be quite so ferocious? And would more Americans be speaking up against the threat of reprisals? (p. MM32)

The question, of course, is what role traditional media players in the United States played in creating that perception of Assange, and with it the license for what Keller described as the "ferocious" responses.

Other media partners were less critical of WikiLeaks. Compare Keller's "dirty white shirt" or "filthy white socks" description to *Der Spiegel's* description that Assange, "wearing a white shirt and jacket and sporting a three-day beard, was even paler than usual and had a hacking cough. 'Stress', he said, by way of apology" (Rosenbach and Stark, 2011). Similarly, Rosenbach and Stark describe Assange as a man who is very difficult to work with but one with whom (after extensive negotiations involving lawyers, dinner, and long negotiations over wine) a deal could be, and was, reached. Keller's vignettes describe someone who was only marginally sane and certainly malevolent. Other media were less critical of WikiLeaks. *El Pais* editor Javier Moreno (2010) claimed that the many hours of a meeting with Assange was insufficient to form a rigorously researched profile, but he could attest that the discussion was purely focused on a common publication calendar and on how critical it was to protect names, sources, and dates that could put people at risk.[6]

It appears that the media organizations that were the most openly associated with the WikiLeaks scoops, and therefore felt most threatened, were the most critical of WikiLeaks. Keller and the *Times*, then, are not innocent bystanders in the perceptions of Assange that made the response to him so ferocious; they are primary movers. It was the *Times*, after all, that chose to run a front-page profile of Assange a day after it began publishing the Iraq war logs in which it described him as "a hunted man" who "demands that his dwindling number of loyalists use expensive encrypted cellphones and swaps his own the way other men change shirts" and "checks into hotels under false names, dyes his hair, sleeps on sofas and floors, and uses cash instead of credit cards, often borrowed from friends" (Burns and Somaiya, 2010, p. A1).

What responsibility does the established press have toward the newcomers in the networked fourth estate not to paint them in such terms that they become fair game for aggressive, possibly life-threatening, and certainly deeply troubling pressures and threats of prosecution? There is a direct intellectual line connecting Jonathan Klein's "you couldn't have a starker contrast between the multiple layers of checks and balances, and a guy sitting in his living room in his pajamas writing what he thinks" (Foxnews.com, 2004) to Keller's "bag lady walking in off the street" (2011, p. MM32), twice denied as a source, not a partner. In combination with the US Administration's clear deference to the traditional media, on the one hand, and its repeated denunciations of, threats to, and multisystems attacks on WikiLeaks and Assange, the need of the incumbent media organizations to assert their identity and shore up their own continued vitality threatens emerging elements of the networked fourth estate. "Multiple layers of checks and balances" are merely one way of creating accountability. The social relations among elite players that make these meetings feasible and that allow Keller to present cables to the Administration are central aspects of what both the government and the incumbents of the fourth estate value; and it is the absence of such relations in the new organizational forms run by social outsiders that is so threatening. The risk is that the government will support its preferred media models, and that the incumbent mass media players will, in turn, vilify and denigrate the newer models in ways that will make them more vulnerable to attack and shore up the privileged position of those incumbents in their role as a more reliable ally-watchdog. This threat is particularly worrisome because it comes as the economics of incumbent media force us to look for new and creative networked structures to fill the vacuum left by the industrial decline of mid-twentieth-century media models.

Collaboration between networked and incumbent models of journalism

The events surrounding WikiLeaks mark the difficulties with what will inevitably become a more broadly applicable organizational model for the fourth estate. This new model will require increased integration between decentralized networked and traditional professional models of information production and concentration of attention.

On the production side, even looking narrowly at the question of leaks, spinoffs from WikiLeaks – OpenLeaks or BrusselsLeaks, efforts by established news organizations like Al Jazeera and the *New York Times* to create their own versions of secure online leaked document repositories – mark a transition away from the model of the leak to one trusted journalist employed by a well-established news organization. The advantages of moving away from this model to the person leaking the documents are obvious. A leak to one responsible organization may lead to nonpublication and suppression of the story. The *New York Times* famously delayed publication of its story on the NSA domestic eavesdropping program for a year (Farhi, 2005). WikiLeaks has shown that by leaking to an international networked organization able to deliver the documents to several outlets in parallel, whistleblowers can reduce the concern that the personal risk they take in leaking the document will be in vain. Major news organizations that will want to receive these leaks will have to learn to partner with organizations that, like WikiLeaks, can perform that function.

Leaking is of course but one of many ways in which news reporting can benefit from the same distributed economics that drive open-source development or Wikipedia. The user-created images from the London underground bombing in 2005 broke ground for this model. They were the only source of images. During the Iranian reform movement protests in 2009, videos and images created by users on the ground became the sole video feed for international news outlets, and by the time of the Tunisian and Egyptian uprisings in early 2011, the integration of these feeds into mainline reporting had become all but standard. Just as in open-source software "given enough eyeballs, all bugs are shallow" (Raymond, 2001); a distributed population armed with cameras and video recorders and a distributed population of experts and insiders who can bring more expertise and direct experience to bear on the substance of any given story will provide tremendous benefits of quality, depth, and context to any story.

But the benefits are very clearly not only on the side of traditional media integrating distributed inputs into their own model. Looking specifically at WikiLeaks and the embassy cables shows that responsible disclosure was the problem created by these documents that was uniquely difficult to solve in an open networked model. The problem was not how to release them indiscriminately or how to construct a system for sifting through these documents and identifying useful insights. Protestations of the professional press that simply sifting through thousands of documents and identifying interesting stories cannot be done by amateurs sound largely like protestations from *Britannica* editors that Wikipedia will never be an acceptable substitute for *Britannica*. At this stage of our understanding of the networked information economy, we know full well that distributed solutions can solve complex information production problems. It was the decision to preserve confidentiality that made the usual approach to achieving large-scale tasks in the networked environment – peer production, large-scale distributed collaboration – unavailable. One cannot harness thousands of volunteers on an open-networked platform to identify what information needs to be kept secret. To get around that problem, WikiLeaks needed the partnership with major players in the incumbent media system, however rocky and difficult to sustain it turned out to be.

Another central aspect of the partnership between WikiLeaks and its media partners was achieving salience and attention. There is little doubt that mass media continues to be the major pathway to public attention, even as the role of Internet news consumption rises (Pew Research, 2011). Both the WikiLeaks case and the brief event study of the $200 million a day story suggest that, at a minimum, ultimate transmission to the main agenda of the population requires transmission through mass media. However important a subject, if it cannot, ultimately, make its way to mainstream media, it will remain peripheral to the mainstream of public discourse, at least for the intermediate future (Zuckerman, 2010; 2011).[7] Networked organizations need a partnership model with traditional organizations in large part to achieve salience.

As more mature sectors across the boundary between traditional organizational models and new networked models show, creating these collaborations is feasible but not trivial. Open-source software is the most mature of these, and it shows both the feasibility and complexity of the interface between more hierarchical and tightly structured models and flat, networked, informal structures (O'Mahony and Bechky, 2008). The informality of loose networks and the safety of incumbent organizations draw different people, with different personalities and values. In looking at the WikiLeaks case, it is difficult to separate out how much of the difficulties in the interface were systemic and how much a function of interpersonal antipathy, Assange's personality, and the *Times's* ambivalence about working with WikiLeaks.[8] In thinking of the events as a case study, it is important not to allow these factors to obscure the basic insight: that collaboration is necessary, that it is mutually beneficial, and that it is hard.

Conclusion

A study of the events surrounding the WikiLeaks documents released in 2010 provides a rich set of insights about the weaknesses and sources of resilience of the emerging networked fourth estate. It marks the emergence of a new model of watchdog function, one that is neither purely networked nor purely traditional, but is rather a mutualistic interaction between the two. It also offers a richly detailed event study of the complexity of the emerging networked fourth estate, and the interaction, both constructive and destructive, between the surviving elements of the traditional model and the emerging elements of the new.

The networked fourth estate will be made up of interaction and collaboration, however difficult it may be initially. The major incumbents will continue to play an important role as highly visible, relatively closed organizations capable of delivering much wider attention to any given revelation, and carrying on their operations under relatively controlled conditions. The networked entrants, not individually, but as a network of diverse individuals and organizations, will have an agility, scope, and diversity of sources and pathways such that they will, collectively, be able to collect and capture information on a global scale that would be impossible for any single traditional organization to replicate by itself. Established news outlets find this partnership difficult to adjust to. Bloggers have been complaining for years that journalists pick up their stories or ideas without giving the kind of attribution they would normally give to journalists in other established organizations. But just as software companies had to learn to collaborate with open-source software developers, so too will this industry have to develop its interactions. One would assume that the networked components of the fourth estate will follow the same arc that Wikipedia has followed: from something that simply isn't acknowledged, to a joke, to a threat, to an indispensable part of life.

The case of WikiLeaks also teaches us that the traditional, managerial-professional sources of responsibility in a free press function imperfectly under present market conditions, while the distributed models of mutual criticism and universal skeptical reading, so typical of the Net, are far from powerless to deliver effective criticism and self-correction where necessary. The future likely is, as the *Guardian* put it, "a new model of co-operation" between surviving elements of the traditional, mass-mediated fourth estate, and its emerging networked models. The transition to this new model will likely be anything but smooth.

In conclusion, the attack on WikiLeaks, in particular the apparent fear of decentralization that it represents, requires us to understand the current decline of the traditional model of the press and the emergence of its new, networked form. At core, the multisystem attack on WikiLeaks, including mass media coverage and framing, is an expression of anxiety about the changes that the fourth estate is undergoing. This anxiety needs to be resisted, rather than acted upon, if we are to preserve the robust, open model of news production critical to democracy in the face of economic and technological change.

Notes

This chapter has been edited by the authors of this volume from a longer paper published by the Harvard Civil Rights Civil Liberties Law Review entitled, "A Free Irresponsible Press: Wikileaks and the Battle Over the Soul of the Networked Fourth Estate".

1. In February 2011, Ariana Huffington, the Huffington Post's founder, sold the website to AOL for $315 million.
2. I exclude here The Weather Channel and Yahoo News from what I consider to be "news outlets." Both are ahead of the Huffington Post.

3. A major Indian news outlet that *Forbes Magazine* described in a 2006 article as "India's top-rated English-language news channel" (Karmali, 2006).
4. "At a point when relations between the news organizations and WikiLeaks were rocky, at least three people associated with this project had inexplicable activity in their e-mail that suggested someone was hacking into their accounts" (Keller, 2011). Assange annotations on this statement: "This allegation is simply grotesque."
5. Assange, in his annotations to Benkler's paper 'A Free and Irresponsible Press: WikiLeaks and the Battle Over the Soul of the Networked Fourth Estate' (2010), explains that the disagreement with Keller was over Keller's decision to kill a piece on Task Force 373, the targeted assassination squad, authored by national security reporter Eric Schmitt, and widely considered by other papers to be one of the most important revelations in the Afghan War logs. A Nexis search of the *New York Times* suggests that, indeed, TF 373 is mentioned only once, in a brief, highly sanitized version: "Secret commando units like Task Force 373 – a classified group of Army and Navy special operatives – work from a "capture/kill list" of about 70 top insurgent commanders. These missions, which have been stepped up under the Obama administration, claim notable successes, but have sometimes gone wrong, killing civilians and stoking Afghan resentment" (Chivers et al., 2010, A1).
6. Thanks to Fernando Bermejo for the pointer and translation.
7. Discussing difficulty of getting Gabon's revolution covered by Global Voices, through the media focus on Egypt and Tunisia.
8. Assange notes that WikiLeaks had been working with individual *Times* reporters since 2007. This is, perhaps, not surprising, at a time when WikiLeaks was less well known, and played a role that fit much more closely the traditional perception of "source." By the time of the embassy cables, WikiLeaks was no longer playing that role, and the relationship was no longer up to the individual reporter writing the story.

References

AFP (2009, May 6). Future of Journalism debated in US Senate. *Google News*, Retrieved from: http://www.google.com/hostednews/afp/article/ALeqM5gWvGizqEZzkGqCUEJZjb6ldVjcBw

Alexa (2012). Ranking, for U.S., for News Site. Retrieved from: http://www.alexa.com/topsites/category/Top/News

Benkler, Y. (2006). *The Wealth of Networks*. Yale: New Haven CT

Benkler, Y. (2010). A Free and Irresponsible Press: WikiLeaks and the battle over the soul of the networked fourth estate. *Harvard Civil Rights-Civil Liberties Law Review*. Retrieved from: http://www.benkler.org/Benkler_Wikileaks_current.pdf

Benkler, Y. and Shaw, A. (2010). A Tale of Two Blogospheres: Discursive Practices on the Left and the Right (Working paper). Retrieved from: http://cyber.law.harvard.edu/sites/cyber.law.harvard.edu/files/Benkler_Shaw_Tale_of_Two_Blogospheres_Mar2010.pdf

Brown, P. (2010, November 2). Obamas' India Trip Costing USA $200 Million PER DAY. Katablog.com. Retrieved from: http://www.katablog.com/display_blog.cfm?bid=0E0FDD3C-B83E-F4FC-82E1FA3F39F534A8

Burns, J. F. and Somaiya, R. (2010, October 24). WikiLeaks Founder on the Run, Trailed by Notoriety. *New York Times*. Retrieved from: http://www.nytimes.com/2010/10/24/world/24assange.html

Chivers, C. J. & al. (2010, July 26). The War Logs: The Afghan Struggle: A Secret Archive. *New York Times*, Retrieved from: http://www.nytimes.com/2010/07/26/world/asia/26warlogs.html

Cooper, A. (2010). *Anderson Cooper 360°* [television program], 4 November, CNN

Downing, J. D. H. (ed.) (2011). *Encyclopedia of Social Movement Media*. Thousand Oaks, CA: Sage

Drudge Report (2010, November 2). Drudgereport.com. Retrieved from: http://www.drudgereportarchives.com/data/2010/11/02/20101102_155942.htm

FactCheck.org (2010, November 3).Trip to Mumbai. Factcheck.org. Retrieved from: http://factcheck.org/2010/11/ask-factcheck-trip-to-mumbai/

Farhi, P. (2005, December 17). At the Times, a Scoop Deferred. *Washington Post*. Retrieved from: http://www.washingtonpost.com/wp-dyn/content/article/2005/12/16/AR2005121601716.html

Federal Trade Commission Staff (2010). Potential Policy Recommendations to Support the Reinvention of Journalism [Workshop transcript], 15 June, 2010. Retrieved from: http://www.ftc.gov/opp/workshops/news/jun15/docs/new-staff-discussion.pdf

Flickr.com (2011). *Flickr*, http://flickr.com/ (home page)

Foxnews.com (2004, September 17). How the Blogosphere took on CBS' Docs [Partial transcript of television program], Special Report with Brit Humes, FOX. Retrieved from: http://www.foxnews.com/story/0,2933,132494,00.html

Friedman, T. (2010a, November 17). Too Good to Check. *New York Times*, Retrieved from: http://www.nytimes.com/2010/11/17/opinion/17friedman.html

Friedman, T. (2010b, December 14). We've Only Got America A. *New York Times*, Retrieved from: http://www.nytimes.com/2010/12/15/opinion/15friedman.html

GAO (1999). 'Report to Congressional Requesters: PRESIDENTIAL TRAVEL: Costs and Accounting For the President's1998 Trips to Africa, Chile, and China'. Retrieved from: http://www.gao.gov/archive/1999/ns99164.pdf

Greenwald, G. (2010, December 14). Attempts to prosecute WikiLeaks endanger press freedoms. Salon. Retrieved from: http://www.salon.com/news/opinion/glenn_greenwald/2010/12/14/WikiLeaks/index.html

N.Karmali (2006, September 18). *News Delhi TV*. Forbes.com, Retrieved from: http://members.forbes.com/global/2006/0918/034.html

Keller, B. (2011, January 30). Dealing With Assange and the WikiLeaks Secrets. *New York Times* Magazine. Retrieved from: http://www.nytimes.com/2011/01/30/magazine/30Wikileaks-t.html

LameCherry (2010, November 2). Joe Biden making his move on Obama. Lamecherry.com. Retrieved from: http://lamecherry.blogspot.com/2010/11/joe-biden-making-his-move-on-obama.html

Leigh, D. and Harding, D. (2011, January 31). WikiLeaks: Strained relations, accusations – and crucial revelations. *The Guardian*. Retrieved from: http://www. guardian.co.uk/world/2011/jan/31/WikiLeaks-embassy-cables-publication

Limbaugh, R. (2010, November 2). Stack of Stuff Quick Hits Page. *The Rush Limbaugh Show*, Retrieved from: http://www.rushlimbaugh.com/home/daily/site_110210/content/01125104.guest.html

The Media Desk (2010, November 2). Election Night: Live Blogging the Media Coverage,11:26 P.M. Carter. On Fox, Huckabee Puts a Price Tag on a State Visit, Media Decoder. *New York Times*, Retrieved from: http://mediadecoder.blogs.nytimes.com/2010/11/02/election-night-watching-the-media-coverage/#carter-on-fox-huckabee-puts-a-price-tag-on-a-state-visit

MMTV (2010, November 3). Fox Business' Bolling attacks Obama's India trip based on price tag White House called "wildly inflated". *Media matters for America*. Retrieved from: http://mediamatters.org/mmtv/201011030048

Moreno, J. (2010, December 19). Lo que de verdad ocultan los Gobiernos. El Pais, Retrieved from: http://www.elpais.com/articulo/internacional/verdad/ocultan/Gobiernos/elpepuint/20101218elpepuint_23/Tes

Murphy, J. (2009, February 11). Dan Rather Statement On Memos. *CBS News*. Retrevied from: http://www.cbsnews.com/stories/2004/09/20/politics/main644546. shtml, date accessed June 7, 2012

O'Mahony, S. and Bechky, B. A. (2008). "Boundary Organizations: Enabling Collaboration among Unexpected Allies". *Administrative Science Quarterly*, 53 (3), pp. 422–459

On theMedia. (2010, July 16). Government Intervention to Save Journalism: Transcript. *On the Media*. Retrieved from: http://www.onthemedia.org/transcripts/2010/07/16/02

Pavlus, S. (2010, November 3). White House debunks "wildly inflated" $200M-per-day price tag for Obama's India trip. *Media Matters for America*. Retrieved from: http://mediamatters.org/blog/2010/11/03/white-house-debunks-wildly-inflated-200m-per-da/172855

Pew ResearchCenter. (2011). Internet Gains on Television as Public's Main News Source, *Pew Research Center for the People and the Press*, Retrieved from: http://people-press.org/report/689/

Powers, D. (2010, November 2). Obama to See India on $200 Million a Day, Michelle Malkin. Retrieved from: http://michellemalkin.com/2010/11/02/india/

Raymond, E. S. (2001). *The Cathedral and the Bazaar: Musings on Linux and Open Soure by an Accidental Revolutionary*. Revised edition. Cambridge, MA: O'Reilly Media

Reid, D. and Teixeira, T. (2010, February 26). Are people ready to pay for online news? *BBC News*. Retrieved from: ttp://news.bbc.co.uk/2/hi/programmes/click_online/8537519.stm

Rosenbach, M. and Stark, H. (2011, January 28). Lifting the Lid on WikiLeaks: An Inside Look at Difficult Negotiations with Julian Assange. *Der Spiegel*. Retrieved from: http://www.spiegel.de/international/world/lifting-the-lid-on-wikileaks-an-inside-look-at-difficult-negotiations-with-julian-assange-a-742163.html

Rusbridger, A. (2011, January 28). WikiLeaks: The Guardian's role in the biggest leak in the history of the world. *The Guardian*. Retrieved from: http://www.guardian.co.uk/media/2011/jan/28/WikiLeaks-julian-assange-alan-rusbridger

Shapiro, C. and Varian, H. R. (1999) *Information Rules: A Strategic Guide to The Network Economy*. Boston: Harvard Business Press

Snopes.com (2010). Foreign Currency. Snopes.com, November 5, http://www.snopes.com/politics/obama/india.asp

Starr, P. (2009, March 1). Goodbye to the Age of Newspapers (Hello to a New Era of Corruption). *The New Republic*. Retrieved from: http://www.tnr.com/article/goodbye-the-age-newspapers-hello-new-era-corruption?page=1

SteveMT (2010). 2nd Update – Obama India Trip: 34 Warships and 1km-long AC Bomb-proof Tunnel!, Dailypaul.com, November 2, http://www.dailypaul.com/node/148219

White, J. (2010, November 2). $200m-a-day' cost of Barack Obama's trip to India will be picked up by U.S. taxpayers. *Daily Mail online*, Retrieved from: http://www.dailymail.co.uk/news/article-1325990/Obamas-200m-day-India-visit-picked-US-taxpayers.html

Worth, R. F. and Kirkpatrick, D. D. (2011, January 27). 'Seizing a Moment, Al Jazeera Galvanizes Arab Frustration', *New York Times*. Retrieved from: http://www.nytimes.com/2011/01/28/world/middleeast/28jazeera.html

Zuckerman, E. (2010). The Attention Deficit: Plenty of Content, Yet an Absence of Interest, Nieman Report, Fall 2010. Retrieved from: http://www.nieman.harvard.edu/reports/article/102448/The-Attention-Deficit-Plenty-of-Content-Yet-an-Absence-of-Interest.aspx

Zuckerman, E. (2010). (2011). Tunisia, Egypt, Gabon? Our responsibility to witness, My Heart's in Accra, 9 February. Retrieved from: http://www.ethanzuckerman.com/blog/2011/02/09/tunisia-egypt-gabon-our-responsibility-to-witness/

2
Following the Money: WikiLeaks and the Political Economy of Disclosure

Benedetta Brevini and Graham Murdock

In a pivotal scene in *All the President's Men,* the Oscar-winning film about the Watergate scandal, Bob Woodward, an ambitious young reporter on the *Washington Post,* goes to meet his anonymous, shadowy, informant, "Deep Throat," in an underground car park. Woodward hopes the encounter will offer clues to possible connections between the burglary at the Watergate Hotel and malpractice in President Nixon's re-election campaign. He is told to "follow the money," a trail that eventually leads to Nixon's impeachment and ignominious departure from office.

The recent controversies surrounding the WikiLeaks' release of material that has embarrassed the Obama presidency, particularly in the area of foreign policy, have focused renewed attention on the role of whistle-blowers and their relation to investigative journalism. This paper follows Deep Throat's advice and asks who has the economic power to direct the resources that underpin public disclosure in the Internet era. We will argue that this power operates along three key dimensions; control over essential infrastructure, particularly the server capacity needed to store large amounts of data; control over the income streams that support radical online disclosure; and control over the analytical labour needed to convert raw information into accessible interpretation and explanation.

WikiLeaks' struggle to establish and sustain itself offers an instructive case study of these three modalities of power in action and demonstrates, in the starkest terms, the contradictory structure of the Internet as the site of a continuous, and intensifying, struggle between openness and closure. Many early observers however failed to grasp the possibility of concentrated power and focussed instead on its openness to public participation.

Dashed hopes: from openness to closure

The public launch of the World Wide Web in the summer of 1991 was greeted with widespread enthusiasm by commentators who saw it as ending the privileged access to Internet capacity that had previously been enjoyed by academic researchers and military personnel and opening the emerging digital networks to the possibility of mass participation. They saw the power centers that had traditionally controlled vertical flows of communication being progressively challenged by horizontal networks of peer-to-peer exchange and collaboration. Citizens would freely share what they knew. With minimal distribution costs, the age of scarcity would come to an end and be replaced by a new era of abundance. For Chris Anderson, the editor-in-chief of *Wired,* the house magazine of techno optimists, "Ideas are the ultimate abundance commodity, which propagates at zero marginal cost. Once created, ideas want to spread far and wide, enriching everything they touch" (Anderson, 2009, p. 75). The traditional gatekeepers of public communication seemed finally set to be consigned to history. Freedom Forum in 1995 was convinced that "the greatest beneficiaries of the information superhighway will be mediaconsumers, who have more control over more information than ever before…. They also hear much of that information raw" (Anderson, 2009, p. 98).

Armed with this extended awareness of the key issues of the day, citizens would enter the "'21st century's electronic version of the meeting place on the hill near the acropolis where 2,500 years ago Athenian citizens assembled,'" holding the powerful to account and extending "decision making from the few in the centre of power to the many outside who may wish to participate" (Grossman, 1995, p. 49). Predictions for the formation of this new "electronic republic" have not been entirely unfounded. Social movements around the world have deployed the Web's networking capacities to publicize platforms, mobilize support, and coordinate action, with varying degrees of success. But hopes for a more general reinvigoration of democratic processes have been progressively dashed as technological potentials have been commandeered by corporate and governmental initiatives designed to reinstitute top-down control.

Forces for closure: marketization, security, geopolitics

To understand why and how this is happening, we need to remember that the Web's arrival as an everyday utility has intersected with economic and political shifts that have shaped its deployment in fundamental ways. Three are particularly relevant to the present discussion: marketization; the consolidation of the security state; and the erosion of the United States' position as the primary global superpower.

Marketization is the primary force driving the neoliberal project of dismantling the public sector and installing market dynamics and market thinking as the unchallenged criteria for organizing and evaluating economic activity (Harvey, 2007). The relentless advocacy of this "market fundamentalism" has pushed through concerted policies of privatization (selling off public assets) and liberalization (opening up monopoly and protected markets), coupled with the relaxation of regulatory controls. As a consequence, corporations have been able to extend their operations into new areas and conduct their activities with less public oversight than before. The financial crash of 2008 and its continuing aftermath has demonstrated, in the most dramatic way, the mounting public costs of this new flexibility. It has also confirmed the migration of control over public life from elected political assemblies to corporate boardrooms (Crouch, 2011).

This new business environment has shaped the development of the Internet in significant ways. Far from producing a multitude of players, the relative lack of regulation, coupled with the emerging terms of competition, have led to the progressive consolidation of control over popular Web usage into fewer and fewer corporate hands. In 2001, the top ten websites accounted for 31 percent of US page views. By 2010, that figure had climbed to 75 percent (Anderson and Wolff, 2010). A recent analysis of the Canadian situation calculated that Google had an 81 percent share of the search engine market (Winseck, 2010). The figures for other major English-speaking markets are even higher, with Google dominating 88 percent of search volume in Australia, 90.5 percent in the UK and 92 percent in New Zealand (Freedman, 2012, p.88). The online market for news, information, and analysis also displays high levels of concentration, with the top 7 percent of sites taking 80 percent of overall traffic in the United Sates and the top 10 outlets, all of which are traditional news providers or major online portals, accounting for over 25 percent of market share (Project for Excellence in Journalism, 2011). Reports of the death of gatekeeping have clearly been greatly exaggerated. Nor are social media, the main sites of peer-to-peer participation, as plural as the more optimistic projections hoped for. The Canadian study cited earlier found Facebook accounting for almost two thirds (63.2 percent) of the market, with Facebook and YouTube together taking 83.6 percent (Winseck, 2010).

The relatively weak public regulation of the Internet has had two further consequences. First, it has encouraged the leading companies, led by Google, to proceed by a series of preemptive strikes, moving into new areas or changing the terms of service unilaterally and responding to public concerns only when there is a significant backlash. Second, where regulatory arrangements are in place, as with decisions over Internet domain names, they tend to be vested in bodies with minimal public accountability.

This hollowing out of public oversight is replicated in the political area by the emergence, in the major Western powers, of the new security states that have developed in the wake of the 9/11 attacks on New York and Washington in 2001, constructed around a combination of secrecy and extended electronic surveillance. Civilian populations are continually monitored from above, in ever more comprehensive ways (see Lyon, 2006), while being denied the information they need to fully evaluate and respond to key strategic decisions. The elevation of considerations of national security over the defence of civil liberties has been replicated in the international arena in two major instances of military adventurism, Iraq and Afghanistan, ostensibly aimed at eradicating key nodes in the global "network of terror." There is now a widespread consensus that these interventions have been badly managed, inconclusive, and counterproductive. This view is shared not only by journalists covering the conflicts (see Chandrasekaran, 2012), but increasingly by insiders. In January 2012, Lt. Colonel Daniel Davis, a serving US officer with 17 years of experience, issued a dossier titled, *Dereliction of Duty II,* that was taken up by the *New York Times* and published in full in *Rolling Stone Magazine,* alleging that the American people were not being told the truth about the incompetence and failures of the mission in Afghanistan (Hastings, 2012). This disillusion has helped fuel a growing sense that the global pre-eminence previously enjoyed by the United States and supported by its major western allies, led by the United Kingdom, is ebbing away, creating new imperatives for action and diplomacy in the international arena. These concerns have increasingly centred on China's ability to move from economic power to political leverage in global geopolitics (see Jacques, 2009; Li, 2009).

This context of persistent volatility in the international arena, continuing emphasis on the need to defeat "terrorism" at home and abroad, escalating civilian surveillance, entrenched official secrecy, combined with widespread corporate disregard for the public interest, has arguably made disclosure of governmental and business malpractice more imperative than ever. But it is exactly at this point that newspapers and broadcasting organizations, the traditional fourth estate, have become both less able and less willing to act as watchdogs against abuses of power. Newspapers are closing on a daily basis. Broadcasters, faced with intensified competition, are increasingly basing their schedules on reality programs, game shows, and other formats that deliver high ratings for minimal outlay. In a cost-conscious environment, investigative journalism ticks none of the requisite boxes. It is time-consuming, takes staff away from other tasks, is expensive to sustain, and raises the possibility of expensive litigation further down the line. The result has been a marked decline. In the United Kingdom, two of the best-known sites of sustained investigation within the commercial media sector, the *Sunday Times* "Insight" team and *World in Action*, the multiple-award-winning television current affairs series, have disappeared, leaving the country's two major public broadcasting organizations, the BBC and Channel 4, to carry even more of the weight. Whether this commitment can be sustained in an increasingly pressured economic climate is an open question, however (Barnett, 2011). In the United States, investigative journalism is in accelerating decline (McChesney and Pickard 2011). Between 2003 and 2009, membership of the Investigative Reporters & Editors (IRE) organization fell by 31 percent (Walton, 2010). Intensified competition and companies' desire to boost balance sheets and share values by cutting operating costs are part of the explanation for this situation, but so too is growth of the Internet's commandeering of classified advertising (a staple income stream for many newspapers) and the miscalculation that led many newspapers to make their content freely available on the Web. It remains to be seen if attracting online display advertising and introducing electronic pay walls will stem the current outflow of income, but predictions are that if these strategies work, they are likely to do so only selectively, for titles like the *Financial Times* that command a specialized audience, or the *New York Times,* which have a solidly established reputation among affluent readers.

So we arrive at a paradox. Because of the economic and political shifts outlined earlier, the need for sustained public scrutiny of corporations and government agencies is arguably more urgent than ever. At the same time, many of the media outlets traditionally charged with this task are less and less able to discharge it.

The promise of WikiLeaks

It was against this background that the launch of WikiLeaks in 2006 was seen by activists and commentators as a major intervention, capable of redressing the balance.

By offering a high-security anonymous drop box supported by cutting-edge cryptography that rendered the original source untraceable, the founders aimed to encourage whistle-blowers working for corporations and government agencies to submit restricted and classified material uncovering deception and malpractice. The material submitted has covered a wide range of organizations and situations, from the Church of Scientology and Barclays Bank to the wholesale corruption practiced by President Moi of Kenya. But the two best-known instances both relate to American foreign policy. In April 2010, WikiLeaks issued the footage that came to be known as the *Collateral Murder* video, showing gunsight images from an Apache helicopter air strike in Baghdad in July 2006 in which an Iraqi journalist was among those killed. In November 2010, WikiLeaks collaborated with major international news organizations to publish cables from within the US State Department, recording diplomats' restricted opinions and observations on the countries and leaders they were dealing with. These and other interventions, have won widespread public and professional recognition. The organization won the *Economist's* New Media Award in 2008 and the Amnesty International UK Media Award in 2009 and in 2010. Julian Assange, the site's founder, was the Readers' Choice for *Time's* Person of the Year in 2010.

For Yochai Benkler, WikiLeaks represents a real "counter-power" that "disrupts the organisational technical form in which governments and large companies habitually control the flow of information about their behaviour in ways that constrain the capacity of others to criticise them" (Benkler, 2011; also see Benkler, Chapter 1 in this volume).

His views are echoed by the United Kingdom's Information Commissioner, who sees WikiLeaks as "part of the phenomenon of the online empowered citizen" (Gilson, 2010). The radical philosopher, Slavoj Žižek, has gone further, claiming that " the aim of the WikiLeaks revelations was not just to embarrass those in power but to lead us to mobilise ourselves to bring about a different functioning of power that might reach beyond the limits of representative democracy" (Žižek, 2011).

These plaudits are strongly reminiscent of the early optimistic projections of the Internet as a force for greater openness and democratization, but, as we have argued, these initial hopes largely ignored the way the Web's potential was being shaped in fundamental ways by the consolidation and recomposition of corporate power. The problems WikiLeaks has faced, which intensified in the aftermath of the publication of the diplomatic cables, offers a vivid case study of that power in action and of its capacity to threaten the viability of radical interventions.

Infrastructure: conditional access

In order to understand how WikiLeaks' platform works, it is useful to rely on a general model that explains how communication on the Internet operates through a series of layers. Lawrence Lessig (2002) has usefully identified three:

> At the bottom is a "physical" layer, across which communication travels. This is the computer, or wires, that link computers on the Internet. In the middle is a "logical" or "code" layer – the code that makes the hardware run. Here we might include the protocols that define the Internet and the software upon which those protocols run. At the top is a "content" layer – the actual stuff that gets said or transmitted across these wires. Here we include digital images, texts, on-line movies, and the like. These three layers function together to define any particular communications system. (Lessig, 2002, p. 23)

The control over content has attracted the most comment. The global survey conducted by the OpenNet Initiative (Deibert, Palfrey, Rohozinski, and Zittrain, 2008) identifies three common rationales for Internet filtering: "politics and power, social norms, and security concerns" (Faris and Villeneuve, 2008, p. 9). Of these, the politically motivated interventions of authoritarian and repressive regimes have attracted the most attention from Western commentators (see Morozov, 2011), particularly in cases where governments require private corporations "whose services connect one online actor to another within their territories to participate in online censorship and surveillance as a cost of doing business in that state" (Zittrain and Palfrey, 2008, p. 31).

Less visible and less remarked on is the control exercised at the next level down in Lessig's (2002) model, the level of code. As Galloway has argued, control is "endemic to all distributed networks that are governed by protocol" (Galloway, 2004, p. 141) and increasingly the technical standards and operating systems that organize and regulate online activity are established by entities that operate with minimal public oversight and accountability. The codes that generate the ranking order of sites on Google's search engine are a case in point. Protected by commercial privilege, this system has the capacity to relegate sites to low rankings, rendering them effectively invisible.

But arguably the most far-reaching potential for control is exercised at the third level down, the level of infrastructure (Lessig, 2002). This potential has increased markedly in recent years, as the capacity to store data has migrated from desktop and laptop machines to the arrays of servers owned by companies selling this service. The list of leading companies operating in the "cloud," as it has come to be called (see Milan, Chapter 11 this volume), includes some of the major computing and Internet companies, led by the Web services division of the Net's largest retailer, Amazon. Whereas other major Internet companies, such as Google, have the resources to operate their own server "farms," small Internet sites that need to store large amounts of data have little or no choice but to pay for remote storage. In the process they cede control.

WikiLeaks' release of the US embassy diplomatic cables triggered strong condemnatory reaction from governments around the world, particularly in the US, whose interests were most directly affected, with Senator Joe Lieberman, Chairman of the Homeland Security Committee declaring that "WikiLeaks' deliberate disclosure of these diplomatic cables is nothing less than an attack on the national security of the United States, as well as that of dozens of other countries" (Lieberman, 2010). Within days, a number of corporations with different connections to WikiLeaks stopped supplying their services.

The WikiLeaks website has been hosted by multiple servers and under various domain names. At the beginning of its activity in 2006, it was hosted by a server based in Sweden called PeRiQuito AB, but it later moved its servers to Amazon Web Services (AWS), which rents computer infrastructure on a self-service basis. On December 1, 2010, Amazon suspended WikiLeaks' service (Davidson, 2010). AWS does not prescreen its customers but it does have Terms of Service, and it gave WikiLeaks' breaching of these terms as the reason for its decision. However, it was revealed that the same day that Lieberman had condemned the cable leaks, he had also declared that he would "be asking Amazon about the extent of its relationship with WikiLeaks and what it and other web service providers will do in future to ensure that their services are not used to distribute stolen, classified information" (Davidson, 2010).

The univocal political reaction across the political spectrum in the United States is in marked contrast with the political response to the 1971 leak of a US Defense Department history of US involvement in Vietnam between 1945 and 1967 (see also McCurdy, Chapter 7, this volume). The study, later dubbed the Pentagon Papers, revealed that successive US administrations had knowingly misled the public about their intentions and had deliberately expanded the scope of the war, instituting bombing campaigns directed at Cambodia and Laos. Concerned that this crucial information had been kept out of the public domain, Daniel Ellsberg, who had worked on the study, photocopied the report and handed it to the *New York Times,* which began publishing extracts in June 1971. On the 29th of June, Mike Gravel, the Democratic senator from Alaska, took advantage of the provision in the US Constitution that protects material entered in the Congressional Record from prosecution, and lodged over 4,000 pages of the Pentagon Papers with the Subcommittee on Public Buildings and Goods, where they were available for public scrutiny. This material was later published as a book by the Beacon Press. It is a mark of the changed political climate outlined earlier that in the case of WikiLeaks, considerations of realpolitik have so comprehensively trumped the defense of the public interest and citizens' right to know what governments are doing in their name and why.

Amazon's cancellation of its infrastructural storage service was repeated at the second level, that of code (Lessig, 2002). On December 2, 2010, EveryDNS, the company responsible for mapping WikiLeaks' domain names, withdrew its services, claiming that the domain name had been subject to multiple Denial of Service (DoS) attacks, which were affecting the overall quality of service the company could offer its clients.

The most far-reaching ability to disrupt WikiLeaks activities lies elsewhere, however, with the financial institutions that process the donations that provide its core economic base.

Following the money

As Golding and Murdock (2005, p. 63) have argued, economic dynamics play "a central role in defining key features of the general environment within which communicative activity takes place." A critical political economy analysis of WikiLeaks' activities requires an examination of its different sources of income to assess the sustainability of WikiLeaks' operations. As shown in Table 2.1, in 2010 WikiLeaks' income was allocated to five major expense categories (Leigh and Harding, 2010; Wau Holland Foundation, 2010).

By monitoring the flows of income coming into WikiLeaks and the costs it incurs, we can begin to identify the vulnerabilities in its project and, by extension, the vulnerabilities of radical Internet platforms more generally.

Table 2.1   WIkiLeaks' expenses 2010

	%	Euros
Campaigns	35.7	143,305
Remuneration	26.0	104,477
Travel	15.4	62,053
Infrastructure	14.7	59,044
Legal advice	8.2	32,944

Source: Wau Holland Foundation (2010).

Card declined: the banking blackout

WikiLeaks' funding model has at its core a German foundation, the Wau Holland Foundation, which processes the personal donations coming into the site. In 2010, €695,000 came through general bank transfers and €635,000 through Wau Holland's account with PayPal, which since 2002 has been owned by eBay, the other major Internet retailer alongside Amazon (Wau Holland Foundation, 2010). Figure 2.1 details the flow of donations to WikiLeaks from January 2010 to August 2011.

The data in Figure 2.1 reveal a clear pattern, with donations peaking directly after the release of particularly politically sensitive material, in April 2010, when the *Collateral Murder* video was published, and again in December 2010, following the release of the diplomatic cables. This second peak was greatly helped by the increased public visibility that WikiLeaks secured through its collaboration in breaking the story with prominent national newspapers in key locations in major western countries. As Fuchs notes, the leading partners, the *Guardian,* the *New York Times,* and *Der Spiegel,* had the "reputational and political power to reach the public, whereas an alternative medium like WikiLeaks is less likely to be recognised [and] read by everyday citizens"(Fuchs, 2011, p. 11), a conclusion supported by the fact that in 2011, whereas WikiLeaks ranked 28, 167th among the world's most accessed websites, the *New York Times* ranked 88th, *Der Spiegel* was 143rd, and the *Guardian* was 168th (Fuchs, 2011).

At the same time, as the figures in Table 2.1 show, WikiLeaks has also allocated a major share of its operating income (35 percent) to launching its own campaigns. These have been aimed at extending the site's international reach, with the double intention of increasing "the global impact of the leaks" (Assange, 2010) and making it more resilient to pressure from individual states and corporations. In pursuing these aims, however, WikiLeaks has bumped up against the concentrated

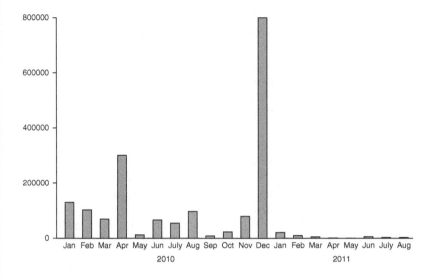

Figure 2.1   Flow of donations to WikiLeaks, 2010–2011
Source: Wau Holland Foundation (2010).

control exercised by the financial institutions that handle donations and the pivotal role played by PayPal in regulating income flow.

On December 3, 2010, PayPal stopped processing donations for WikiLeaks (Poulsen, 2010), explaining its decision as follows: "PayPal has permanently restricted the account used by WikiLeaks due to a violation of the PayPal Acceptable Use Policy, which states that our payment service cannot be used for any activities that encourage, promote, facilitate or instruct others to engage in illegal activity" (WikiLeaks, 2011).

Later, in February 2011, PayPal also suspended the account of Courage to Resist, an organization collecting funding for the defense of Bradley Manning, the soldier who originally leaked the cables. After about a month of suspension, PayPal decided to reintegrate the account, claiming that the decision "had nothing to do with WikiLeaks" (WikiLeaks, 2011; PayPal, 2011).

The corporate attack on WikiLeaks, however, continued and extended to all the major financial institutions dealing with the site. In December 2010, Swiss PostFinance froze the account for Assange's legal defense in Switzerland. The reason this given time was stated as follows:

Julian Paul Assange. The Australian citizen provided false information regarding his place of residence during the account opening process. Assange entered Geneva as his domicile. Upon inspection, this information was found to be incorrect. Assange cannot provide proof of residence in Switzerland and thus does not meet the criteria for a customer relationship with PostFinance. For this reason, PostFinance is entitled to close his account (PostFinance, 2010).

Bank of America, Visa, and MasterCard also decided to discontinue any services for WikiLeaks. MasterCard stated that it was "taking action to ensure that WikiLeaks can no longer accept MasterCard-branded products allegedly in order to prevent illegal activity" since, as the spokesperson for the company, Chris Monteiro, explained, "MasterCard rules prohibit customers from directly or indirectly engaging in or facilitating any action that is illegal" (McCullagh, 2010).

Visa joined the financial shutdown in December 2010, declaring that "Visa Europe has taken action to suspend Visa payment acceptance on WikiLeaks' website pending further investigation into the nature of its business and whether it contravenes Visa operating rules" (Eichenbaum, 2010).

Soon after, Bank of America followed. Once again, the official excuse was the breach of internal contractual policies: "This decision is based upon our reasonable belief that WikiLeaks may be engaged in activities that are, among other things, inconsistent with our internal policies for processing payments" (Schwartz, 2010).

Meanwhile, Apple was offering an alternative funding option for WikiLeaks, launching a dedicated application for the iPad and iPhone that guaranteed access to WikiLeaks documents. One dollar from every purchased application (at £1.19) would have been donated to WikiLeaks. The application was launched on December 17, 2010, but three days later Apple removed it from its Apple store on the grounds that "it violated our developer guidelines. Apps must comply with all local laws and may not put an individual or targeted group in harm's way" (BBC News, 2010).

As the data in Figure 2.1 show, the comprehensive financial blockade had a devastating impact on the flow of donations after December 2010, with Assange claiming that the site had lost 95 percent of its income (Guardian, 2010). Faced with this severe squeeze, the platform was forced to temporarily suspend its publishing activities in October 2011; it stated, "In order to ensure our future survival, WikiLeaks is now forced to temporarily suspend its publishing operations and aggressively

fundraise in order to fight back against this blockade and its propo-
nents" (WikiLeaks, 2011). As a consequence, most of the core staff were redeployed on strategies
for securing new sources of income As Kristinn Hrafnsson, the site's
spokesperson explained, "donations are now mostly limited to bank
transfers (most of them through WHF (Wau Holland Foundation)). On
top of that, there has been some income from the sales of merchandise
with WL logos etc that Spreadshirt [the website spreadshirt.com] has
been selling online" (Hrafnsson, 2012).

Analytical labour: cooking raw data

A critical political economy approach to communicative activity is not,
however, confined to analyzing how variable sources of funding affect
the viability and diversity of cultural production. It is also centrally
concerned with the labour processes that organize production on a
practical basis.

In the *Grundrisse*, the extensive set of notes and conjectures that Marx
compiled in preparation for drafting his master work, *Capital*, he introduces the idea of the "general intellect" or as he also calls it, the "social
intellect" or "general social knowledge." His remarks are tantalizingly
brief, and he never returned to them in his later work (Toscano, 2007),
but in a key passage he argues that "general social knowledge has become
a direct force of production" (Marx, 1973, p. 706), a remark that some
commentators have found startlingly prescient. As Nick Dyer-Whiteford
has argued, read through a particular lens, his discussion of the gener-
alization of productive intellectual and creative capacities is "eminently
recognisable as a portrait of what is now commonly termed an "information society" or "knowledge economy" (Dyer-Whiteford, 1999, p.486).
For early enthusiasts, the Internet's horizontal connectivity and ability
to support spaces where participants could pool their knowledge and
skills to create cumulative resources would play a central role in real-
izing the democratic potential of the new digital environment.

As the prefix "wiki" suggests, Assange originally envisaged WikiLeaks
as a demonstration of the principle of open collective production in
practice, providing a space in which users could build on the base information by adding their own material and annotations. As he explained
at the 4th Annual Logan Investigative Reporting Symposium at the
University of California, Berkeley, in April 2010:

Our initial idea – which never got implemented – our initial idea was that, look at all those people editing Wikipedia. Look at all the junk that they're working on. Surely, if you give them a fresh classified document about the human rights atrocities in Fallujah, that the rest of the world has not seen before, that, you know, that's a secret document, surely all those people that are busy working on articles about history and mathematics and so on, and all those bloggers that are busy pontificating about the abuses in Iraq and Afghanistan and other countries and other human rights disasters, who are complaining that they can only respond to the NY Times, because they don't have sources of their own, surely those people will step forward, given fresh source material and do something (Assange, 2010).

However, things went differently, and he soon found that people were not interested in the material released online without a professional interpretation (Assange, 2010). The raw data needed to be cooked by accessible and authoritative analysis, and this labour entailed costs. Despite the rhetoric of abundance and zero marginal costs, online platforms, from web-publishing ventures to disclosure platforms, do not develop for free. They require substantial labour to operate and sustain. As Andrew Graham has noted, "The fixed costs of producing content for the Internet are not falling as fast as might be supposed. This is because a major component of these fixed costs is not equipment, but people – and not just individual people, but teams of people" (Graham, 2001, p. 150). This logic applies with particular force to radical platforms, as Curran and Witschge (2010) demonstrate in their study of the website OpenDemocracy. As they point out, although "the Internet lowers costs by transferring print and reproduction costs to the user...e-zine still had to spend money. Its largest outlays were on the salaries of staff to commission, subedit, and publish (i.e., code, lay out, and present) content, and to administer its business; payments to contributors; and office overheads" (Curran and Witschge, 2010, p. 20).

In its early days WikiLeaks announced that it could draw on the labor of a substantial team of volunteers, but as Daniel Domscheit-Berg notes in his memoir of working for the site: When we claimed that several thousand volunteers and hundreds of assistants supported us, this wasn't perhaps a direct falsehood, but that number included everyone who had signed up for our mailing list.... But they didn't do anything at all. They were just names. Not even names, really, just numbers" (Domscheit-Berg, 2011, p. 22).

The effective work of checking and verifying the data submitted and administering the day-to-day running of the site is done by a small team of permanent staff, and although some agreed to work for free for several months in 2010, as the data in Table 2.1 show, "remuneration" was the second highest component of costs (after expenditure on campaigns) with payments of €104 ,000 to key employees and of €66,000 to Assange (Leigh and Harding, 2010). But the true costs of interpreting the raw data and presenting it in readily attractive forms do not appear on that list, since in a number of key cases, exemplified by the release of the US diplomatic cables, they were transferred to selected mainstream media organizations.

As we noted earlier, this "outsourcing" has the advantage of increasing the visibility and impact of the material released, but it also significantly reduces costs. As Assange has conceded, "It's really a matter of logistical overhead, in that in a large media organization, you can enter into a negotiation with it and then use all its resources to get something through, whereas dealing with a hundred freelancers or bloggers requires pretty much the same costs, but times a hundred" (Assange, 2010).

This strategy of piggybacking on the resources provided by established news media raises the question of how far a platform can claim to be a radical alternative channel for disclosure if it lacks the resources to interpret the raw data it presents in a thoroughgoing way and is obliged to relinquish its editorial independence.

The future of disclosure

In February 2012, WikiLeaks published the *Global Intelligence Files,* over five million internal e-mails from within Stratfor, a company providing confidential intelligence to a range of major corporations and US government agencies, confirming that despite the pressures placed on it, the platform is still able to attract and process material that reveal significant governmental and corporate evasion and malpractice. In March, the hacker group Anonymous collective launched Par: AnoIA (Potentially Alarming Research), a new dedicated data store for leaked material, partly in response to what they saw as the slow pace of disclosures from Wikileaks, and in the hope that researchers and journalists would use it as a basis for stories and analysis. The analysis presented here, however, raises questions about the longer term future of online disclosure.

Given WikiLeaks' inability to fully interpret the data it collects using solely its own internal resources, it is not particularly surprising that one of the newly proposed disclosure platforms, OpenLeaks, announced in January 2010 by Daniel Domscheit-Berg, opted to fundamentally change its operating mode.[1] As the site's publicity explains:

> Our intention is to function, as much as possible, as a mere conduit (akin to the telephone exchange and the post) between the whistle-blower and an organization of their choice. This means that OpenLeaks does not accept submissions or publish leaked material directly. (OpenLeaks, 2011)

In other words, the new platform aims to facilitate online publishing by acting as an intermediary between whistle-blowers and the publishing opportunities provided by "members of our community: NGOs [nongovernmental organizations], media, independent organizations, and more" (OpenLeaks, 2011).

This development, if it becomes a template for future ventures, suggests that standalone radical platforms capable of transforming information into useable knowledge by providing authoritative contextualization and interpretation are not economically sustainable. It also suggests that, far from being overtaken by the torrent of data flowing over the Internet, high-end analytical journalism remains an indispensable resource for full citizenship. Funding this work requires creative solutions since, as we noted earlier, in the present commercial environment, investigative journalism is a threatened species.

One way of minimizing commercial pressures is to seek support from charitable foundations. This option has been pursued with some success by ProPublica in the United States, funded substantially by the Sandler Foundation, and the Bureau of Investigative Journalism in the United Kingdom, established with monies from the David and Elaine Potter Foundation. Both organizations have been awarded prestigious prizes for their investigative journalism, ProPublica winning the Pulitzer Prize in successive years (2010 and 2011) and the Bureau taking the Amnesty International in 2012. Foundation support presents two problems, however. First, there is no absolute guarantee that funding will continue at a level sufficient to meet increasing costs and commitments over the longer term. Second, despite assurances of independence, there always the possibility that funders will intervene in policy decisions. The past record of the Ford Foundation, one of ProPublica's current backers, on this score suggests that progressive media reform movements would be unwise to rely mainly or wholly on "the support of liberal philanthropists" (Barker, 2008, p. 10).

The main alternative is to fund investigative journalism out of taxes levied on commercial media organizations and usage. Robert McChesney and John Nichols have proposed that funds raised from taxing consumer electronics, advertising, mobile phone subscriptions, and the use of the broadcast spectrum should be placed in a dedicated media fund. This would be used to support a Citizenship News Voucher scheme, giving "every American adult $200 ... to donate money to any non-profit news medium of her choice," with the proviso that everything produced should be made freely available on the Internet (McChesney and Nichols 2010, p. 201). They admit that this "program may not develop exactly the type of journalism our greatest thinkers believe is necessary" but urge doubters to put "their faith in the judgement of the American people" (p. 205). Dan Hind (2012) takes this argument further, arguing that public funding for investigative journalism should be contestable. Monies raised from taxation would be held by independent trusts. Journalists, and anyone else with an investigative proposal, would then pitch their ideas to open meetings, with the public voting for those they wanted to support. By shifting final decisions over investigative priorities from media professionals to the public at large, public commissioning would, so the argument goes, ensure that effort was devoted to "matters of deep general concern that cannot secure support in the existing commissioning institutions" (Hind 2012, p. 161). This system might work in areas where there is already an established body of popular concern, such as proposals to roll out commercial plantings of genetically modified crops or build more nuclear power stations, but it doesn't address issues that are concealed from public view or ones where a public proposal for investigation would put anyone providing inside information at risk and allow culpable corporations or government agencies time to devise a public relations counteroffensive or destroy vital evidence. As the experience of WikiLeaks confirms, maximum impact is achieved precisely by keeping an investigation under wraps until it is completed and published in a coordinated release, not only on the Internet but across major print and broadcast news sites that have high credibility.

The centrality of established media outlets in both producing and publicizing authoritative investigation is further underlined by the key role played by the new digital majors in regulating WikiLeaks' Internet access and use. It was the largest online retailer, Amazon, that cut off access to the servers on which significant segments of the WikiLeaks site's data was stored, and a subsidiary of one of its main retail rivals, e-Bay, that initiated the financial blockade of donations. And it was Apple, the leading force in developing the smartphones and tablets that are increasingly displacing laptops and desktops as points of entry to the Net, that cancelled the application that could have provided WikiLeaks with an alternative source of income. In none of these instances was any account taken of the potential public interest of the material being released.

The increasing control exercised by the leading commercial corporations points to the continuing need for counterinstitutions based on ideals of public service. As the experience of WikiLeaks demonstrates, the long-term future of radical disclosure is ultimately tied up with the development of a network of publicly owned and accountable supporting organizations, from server farms to banks. This is a tall order, but it is no less than what the challenges of reinvigorating democracy in contemporary conditions demand.

Note

1. OpenLeaks was supposed to start its operations in January 2011 but, at the time of writing, it is still not functioning.

References

Anderson, C. and Wolff, M. (2010 August 17). The Web Is Dead; Long Live the Internet: Who's to Blame: Them *Wired* Retrieved from http://www.wired.com/magazine/2010/08/ff_webrip/
Anderson, C. and Wolff, M. (2009). *The Future of a Radical Price*. New York: Hyperion
Assange, J. (2010). Julian Assange in Berkley, retrieved from http://zunguzungu.wordpress.com/2010/12/12/julian-assange-in-berkeley/
Assange, J. (2011). Hans Ulrich Obrist In Conversation with Julian Assange, Part I, *e-* Flux Retrieved from http://www.e-flux.com/journal/in-conversation-with-julian-assange-part-i/
Barker, M. J. (2008). 'The Liberal Foundations of Media Reform? Creating Sustainable Funding Opportunities for Radical Media Reform', *Global Media Journal: Australian Edition*, Vol 1, No 1. Retrieved from http://www.commarts.uws.edu.au/gmlou/2008_1-toc.html
Barnett, S. (2011). *The Rise and Fall of Television Journalism: Just Wires and Lights in a Box?* London: Bloomsbury
BBC news (2010 December 22). Apple removes iPhone WikiLeaks app from iTunes, *BBC News*. Retrieved from http://www.bbc.co.uk/news/technology-12059577
Benkler, Y. (2011). Networks of power, degrees of freedom. *International Journal of Communication* 5, pp. 721–755

Chandrasekaran, D. (2012). *Little America: The War within the War for Afghanistan.* London: Bloomsbury Publishing

Crouch, C. (2011). *The Strange Non-Death of Neo-Liberalism.* Oxford: Polity Press

Curran, J. and Witschge, T. (2010). *Liberal Dreams and the Internet.* In Fenton, N. Ed. New Media, Old News: Journalism and Democracy in the Digital Age. London: Sage

Davidson, A. (2010 December 1). Banishing WikiLeaks *New Yorker.* Retrieved from http://www.newyorker.com/online/blogs/closeread/2010/12/banishing-WikiLeaks.html

Deibert, R., Palfrey, J., Rohozinski, R., and Zittrain, J. (2008). *Access Denied: The Practice and Policy of Global Internet Filtering,* Retrieved from http://access.opennet.net/

Dyer-Whiteford, N. (1999). *Cyber Marx Cycles and Circuits of Struggle in High-Technology Capitalism.* Chicago: University of Illinois Press

Domscheit-Berg, D. (2011). *Inside WikiLeaks – My Time with Julian Assange at the World's Most Dangerous Website,* New York: Random House

Eichenbaum, P. (December 7, 2010). MasterCard, Visa Europe Halting Payments to WikiLeaks, *Bloomberg News.* Retrieved from http://www.bloomberg.com/news/2010-12-07/mastercard-visa-europe-suspend-use-of-brands-b y-WikiLeaks-joining-paypal.html

Faris, R. and Villeneuve, N. (2008). "Measuring Global Internet Filtering" in Deibert, R. et al. *Access Denied: The Practice and Policy of Global Internet Filtering,* Retrieved from http://access.opennet.net

Freedom Forum (1995). "Information Superhighway" in Altschiller, D. *The Information Revolution,* New York and Dublin: Wilson

Freedman, D. (2012). "Web 2.0 and the death of the blockbuster economy" in Curran, J. Fenton, N. and Freedman, D. *Misunderstanding The Internet,* London: Routledge

Fuchs, C. (2011). "WikiLeaks: power 2.0? Surveillance 2.0? Criticism 2.0? Alternative media 2.0? A political-economic analysis". *Global Media Journal Australian Edition,* 5(1)

Graham, A. (2001). 'The Assessment: Economics of the Internet', Oxford Review of Economic Policy, 17 (2)

Grossman, K. L. (1995). *The Electronic Republic: Reshaping Democracy in the Information Age.* New York: Viking

Guardian (2010 December 7). The arrest of Julian Assange: as it happened, *The Guardian.* Retrieved from http://www.guardian.co.uk/news/blog/2010/dec/07/WikiLeaks-us-embassy-cables-live-updates

Galloway, A. (2004). *How Control Exists After Decentralization Cambridge,* Massachusetts: MIT Press

Gilson, D. (2010 19 May). 'WikiLeaks gets a facelift', *Mother Jones,* Retrieved from http://motherjones.com/mojo/2010/05/WikiLeaks-assange-returns

Harvey, D. (2007). *A Brief History of Neoliberlaism.* Oxford. Oxford University Press

Hastings, M. (2012). "The Afghanistan Report the Pentagon Doesn't Want You to Read", *Rolling Stone,* February 10th.http://www.rollingston.com/politics/blog/national-affairs/the –afghanistan-report-the –pentagon-doesn't-want-you-to-read-20120210. Retrieved August 1, 2012

Hind, D. (2012). *The Return of the Public: Democracy, Power, and The Case for Media Reform*. London: Verso

Hrafnsson, K. (2012). Email correspondence with Kristinn Hrafnsson, spokeperson WikiLeaks, 5th of October 2012

Jacques, M. (2009). *When China Rules The World: The Rise of the Middle Kingdom and the End of The Western World*. London. Allen Lane

Leigh, D. and Harding, L. (2011). *WikiLeaks: inside Julian Assange's War on Secrecy*. London: Guardian Books.

Minqui, L. (2009). *The Rise of China and The Demise of the Capitalist World Economy*. New York. Monthly Review Press

Lieberman, J. (2010 November 28). Lieberman Condems new WikiLeaks disclosures Retrieved from http://lieberman.senate.gov/index.cfm/news-events/news/2010/11/lieberman-condemns-new-WikiLeaks-disclosures

Lyon, D. (2006). (ed.) *Theorizing Surveillance: The Panopticon and Beyond*. London. Taylor and Francis

Marx, C. (1973). *Grundrisse*. Harmondsworth: Penguin

McHesney, R. W. and Nichols, J. (2010). *The Death and Life of American Journalism: The Media Revolution that Will Begin the World Again*. New York. Nation Books

McChesney, R. W. and Pickard, V. (eds) (2011). *Will the Last Reporter Please Turn Out the Lights: The Collapse of Journalism and What Can be Done to Fix It*. New York. The New Press

McCullagh, D. (December 6, 2010). MasterCard pulls plug on WikiLeaks payments, *News.cnet* Retrieved from http://news.cnet.com/8301-31921_3-20024776-281.html

Morozov, E. (2011). *The Net Delusion: How Not to Liberate the World*. London: Allen Lane

Murdock, G. and Golding, P. (2005). Culture, communications and political economy. In *Mass media and society*, James Curran and Michael Gurevitch (eds). London: Hodder. pp. 60–83

OpenLeaks (2011). *What is OpenLeaks? OpenLeaks.org*, Retrieved from http://openleaks.org/content/faq.shtml

PayPal (2011 February 24). PayPal Statement on Courage to Resist Situation, PayPal Blog. Retrieved from https://www.thepaypalblog.com/2011/02/paypal-statement-on-courage-to-resist-situation/

PostFinance (2010 December 6). WikiLeaks: PostFinance ends business relationship with Assange, Retrieved From https://www.postfinance.ch/en/about/info/press/2010/message20101206.html

Poulsen, K. (2010 December 4). PayPal Freezes WikiLeaks Account, *Wired* Retrieved From http://www.wired.com/threatlevel/2010/12/paypal-WikiLeaks/

Project for Excellence in Journalism (2011 May 9). Navigating News online, *Journalism.org* Retrieved from http://www.journalism.org/analysis_report/top_25

Schwartz, N. (2010 November 18). Bank of America Suspends Payments to WikiLeaks, *New York Times* Retrieved From http://www.nytimes.com/2010/12/19/business/global/19bank.html

Toscano, A. (2007). From Pin Factories to Gold Farmers: Editorial Introduction to a Research Stream on Cognitive Capitalism, Immaterial Labour, and the General Intellect, *Historical Materialism* 15 (1)

Walton, M. (2010). "Investigative Shortfall", *American Journalism Review*, http:// www.ajr.org/article.asp?id=4904

Wau Holland Foundation (2010). "Project 04: Enduring freedom of information". Preliminary transparency report, 2010

Whalen, J. and Crawford, D. (2010 August 23). How WikiLeaks Keeps Its Funding Secret *Wall Street Journal*, Retrieved From http://online.wsj.com/article/SB1000 14240527487045541045754362319268531 98.html

WikiLeaks (2011). WikiLeaks: Banking Blockade and Donations Campaign, Retrieved from http://WikiLeaks.org/Banking-Blockade.html

Winseck, D. (2011). 'Media and Internet Concentration in Canada, 1984–2010', *Mediamorphis*, Retrieved from http://dwmw.wordplus/2011/09/03 media-an-in-ternet-concentration-in canada-1984-%E2%80%93–2010/

Zittrain, J. and Palfrey, J. (2008). Internet Filtering: the Politics and Mechanisms of Control, Deibert, R. et al. *Access Denied: The Practice and Policy of Global Internet Filtering*, Retrieved from http://access.opennet.net

Žižek, S. (2011). Good manners in the age of WikiLeaks. *London Review of Books* 33 (3). Retrieved from http://www.lrb.co.uk/v33/n02/slavoj-zizek/ good-manners-in-the-age-of-WikiLeaks#fn-ref-asterisk

3
The Leak Heard Round the World? Cablegate in the Evolving Global Mediascape

Lisa Lynch

On March 6, 2011, 100 days after US diplomatic cables leaked by WikiLeaks first appeared in the European and American press, an editorial on the WikiLeaks website celebrated the effects of the disclosures:

> [In recent months] ... the Tunisian revolution has removed a dictator of 23 years, we now know Arab countries urged America to take military action against Iran, why China cracked down on Google, that the UK government offered to "protect US interests" during its Iraq war inquiry ... how the Yemeni government agreed to cover up US airstrikes on its soil, and that US diplomats were ordered to become spies and steal the DNA and other information from UN staff and NGO's (WikiLeaks 2011a).

Given that Cablegate coverage was fading from the news outlets that had first brought the leaks to the public – the *New York Times*, the *Guardian*, *El País*, *Le Monde*, and *Der Spiegel* – the editorial was intended to challenge skeptics who claimed nothing much had come from the leaked tranche of diplomatic documents. But WikiLeaks also wished to make a strong case for Cablegate's continuing relevance: since these original outlets, or "media partners,"[1] had published only 2 percent of about 250,000 documents, further disclosures should be expected. To circulate the cables more effectively, WikiLeaks announced, the group would begin a second phase of distribution, sending selected cables to a wide variety of print, broadcast, and online-only outlets around the globe.

By mid-2011, these new WikiLeaks media partners would include the *Sunday Star Times* (New Zealand), *Folha de São Paulo* and *O Estado de Sao Paulo* (Brazil), *Novaya Gazeta* (Russia), *RUV* (Iceland), *Al Akhbar* (Lebanon), *Al-Masry Al Youm* (Egypt), *El Comercio* (Peru), *L'Espresso* (Italy), *Daily Nation* (Kenya), *CIPER* (Chile), and over 70 other media outlets. Sifting through the cables, this second group of journalists discovered stories that WikiLeaks' original media partners[2] had not found sufficiently newsworthy, including stories about Venezuelan oil contracts; African arms sales; influence-mongering in the Congo; backroom deals brokered in Peru; and a US diplomat's dismissal of Irish politicians. WikiLeaks founder Julian Assange lauded the journalism from this second group of media partners, claiming that their reporting had more direct impact than the first wave of cable reporting (Goodman 2011). Yet for the most part – though accessible online[3] – these new disclosures went unacknowledged by WikiLeaks' original partners as well as by other mainstream Western media outlets: they were thus effectively invisible to Western media audiences.

In the wake of Cablegate, much has been written about how WikiLeaks' initial release of cables demonstrated radical changes in the production and circulation of news. Scholars and media observers have focused on WikiLeaks' status as a "stateless news organization" (Rosen 2010) and on its commitment to radical transparency (Sifry 2011, Žižek 2011). They have explored the new collaborations that emerged between American and European news outlets (Leigh and Harding 2011, Keller 2011) and have noted that WikiLeaks has facilitated the emergence of "data journalism" as a means of handling large quantities of documents (Beckett 2012a). But consideration of the implications of the WikiLeaks phenomenon for journalism often overlooks the role played by the second wave of cable releases, which continued throughout the spring and summer of 2011. This omission has been unfortunate, as understanding WikiLeaks' efforts to build an international network of media "partners" is key to understanding the organization's relationship to journalism – not just journalism as practiced in legacy outlets in the United States and Europe, but journalism as a global practice.

Looking beyond WikiLeaks' initial media partnerships at the second phase of Cablegate reporting, this chapter focuses on the tension between journalism as an endeavour facilitated by expanding networks of communicative and commercial exchange and journalism as a regional enterprise shaped by regional politics and markets. I suggest that in their efforts to globalize the impact of Cablegate by diversifying its media partnerships, WikiLeaks was aided by and facilitated such new forms of exchange, but also underestimated the legal, commercial, and institutional challenges to the idea of a truly global mediascape. In the wake of Cablegate, WikiLeaks has been identified as facilitating a global public sphere (e.g., Kappert 2010; Saunders 2011; Dijkman 2012), or a space in which global political and social issues might be debated in a supranational setting. Here, I consider whether WikiLeaks' reliance on the mainstream press proved an asset or a liability in their attempts to spur a global conversation about US influence in world affairs.

The phantom global public

The idea of a "global public sphere" extends from the Habermasian notion of a space outside the control of the state, in which the circulation of information and opinion could potentially shape governance (Habermas 2000). It likewise extends from the presupposition in much American and European media scholarship that the mass media are uniquely suited to foster such a space of discourse. However, the notion of a global public sphere modifies Habermas's idea of a sphere mediating between states and their citizen-subjects. Instead, theorists of the global public sphere argue that as communications become less regionally constrained due to Internet and satellite technology, a space of discursive engagement outside of the nation-state can emerge to facilitate the emergence of global civil society (e.g., Dahlgren 1995; Tomlinson 1999; Fraser 2005; Castells 2008).

For at least a decade, there has been heated debate over the nature of this reconstituted public sphere, frequently focusing on the role professional journalism might play in constituting a global public. Volkmer (2005:151) has suggested that an increase in satellite broadcast transmissions has brought about "a new extra-societal political territory" composed of transnational individuals and communities. Boyd-Barrett and Thussu (1992), as well as other scholars, have noted that in the wake of media globalization, traditional flows of media from the global North to the global South have been disrupted by media "contra-flows" that shape new forms of global understanding and dialogue by challenging historical patterns of dominance. And Peter Berglez has argued that global crises such as climate change have resulted in the emergence of "global journalism," a new form that "transcends the domestic–foreign dichotomy" to produce accounts of "complex relations and flows across national borders and continents" (2008).

However, critics have argued that even in the face of these changes, the often balkanizing and exclusionary tendencies of legacy media remain in place, making it difficult to imagine mainstream media outlets as a platform for a new communications order. For example, Hjarvard notes

that "international" broadcast stations such as CNN often simply repro-
duce Western news interests for an elite international news audience
(2001). Thussu himself (2000) has cautioned against an easy embrace of
the ascendancy of "contra flows," noting that that these regional disrup-
tions, despite their significant local effects, rarely pose a challenge to
the hegemonic structure of global media.[4] These scholars and others see
globalization in media as inextricable from increasing corporate control
of the media. Such control perpetuates or accelerates historic power
imbalances, including elite control within the nation state and overall
dominance of the global North over the global South (Artz 2012).

As news media have increasingly moved online, some scholars have
pointed to an emerging "networked" structure of news that resembles
computer networks in breadth of distribution and rhizomatic spread,
arguing that such "networked journalism" blurs formerly rigid lines
between national news spaces (Heinrich 2011). But recent scholarship
on media law has tended to sharply qualify the degree to which the
Internet might serve as a force to overcome either the legal challenges
faced by legacy media or their limited scope of coverage. Early ideas of
the Internet as a lawless space (Ludlow et al. 1996) have given way to
cautious appraisals of the role of states in controlling access and use of
the Internet (Goldsmith and Wu 2006), surveys of the ways in which
filtering and censorship have changed the information landscape worldwide (Deibert et al. 2010), analyses of the use of "intermediary censorship" by Internet service providers, and explorations of new trends in
international libel law that have produced a chilling effect on publication worldwide (Abah 2008).

Skeptics such as McChesney and Foster (2011) point to the deep
implication of the online space in a capitalist logic that runs counter
to the emancipatory claims made on its behalf, as well. As demonstrated by the various takedowns of WikiLeaks-related sites in the wake
of Cablegate, the Internet should not be seen as a public sphere, but
rather a "quasi public sphere" that is ultimately managed by private
interests (Tufekci 2010). For journalistic organizations, those interests
are often regional, leading scholars to argue that unless markets and
audiences are truly denationalized, it is difficult to imagine how media
might transcend these local imperatives and engender global exchange
(Chalaby 2005).

This brief summary should suggest why WikiLeaks' choice to work
with the mainstream press is a productive case study in exploring
the media's role in shaping a global public. Once the group realized
the significance of the US intelligence materials in their possession,

WikiLeaks decided to shift their customary practice of using the Internet to disseminate leaked information on their own website, with the hope that partnering with the media would give their material far more public exposure (Obst 2011; Goodman 2011) and thus create the global political firestorm they believed such disclosures merited. Their final hybrid publishing plan, in which WikiLeaks released cables on their own website only after they had been vetted and redacted by the mainstream media, traded the group's customary autonomy for unprecedented media focus on the organization and its leaked cables. When this plan faltered, WikiLeaks chose not to abandon the idea of media collaboration, but to partner more "globally" with professional media outlets, in order to maximize the impact of the leaks.

WikiLeaks goes global: searching for local and regional media partners

As Cablegate unfolded, WikiLeaks' hopes for the impact of their leak were suggested by comments made on the group's Twitter feed. Several days before the embargo was lifted, WikiLeaks tweeted "the coming months will see a new world, where global history is redefined" (WikiLeaks 2010a). On December 10, after WikiLeaks and Cablegate had become worldwide news, the group tweeted "the last time there was a leak like this, Noah built himself a boat" (WikiLeaks 2010b). Drawing a connection between Cablegate and a flood of Biblical proportions, WikiLeaks suggested the leak would have ripple effects – in this case, political ones – reaching across the planet.

But if WikiLeaks' plan to redefine global history hinged on "exploiting the network of the mainstream media" (Beckett 2012b), the weeks after the Cablegate launch revealed the initial limitations of such an exploit. Cable stories in the *New York Times*, the *Guardian, El País, Le Monde,* and *Der Spiegel* had a broad geographic range, but they were intended for the elite European and American media audiences they served and thus reflected historical patterns of imperial or neoimperial news flows (Meyer 1989). Thus, though the *Guardian* wrote about a selection of cables from Italy, Egypt, and Lebanon; the *New York Times* wrote about countries including Russia and Kenya; and *El País* wrote about cables relating to Mexico and Central and Latin America, these outlets still filtered out cables that were relevant *only* to regional media outlets whose audiences did not overlap with their own.

To balance out this underrepresentation, Assange and his colleagues began approaching additional outlets, even as the initial media partners continued to publish disclosures. Some of these newer publications were as established and influential as WikiLeaks' initial partners – for example, *Asahi Shimbun*, a Japanese paper with a circulation of nearly eight million. But others, such as online Guatemalan outlet *Plaza Publica*, or the French data journalism startup *Mediapart*, were relatively new and had audiences in the thousands or tens of thousands. The outlets varied in terms of their political agendas as well; in countries with politically polarized media, an effort was made to choose publications across the political spectrum, deliberately attempting to "triangulate" by giving cables to publications with opposing political views (Satter 2011). What they had in common, however, was an interest in seeing which cables the initial media partners had overlooked that might be of interest to their own readers.

In addition to these "official" media partners, a second set of media outlets gained access to the diplomatic cables beginning in late January of 2010. *Aftenposten*, a Norwegian newspaper and subsidiary of the Schibsted Group, received the full set of cables from an undisclosed intermediary, sharing them with sister publications in the Schibsted Group as well as with select media outlets in Europe. Several further media outlets, including Israel's *Haaretz*, remained coy about how they obtained cables, neither denying contact with WikiLeaks nor affirming that they had entered into a formal partnership (Melman and Hendler 2011).[5] In some cases, this led to confusion about who WikiLeaks had established partnerships with, complicated by the fact that WikiLeaks claimed to have relationships with some papers (including *Aftenposten*) that denied having worked with the group directly.

Such exceptions aside, however, media outlets that obtained diplomatic cables in late 2010 through mid 2011 did so by entering into an agreement with WikiLeaks, and WikiLeaks followed a largely consistent strategy in establishing these relationships. Once media outlets were chosen, Assange or a WikiLeaks staff member contacted individual journalists via e-mail, inviting them to London to meet with the group. When journalists arrived in London, they were asked to sign a memorandum of understanding that requested redaction of sensitive information. They would then leave with an encrypted flash drive containing the cables. If a personal visit proved impossible – as in the case of *Asia-Plus* in Tajikistan or Lebanon's *Al-Akhbar* – files were delivered via digital dropbox and agreements were signed remotely (Khamidova 2011). Reporters at these papers then selected key cables and wrote analyses that were usually published online on their outlet's website with hyperlinks to the WikiLeaks cable database.

Cablegate: a global media story?

A survey of the sourcing and coverage of the reporting done on Cablegate by these outlets suggests the difficulty of producing "global journalism" in a media environment dominated by segmented market interests. Though Assange argued that distribution of cables to a second set of media partners had "subverted the filter of the mainstream press" (Goodman 2011), what actually happened was that these newer partners wrote stories that circulated in the regional press or in the blogosphere, but rarely attracted the attention of international media outlets. In part because they had already chosen the cables they found newsworthy, WikiLeaks' initial media partners rarely picked up stories from this second round of reporting. In one notable exception, *Asahi Shimbun* in May 2011 reported on a cable detailing US ambivalence about the planned relocation of the Okinawa military base, prompting a follow-up piece in the *New York Times*. However, the controversial US base was of direct interest to both US and Japanese audiences. The gap between the coverage in the regional publications and Euro-American press was reflected in an article in *Foreign Policy* summing up a few of the more important disclosures from WikiLeaks' second set of media partners; it was titled "The WikiLeaks You Missed" (Keating 2011).

WikiLeaks' second set of media partners, though they added considerably to the overall coverage of Cablegate, thus did not "subvert" the filter of the Western press by bringing global attention to stories the first partners had missed. Yet even if their stories did not find a global audience, Cablegate journalists writing for the second set of media partners often described their cable analyses as part of a larger international effort. This sense of shared mission is evident in a series of feature articles – usually included as part of a media outlet's packaging of their WikiLeaks exclusives – in which journalists from places including El Salvador, Nicaragua, Australia, New Zealand, Argentina, Ireland, Italy, and Guatemala use a similar blend of awe and whimsy to describe how they obtained the cables. Writing of his typically secretive and circuitous journey to Ellingham Hall (the English country estate where Assange remained under house arrest during the second phase of the cable distribution), Phillip Dorling of the *Sydney Morning Herald* noted that the house was "a marvelous example of Georgian elegance, a relic of the pre-industrial age...on the walls of the drawing room, in effect the WikiLeaks operations room, paintings of long-dead defenders of empire, mostly in scarlet uniforms, looked down on a tangle of laptops, printers, wires and power cables" (Dorling 2010). In a story titled

"The Ghost Road Towards WikiLeaks," Martin Pellecer, editor of the Guatemalan paper *Plaza Publica*, gave his WikiLeaks contact the nickname Alsan and compared negotiations with WikiLeaks with a journey to "a thick forest, like in Cobán or Narnia, where one hardly sees the sunlight (Pellecer 2011)." Describing his first, unsuccessful contact with WikiLeaks (he later travelled to London to meet Assange), the editor of the Salvadoran paper *El Faro* describes a false start that seems drawn from the pages of a detective novel:

> I received the first email in February of this year. The sender's name was indicated simply as "WL WL" and the message read: "I am writing from WikiLeaks in England. Right now, we have in our possession documents of political significance for El Salvador ... " I didn't believe him. I was not going to give away my information "in a secure way," to a stranger who supposedly was from Wikileaks ... so I deleted the mail (Dado 2011).

Other accounts detailed abandoned train stations, shadowy figures, anonymous phone calls, and further examples of what a reporter described as "spy-novel subterfuge" (Hager 2010).

Collectively, these narratives conveyed excitement at becoming part of the WikiLeaks phenomenon, an excitement that stemmed in part from gaining access to insights about the workings of power. Brazilian reporter Natalia Viana wrote that when she gained access to the cables, "I felt like a fly going into an open window of power, listening in on everything that was going on" (Viana 2011b). Ironically, such access often resulted in a disempowering awareness of how global geopolitics was shaped by US strategic interests. In consequence, frustration with the often smothering force of US "soft power" characterized many of the editorials written by the second wave of media partners. Mexico's *La Jornada* described how the cables revealed that the United States had "penetrated" Mexico, especially though oversight of the country's drug laws (*La Jornada* 2011). India's *The Hindu* noted that "the diplomatic cables leaked by the WikiLeaks have provided a rare insight into how the United States has sought to exert pressure and influence policymaking in India" (Vyas 2010). *Asahi Shimbun* wrote of "shocking" tactics among US diplomats (2011a). And the *Irish Independent* observed:

> It is clear from the cables Ireland enjoys a very "special relationship" with our allies in Washington. But this does not appear to be a relationship of equals. In the global political arena, our own interests

generally mirror that of the US, and this is vividly reflected in the Ireland Cables. But on those occasions when our interests diverge, the US State Department is never shy about showing their displeasure (Doran 2011).

Some editorials argued that this unequal relationship meant US diplomats were unable to look beyond their own interests to accurately appraise a country's political or social situation. In their introduction to a special section on cables regarding the Middle East, the English edition of the Egyptian paper *Al Masry Al Youm* cautioned that the cables were more a reflection of American misperceptions than Egyptian realities:

> As authoritative as these US diplomats strive to appear, their cables should be read for what they are: indicative of an often warped reading of reality and a reflection of anxiety regarding the precarious position that the US faces...confronting challenges that nascent powers pose to its global hegemony. (K. Fahmy 2010)

Such examples suggest that, for all the particularities of regional reporting, a common aversion toward the idea of US dominance became a unifying theme in these outlets' approach to the diplomatic cables, making much of the second wave of Cablegate reporting read like part of a shared endeavour.

Sometimes, of course, cable reporting *was* a shared endeavour. In the process of working with the cables, journalists and media outlets shared information and resources, even forming strategic partnerships across national borders. The close relationship between several of WikiLeaks' initial media partners was the most widely touted instance of such international interchange. But even as the *Times* and the *Guardian* were publishing their first cable stories, a group of international journalists was also working out of Ellingham Hall, posting stories to the WikiLeaks website, providing what one reporter described as "a spice of multiculturalism" to the largely European group of activists at Ellingham (Viana 2011). And after the second phase of cable distribution was underway, a series of networks between reporters in different countries evolved, often for the purposes of creating strong regional responses to the cables. In Central America, Costa Rican journalists requested and received permission to collaborate with Nicaraguan journalists to analyze cables (Segnini 2011). In the United States, the news magazine the *Nation* partnered with *Haïti Liberté* to distribute their reports on cables concerning Haiti, drawing on the local expertise of those reporters while bringing the cables to a wider audience. Though some of these partnerships were situational, the ability of journalists to share Cablegate resources through both formal and informal international partnerships became one of the defining features of the second phase of cable distribution, as journalists drew on and expanded existing networks of investigative practitioners to share new disclosures, suggest search practices for cable databases, and discuss the implications of Cablegate in their home regions.

The idea that Cablegate helped to foster a community of journalists seemed especially significant to small media outlets and freelancers, who at times suggested that collaboration with WikiLeaks made them members of an elite group or provided a seal of approval for a new type of journalistic practice. One American freelancer claimed "being invited to collaborate with WikiLeaks is a great accomplishment in the life of an independent journalist ... it means that others recognize you have done great work and will be remembered. It also means earning respect and credibility" (Breda 2011). The Guatemala news site *Plaza Publica* argued that WikiLeaks chose *Plaza Publica* over other Guatemalan newspapers because they were "a serious, independent media outlet that covered the those at the margins of society and promoted human rights" (Pellecer 2011). And an editorial in *Mediapart*, an online outlet for French journalists, described the site's partnership with WikiLeaks as a "reflection of the new alliance formed by the digital revolution between professionals and amateurs, journalists and activists, news professionals and citizen whistleblowers" (Bonnet 2011).

But if WikiLeaks' second set of media partners at times characterized involvement with WikiLeaks as a privilege, they also frequently described the publishing of Cablegate stories as a responsibility. Large or small, politically conservative or left-leaning, Western or non-Western, WikiLeaks' media partners justified their coverage in terms of their larger journalistic obligation to readers. In Ecuador, *El Universo* (2011) claimed that "like other national media, *El Universo* believes this information is in the public interest and should be published." In Japan, an editorial in *Asahi Shimbun* (2011b) noted the cables were "an opportunity to test our capability and responsibility as a media organization." In Mexico, *La Jornada* defended the publication of the cables by asserting "this newspaper believes that the dissemination of truth and the right of citizens to information is an indispensible factor of legality, democratic normality, accountability, and national sovereignty, and a basic obligation of journalism" (*La Jornada* 2011). In Israel, *Haaretz* referred to "a newspaper's basic commitment to its public of readers" (Melman 2011).

Read collectively, these framing editorials gesture towards an international consensus about the obligation of a newspaper to publish information that is truthful and in the public interest. In other words, they might be seen as an argument for what Stephen Reese has described as the emergence of a "global journalism ethic" (2008), in which truth-telling in the public service is privileged by journalists worldwide. But stepping back from the editorial commentary to look at the actual reporting done by these publications shows that despite the rhetoric, media outlets did not always live up to their promises of accountability and responsibility. In Russia, the dissident paper *Novaya Gazeta*, one of the two publications given access to the cable database, declared their intention to "expose corruption at the highest political strata," (Anin 2010), but then published only of handful of stories of the cables WikiLeaks supplied; indeed, the paper's editor remarked later that there were "not really any big revelations" in their coverage (Costa 2012). In Argentina, the online publication *Tribuna de Periodistas* criticized the paper *Pagina 12* for failing to publish cables critical of the government; shortly afterward the reporter who had obtained the cables for *Pagina 12*, Santiago James O'Donnell, went on to write a book, *Argenleaks*, about the constraints imposed by that paper (Toro 2011; Becerra 2011).

Beyond merely overpromising disclosures, a number of media outlets were charged with reporting on cables selectively to promote a certain political agenda. This was not surprising – in fact, Assange had anticipated it in his plan to "triangulate" the distribution of cables by choosing media outlets with opposing political viewpoints. But in some cases, politically motivated media outlets were accused of deliberately misrepresenting the contents of specific cables. For example, the pro-Kremlin *Russky Reporter* was accused of altering the meaning of cables written by US diplomats in Tbilisi during the Russia-Georgia war in August 2008 (Bigg 2010). And an Islamabad-based news service went one step further, fabricating cables that asserted Indian spies were supporting Islamist militants in Pakistan's tribal region (Walsh 2010). The cables were then picked up by several major Pakistani newspapers.

Though inaccuracies or deceptions in cable reporting were the exception rather than the rule, the gap between how some media outlets described their Cablegate coverage and the actual choices these outlets made in selecting, interpreting, and publishing cables suggests that the gesture towards a global journalism ethic evident in Cablegate reporting was more window dressing than a reflection of practice. But it would be simplistic to assume that media outlets whose Cablegate reporting was flawed or insubstantial were simply flouting journalistic principles because of a political agenda or their own economic interests. In many cases, journalists and editors justifiably feared reprisals for publishing cable stories that reflected badly on public figures in their home countries.

Controlling the message: cable reporting and reprisals

WikiLeaks' decision not to limit themselves to their initial publishing arrangements, but instead to seek out a broad spectrum of media partners, proved an innovative and often quite effective method of distributing information that might otherwise have gone unreported. At the same time, it should be noted that in many regions – including China (and most of Asia with the exception of Japan), most countries in Africa, and most of the Arab world – WikiLeaks was either unwilling or unable to establish media partnerships. In the wake of Cablegate, a survey of the fallout from Cablegate reporting from these regions areas suggests why partnerships would have been challenging. Though it is undoubtedly the case that some regional papers reported on controversial stories in their home countries through reference to the US diplomatic cables, it is also true that stories were often suppressed by censorship, self-censorship, and filtering, and that journalists and media outlets faced consequences for daring to publish.

Soon after the first cables were released, some governments simply blocked access to WikiLeaks itself or to publications discussing cables related to their countries. WikiLeaks' media partner in Lebanon, the left-wing newspaper *Al-Akhbar*, was hacked and taken offline in response to reporting on cables relating to Saudi Arabia (Kenner 2010). Saudi authorities also blocked access to this site, as well as to the London-based Arab news outlet *Elaph*. In Morocco, *El País* and *Le Monde* were blocked after publishing articles on cables (Black 2010). The Chinese government blocked access to the WikiLeaks website after the *New York Times* reported that a cable had linked China's Politburo to the December 2009 hack of Google's computer systems (Kan 2010), and Chinese government officials directed local media outlets to stop reporting on the cables (Smith 2010).

In addition to externally imposed efforts to block cable reporting, media outlets in some regions quietly or explicitly self-censored in response to perceived legal or political pressures. There was little coverage in Egypt of cables concerning presidential succession and the role of the army (Black 2010). Similarly, the Pakistani media ignored cables that reflected poorly on the military in that country (Walsh 2010). In the Bahamas, the *Nassau Guardian*, after partnering with WikiLeaks, acknowledged that it could not publish all of the cables due to local libel law – what the paper described as a "troublesome legal climate" surrounding publication (Dames 2011).

When controversial cables did become the focus of media attention in countries with more restrictive media systems, libel charges were sometimes levied to retaliate against publishers. In Zimbabwe, the wife of president Robert Mugabe filed a libel suit against the Harare-based paper the *Standard* for quoting from a WikiLeaks cable; she said that the nation's respect for her had decreased "to the point of disappearance" due to information in the cable (Reporters Without Borders 2011a). Former Zimbabwean information minister Johnathan Moyo sued the *Daily News* over their cable coverage, and Reserve Bank of Zimbabwe Governor Gideon Gono sued the *Standard* for $12.5 million (Reporters Without Borders 2011b). In Indonesia, government officials even attempted to sue two Australian newspapers – the *Age* and the *Sydney Morning Herald* – for $1 billion in damages after they published reports on cables concerning President Susilo Bambang Yudhoyono (*Jakarta Globe* 2011).

In Thailand, where strict *lèse majesté* laws forbid making negative remarks about the royal family, Scottish reporter Andrew MacGregor Marshall caused a sensation with a story about several diplomatic cables that cast the royal family of Thailand in an unflattering light. At the time, the Singapore-based Marshall was employed by *Reuters*, but the wire service refused to publish his report. Marshall thus resigned from *Reuters* and published in the British paper the *Independent* and in the US-based journal *Foreign Policy*. In an editorial published in the *Independent*, he asserted that professional ethics dictated that he publish his story despite the implications for his career (MacGregor Marshall 2011).

Aside from legal sanctions, some reporters faced violence or threats of violence after the publication of cable stories. In Panama, cables were originally given only to *EPASA*, a paper loyal to the current Martinelli administration, and stories on cables critical of the government went unreported (Ornstein 2011). But when WikiLeaks added *La Prensa* to their roster of media partners, that paper proved bolder in its selection of cables. In response, reporters from *La Prensa* were threatened in a series of videos circulated on YouTube (Medel 2011), an action that provoked concern from journalists' rights groups. In Honduras, a radio journalist who had reported on cables narrowly escaped an ambush of masked gunman in May 2011 (Greenslade 2011).

Finally, in some cases the consequences for writing about WikiLeaks have been implicit rather than explicit. In March of 2011, Ojolede Dele, publisher of the Nigerian newspaper *Next*, seemed lighthearted about the reaction to his controversial cable reporting, declaring:

> We have angered the president, made an enemy of the Speaker, failed to recommend ourselves highly to our most senior justices...and of course (former Nigerian foreign minister) Mr. Maduekwe, who used to call me his "in-law"...probably will never speak to me again as long as he lives. (Dele 2011)

Shortly after writing this editorial, however, *Next* ceased publishing cable stories; in late September, Dele announced that the paper was ceasing to publish entirely. Though no other publications have met their demise in the wake of Cablegate reporting, it is impossible to know how many journalists, editors, and publishers refrained from writing particular stories in order to keep themselves and their publications from harm.

Conclusion: Cablegate reporting beyond the second wave of media partners

By late summer of 2011, after months of secret deals, document hand-offs, and untold hours spent analyzing, contextualizing, and verifying information, fewer than 10 percent of the cables had been analyzed and made publicly available by the first and second set of media partners combined. This figure represented a significant increase over the 2 percent figure noted by WikiLeaks in March 2011, but it left a vast number of cables inaccessible to the public. As publication of the cables slowed, WikiLeaks activists became frustrated with what seemed to be their partners' inattention to the considerable number of remaining cables (*Telegraph* 2011).

At the end of August, however, everything changed. When a decrypted file containing the Cablegate cables turned up on a publicly accessible server, WikiLeaks decided to release all of the unpublished cables themselves – first in large batches according to region, then in their entirety in the form of a downloadable compressed file. The mass release of the cables was immediately condemned by the initial-media partners, who issued a statement declaring they had understood that cables would not be released unless they were vetted and redacted by professional news organizations (Ball 2011). In a press release, WikiLeaks defended the release by asserting "the decision to publish [the] cables was taken in accordance with WikiLeaks' commitment to maximising impact, [as] the cables that [have] been reported on ... demonstrate a less than satisfactory representation on the world map" (2011b).

WikiLeaks' framing of the mass release as a means to maximize the impact of their source material suggested that the group had had second thoughts about their earlier decision that the cables would have more impact when released through collaboration with the mainstream media. Indeed, revelations in the weeks that followed underscored the limits of those collaborations. WikiLeaks encouraged readers to "crowd-source" the analysis of the remaining cables, reporting their results on Twitter through the hashtag #WLFIND and on the WikiLeaks forum (WikiLeaks 2011b). In this third wave of cable reporting – beginning at the very end of August 2011 and continuing through the fall – scores of reports from the now-accessible cable database were discovered, not only by bloggers, independent journalists, and curious observers, and many subsequently drew attention from media outlets that did not previously have access to the cables in question. These included stories about Chevron's activities in Ecuador (*La Hora* 2011), a *Taipei Times* piece on China's perspective on Taiwan (Hsiu-Chuan 2011), and a story on the Mexican casino industry (*Prensa Latina* 2011). Two of the more significant concerned the health of Zimbabwean President Robert Mugabe (*BBC* 2011) and a UN investigation of an incident in Iraq in which an American soldier shot a child in the head (Schofield 2011). The latter story was picked up by major US papers and also ran in the *Tehran Times*. CNN later drew a link between coverage of the cable and US President Obama's declaration that US troops would leave Iraq by the end of 2011 (CNN 2011).

Though the cumulative impact of this third wave of cable reporting was less than that of either the first or second wave of cable reports, the very existence of significant stories that had been excluded by the filter of the mainstream press, even in the wake of expanded media partnerships, raised the question of what might have occurred had WikiLeaks released the entire tranche of cables at the very beginning of November 2010, instead of waiting until late the following year. Working with the mainstream press had allowed WikiLeaks to keep Cablegate cables in the spotlight for over nine months, but it had also transformed the cables into a commodity offered for public consumption only when the benefit to the professional media outweighed the costs of publication. Made freely available, the cables became something else: less interesting to mainstream media outlets seeking exclusive access to information, but more available to groups rendered marginal by the institutional structure of such media outlets. Had the material been available to such groups from the outset, could Cablegate could have been the impetus for a real challenge to the hegemony of institutional media, to global information flows, and to the ability of governments to restrict access to information by suppressing their national media?

Such a conjecture is provocative, but unlikely. WikiLeaks may have made a Faustian bargain in partnering with the mainstream press, but in the absence of that partnership, it is doubtful that alternative information pathways would have brought the leaked cables to broad public attention. The real question is whether WikiLeaks' strategy of "maximizing the impact" of Cablegate might have been the wrong plan in the first place. Perhaps in searching for the illusory "global public" conjured by the international media system, WikiLeaks lost sight of its own public, overextending itself in an effort to create a media event that was only rhetorically linked to the sort of political change the group had hoped for.

There is evidence that WikiLeaks realized this mistake right at the end of Cablegate. Even as the future of the organization itself became unclear, WikiLeaks has begun making efforts to sustain the conversation by fostering a sense of community among supporters. They promoted local WikiLeaks interest groups, expanded its online forums, and even backed a peer-to-peer network for activists named Global Square. It is too early to tell whether these efforts might be successful, or whether their continued existence might be too closely tied to an organization whose own survival is in question. But they exist, for the most part, entirely apart from the mainstream press, and harken more closely to WikiLeaks' roots in information activism. They are, in short, a grassroots effort to strengthen *their* public, rather than a top-down effort to constitute "a new world, in which global history is redefined."

Singular in scale and ambition, Cablegate was ultimately a bold, if flawed, attempt to use the existing media infrastructure to promote political change on the global scale. As a case study of an effort to build a global public sphere through the mainstream press, the mixed successes of Cablegate reporting illuminate how legal, commercial, and institutional challenges conspire to ensure that such a space "does not exist save in an embryonic – or at best nascent – form" (Curran and Witschge 2010, p. 103). And yet WikiLeaks' decision to task a globally distributed range of media outlets with the analysis of their leaks might also be seen as prefiguring a new stage in the evolving practice of global journalism, in which a shared archive of data becomes the basis for a collective (if not collaborative) effort to author a story with global implications. Perhaps the most enduring legacy of Cablegate will be that WikiLeaks provided a new means for professional journalists outside of the "old democracies" of the West to forge and exploit new networks of communication while participating in reporting on a global story. Though the challenges remain vast, perhaps a newly globalized community of journalists might serve in the future to mitigate the downsides of the institutions they inhabit.

Notes

1. I would like to acknowledge the research assistance of Anna Meshcherova, who helped to sift through the reporting done by WikiLeaks' research partners and assisted with translations from Russian and Spanish.
2. It should be noted here that the initial media outlets working with WikiLeaks disputed WikiLeaks' claim that they were "media partners," insisting instead that WikiLeaks was a source.
3. All of WikiLeaks' media partners had an online presence; though some cable stories were published online, there is no evidence of cable stories that appeared in print or broadcast media that did not also appear online.
4. One notable exception has been the "contra-flow" created by the Qatari television network Al Jazeera, which has indeed changed the global conversation about the Middle East (Sakr 2005). Ironically, one effect of the release of the cables was the disillusioning revelation that the head of Al Jazeera had been taking guidance from the US government (Kirkpatrick 2011).
5. WikiLeaks has since claimed that Haaretz received the cables from David Leigh of the *Guardian*.

References

Abah, A. L. (2008). Trends in international internet defamation suits. *International Communication Gazette*. LXX, 6 (December), 529–546

Anin, R. (2010, December 22). An "Assange" on both your houses! Novaya Gazeta (English edition). Retrieved from *NovayaGazeta.ru*

Appadurai, A. (1996) *Modernity at Large: Cultural Dimensions of Globalization*. Minneapolis: University of Minnesota Press

Artz, L. and Kamalipour, Y. R. (eds) (2003). *The Globalization of Corporate Media Hegemon*. Albany: SUNY Press

Asahi Shimbun Editorial Board (2011, April 4). Why The Asahi Shimbun is reporting about US diplomatic cables. The Asahi Shimbun. Retrieved from http://www.asahi.com/english/

Asahi Shimbun Editorial Board (2011, May 5). Leaked documents reveal shocking Japan-US diplomacy. The Asahi Shimbun. Retrieved from http://www.asahi.com/english/

BBC Reporting Staff (2011, September 5). WikiLeaks: Zimbawe's Robert Mugabe 'has cancer'. Retrieved from http://www.bbc.co.uk/news/world-africa-14790747

Ball, J. (2011, September 2). WikiLeaks publishes full cache of unredacted cables. *The Guardian*. Retrieved from http://www.guardian.co.uk/media/2011/sep/02/wikileaks-publishes-cache-unredacted-cables

Becerra, M. (2011, August 25). 'Wikileaks y las zonas erróneas del periodismo y la política'. El Ruido de las Nueces. Blog Retrieved from http://www.elruidodelasnueces.com.ar/?p=7972

Beckett, C. and Ball, J. (2012a). *WikiLeaks: News in the Networked Era*. Cambridge: Polity Press

Beckett, C. and Ball, J. (2012b). 'Wikileaks: Lessons for Press Policy and Regulation'. LSE Media Policy Project Blog, 22 February 2012. Blog Retrieved from http://blogs.lse.ac.uk/mediapolicyproject/page/6/

Berglez, P. (2008, December). 'What is Global Journalism?', *Journalism Studies*, IX, 6, 845–858

Bigg, C. (2010, December 13). 'Critics allege Russian magazine is misrepresenting WikiLeaks cables'. Radio Free Europe/Radio Liberty. Retrieved from *rferl.org*

Black, I. (2010, December 17). How Arab governments tried to silence WikiLeaks. *The Guardian*

Bonnet, F. and Plenel, E. (2011, February 13). Mediapart becomes new media partner for WikiLeaks. Retrieved in English from http://www.mediapart.fr

Boyd-Barrett, O., and Thussu, D. K. (1992). *Contra-flow in Global News. International and Regional News Exchange Mechanisms*. London: John Libbey

Breda, T. (2011, May 22). "We will continue working even if Julian Assange is in jail." *The Narco News Bulletin*. Retrieved from http://www.narconews.com/Issue67/article4417.html

CNN Wire Staff (2011, October 21). Obama: Iraq war will be over by year's end; troops coming home. Retrieved from *http://articles.cnn.com/*

Castells, M. (2008). "The New Public Sphere: Global Civil Society, Communication Networks, and Global Governance", *The Annals of the American Academy of Political and Social Science*, DCXVI, 1 (March), 78–93

Curran, J. and Witschge, T. (2010). "Liberal Dreams and the Internet" in N. Fenton (ed.) *New Media, Old News: Journalism and Democracy in the Digital Age*. London: Sage

Dado, C. (2011, May 23). Como llegar a WikiLeaks. Blog, retrieved from http://www.elfaro.net/es/201105/noticias/4153/

Dames, C. (2011, September 5). 250,000 WikiLeaks cables made public. Editorial in The Nassau Guardian

Deibert, R. J., Palfrey, J. G., Rohozinski, R. and Zittrain, J. (eds) (2010). *Access Controlled: The Shaping of Power, Rights and Rule in Cyberspace*. Cambridge: MIT Press

Dijkman, L. (2012). 'Do You Want To Know a Secret? WikiLeaks, Freedom, Democracy', *Amsterdam Law Forum* IV, 2, 49–64

Doran, S. (2011, May 31). WikiLeaks: The Irish Independent lifts the veil of diplomatic secrecy via 1,903 US Embassy cables. The Irish Independent

Dorling, P. (2010, December 11). How I met Julian Assange and secured the American embassy cables. Sydney Morning Herald

ElUniverso Editorial Board. (2011, April 6). 'WikiLeaks gives the cables to El Universo'. El Universo

Fahmy, K. (2010, December 26). When Historians Read WikiLeaks. *Egypt Independent*. Retrieved from http://www.egyptindependent.com/opinion/when-historians-read-wikileaks

Fraser, N. (2005). 'Transnationalizing the Public Sphere' in M. Pensky (ed.) *Globalizing Critical Theory*. Lanham: Rowman & Littlefield

Goldsmith, J. and Wu, T. (2006). *Who Controls The Internet? Illusions of a Borderless World*. Oxford University Press

Goodman, A. (2011, July 5). Video Interview with Julian Assange and Slavoj Žižek. *Democracy Now*. Can be accessed at http://www.democracynow.org/blog/2011/7/5/watch_full_video_of_wikileaks_julian_assange_philosopher_slavoj_iek_with_amy_goodman

Greenslade, R. (2011, May 3). Honduras radio journalist escapes ambush. Greenslade Blog. *The Guardian*

Habermas, J. (2000). "The Public Sphere" in P. Marris and S. Thornham (eds) *Media Studies: A Reader*. New York: NYU Press

Hager, N. (2010, December 19). WikiLeaks cloak and dagger. Sunday Star-Times. Retrieved from http://www.stuff.co.nz/sunday-star-times/features/4471086/WikiLeaks-cloak-and-dagger

Heinrich, A. (2011). *Network Journalism: Journalistic Practice in Interactive Spheres*. New York: Routledge

Hjarvard, S. (2001). "News Media and the Globalization of the Public Sphere" in S. Hjarvard (ed.) *News In A Globalized Society*. Goteborg: Nordicom Press, pp. 17–39

Hsiu-Chuan, S. (September 11, 2011). WikiLeaks: China does not support 'mutual non-denial': cable. *Taipei Times*. Retrieved from http://www.taipeitimes.com/News/taiwan/archives/2011/09/11/2003513008

Jakarta Globe Reporting Staff. (2011, March 15). Australian papers sued for $1 billion over WikiLeaks claims. *The Jakarta Globe*. Retrieved from http://www.thejakartaglobe.com

Kan, M. (2010, November 30). China blocks access to WikiLeaks. Article in *Computerworld*. Retrieved from http://www.computerworld.com

Kappert, I. (2010, December 1). WikiLeaks makes real a global public sphere. Article in *Die Tageszeitung*. Retrieved from http://worldmeets.us/dietageszeitung000014.shtml#axzz1zpJ8u33h

Keating, J. E. (2011, July 1). The WikiLeaks you missed. Article in *Foreign Policy*.

Keller, B. (2011). Introduction to *Open Secrets: WikiLeaks, War and American Diplomacy*. New York: New York Times Books

Kenner, D. (2010, December 9). Al-Akhbar hacked. *Foreign Policy Passport Blog*. Retrieved from http://blog.foreignpolicy.com/posts/2010/12/09/al_akhbar_hacked

Khamidova, P. (2011, May 16). Asia-Plus becomes partner of WikiLeaks. *Asia-Plus*. Retrieved from http://news.tj/en/news/asia-plus-becomes-partner-wikileaks?utm_source=twitterfeed&utm_medium=twitter

Kirkpatrick, D. D. (2011, September 20). After disclosures by WikiLeaks, Al Jazeera replaces its top news director. *The New York Times*

LaJornada Editorial Staff. (2011, February 10). The Transformative power of sunshine. *La Jornada*

Leigh, D. and Harding, L. (2011). *WikiLeaks: Inside Julian Assange's War on Secrecy*. London: Guardian Books

Ludlow, P., ed. (1996). *High Noon on the Electronic Frontier: Conceptual Issues in Cyberspace*. Cambridge: MIT Press, Bradford Series

Marshall, A. M. (2011, June 23). Why I decided to jeopardise my career and publish state secrets. Article in *The Independent*. Retrieved from http://www. independent.co.uk/opinion/commentators/andrew-macgregor-marshall-why-i-decided-to-jeopardise-my-career-and-publish-secrets-2301363.html June 23, 2011

McChesney, R. W. and Foster, J. B. (2011). 'The Internet's Unholy Marriage to Capitalism', *Monthly Review*, LXII, 10 (March)

Medel, M. (2011, April 12). Videos attack Panamanian journalists who published unflattering WikiLeaks cables. *Journalism in The Americas Blog*. Retrieved from http://knightcenter.utexas.edu/

Melman, Y. and Hendler, S. (2011, April 4). The Israel file. *Haaretz News*. Retrieved from http://www.haaretz.com/news/haaretz-wikileaks-exclusive/wikileaks-the-israel-file-1.354874

Melman, Y. and Hendler, S. (2011, April 15). The power of words once spoken. *Haaretz Weekend*. Retrieved from http://www.haaretz.com/weekend/week-s-end/the-power-of-words-once-spoken-1.356143

Meyer, W. H. (1989). "Global News Flows: Dependency and Neo-Imperialism", *Comparative Political Studies*, XXIII, 3

Olojede, D. (2011, March 28). My Wiki moment. [Originally at 234next.com] Retrieved from *http://groups.yahoo.com/group/Naija-news/message/6730*

Ordaz, P. (2010, December 2). Mexico: Un ejercito dividido incapaz de vener a los narcos. El Pais

Ornstein, O. (2011, March 17). How Assange gave Martinelli exclusive access to Panama cables. Article at Bananamarepublic.com Retrieved from http://www. bananamarepublic.com/2011/03/17/wikileaks-how-assange-gave-martinelli-exclusive-access-to-panama-cables/

Pellecer, M. R. (2011, August 16). El Camino de los fantasmas (hacia los WikiLeaks). Plazapublica.com. Retrieved from http://plazapublica.com.gt/content/el-camino-de-los-fantasmas-hacia-los-wikileaks

Prensa Libre reporting staff. (2011, September 6). Crimen pactó con casinos y autoridades de NL, revela cable de WikiLeaks. Prensa Libre

Reese, S. D. (2008). 'Theorizing a Globalised Journalism' in M. Loffekhilz and D. Weaver (eds) *Global Journalism Research: Theories, Methods, Findings*. Oxford: Blackwell

Reporters Without Borders Reporting Staff (2011, September 16). Former Minister sues Daily News over stories quoting WikiLeaks cables. Retrieved from http://en.rsf.org/zimbabwe-   former-minister-sues-daily-news-16–09–2011,41009. html

Reporters Without Borders Reporting Staff (2010, December 22). First Lady sues weekly for quoting WikiLeaks cables. Retrieved from http://en.rsf.org/zimbabwe-first-lady-sues-weekly-for-quoting-22–12–2010,39129.html

Rosen, J. (2010, July 26). The Afghanistan war logs released by WikiLeaks. The World's First Stateless News Organization. Retrieved from http://pressthink. org

Sakr, N. (2006). 'Challenger or Lackey? The Politics of News on Al-Jazeera' in D. K. Thussu (ed.) *Media On The Move: Global Flow and Contra-Flow*. New York: Routledge

Satter, R. G. (2011, January 25). AP Interview: WikiLeaks Seeks More Media Partners. Retrieved from http://www.guardian.co.uk/world/feedarticle/946 8530

Saunders, R. A. (2011, June 24). WikiLeaks are not terrorists – a critical assessment of the "Hacktivist" challenge to the diplomatic system. *Globality Studies Journal* No.25. Retrieved from http://globality.cc.stonybrook.edu

Schofield, M. (2011, August 31). WikiLeaks: Iraqi children in US raid shot in the head, U.N. says. *McClatchy Newspapers*. Retrieved from http://www. mcclatchydc.com/2011/08/31/122789/wikileaks-iraqi-children-in-us.html

Segnini, G. (2011, March 1). Our meeting with WikiLeaks in London. La Nacion

Sifry, M. L. (2011). *WikiLeaks and the Age of Transparency*. New York: OR Books

Smith, F. (2010, November 29). China directs local media outlets to stop reporting WikiLeaks content. *The Next Web*. Retrieved from http://thenextweb.com/asia/2010/11/29/china-directs-local-media-outlets-to-stop-reporting-wikileaks-content

Telegraph Reporting Staff. (2011, August 26). Frustrated WikiLeaks releases thousands of US diplomatic cables. *The Telegraph*. Retrieved from telegraph.co.uk

Thurman N. (2007). 'The Globalization of Journalism Online: A Transatlantic Study of News Websites and Their International Readers', *Journalism*, VIII, 3, 285–307

Thussu, D. K. (2005). 'Mapping Media Flow and Contra-Flow' in D. K. Thussu (ed.) *Media On The Move: Global Flow and Contra-Flow*. New York: Routledge

Thussu, D. K. (2000). *International communication: Continuity and Change*. London: Hodder Arnold.

Tomlinson, J. (1999). *Globalization and Culture*. Cambridge: Polity Press

Toro, E. (February 21, 2011). Incomprehensible: Why did WikiLeaks/Pagina 12 choose to filter cables? *Periodico Tribuna*. Can be retrieved in Spanish from *http://www.periodicotribuna.com.ar/8407-inentendible-por-que-wilkileaks-eligio-a-pagina12-para-filtrar-cables-secretos.html*

Tufekci, Z. (December 22, 2010). WikiLeaks exposes Internet's dissent tax, not nerd supremacy. *The Atlantic*. Retrieved from http://www.theatlantic. com/technology/archive/2010/12/wikileaks-exposes-internets-dissent-tax-not-nerd-supremacy/68397/

Viana, N. (2011a, January 27). Julian Assange Interviewed by the Brazilian People. *The Narco News Bulletin*. Retrieved from http://narconews.com/Issue67/article4305.html

Viana, N. (2011b, December 5). Julian Assange's WikiLeaks: Ten days that changed the world. *Huffington Post*. Retrieved from http://www.huffingtonpost.com/2011/12/05/julian-assange-wikileaks_n_1129355.html

Volkmer, I. (2005). "News In The Global Public Space" in S. Allan (ed.) *Journalism: Critical Issues*. Berkshire: Open University Press

Vyas, N. (December 23, 2010). WikiLeaks gives an insight into US presence. *The Hindu*

Walsh, D. (December 9, 2010). Pakistani media publishes fake cables attacking India. *The Guardian*

WikiLeaks (November 22, 2010a). The coming months will see a new world, where global history is redefined. Twitter.com

WikiLeaks (December 6, 2010b). Cablegate: Boy, the last time there was a leak like this, Noah built himself a boat. Twitter.com

WikiLeaks (March 7, 2011a). 100 days of Cablegate. WikiLeaks.org

WikiLeaks (August 28, 2011b). Global – WikiLeaks statement on the 9 month anniversary of Cablegate: Release of 133,887 cables. WikiLeaks.org

WikiLeaks (September 1, 2011c). Shining a light on 45 years of US diplomacy, it is time to open the archives forever. Twitter.com

Žižek, S. (January 20, 2011). Good manners in the Age of WikiLeaks. *London Review of Books*

4
WikiLeaks and the Public Interest Dilemma: A View from Inside the Media

Chris Elliott

Definitions of the public interest are not easy. It's an abstract concept that in a postmodernist age may appear a little pompous and an idea that lags some way behind – in that version of the phrase rather more knowingly used in newsrooms – the racier interest of the public.

However, the definition is one that is at the heart of the Leveson Inquiry,[1] which is currently grappling with the soul of the United Kingdom's newspaper industry. Whether the inquiry comes up with a wider, deeper definition of public interest than the current Press Complaints Commission[2] version may not be known for some while, as reports are yet to be written. But key to the issue are two questions: What, if anything, gives editors the right to decide what is in the public interest? And what weight should the potential for harm to individuals be given in making that decision? Or, in another form, Can the potential harm to individuals override the public interest in publication?

Questions of this kind were very much in the foreground of the minds of journalists at the *Guardian* when the newspaper tackled the mass of WikiLeaks documents in 2010.

As the *Guardian*'s readers' editor – an internal ombudsman on behalf of readers – I interviewed key *Guardian* journalists and editors for three columns that discussed the way they had tackled the issue in relation to WikiLeaks; the contents of these columns form the basis for this chapter.

In all there was a mass of some 750,000 documents and cables. There were at least five significant tranches of material released from the mass that was allegedly leaked by US intelligence analyst Bradley Manning to WikiLeaks. There was the Apache helicopter video showing the apparent casual killing of a dozen Iraqis, including two Reuters journalists; the

Afghan war logs; the Iraq war logs; the US embassy cables; and finally the Guantánamo files. In the beginning there was an unusual level of collaboration around the world among journalists working on the embassy cables and both sets of war logs.

The *Guardian's* involvement began with the release of the Afghan War Logs. In this and the next two releases, WikiLeaks cooperated with the *Guardian*, which brought together a group of papers, including the *New York Times*, to assess and edit the material. After that there was the well-documented falling-out between Julian Assange, the founder of WikiLeaks, and the *Guardian* and the *New York Times*.

The journalists and editors preparing this material for publication knew from the outset that the government and military on both sides of the Atlantic would argue that any publication of material would put the lives of soldiers and agents at risk. Could the journalists mitigate the risks to the extent where they could successfully argue that public interest outweighed the minimal risks left?

The story of the Afghan War Logs, which are tens of thousands of internal US tactical reports by troops operating in Afghanistan between January 2004 and December 2009, was published in July 2010.

There was immediate criticism from both governments and individuals of the publication. Critics focused on the risk to soldiers on the ground and to those Afghans who have cooperated with NATO forces. Much of the anger came from other papers, but the *Guardian* received only two complaints from readers who believed the newspaper was wrong to publish.

Nick Davies, who brokered the original deal to gain access to the WikiLeaks documents, says:

> The first time I spoke to Julian Assange [in Brussels in mid-June], before I saw the documents I said there are two issues: one, there may be nothing of interest here, and two, there must be a risk that publication would put people on the ground at risk. There was always a big shining light on that right from the outset. It's not our job to get people killed and I am not interested in publishing anything that might get someone killed. There were 92,000 documents and we published fewer than 300 of them. Each one was read from top to toe with the conscious aim of excluding anything that might endanger people on the ground(...). We, as journalists, have to make our own judgments. (David, quoted in Elliott, 2010)

The documents themselves were classified as "secret" in the United States. The equivalent in the United Kingdom is "confidential." That is lower than a "top secret" classification in the United Kingdom.

At the *New York Times*, where the US-based American journalists have the benefit of the First Amendment to the Constitution, a key section of which is "Congress shall make no law...abridging the freedom of speech, or of the press," they nevertheless took a slightly different approach.

Eric Schmitt, one of the authors of the *New York Times* piece said:

> I can't speak for the newspaper as a whole, but I've received a handful of emails complaining about this point [secrecy of the documents] so I expect we've received several complaints. On this story, as with all sensitive military/ intelligence/ national security articles, we took great care to mitigate any threat to US service members, Afghan security forces and informants working with the US in Afghanistan; as well as US national security, and sensitive sources and methods. We redacted [removed] the names and other identifying details from the incident reports we published in the Times. Before publication, we asked the White House, CIA and Defense Department if they had any objections to specific information being made public. They had a couple of specific requests, which we honoured because we did not feel their omission would lessen the impact of the articles. Since publication, we have not received any specific complaints on this point from the Pentagon. (Schmitt, quoted in Elliott, 2010)

In the United Kingdom, newspapers are encouraged to approach the Defence Press & Broadcasting Advisory Committee (DPBAC), which is not part of the Ministry of Defence, but is nevertheless chaired by the permanent Under-Secretary of State for Defence.[3] The role of the committee, which has press and broadcasting members but no one from the *Guardian,* is to advise publications on matters of national security. The *Guardian,* fearful of legal action that might have prevented publication, did not approach it.

The public interest test was again "front and centre" when the *Guardian* published a series of stories based on the 250,000 US diplomatic cables held by WikiLeaks. This time – with a dozen or so e-mails of protest at their publication – the theme of public interest in publishing the stories was explored in a series of pieces that have sat alongside the coverage in print and on the *Guardian*'s website. They included articles by Simon Jenkins (2010);Timothy Garton Ash (2010); Max Frankel (2010), a former *New York Times* editor who dealt with the Pentagon Papers; and a note by the editor-in-chief of the *Guardian* that aimed to tackle the issues of justification.

Among those who e-mailed and posted comments on the WikiLeaks stories online (I read through about 1,000 of the e-mails and posts on these articles), most agreed that publication was the right thing to do. But a substantial minority held a different view. Their arguments were not just that the *Guardian* had endangered lives, but that it had also made the business of governments impossible, relayed insignificant diplomatic tittle-tattle to sell newspapers, and encouraged treason and theft. And would we be sending money to Bradley Manning's defence team? (No, the *Guardian* covered the story after the material was downloaded. We did not encourage anyone to do so. But we have followed and publicized Manning's detention and trial closely.)

One view, posted at the end of a Simon Jenkins article (Jenkins, 2010) that argued "The job of the media is not to protect power from embarrassment," said:

> As much as I love the *Guardian* and use it as a primary source of news...this stinks...I ask who on staff at the *Guardian* is qualified to determine whether there is harm done by the selective release of this information? Who actually made these decisions?...You want to know where the harm will come? The whole point of making these cables available to so many of its [US government's] employees was to make it easier for the likes of Anne Patterson [a US envoy in Pakistan] to have the ability to see the forest for the trees...to connect the dots..."(Jenkins, 2010)

Another reader expressed a powerful case for publication in the public interest:

> The importance of these documents may not be in their content as sensational revelation, but merely in the fact that there is now proof of what was known...There is the revelation in minutiae of a shadow world, inhabited by the powerful who take it upon themselves to play the game of life for us...Private Manning, who may have leaked these docs, may in fact be a greater defender of democracy than Clinton, Rice, Bush, Obama etc." (Elliott, 2010)

In May 2011, the final tranche of the WikiLeaks files was published by the *Guardian* and other newspapers. By then the divisions between Julian Assange and the *Guardian,* as well as between Assange and the *New York Times,* had led him to align himself with a different group of newspapers. In the end there was a scramble to publish, but the issues around public interest and the morality of publication were the same.

In my opinion the Guantánamo coverage was the investigation that has most tested the decision-making process around the disclosure of information that may put at risk the lives of people named in the leaked documents.

Although we had only two letters of complaint from the public – in all, the *Guardian* received less than 20 formal letters of complaint throughout the whole series – there was a complaint from the lawyer of one of the detainees.

The stories emerged out of 765 military dossiers, known as detainee assessment briefs. The files, which were brought to the *Guardian* by the *New York Times*, tell, through the eyes of the US military, the story of the inmates of Guantánamo Bay, where hundreds of alleged Islamist terrorists from around the world have been taken for interrogation by US forces. The *Guardian*'s deputy editor, Ian Katz, said: "There was a lot of debate with the NYT about the redaction policy and our position was identical to the NYT" (Elliott, 2011).

The central ethical issue over identification came with a man named in the files as Adil Hadi al Jazairi Bin Hamlily (Elliott, 2011). In the case of Hamlily, the *Guardian* has been criticized by his lawyer, Clive Stafford Smith, for using material from the files that disclosed that he worked for MI6 (Stafford Smith, 2011). Stafford Smith denies that his client has ever done so (ibid., 2011).

Ian Katz, deputy editor of the *Guardian,* said that before publication the editorial team took the view that, while the *Guardian* does not generally identify serving MI6 officers, Hamlily's work was in the past, reaching back more than 10 years. In addition, he had, according to the files, double-crossed the British and was an active terrorist during that time (Elliott, 2011).

The *Guardian* had decided not to identify another detainee after representations by his lawyer.

Nearly two years after the first tranche was published, there is still no evidence that any individual has been killed as a result of the publication of the files. I still believe that their publication was in the public interest but the buck stops with the editor-in-chief, Alan Rusbridger (Elliott, 2010).

I asked him after the first tranche was published by the *Guardian* whether he thought we were right to do so. He said:

> Our starting point was that we were not going to just put things out there. The alternative was just a gigantic dump of raw information. I think that what we have done is a good thing, not a bad thing.

We were very careful to do our best to put it in context, treat it with caution. If you read the coverage you can see that there was real scepticism about the quality of some of that information. We were very careful to vet everything we published, using advice from regional specialists ... "

"We satisfied ourselves that that we hadn't broken our own internal rules in the way we handled these documents. We generally don't identify serving intelligence operatives or their contacts, although you can never say, never. I don't believe we have ever done so." (Rusbridger, quoted in Elliott, 2010)

In fact that convention, however strongly embedded in the *Guardian*'s approach to journalism, is not part of its editorial code of conduct.

Isn't it arrogant for an editor to think that he or she is in a position to decide what would cause harm and what wouldn't? Rusbridger said:

In the end you weigh up what you believe to be public good against public harm, you try to minimize the harm by highlighting public material of most public interest. You have a discussion about whether journalists should make those decisions but what it comes down to is whether you believe in the fourth estate. Alternatively you leave these decisions to be taken by elected officials or parliament but I believe that would mean that virtually no material would be released." (Rusbridger, quoted in Elliott, 2010)

And that's really the nub of the issue: public good against public harm. I once thought journalists should try to develop a really detailed "cut out and keep" definition of the public interest, but I have changed my mind. When I think of WikiLeaks – and phone hacking – the robust general guidance of the Press Complaints Commission provides a good place to start. After that, each case should be judged on its merits, remembering, as Andrew Sparrow, the *Guardian*'s award-winning blogger, has said, that society changes and needs to redefine what the public interest entails for each generation.

Notes

1. The Leveson Inquiry is a UK public inquiry into the culture, practices, and ethics of the British press following the News International phone hacking scandal in July 2011.

2. The PCC is the self-regulatory body for British printed newspapers and magazines, consisting of representatives of the major industry players in the United Kingdom.
3. Permanent under-secretaries are the most senior civil servants of a British government department.

References

Elliott, C. (August 9, 2010). Open door. The readers' editor on ... the moral and legal implications of publishing the war logs. *The Guardian*. Retrieved from http://www.guardian.co.uk/commentisfree/2010/aug/09/afghanistan-war-log s-readers-editor

Elliott, C. (May 2, 2011). Open door. The Guantánamo files. *The Guardian*. Retrieved from http://www.guardian.co.uk/commentisfree/2011/may/02/ope n-door-guantanamo-files-wikileaks

Jenkins, S. (November 28, 2010). US embassy cables: The job of the media is not to protect the powerful from embarrassment. *The Guardian*. Retrieved from http://www.guardian.co.uk/commentisfree/2010/nov/28/ us-embassy-cables-wikileaks

Garton Ash, T. (November 28, 2010). US embassy cables: A banquet of secrets. *The Guardian*. Retrieved from http://www.guardian.co.uk/commentisfree/2010/ nov/28/wikileaks-diplomacy-us-media-war

Frankel, M. (December 1, 2010). WikiLeaks: Secrets shared with millions are not secret. *The Guardian*. Retrieved from http://www.guardian.co.uk/ commentisfree/cifamerica/2010/nov/30/wikileaks-secrets-pentagon-papers

Stafford Smith, C. (April 27, 2011). These Guantánamo claims against my client are based on ignorant gossip. *The Guardian*. Retrieved from http://www. guardian.co.uk/commentisfree/2011/apr/27/guantanamo-bay-adil-hadi-jazair i-bin-hamlili?INTCMP=SRCH

5

"Something Old, Something New ... ": WikiLeaks and the Collaborating Newspapers – Exploring the Limits of Conjoint Approaches to Political Exposure

Hopeton S. Dunn

Introduction

New media are now contributing to the democratization of access to information, its creation, and its consumption. This has effectively altered the coveted gatekeeping and public agenda setting roles usually ascribed to traditional media. At the same time, a new relationship is emerging between these Web 2.0 media platforms and their traditional media counterparts, especially print media. While newspapers sometimes rely on less encumbered online sources for cutting-edge news exposés, the new-media entities also often count on the long-established traditional media institutions to provide credibility and critical analysis of new media's Web-generated news content. It is this notion of a conjoint approach to political exposure that was evident in the WikiLeaks engagement of and association with traditional news entities such as the *New York Times*, the *Guardian*, *Der Spiegel*, the *Jamaica Gleaner*, and other newspapers as outlets for its classified secret content. The chapter argues that this collaboration, although an uneasy marriage of necessity, may eventually settle into a stable cohabitation of the public sphere and will help to redefine the character of media and the meaning of "news."

This conjoint approach to political exposure, regarded by some traditionalists as simply the interplay between new Web sources and established media outlets, will likely evolve well beyond this into new hybrid forms of investigative journalism. WikiLeaks and other news blogs and online entities will continue to shape the nature of public deliberation on media content while challenging and disrupting existing or settled tenets of "proper" journalism. As the public demand for greater transparency in government and corporate life intensifies and a more organized, connected, and broadened civic culture of information flow emerges, there will be heightened attention to these collaborative public-interest exposés, which are viewed as being beyond conventional reporting modalities.

It would appear that WikiLeaks is symptomatic of a larger new-media movement whose interaction with, and disruption of, traditional media platforms will likely increase in the foreseeable future. The variety in reporting and news delivery methods will endure, but with considerable convergence and overlap. With specific reference to the collaboration between WikiLeaks and certain mainstream media outlets in exposing newsworthy political information, it is argued here that there is no need to worry about whether WikiLeaks will lead to the demise of traditional media. Instead, it would seem that WikiLeaks, as just one of many such entities that have been empowered and emboldened by new online convergences described as Web 2.0, has catalysed changes in how traditional media retrieve raw data for analysis and for news presentation in the context of communications convergence and an increasingly activist global public.

The chapter further argues that, despite differing sources and delivery platforms, news media must strive to retain their standards-bearing role of providing truthful, credible, and balanced output, in line with the ethical principles that have guided the journalism profession over the past century, while exploring opportunities for reform. What will and ought to change are the outmoded news values that currently define what is worthy of coverage and what may be exposed and when. In this way, a mutually beneficial relationship may be struck between entities such as WikiLeaks, with a more open and emergent attitude to news, and the more traditional media, with often fixed notions of what should be reported and how.

While longer-established media will continue to espouse the key tenets and twentieth-century standards of public journalism, the concept of news will evolve and will be redefined in the twenty-first century by new and emerging players, with news being regarded not just as "current" information but also as "currently available" information. In these circumstances, it appears that the unrelenting commitment to truth and balance will be pursued not just through conventional verification of data and the use of a diversity of information sources, but also through the use of emerging technologies that can enable more rapid, unauthorized disclosure of suppressed or concealed information, particularly relating to injustice and corruption in both the public and private sectors. It will be for the longer-established media to evaluate these unconventional sources and regard the "public interest" as being served through what Dahlgren (2000) posits as the emergence of a new "civic culture," understood as "collective meaning making."

Framing the WikiLeaks story

The leaking of the Pentagon Papers in 1971 (discussed in Chapter 7 of this volume) provides a significant antecedent to the WikiLeaks disclosures, differentiated in reach and impact by the technology game changer occasioned by the Digital Age. The current notably transformative period represents the age of globalization, in which the meaning of geographic distance is altered and geographical boundaries are redefined. It facilitates convergence, mobility, ubiquity of access, and the overlap and interconnection of communication by potentially bringing all media onto a single digital platform. In this domain there is seamless interaction and transmission of voice, video, and text. These sources of data can be stored and delivered anytime, anywhere, in a digital format via the Internet. It's an age that enables "always on" access to information.

The media industry in particular has adopted and adapted the Internet to reach new audiences, to segment and cater to niche markets, to enable greater coverage of events and newsworthy issues and to reach out beyond the geographical borders of the traditional news entities. Perhaps a defining force behind the integration of traditional media and Internet enabled media forms is the emergence of new business and distribution models, new delivery and user platforms and changing media content and consumption patterns. Table 5.1 below aptly captures this paradigm shift, using the status quo in 2006 as comparator to that anticipated in a 2012 scenario. The contrast is striking both in terms of technology's role and consumer habits. In the new communications paradigm, consumers are more emboldened by Web 2.0 technologies to create their own media content. The traditional media entities, driven by commercial imperatives, must integrate this into their business models, but without compromising too much on their storied gatekeeping roles, to assure accuracy and depth in news reporting.

Not only are the differences clear, but the linkages and continuities are also evident. What is now referred to as "new media" operate in association with the pre-existing network of more traditional media outlets.

Table 5.1   Changing characteristics of media

Predominant Characteristics in 2006	Predominant Characteristics in 2012
Technology Trends	**Technology Trends**
Platform owners as gatekeepers	Ubiquitous IP network for cross-platform delivery
Barriers to content creation	Ease of content creation, production, and management
Channel-centric device	Converged capability devices
Consumer Trends	**Consumer Trends**
Content for the masses	Niche and personalized content
Content push	Content push, pull, and interact
Mass marketing	Targeted and personalized marketing
Limited consumer-generated content and sharing	Mainstream consumer-to-consumer content
Timed release of content	"Always on" content sources continually updated

Source: Adapted from Deloitte MCS Limited UK, as cited in Bueti and Obiso, 2007.

Unlike the traditional media of radio, television, and print, which can be defined in terms of a particular technology, new media are device-, platform- and application-neutral. New media also envelop citizen or social media, where individuals not only consume content, but are also active producers of content in the role of "prosumers" (Toffler, 1980).

Two defining characteristics of emerging media systems in this new digital paradigm are first, that they can deliver unique, individualized information simultaneously to an infinite number of persons globally and second, that the content can be accessed, modified, and shared by all players involved. These are the equivalents of publishers, broadcasters, and consumers. The emergent twenty-first-century media are characterized not only by converged and digitized technologies, but also by a capacity for low-cost addressability and "massification" of content distribution at the same time (Dunn, 2008). These features are among those that traditional media have found to be highly attractive in new media.

Perhaps the greatest strength of the Internet-based new media platforms is the degree of power that they have now reposed within users of the technologies. They can easily crowdsource ideas (obtain by soliciting contributions from a large group of people) and solutions, create and consume content, and interact across borders, without ever interfacing with the traditional media forms. It is this complex ecology that WikiLeaks inhabits and the framework within which it ought to be understood. The modus operandi of WikiLeaks presents a scenario where these new Web 2.0 platforms enable the spread of information that may have been previously unavailable to the global public. Furthermore, the new platforms allow for an unprecedented volume of information to be released at any one time, which perhaps has caused the most concern to critics of WikiLeaks.

Transborder flows and the network society

A useful point of departure in remapping the issues generated by the emergence of WikiLeaks is the notion of the network society, as argued by Castells in his seminal book, *The Rise of the Network Society* (2000). He speaks of the new communications channels, with their many and varied systems of message distribution, as extending our global consciousness. Castells suggests that we have moved into a network society from an information society; the network society is defined as one which goes beyond primarily content in the form of data to also embrace distribution infrastructure, data management and the linkages between content producers and consumers. He argues that although previously data would tend to be monopolized, the power and reach of media networks now are greater than those of the state. He notes that the information brokers that can create new networks will have more influence on economic, social, and political life. It is not farfetched to consider WikiLeaks as being one of these influential transborder information brokers that has already reached beyond the grip of the state.

WikiLeaks may also be understood within the context of theories about the roles of and the relationship between the Internet and traditional media. Prior to the launch of the World Wide Web in the 1990s, traditional media were the primary outlets by which the public received their daily diet of information. Television, radio, and newspapers were explicitly the content and price deciders on both sides of the media market. Consumers had very little choice about what to view on television, listen to on radio, or read in their newspapers. Similarly, advertisers, the main source of revenue on the commercial side of the media business, had little bargaining power over the rates that they were charged. Newspaper editors and/or owners wielded significant power in society and, through skillfully managing the dissemination of information into the public domain, they were able to goad the public to react in particular ways. Theorists such as Cohen (1963) recognized this power of the media as "agenda setting." This was argued as a role of media in prescribing, if not what audiences should actually think, then, stunningly, what audiences, including public actors, must think about (Cohen, 1963, p. 13).

Consistent with this perspective, McCombs and Shaw (1972) noted that "in choosing and displaying news, editors, newsroom staff, and broadcasters play an important part in shaping political reality. Readers learn not only about a given issue, but also how much importance to attach to that issue from the amount of information in a news story and its position." In the preceding decade, Dearing and Rogers (1963) had conducted research along similar lines to establish the salience of media highlights to the public agenda. This was indeed the golden era of influence of media gatekeepers on the public sphere.

New media and the Internet have given rise to a dilution of this aspect of centralized media power by distributing more widely the points of origin and dissemination of news. Themselves increasingly significant sources of news, Internet blogs have engendered a remarkable reconceptualization or extension of agenda setting. These new Internet-based content streams may in fact play a crucial role in redefining what constitutes news, and they could eventually impose this on the traditional media platforms. Websites and web-logs (blogs) such as TMZ and Huffington Post, as well as viral videos on YouTube, for example, have become major sources of news and serve as important points of discussion in traditional media. On this specific point, Meraz (2009) empirically tested this notion and found that traditional media's agenda-setting power is no longer universal or singular. It seems that independent blog platforms redistribute power between traditional media and citizen media. "Traditional media's agenda setting is now just one force, though still an important one, among many competing influences. Unlike traditional media platforms, independent online networks are utilizing the blog tool to allow citizens more influence and power in setting news agendas," Meraz notes (2009, p. 701). But, in addition to blogs, there are also sites for professional updates and interpersonal interaction such as LinkedIn and more broad-based social networking and blogging sites, such as Facebook, Pinterest, Twitter and Google+, all of which offer their own means of news and information flow, interaction, sharing, and service provision.

Against this background of the increasing growth in online information channels and in the diversity of alternative media, the reduction in dominance of traditional media such as newspapers and cinema has become evident. Althaus and Tewksbury (2000) note that

> while this does not mean that new media inevitably supplants old media, the historical patterns of competition among mass media

provide strong support for aspects of the replacement hypothesis. In the United States, motion pictures, radio, newspapers, and network television all declined in popularity as newer media technologies were developed and diffused (p. 24).

Althaus and Tewksbury, in support of McCombs, ascribe the observed relationship between new and old media to the theory of relative constancy. This means that when newer media enter the market, spending on existing media tends to decline, because audiences have limited amounts of money and time, which must be reallocated across both old and new media (see also Althaus and Tewksbury, 2000).

The Internet in particular has fragmented and perhaps contracted the audience base of traditional media, given user constraints on time and money, as the constancy theory purports. The newfound liberation of audiences to create and consume content, as enabled by new Web 2.0 platforms, has arisen as the pre-eminent reason for the observed diversity in media platforms and channels. These developments lay the basis for Henry Jenkins's "participatory culture" hypothesis, which postulates, inter alia, that patterns of media consumption have been profoundly altered by the new media technologies and citizens are now able to archive, annotate, appropriate, and transform media content in a way unthinkable before (Jenkins, 2009). This analysis of participatory culture enables a better understanding of how WikiLeaks operates: as an innovative means of online content aggregation and as a repository for crowdsourcing of key data.

Hardey (2007) notes that for people globally, new media through Web 2.0 represent a "new degree of agency in constructing their engagement with resources and other users so that it is easy to form and interact with social and technological networks." He argues that "Web 2.0 is inherently social so that users are central to both the content and form of all material and resources" (Hardey, 2007, p. 60). This could be contrasted with the emergence of the Internet in the 1990s, which, while helping to ease the bottlenecks associated with the traditional media, was still in its own way exclusive and liable to be used and appropriated mainly by both economic and technology elites. It is this new degree of agency, enabled by the Web 2.0 platforms, that constitutes a distinct newness about this phase of media transition. It is also this new phase of media transition that now may make public deliberation more intense, diversified, and complex, through channels like WikiLeaks.

There is the additional dimension of public deliberations on leaked political and economic information that is enabled by the new media and Internet-based technologies. This concerns the whole notion of the transnational "citizen" or "unbounded" citizenship. Emerging information and communications technologies have allowed and facilitated greater degrees of interactivity and collaboration between people globally, irrespective of their legal citizenship. New media and the Internet are being used to mediate discussions and debates about politics, economics and social issues, and can transfer and translate them into real conclusions for action drawn in online public deliberations in at least three ways: 1) they act as tools to organize social movements at the national and transnational level, 2) they can also be used to coordinate both offline and online behaviour, and 3) they are potent conduits that can mediate transnational discussions and hence give rise to a transnational public sphere (Cammaerts and Audenhove, 2005).

In relation to the WikiLeaks story, this notion of a transnational public sphere creates an interesting dynamic between traditional media and the new-media platform. Under anonymous cover, people all over the world can secretly upload information to the whistle-blowing site. WikiLeaks in turn depends on the traditional outlets at the national level to analyse and extract meaning and purvey that meaning and conclusion to audiences within their national domains. As recounted by *New York Times* reporter Bill Keller, however, the handling of the volumes of information presented by WikiLeaks did not absolve the papers from exercising care in their own reporting. He noted that what they had done was "to fashion coherent and instructive reporting from a jumble of raw field reports" ... supplying "context, nuance and skepticism" (Keller 2011).

It can also be argued that the information released by WikiLeaks only served to heighten the understanding by people about events, aspects of which were already known. For example, Bill Keller credits the WikiLeaks cables for helping to propel the Arab Spring. The complex relationship between new media platforms and civic life is evident. Both traditional and new media can be catalysts for civic action against political and corporate nepotism and political repression. Rather than being simply a disruptive force to information dissemination and agenda-setting conventions WikiLeaks, or other similar platforms, can also provide a useful complement to conventional media forms in relaying prohibited information that is nevertheless considered vital to public discourse and action.

WikiLeaks, the public sphere and the case of the *Jamaica Gleaner*

As indicated earlier, numerous newspapers globally entered into arrangements with the WikiLeaks organization and its founder Julian Assange to publish information from secret documents, especially regarding diplomatic relations with the United States. Many observers in the Caribbean were surprised when the politically conservative Gleaner Newspaper group announced its intention to join in publishing the controversial WikiLeaks content, exposing among other things secret cables between the US Embassy in Kingston and the State Department in Washington. The documents were originally obtained by WikiLeaks under circumstances regarded in the United States as illegal.

In presenting its decision to partner with WikiLeaks, the *Gleaner's* editor-in-chief declared as follows:

> After intense discussion, the *Gleaner* took a decision to partner with independent non-profit media organisation Wikileaks to provide Jamaicans with information out of dozens of secret cables from the United States Embassy in Kingston.
>
> The diplomatic cables touch on various issues of Jamaican life and reflect the views and opinions of US Embassy officials based on conversations, documents and formal briefings.
>
> We took the decision to publish stories from these documents because we feel Jamaicans have a right to this kind of information. We agree with Wikileaks that a healthy, vibrant and inquisitive media play a vital role in making any country a better place to live and work. (Editorial, the *Gleaner*, May 21, 2011)

In the month that followed, the *Gleaner* published a steady stream of disclosures, including 25 front-page lead stories and a large number of sidebars and commentaries. Most of the instances of disclosures reported by the *Gleaner* took place in 2009 – that is, two years earlier. Nevertheless they created major interest as headline news on a daily basis, with members of the public eagerly awaiting the next edition of the newspaper. The articles generated excitement among readers of a kind not recently seen, and were the source of anxiety among sections of the political elites, whose secret contacts with the US Embassy could be disclosed at any time.

It is clear that the *Gleaner* newspaper, despite a background steeped in conventional journalism, recognized the benefits of linking with WikiLeaks to disclose secrets that would not otherwise be available to the Jamaican and global public. In a statement on July 13, 2011, the *Gleaner* reaffirmed its satisfaction with the initiative in publishing the WikiLeaks exposes. It did not matter that these reports were two years old. News was now being regarded as what we earlier called "newly available information," and not necessarily current information. While the financial rewards or increased readership would no doubt have played an important role in the newspaper's decision making, the owners of the *Gleaner* must also have perceived reputational and public-interest advantages in establishing the alliance. Something old was linking with something new to conjointly provide useful public insights into the conduct of national and international affairs that affect people's lives. The newspaper was prepared to risk association with a questionable Web-based partner, but there was a recognition that the *Gleaner* could not have done it alone, nor could WikiLeaks.

The *Gleaner*'s publication of the US diplomatic cables out of Jamaica as supplied by WikiLeaks generated a robust public debate about the public issues raised. Both in this instance and elsewhere, WikiLeaks and other similar entities will continue to shape the nature of public deliberation because of the technologies that now facilitate a more organized, connected, and a broadened "civic culture" and a more receptive context for conjoint exposés.

Dahlgren (2000) notes that "civic culture" underscores the idea of culture, defined as collective meaning making. He comments: "One could say that civic culture resides within civil society, but this is not the whole story, since civic culture shores up full-blown political participation as well, not just the pre- or proto-political activity normally gathered under the civil society label. Also, civic culture is not equivalent to the public sphere, though one could say that the public sphere is in part made possible by suitable features of a 'civic culture.'" (p. 336).

Dahlgren further notes that "normatively, a civic culture does not presuppose homogeneity among its citizens, but in the spirit of civic republicanism, it does suggest minimal shared commitments to the vision and procedures of democracy" (p. 336). Ostensibly, the notion of a civic culture with shared passion and enthusiasm for democratic principles among its members is a fertile space for whistle-blowers such as WikiLeaks to thrive. And, with expanded access to the Internet by millions of people globally, the nature of public discussions on these electronic spaces is increasingly forcing established media and political elites to take notice.

Sustainability and the future

There are many interrelated factors that predispose mainstream print media to host or publish content from Web channels such as WikiLeaks and that influence the relationship between both sides. From a business standpoint, we know that many new media outlets lower the barriers to entry into media markets and significantly lower production and reproduction costs. Additionally, there are now multiple content production and distribution channels, consistent with media ecology theories (Innis, 1951; McLuhan, 1962 and 1964; Postman, 1985 and 1992; Ong, 1982). Traditional media platforms such as newspapers are seeing significantly decreasing revenues and are therefore in need of fresh and explosive material to attract new readers or subscribers and therefore new or increased advertising revenues. On the other hand, WikiLeaks, despite its attempt with the earlier release of the Apache videos and controversially titling the video *Collateral Murder,* did not gain the momentum and public attention that it desired. This is something that Assange frequently recounted to his associates. Therefore, he needed to reach the markets and the skill sets of the mainstream media professionals. There are also crucial behavioural issues at play, that is, whether each "partner" will believe it is beyond the scrutiny and public reprimand of the other. It is precisely this idea that emerged when the *Guardian* and the *New York Times* reported on the allegations of sexual misconduct by Assange, reports that Assange strongly denied, and he criticized his print collaborators for publishing the allegation. Given these observations, a major factor that will influence the future of WikiLeaks and the sustainability of its relationship with traditional media forms is the perception of the legitimacy of WikiLeaks as a journalistic entity, regardless of whether it is controversial.

Journalists and media entities in the traditional sense of the terms exercise freedom of expression to publish material deemed important and relevant to the public interest, even if their sources obtained the information illegally. In the United States, there is the famous case of *Bartnicki v. Vopper,* in which the Supreme Court ruled that when an individual receives information from a source who has obtained it unlawfully, that individual may not be punished for publicly disseminating the information "absent a need of the highest order." In other words, no media entity should and can be prosecuted for reporting any information retrieved from WikiLeaks, once the reports satisfy the canons of "public interest" journalism. Geoffrey Storre, professor and former dean of the University of the Chicago Law School, in testimony before Congress on WikiLeaks observes that, in relation to the *Bartnicki v. Vopper* ruling:

> If we grant the government too much power to punish those who disseminate information, then we risk too great a sacrifice of public deliberation. If we grant the government too little power to control

confidentiality at the source, then we risk too great a sacrifice of secrecy. The solution is to reconcile the irreconcilable values of secrecy, on the one hand, and accountability, on the other, by guaranteeing both a strong authority of the government to prohibit leaks, and an expansive right of others to disseminate information to the public. (US Government 2010, p. 8)

Clearly, from a legal perspective, traditional media were well within their legal rights to share the leaked information (redacted and analysed) for public deliberation. But the legal status of WikiLeaks itself remains unresolved. Abbe D. Lowell, also testifying before the US Congress, noted that the prosecution of WikiLeaks or of Julian Assange, its progenitor, would be unprecedented because it

> would be applying the law to (a) non-government official, (b) who had no confidentiality agreement, (c) who did not steal the information, (d) who did not sell or pay for the information involved, (e) who was quite out front and not secretive about what he was doing, (f) who gave the U.S. notice and asked if the government wanted to make redactions to protect any information, and (g) in a context that can be argued to be newsgathering and dissemination protected by the First Amendment. If the Act applies to this disclosure, then why does it not apply as well to the articles written by *The New York Times* and other traditional media with the same disclosures? (US Government, 2010, p. 33)

To prosecute the organization, as one state in the US contemplated doing, under espionage legislation, is to travel a dangerous and unprecedented road. For in the event that WikiLeaks is prosecuted for an act that is akin to a form of investigative journalism, it would establish a dangerous precedent, which could be applied to prosecuting the traditional media, should similar circumstances arise in their hallowed "investigative journalism" output in future.

International principles of professional ethics in journalism, while speaking to the rights of people to accurate information, also stress the notions of social responsibility and commitment to objective reality (Shrivastava, 1998, p.177). David Leigh, from the *Guardian* newspaper, is repeatedly quoted as saying that "neither us nor *Der Spiegel* nor *The New York Times* was ever going to print names of people who were going to get reprisals, anymore than we would do on any other occasion." Additionally Leigh notes that "we were starting from: 'here's a document. How much of it shall we print?' whereas Julian's ideology was: 'I shall dump everything out and then you have to try and persuade me to cross a few things out.' We were coming at it from opposite poles" (Ellison 2011). It is this more radical position taken by Assange that led to the revealing of civilians'[1] names in the Afghanistan files. But it is that same attitude that has secured the disclosures that the newspapers are keen to publish, even in edited form.

It is Assange's radical position that in a way demonstrates the bolder, more catalytic and critical role that mainstream media entities must play in this increasingly corrupt global environment in order to better give effect to this emerging, inchoate, and dynamic relationship. They need each other. Because without the strictures and the standards of professional journalism and the frameworks of self-regulation in main-stream media, online whistle-blowing organizations run the risk of compromising the security, lives, and reputations of countless people. But equally, without the boldness of WikiLeaks, wrongdoing or corruption in government and corporate circles might have gone unreported.

Perhaps the modus operandi of posting unredacted documents was a direct function of the personality type and disposition of its leader, Julian Assange, qualities that are not always shared by others operating in the same domain. As is widely known, one of his key lieutenants, who was displeased about the posting of sensitive information online, has now decided to form his own breakaway whistle-blowing entity called OpenLeaks. This he has done, ostensibly, in a bid to ensure that whistle-blowing is done responsibly and does not compromise the security of innocent people. Despite this development, it remains the absolute imperative and duty of mainstream media to retain their ethical essence while reviewing and reforming the rules of defamation, reimagining the essence of news, and pushing back boundaries of acceptable journalism. A key start in this process of self-reflection on both sides is to ask the question: "Responsible to whom?"

Conclusions

The empirical and theoretical evidence discussed here suggests that new media and Internet technologies are now contributing to the democratization of access to media content creation and consumption. This has impacted the gatekeeping and public agenda setting roles usually played by traditional media. In this sense, a new form of relationship is emerging between these new media entities and traditional media, in that the latter rely to some degree on the former for news. But, there are also instances in which the new media entities must rely on the traditional media to provide credibility, analysis, and prominence of the exposés originating in new media. Emma Heald refers to this "symbiotic" relationship as it concerns WikiLeaks and is summed up in the words of Sylvie Kauffman, former editor of *Le Monde*, France: "I don't think any of us alone could have got the documents, but WikiLeaks couldn't do anything with them without us. WikiLeaks needed the reputation and expertise of mainstream media journalists to make the most of the information in its hands" (quoted in Heald, 2012).

We surmise that while this conjoint form of relationship ostensibly will continue, largely for commercial reasons, traditional media must not only remain vigilant in protecting and upholding the fundamental tenets of journalism, but must also examine opportunities for reform. In many countries, changes to the defamation laws are required that would allow for greater engagement in investigative work without attracting the existing levels of exposure to charges of libel. While retaining their ethical safeguards, traditional media will also need to continue to re-examine their notions of what is news and to alter conventional ideas of what are appropriate as news sources. New media, for their part, must be allowed to emerge with their own radical traditions, while eventually coming to embrace even the most basic editorial principles. These include commitment to thorough and careful analysis, the verification of data accuracy, protection of sources, and the seeking out of alternative information sources. In the meantime, it is important that new media be allowed to drive the emerging radical culture of disclosure, largely unencumbered by traditional constraints. WikiLeaks clearly filled an important vacuum, and the series of events that have transpired in the saga have opened up the dialogue on journalistic standards, regulation, ethics, and law for both new and traditional media, if nothing else.

New entrants to the media landscape, such as WikiLeaks, facilitated by Internet and Web 2.0 technologies, are important catalysts to engender greater depth, boldness, and new information flows, to stimulate traditional media, and to fuel more robust public discourse. Conventional media such as newspapers have operated in this information-gathering role for centuries, with varying degrees of success. And despite their waning readership, such established news organizations continue to hold accumulated public trust and credibility over centuries of their operation. It would seem therefore to be in the public interest that these traditional outlets that we call in the title "something old" should link with new forms like whistle-blower sites that may be called "something new" to create a more potent, hybrid form of journalistic practice for greater public probity.

Applying Jenkins and Hardey's ideas about renewed agency to this dynamic media ecology, we can only postulate that the nature of political exposure and the process of public deliberation on these issues have been irrevocably altered, even though we do not and cannot yet know the full extent of the changes. We have seen the beginnings of this putative marriage of convenience that will likely be uneasy and delimited by differing histories, culture, and modus operandi. There will be predictable ups and downs. But they need each other in order to survive, and if the early tentative steps towards collaboration are sustained, civic discourse will be enriched by both new and the older entities, which may become indistinguishable in their core journalistic norms in the future.

Note

1. These documents published by WikiLeaks in 2010 comprised detailed internal U.S. military logs on the war in Afghanistan. It was felt that the publication of the names of civilian informants would endanger their lives.

References

Althaus, S. and Tewksbury D. (2000). Agenda Setting and the "new" News: Patterns of Issue Importance Among Readers of the Paper and Online Versions of the *New York Times*, *Communications Research* 29 (2), 180–207

Bueti, C. and Obiso, M. (2007). Content Delivery Platforms in a Converging World. Retrieved June 30, 2012 from http://www.itu.int/osg/spu/stn/digital-content/Presentations/Day1/Session4/21%20June-Bueti-Obiso.pdf

Cammaerts, B. and Audenhove, L. (2005). Online Political Debate, Unbounded Citizenship, and the Problematic Nature of a Transnational Public Sphere. *Political Communication* 22, 179–196

Castells, M. (2000). *The Rise of Network Society*. Oxford: Blackwell Publishers

Cohen, B. (1963). *The Press and Foreign Policy*. Princeton: Princeton University Press

Dahlgren, P. (2000). The Internet and the Democratization of Civic Culture. *Journal of Political Communication* 17, 335–340

Dearing, J. W. and Rogers, E. M. (1966). *Agenda Setting*. London: Sage

Dunn, H. (2008). Regulating the Changing Face of Electronic Media in Jamaica. Retrieved June 25, 2012 from http://www.broadcastingcommission.org/speeches_and_presentations#speeches-and-presentations

Ellison, S. (February 11, 2011). The Man Who Spilled the Secrets. Retrieved September 10, 2012 from http://www.vanityfair.com/politics/features/2011/02/the-guardian-201102

Gleaner Newspaper Online. (July 13, 2011). WikiLeaks: What We Published. Retrieved August 15, 2012 from http://jamaica-gleaner.com/gleaner/20110713/lead/lead6.html

Gleaner Newspaper Online. (May 22, 2011). Wikileaks Secrets! Busted. Retrieved August 15, 2012 from http://jamaica-gleaner.com/gleaner/20110522/lead/lead1.html

Hardey, M. (2007). The City in the Age of Web 2.0: A New Synergistic Relationship between Place and People. *Information, Communication, & Society 10* (6), 867–884

Heald, E. (2012). The Impact of WikiLeaks on Professional Media. Retrieved June 20, 2012 from http://www.editorsweblog.org/2012/02/16/the-impact-of-Wiki Leaks-on-professional-media

Howard, P. (2011). *Castells and the Media.* United Kingdom: Polity Press

Innis, H. A. (1951). *The Bias of Communication.* Toronto: University of Toronto Press

Keller, Bill. (2011, January 26). Dealing with Assange and the WikiLeaks Secrets. *The New York Times*

Lagerkvist, A. (2009). Transitional Times: "New Media", Novel Histories and Trajectories. *Nordicom Review 30*(1), 3–18

Leigh, D. and Harding, L. (2011). *WikiLeaks. Inside Julian Assange's War on Secrecy.* Great Britain: Guardian Books

Jenkins, H. (2009). *Confronting the Challenges of Participatory Culture: Media Education for the 21st Century.* Chicago: MacArthur Foundation

McCombs, M. E., and Shaw, D. L. (1972). The Agenda-Setting Function of Mass Media. *Public Opinion Quarterly 36*, 176–187

McLuhan, M. (1962). *The Gutenberg Galaxy: The Making of Typographic Man.* Toronto: University of Toronto Press

McLuhan, M. (1964). *Understanding Media: The Extensions of Man.* New York: Mentor

Meraz, S. (2009). Is there an Elite Hold? Traditional Media to Social Media Agenda Setting Influence in Blog Networks. *Journal of Computer-Mediated Communication 14*, 682–707

Ong, W. (1982). *Orality and Literacy: The Technologizing of the Word.* New York: Methuen

Postman, N. (1985). *Amusing Ourselves to Death: Public Discourse in the Age of Show Business.* New York: Penguin

Postman, N. (1992). *Technopoly: The Surrender of Culture to Technology.* New York: Knopf

Press, A. L., Williams, Bruce, A. (2010). *The New Media Environment: An Introduction.* Oxford: Wiley-Blackwell

Russell, A. (2011). *Networked: A Contemporary History of News in Transition.* Polity Press

Shrivastava, K. M. (1998). *Media Towards 21st Century.* New Delhi India: Sterling Publishers Private Ltd

Toffler, A. (1980). *The Third Wave.* New York: Bantam Books

US Government. (2010). Espionage Act and the Legal and Constitutional Issues Raised by WikiLeaks. Hearings before the Committee of the Judiciary House of Representatives. One Hundred Eleventh Congress. Second Session. December 2010. Retrieved August 29, 2012 from http://judiciary.house.gov/hearings/printers/111th/111-160_63081.PDF

6
WikiLeaks and Whistle-blowing: The Framing of Bradley Manning

Einar Thorsen, Chindu Sreedharan, and Stuart Allan

Introduction

Inquiries into freedom of expression and the rights of the press frequently highlight examples where ordinary individuals have taken it upon themselves to leak information to a journalist with the aim of exposing corruption, maleficence, or injustice. Hollywood films have contributed to a certain mythology surrounding whistle-blowing. *All the President's Men*'s (1976) depiction of the covert informant "Deep Throat" in the Watergate scandal is an especially well-known example; others include *The China Syndrome* (1979), *Norma Rae* (1979), *Silkwood* (1983), *The Insider* (1999), *The Constant Gardener* (2005), *The Informant* (2009), and *The Whistleblower* (2010). In real life, whistle-blowers usually wish to remain anonymous, relying on the journalists to uphold the principle of "protecting their sources" to safeguard them from reprisals. The journalist–whistle-blower relationship can be challenging to negotiate at the best of times, and the whistle-blowing site WikiLeaks has transformed it in profound ways.

This chapter contributes to current debates surrounding WikiLeaks and whistle-blowing by focusing on the alleged activities of Bradley Manning, the US soldier accused of providing classified military documents to WikiLeaks. Following a discussion about the complex definition of whistle-blowing, it will draw upon published descriptions of how Manning came to be in possession of the sensitive military materials documenting US involvement in Iraq and Afghanistan, the steps he ostensibly took to leak them, and the involvement of WikiLeaks in placing them in the public domain. The second part of the chapter will focus on a comparative study of online news framing of Manning in the ensuing reportage and commentary published on the websites of the *Guardian* (guardian.co.uk), the *New York Times* (nytimes.com), and *Der Spiegel* (spiegel.de/international). On this basis, the chapter will develop its argument regarding news coverage of Manning as a whistle-blower, but also will investigate wider questions about WikiLeaks as an alternative platform that encourages whistle-blowing to flourish. It will conclude by exploring the implications of the Manning case for journalism's role in a modern democracy, with particular reference to its capacity to speak truth to power.

Whistle-blowing: a complex concept

Whistle-blowing, a term coined by US civic activist Ralph Nader in 1971 (Bollier, 2002), is generally seen as the activity of calling attention to wrongdoing (Calland and Dehn, 2004, p. 2). It is a distinct act of dissent (Elliston et al., 1985), a special form of dissidence in which "a member or former member of an organization goes outside the organization or outside normal organizational channels to reveal organizational wrongdoing, illegality, or actions that threaten the public" (Petersen and Farell, 1986, p. 5). It typically involves inside informants who want to expose "actual nontrivial wrongdoing" by collaborating with the media (Johnson, 2003, pp. 3–4). The coinage is believed to have come about to avoid the negative connotations associated with words such as *informant, snitch, traitor,* and so forth. A whistle-blower is usually cast in a positive light; that is, as someone who discloses confidential information to the press reluctantly, in the belief it is necessary to do so because public attention must be directed to a perceived wrong, crime, or injustice. As Daniel Ellsberg, the former US military analyst who released the Pentagon Papers to the *New York Times* in 1971, puts it in *Secrets: A Memoir of Vietnam and the Pentagon Papers*, "Telling the truth, revealing wrongly kept secrets, can have a surprisingly strong unforeseeable power to help end a wrong and save lives" (Ellsberg, 2002, p. 4; see also Campbell, 2011).

In addition to Ellsberg, and the covert informant Deep Throat in the Watergate scandal mentioned earlier, several individuals whose place inside an organization has afforded them access to otherwise secret or classified information have originated noteworthy news stories. Peter Buxton, the US Public Health Service epidemiologist who collaborated with Associated Press reporter Jean Heller to expose the Tuskegee syphilis experiment in 1972 (see Thomas and Quinn, 1991); Philip Agee, the former Central Intelligence Agency case officer who accused the CIA of supporting death squads and military dictatorships in 1975; Mordechai

Vanunu, the nuclear technician who leaked details of the Israeli nuclear program to the *Sunday Times* in 1985; Jeffrey Wigand, who worked with CBS's *60 Minutes* in 1996 to allege how the tobacco company Brown & Williamson manipulated nicotine content in cigarettes to addict smokers (see Brenner, 1996); and Sherron Watkins, who helped uncover the Enron crisis in 2001 are among the other significant whistle-blowers to emerge over the years.

Whistle-blowing may be aptly characterized as one of several actions frequently referred to under the umbrella term of "leak" in news reporting. *Leak,* in this sense, came into being in the early twentieth century, "specifically to mean an inadvertent slip of information picked up by reporters." Today it is used to broadly mean "an array of practices involving the accidental and strategic sharing of information, including whistle-blowing, settling grudges, culling favours, drawing attention to policy initiatives, signalling foreign governments, and releasing trial balloons so as to discern early public response" (Zelizer and Allan, 2010: 68). Whistle-blowing thus is a distinct kind of leaking, commonly perceived to be deliberate and driven by an idealistic motive, and as such, an act of honour, "an epithet...conjuring up the image of a responsible (and brave) employee" (Myers, 2004, p. 104). As noted above, a number of fictional portrayals of whistle-blowers as heroes and experts have been featured in the entertainment media over the years (Johnson, 2003, p. 4). Wahl-Jorgensen and Hunt (2012) reaffirm this positive depiction, suggesting that their research shows news representations of whistle-blowing tend to be reported in positive terms. Through a longitudinal content analysis of the UK national press covering 1997–2009, they make three key observations about how the news media view whistle-blowing: a) it is newsworthy, taken seriously by the media, and "mostly covered in neutral or positive ways"; b) "the acts of whistle-blowing which receive most media attention fit with the existing news agenda and prevailing social and economic trends"; and c) journalist narratives possibly construct whistle-blowers "as heroic, selfless individuals to establish the legitimacy of their claims of systemic wrongdoing in the public interest" (Wahl-Jorgensen and Hunt, 2012, p. 399).

Such media constructions of what constitutes whistle-blowing and indeed how it might be perceived can be understood and analysed through the process of news framing. Reese (2004, p. 11) defines frames as *"organising principles* that are socially *shared* and *persistent* over time, that work *symbolically* to meaningfully *structure* the social world."Similarly, de Vreese (2005, p. 51, emphasis in original) highlights framing as "a dynamic *process* that involves frame-building (how frames emerge) and frame-setting (the interplay between media frames and audience predispositions)." That is, news framing refers to the manner in which news reports emphasize particular values or facts in a story, subsequently promoting certain interpretations or public perceptions of events or individuals (see also Entman, 1993; 2004). Framing of news is frequently contested and is the subject of intense negotiation among journalists, their sources, and editors – not least concerning the narrative conventions guiding how events and sources are reported. This tension between competing definitions and stakeholder interests is particularly worthy of study in relation to whistle-blowers and information leaking, given whistle-blowing's complex legal definitions and the potential such acts have to challenge established forms of power.

Despite legislation that exists in several countries to protect it, whistle-blowing is fraught with the threat of legal repercussions, for both the whistle-blower and the journalist concerned. This is particularly true when the leak involves government material. In fact, several countries, including India, Malaysia, New Zealand, the Republic of Ireland, and the United Kingdom, possess an Official Secrets Act or equivalents such as the Espionage Act in the United States, to prohibit the dissemination of information classified as vital to protect national security interests. According to Richard T. De George's Standard Theory (1990), whistle-blowing is permissible not just if the information is in the public interest. The whistle-blower must also have "evidence that would convince a reasonable, impartial observer" that his or her "view of the threat is correct" (cited in Davis, 1996, p. 7). But even with such evidence, whistle-blowers could face legal sanctions. Often their status as a whistle-blower is contested, with the organization they leaked information from claiming the act as a "wrongdoing" deserving punitive actions. Public opinion could also be polarized, and – as happened with Daniel Ellsberg, Philip Agee, and Mordechai Vanunu – a whistle-blower could face a prison term, and it is only in time, with the benefit of hindsight, that an informant is sometimes seen as a legitimate whistle-blower. In other words, what may be initially reported as an act of treason or subversion may eventually be re-inflected as a selfless – even heroic – commitment to social justice.

Digital communication technologies have added another layer of complexity to whistle-blowing. Not only has the physical act of leaking and disseminating information become easier, the Internet has empowered digital citizens, providing them with the capability of whistle-blowing without the help of traditional media organizations (see also

Sreedharan, Thorsen and Allan, 2012). Prior to the emergence of the Web and citizen journalism, the status of whistle-blower could be counterpoised against that of the journalist in relatively straightforward terms. The relationship was symbiotic, with both parties benefiting from the other's involvement, and it was also hierarchical, in that the decision of whether or not to proceed rested with the journalist's news organization. In other words, the whistle-blower was reliant upon the journalist to translate what s/he had witnessed – typically evidenced in a document of some description – into a news story of interest to the public, and quite possibly in the public interest. In a digital age, however, the normative rules of this reciprocity have been recast, with the whistle-blower increasingly able to bypass the journalist altogether. Consequently, new forms of whistle-blowing are flourishing across diverse platforms. In the next section, we examine WikiLeaks, the most controversial of whistle-blowing operations to emerge in recent years.

WikiLeaks and whistle-blowing

"A Wiki for Whistle-Blowers" was the title of a January 2007 *Time* magazine article by Tracy Samantha Schmidt (2007), one of the very first blips about WikiLeaks on radar of the mainstream media. Described as a "bold new collective experiment in whistle-blowing," the fledgling website was credited with putting into motion a system that would "protect leakers' identities while exposing government and corporate corruption worldwide." With the prospect of more than one million leaked documents being posted online by March, when it was anticipated that the website would go live, *Time* enthused about WikiLeaks' potential as a global forum for examining confidential materials.

For its part, WikiLeaks positioned itself as a nonprofit media organization aimed at facilitating "an innovative, secure and anonymous way for independent sources around the world to leak information." It offered an electronic drop box, with "military-grade encryption protection," to which potential whistle-blowers could upload the information. The drop box, as WikiLeaks made it clear on its website, was designed to keep the identity of the leaker "hidden from everyone, including WikiLeaks." Julian Assange, the chief spokesperson and co-founder of WikiLeaks, envisaged it as an "uncensorable" enterprise of "ethically leaked" documents.

The journalistic underpinnings of WikiLeaks' operational rationale was an issue right from the start. For most news organizations it was less a question of how best to describe the website's role in providing access to sensitive information than an issue of whether to acknowledge it at all. Journalistic attention would be seldom directed at WikiLeaks in the months ahead, even though news stories based on documents it put into public circulation steadily enhanced its reputation among hackers, activists, campaigners, and investigative reporters. Documents the site released helped generate many news reports, including stories focusing on the treatment of prisoners at the detention centre in Guantánamo Bay, Cuba; allegations of corruption in a Swiss-based bank; secret information about the internal organization of the Church of Scientology; Republican vice presidential candidate Sarah Palin's use of private e-mail to sidestep public record laws; and details about the far-Right British National Party (BNP) membership.

WikiLeaks' growing reputation within Internet circles was subject to polarized debate in the blogosphere. Advocates enthused about its "fourth estate" role as a vital "check against tyranny" in the fight for a "more open and transparent society." Detractors, in sharp contrast, pounced on what they perceived to be the site's reckless violation of secrecy for its own sake, issuing grave warnings about implications for national security. Meanwhile, several news outlets somewhat begrudgingly began to acknowledge the site as a "journalistic tool" (*Time*'s initial definition). This status was reinforced, in turn, by related forms of public recognition for the site's activities, such as the *Economist*'s 2008 New Media Award as well as credit from the *Index on Censorship* for being "an invaluable resource for anonymous whistle-blowers and investigative journalists." In June 2009, WikiLeaks earned a second new media award, this time from Amnesty International, for exposing "extra judicial killings and disappearances" in Kenya.

WikiLeaks became front-page news around the world when it published *Collateral Murder*, a controversial video footage that showed US soldiers in an Apache helicopter killing a group of civilians in Iraq, including two Reuters journalists. The American military statement was that the soldiers were engaged in an active firefight, and those killed were insurgents, but the leak challenged this version. In placing the video into the public domain, WikiLeaks succeeded where Reuters had failed. The latter had actively petitioned the US military to release the footage of the military operation since July 25, 2007, but had made no progress until a whistle-blower used WikiLeaks' anonymous drop box facility.

The next major milestone in WikiLeaks' history of unorthodox whistle-blowing came in the second half of 2010, with the publication of what came to be known as the "war logs" – more specifically, the Afghan War

Logs and the Iraq War Logs. The attention the *Collateral Murder* video brought the whistle-blowing organization had spurred the *Guardian,* in the United Kingdom, to track down Assange and make a case for sharing information with other media outlets (Ellison, 2011). The discussions that followed saw WikiLeaks working with three major news outlets – the *Guardian,* the *New York Times* and the German *Der Spiegel* were on board – on one of the largest leaks in US military history. The publication of the Afghan War Logs saw 91,731 classified documents, covering a six-year period of US engagement in Afghanistan, being placed in the public domain. Assange released a second set of documents to his media partners almost simultaneously. The Iraq War Logs comprised 391,832 documents, recording aspects of the war in Iraq from January 1, 2004 to December 31, 2009, and they were published on October 22, 2010. A month later, on November 28, 2010, WikiLeaks began the release of Cablegate, a cache of 251,287 confidential diplomatic cables from 274 US embassies around the world. By now, Assange's media partners had grown to include *Al Jazeera,* the London-based Bureau of Investigative Journalism, *El País* of Spain, and *Le Monde* of France.

Manning the whistle-blower vs. Manning the villain

Private First Class Bradley Manning, a US soldier in his twenties, is the man accused of uploading the *Collateral Murder* video, the war logs, and embassy cables to WikiLeaks' drop box. Widely reported to have had an unhappy childhood, he evidently appeared to have found military life stressful. His gay identity and diminutive physique singled him out for harassment by some of his colleagues, according to some news profiles (see also Chapter 7 by McCurdy in this book). In October 2009, Manning was posted as an intelligence analyst to a base near Baghdad, and it is here that he is believed to have accessed the classified information he allegedly leaked. Ironically, Manning was tied to the leaks by what is arguably another act of whistle-blowing, this one by a Californian computer hacker named Adrian Lamo.

Initially the source of the war logs was identified as "Bradass87," a person who initiated a series of instant messages (IMs) with Lamo, including one which asked: "Hi... how are you?... im an army intelligence analyst, deployed to eastern bagdad... if you had unprecedented access to classified networks, 14 hours a day, 7 days a week for 8+ months, what would you do?" In the days that followed, Bradass87 explained that someone he knew (presumably Bradass87 himself) had been downloading, compressing, and encrypting the data onto blank

CDs labelled as Lady Gaga's music, before uploading it to WikiLeaks. "i want people to see the truth," he was quoted as stating. "It's open diplomacy...it's Climategate with a global scope and breathtaking depth...its beautiful and horrifying...It's public data, it belongs in the public domain." Lamo contacted US authorities and provided them with a printout of Bradass87's online chat, which led to Manning's arrest. "I wouldn't have done this if lives weren't in danger," Lamo told Wired.com after Manning was held. "He was in a war zone and basically trying to vacuum up as much classified information as he could, and just throwing it up into the air" (Poulsen and Zetter, 2010).

The days following the publication of the war logs witnessed extensive media reportage about the leaks. A key feature of the coverage revolved around what appeared to be a concerted effort by US officials to discredit the individuals thought to be responsible for the leaks. In 2010 this focus was almost exclusively on WikiLeaks' Julian Assange. Different official lines were put forth to counter WikiLeaks, chiefly concerned with how the revelations would harm US national security. US Joint Chiefs of Staff Chairman Admiral Mike Mullen claimed the leaks had put the lives of soldiers and informers at risk in Afghanistan, and accused WikiLeaks of having blood on its hands (Jaffe and Partlow, 2010). Republican Peter King of the US House of Representatives' Homeland Security Committee requested that the Obama administration "determine whether WikiLeaks could be designated a foreign terrorist organization," and reportedly asked Attorney General Eric Holder to "criminally charge Assange under the Espionage Act" (McCullagh, 2010). Running parallel to this were reports of Swedish police investigations against Assange, who was accused of violating two women with whom he had been sexually involved. The story was treated as a lurid scandal by the international media, with commentators engaging in extensive conjecture about the specific details of the case, in part fuelled by different legal definitions of what constitutes rape in Swedish law and in part by the lack of clear information about what had actually transpired. Assange repeatedly denied the claims of rape and, at the time of writing of this chapter in 2012, has sought to avoid extradition to Sweden by seeking asylum in Ecuador.

Such were the attempts to discredit the man who facilitated the whistle-blowing; the alleged whistle-blower fared even worse. After his arrest, Manning was held as a maximum custody detainee, in severely harsh conditions. These reportedly included being kept in solitary confinement for 23 hours a day and being forced to strip naked at night, prompting United Nations investigator Juan Méndez to formally accuse the US military of torture. The pretrial treatment meted out to the alleged whistle-blower was, Mendez said in his report to the UN, "cruel, inhumane and degrading" and "violated his physical and psychological integrity as well his presumption of innocence" (Pilkington, 2010). Outside the prison walls, moreover, the US government officials were presenting him as a disloyal soldier who had betrayed his country. Republican Peter King focused his attention on Assange and WikiLeaks; another prominent Republican, Mike Huckabee, went a step further, saying whoever "leaked that information is guilty of treason" and that "anything less than execution is too kind a penalty" (Beltrone, 2010).

Despite these ferocious attacks on Assange and Manning, the news organizations that worked with WikiLeaks attracted comparatively little criticism from government sources or media commentators for their role in reporting the leaked information. Instead, their efforts to help redact sensitive information from the leaks and protect civilians were emphasized. News organizations were also actively involved in shaping the portrayal of the various stakeholders in their reporting. Drawing on a selection of findings generated by a larger research project conducted by the authors, this chapter will now turn to a discussion of how Manning was portrayed in online news reports, examining WikiLeaks' three initial media partners for the Afghan War Logs – the *Guardian* (United Kingdom), the *New York Times* (United States), and *Der Spiegel International* (Germany).

Framing Bradley Manning

Our study tracked the news reporting of Bradley Manning's apparent involvement in the leaking of US classified information to WikiLeaks. It mapped the volume of articles that referred to him by name from January 2010 to May 2012, the news framing, and the lead sources used. Of interest was the manner in which Manning was portrayed on the three websites: guardian.co.uk, nytimes.com, and spiegel.de/international – in the face of political attacks over his status as a whistle-blower or otherwise, as discussed above. We chose these news organizations because of their close work with WikiLeaks as initial media partners for the Afghan War Logs and because of the international attention they garnered for their coverage associated with WikiLeaks as a consequence. Overall we identified 405 articles that explicitly referred to Manning in this time period, with the majority (311 or 77 percent) of these published by the *Guardian*. The *New York Times* published 82

Table 6.1   Manning's media coverage, 2010–2012

Year	Der Spiegel	*Guardian*	*New York Times*	Total
2010	4	76	31	111
2011	8	195	41	244
2012	0	40	10	50
Total	12	311	82	405

Source: *Authors' own elaboration.*

articles and *Der Spiegel International* published only 12 articles. Here it is important to note that the present research covered only articles published in the English language; it does not reflect *Der Spiegel*'s potentially more extensive German coverage. It is nevertheless telling that the newspaper published a very restricted selection of articles to its international audience.

While it is difficult to discern much about the pattern of *Der Spiegel International*'s coverage based on just 12 articles (see Table 6.1), it is worth noting how closely the two other websites match over time. Though the number of articles referring to Manning differ significantly, the trend lines of the *Guardian* and the *New York Times* are closely aligned, demonstrating a similar editorial judgment regarding the relative proportion of their respective coverage.

None of the news websites made any explicit reference to Manning until June 2010, when excerpts from the alleged chat logs between Lamo and the US soldier started appearing. The first article to mention Manning was published by the *New York Times* on June 7, 2010 ("Army Leak Suspect Is Turned In, by Ex-Hacker"), one day after *Wired* magazine's first publication of transcripts pertaining to the Lamo-Manning chats. The *Guardian* followed on June 11, 2010 with "Pentagon hunts WikiLeaks founder Julian Assange in bid to gag website," and *Der Spiegel International*'s first article was published over a month later, on July 27, 2010, entitled "The Whistleblowers: Is WikiLeaks a Blessing or Curse for Democracy?."

Significant spikes in coverage followed, as demonstrated in Figure 6.1, in December 2010 and January 2011, when WikiLeaks was at the centre of a digital information war in the aftermath of the US embassy cables leak.[1] Further peaks in the coverage were identified in March 2011, when another 22 charges were levied against Manning; in December 2011, when the Article 32 hearing (the preliminary hearing in US military court) against Manning commenced; in February 2012, when Manning

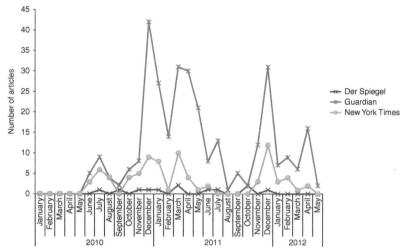

Figure 6.1 Number of articles referring to Bradley Manning in three major newspapers
Source: Authors' own elaboration.

was ordered to stand trial; and in April 2012, relating to Manning's pretrial hearing.

Whistle-blower and victim

Tracking references to Manning in the articles on the respective news websites provides an overview of the relative news value his story yielded over time. In order to further understand the nature of how he was depicted in news reports, we conducted a framing analysis, examining framing and source usage in 405 articles published across the three websites.[2] Overall, we identified five different ways the news websites described Manning – framing him in terms of a whistle-blower, victim, villain, hero, or as entertainment. Each of these will be defined in turn below, with a comparative analysis of how this framing featured across the three websites. Some news articles also combined different ways of framing Manning, which was accommodated in our analysis by coding a secondary framing[3] where present (see Table 6.2).[4]

Overall, the most prevalent framing of Manning was as a whistle-blower, evident as primary framing in 52 percent of articles examined. The whistle-blower framing was identified by a portrayal of Manning as someone who has disclosed information, exposing or potentially exposing wrongdoing or corruption or information that

Table 6.2   Tally of how the articles framed Manning

Primary Frame	Secondary Frame	Der Spiegel	Guardian	New York Times	Total
Entertainment	Hero		2	1	3
	Victim		1		1
	None		19	1	20
Hero	Victim		3	1	4
	Whistle-blower		3		3
	None		14	1	15
Victim	Entertainment		1		1
	Hero		3	1	4
	Whistle-blower	3	14	6	23
	None		98	15	113
Villain	Victim		2		2
	Whistle-blower		1		1
	None		3	1	4
Whistle-blower	Hero	1	3		4
	Victim	2	33	7	42
	Villain		1	3	4
	None	6	110	45	161
		12	311	82	405

Source: Authors' own elaboration

might be embarrassing to the US government. While the illegality of these acts of leaking might be acknowledged in the article, his portrayal was neither praised nor condemned. A good example of this can be found in the *Guardian's* first report to explicitly mention Manning by name. The article introduces him in its lead as "Soldier Bradley Manning said to have leaked diplomatic cables to whistleblower." Later the article reinforced this by noting that "the soldier, Bradley Manning, also claimed to have given WikiLeaks 260,000 pages of confidential diplomatic cables and intelligence assessments" (McGreal, guardian. co.uk, June 11, 2010).

Framing Manning in terms of a whistle-blower was not limited to the initial days of the sample period and could be seen across the timeline on all three websites (see Figure 6.2). *Der Spiegel International* refers to the US soldier as the "suspected WikiLeaks informant" in a June 14, 2011, article; in another, on July 18 of the same year, he is presented as "the alleged source of secret US government documents for WikiLeaks." Similar language was identified in the *New York Times*: "A military judge at Fort Meade refused Thursday to throw out a charge that Pfc. Bradley Manning, accused of leaking government files to the anti-secrecy Web

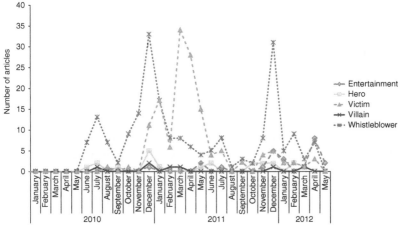

Figure 6.2 Framing of Bradley Manning over time
Source: Authors' own elaboration.

site WikiLeaks, aided the enemy, identified as Al Qaeda" (Reuters, "Maryland: Wikileaks Charges Stand," nytimes.com, April 27, 2012).

Although early reporting of Manning in 2010 drew primarily on the whistle-blower framing, the focus then shifted towards framing him as a victim, as demonstrated in Figure 6.2. This framing emerged in December 2010 and January 2011 and peaked as the primary framing mechanism in March–May 2011, with another peak in this framing evident in December 2011. Overall 35 percent of the articles in our sample described Manning using language associated with victimhood. Within these articles he was portrayed as someone who had been in some way unfairly or improperly treated. This framing of Manning as a victim was identified by the journalist or by cited sources that described unfair coverage in the media or statements made about Manning; unacceptable custody conditions (e.g., "inhumane treatment"); descriptions of Manning as a scapegoat or being used as a pawn; suggestions that his trial might be unfair or in some way biased; or finally suggestions that improper or unfair treatment during his time in the army were a factor contributing to his subsequent actions. The *Guardian* article titled "The lonely battle against solitary confinement" is a good example of this particular style of framing:

For more than seven months, Manning has been held in 23-hour-a-day solitary confinement at a Marine brig in Quantico, Virginia, denied sunlight, exercise, possessions, and all but the most limited contact with family and friends. The conditions of his detention are being discussed, lamented and protested throughout the left-leaning blogosphere, and few of those taking part in the conversation hesitate to describe Manning's situation as "torture." (Ridgeway and Casella, guardian.co.uk, January 19, 2011)

Not only does this passage highlight Manning's extraordinary imprisonment conditions in emotive language, it also notes that "the left-leaning blogosphere" is even more severe in its definition of his situation. Manning is not just a prisoner, but implicitly a victim of "solitary confinement" and "torture." In another report, the *Guardian* notes how "after 17 months of pre-trial imprisonment," Manning is "finally going to see the inside of a courtroom." The story continues:

Though it is Manning who is nominally on trial, these proceedings reveal the US government's fixation with extreme secrecy, covering up its own crimes, and intimidating future whistleblowers.

Since his arrest last May in Iraq, Manning has been treated as one of America's most dastardly traitors. (Greenwald, guardian.co.uk, December 14, 2011)

Only in a very small number of instances was Manning framed as a hero, with 5 percent of the articles portraying him as someone who had acted in a noble or courageous manner. This framing was defined by his actions, described to have advanced the cause of freedom of information and anti-privacy; portrayed as morally right and justifiable; or of importance due to providing information that needed to be in the public domain. A case in point is the article titled "Bradley Manning's quest for justice" by Logan Price in the *Guardian*'s Comment is Free section, where Manning is presented as one who "holds to a higher standard of truth" than that of the court in which he is being tried. The framing is also evident in *Der Spiegel International*'s article on December 15, 2011 titled "US Determined to Punish Bradley Manning," in which former US military analyst Daniel Ellsberg, responsible for leaking the Pentagon Papers in 1971, is shown as "no longer thinking about the past." Instead Ellsberg is focusing on Manning as "unreservedly a hero" for the information his acts helped uncover. The *Guardian* also headlined that "History will remember Bradley Manning better" (Goodman, guardian.co.uk, December 21, 2011) and reported on his nomination for the Nobel Peace Prize by the Movement in the Icelandic Parliament (Siddique, guardian.co.uk, October 7, 2011).

Despite the staunch political rhetoric against Manning discussed in the previous section, framing him in terms of a villain was only evident in 2 percent of the articles in our study. This framing was identified by a portrayal of Manning as someone who acted immorally and without justification, his actions being seen as having put national security or the security of individuals at risk. Thus, in the *New York Times*'s "Loophole May Have Aided Theft of Classified Data" (July 8, 2010), Manning is labeled as the soldier who "exploited a loophole in Defense Department security" and "smuggled highly classified data out of his intelligence unit on a disc disguised as a music CD by Lady Gaga." Another article titled "Why I called Bradley Manning treatment 'stupid,'" which appeared in the Comment is Free section of the *Guardian* (March 29, 2011), former US Department of State spokesman P. J. Crowley presents Manning's alleged action as having "placed the lives of activists around the world at risk," and said that "Private Manning is rightly facing prosecution and, if convicted, should spend a long, long time in prison." Thus, in general, the news websites steered clear of the villain frame on their own, the coverage taking on that hue only where the articles were directly sourced from those involved in prosecuting Manning. One important reason for this arguably is the dominance of Manning supporters as sources in the coverage, which is discussed in further detail below.

Finally, some 6 percent of the articles (see Table 6.2) were identified as framing Manning in terms of entertainment. These were primarily articles published by the *Guardian* in relation to the stage performance of the play *The Radicalisation of Bradley Manning*. For example, a review by *Guardian* theatre critic Michael Billington appeared on April 19, 2012 and presents the performance as "a highly watchable, fact-inspired fictional play," which zigzags "through the last 10 years of Manning's life to produce an impressionistic biography." The review also portrays Manning as a victim, and sympathy for Manning is evident when, for instance, Billington speaks of Manning's "appallingly delayed trial."

When examining the proportional use of each framing for the respective news websites (see Figure 6.3 below), we found that both *Der Spiegel International* and the *New York Times* was primarily framing Manning in terms of a whistle-blower (75 percent and 67 percent of articles, respectively), and to a lesser extent as a victim (25 percent and 27 percent of articles, respectively). Indeed in the case of *Der Spiegel International*, whistle-blower and victim were the only frames used. Although the

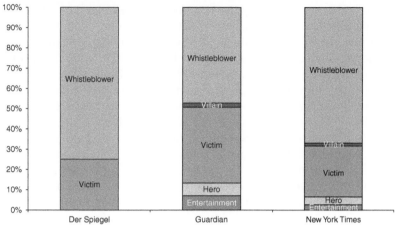

Figure 6.3   Primary framing of Bradley Manning
Source: Authors' own elaboration.

Guardian was also primarily framing Manning in terms of a whistle-blower (47 percent of articles), a significant proportion of its articles implied that he was a victim (37 percent).

As noted above and demonstrated in Table 6.2, some articles contained more than one way of framing Manning. The secondary framing was most frequently used to reinforce the primary framing (e.g., whistle-blower first and victim second), as opposed to providing balance between competing framing positions (e.g., hero first and villain second). Whistle-blower as the primary framing and victim as the secondary framing was the most popular combination, with 10 percent of the articles incorporating these in this order. Another 6 percent of articles reversed the logic, with victim as the primary framing and whistle-blower as the secondary framing. It is worth noting that any combination including hero or villain framing (e.g., whistle-blower–hero, whistle-blower–villain, hero-victim, etc.) did not penetrate more than 1 percent of the articles in our study. In other words, the polar emotive positions of hero or villain were not associated with Manning's status as a whistle-blower or victim in how the articles were framing his depiction.

The *New York Times*'s report "Private in WikiLeaks Spying Case Goes to Court" on December 16, 2011, exemplifies how framing was combined. After introducing Manning as "the Army private accused in the most famous leak of government secrets since the Pentagon Papers," the frame shifts to one of empathy and victimhood in later paragraphs. Manning is in the second part of the article presented as a youth who "turns 24 on Saturday," "a slight figure in black-rimmed glasses," who "faces a possible sentence of life in prison." The story goes on to discuss his prison conditions and how he was "held in isolation and forced to strip off his clothing and sleep in a tear-proof smock, a measure military officials said was necessary because he might be a suicide risk." The article, in other words, combines the initial framing of Manning as a whistle-blower with a latter framing of him as a victim.

Sources on Bradley Manning

Supporters of Bradley Manning were the most frequent primary and secondary sources in articles that made explicit reference to him (see Figure 6.4). Some 14 percent of articles overall used Manning supporters as the primary source and 12 percent of articles used supporters as the secondary source. This dominance of sources sympathetic to Manning might go some way to explain why the websites were framing him predominantly as a whistle-blower and victim, as discussed above. Such sources included, among others, activists and demonstrators advocating Manning's release, Julian Assange, Manning's legal team, and other legal experts. The pro-Manning activists identified the US soldier as someone who had done the "right" thing – some saw him as a "hero," a "patriot," a name worth a place in the history as well – and someone who was being victimized for his alleged actions. Thus, according Jeff Paterson of Courage to Resist, who helped raise funds for Manning's legal expenses, he is a soldier "who gave them all this information." Moreover, famous whistle-blower Daniel Ellsberg identified "kindred spirits" in Manning and Assange since "they were willing to go to prison for life, or be executed, to put out this information" (cited in Burns and Somaiya, nytimes.com, October 23, 2010).

Unsurprisingly, Manning's lawyers endeavoured to portray him in terms that would evoke sympathy. Accordingly, in a report about Manning's trial in the *Guardian*, the lawyers spoke about him as "a troubled young soldier whom the Army should never have deployed to Iraq or given access to classified material" (guardian.co.uk, 15 March 15, 2012). In another report on the *New York Times* website, his lawyer, David Coombs, compared his actions to a soldier speaking to a major newspaper – which, since he did not intend to provide information to the enemy, constituted nothing more than negligence (Thompson, nytimes.com, December 20, 2011).

The US military was the second most prominent source in our study, appearing as primary source in 8 percent of articles and as secondary source in 4 percent of articles. Beyond this, the articles in the sample relied on the authors' own analysis or commentary (primary source in 5 percent of articles), and on other media organizations (primary source in 3 percent of articles). The emphasis on primary sources does differ, depending on the news websites, as demonstrated in Figure 6.4. Here it is particularly worth noting that the *New York Times* relied more on military sources for a proportion of its coverage than the other two websites did (primary source in 35 percent and secondary source in 22 percent of the *New York Times* articles). The *Guardian* and *Der Spiegel* both had Manning supporters as their most prominent primary source (34 percent and 67 percent of its articles, respectively), and similarly the most prominent secondary source (46 percent and 50 percent, respectively).

The *New York Times* and *Der Spiegel International* gave the most promi- nence to US government sources, with 9 percent and 17 percent, respec- tively, of their articles using this as a primary source. By comparison only 1 percent of *Guardian* articles used US government sources as a primary source. However, the greater use of US government and mili- tary sources, particularly within the *New York Times*, does not appear to have increased that website's framing of Manning as a villain.

Only the *Guardian* made use of Manning as a primary or secondary source; he appeared as primary source in 3 percent of its articles. WikiLeaks was also an infrequent source, despite its campaign in support of Manning. Again, the *Guardian* was the only website where WikiLeaks was used as a primary source (3 percent of all its articles), although the *New York Times* used WikiLeaks as a secondary source in 11 percent of its articles. *The Guardian* used WikiLeaks as a secondary source in only 2 percent of its articles. These sources are connected with framing Manning in terms of a whistle-blower and victim, as opposed to a hero, which might be expected, given the aforementioned campaign to vindicate him. Instead, the portrayal of Manning as a hero was mainly associated with WikiLeaks supporters and, in the case of the *Guardian,* with the author of the article.

As mentioned in the previous section, there were only three arti- cles wherein Manning was framed as a villain in more than a passing mention, all published on the *Guardian* website. Two of the articles used military as the primary source, one with the US government as a secondary source and the other with a supporter as a secondary source. The third article was an opinion column, contrasting the framing of Manning as a villain and a victim.

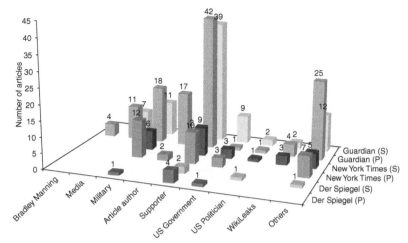

Figure 6.4 Primary(P) and secondary(S) sources in articles with Bradley Manning

Source: Authors' own elaboration.

Conclusion

Despite the reportedly staunch US political rhetoric against Manning and his ongoing military trial, this study has demonstrated how the media representation of him had a very different emphasis. The three news websites analysed – the *Guardian* (guardian.co.uk), the *New York Times* (nytimes.com) and *Der Spiegel* (spiegel.de/international) – portrayed Manning mostly as a whistle-blower. Villain framing of Manning was noticeably subdued – almost to the point of absence – in the coverage. Similarly, hero framing was less pronounced, despite the wave of international sympathy for Manning and the prevailing view in some literature that whistle-blowers are seen as selfless and heroic. News organizations, in other words, attempted to present him mostly in neutral ways – not dissimilar to Wahl-Jorgensen and Hunt's (2012) observation of media representation of whistle-blowers discussed at the outset.

Sympathy for Manning was, nevertheless, evident in the coverage we analysed – especially through the framing as a victim. This may be explained in part by a reliance on Manning supporters as primary and secondary sources (particularly prominent on the *Guardian* website). US military sources were also frequent as the second most dominant source. In this, the *New York Times* relied more heavily on "elite sources" – though this did not show a proportionate increase in framing Manning as a villain. Such emphases in source selection and framing may also reflect the editorial priorities of the news organizations within this study (selected for their early collaboration with WikiLeaks). Here a larger study encompassing a broader range of news organizations may shed further light on ideological tensions and complexities in framing choices of alleged whistle-blowers.

Indeed it is important to note there is more than one way of defining Manning's status, dependent in part on one's moral interpretation of his alleged acts, and also the legal or normative framework against which he is assessed. Such complex conceptual arguments, as touched upon in the outset of this chapter, may also contribute towards the competing news framing choices evidenced in our analysis. Tensions are also reflected in how the culture of whistle-blowing is changing over time. Digital communication technologies have enabled leaking and dissemination of classified information on an unprecedented scale, not least demonstrated by the success of WikiLeaks and the emergence of similar websites. Some news organizations have even sought to reclaim the traditional hierarchical gatekeeping function by establishing anonymous online drop boxes of their own. Leaking classified information is, in other words, actively encouraged across a range of platforms. This, in our view, is transforming not only how whistle-blowing is operationalized, but also how people leaking information are defined – legally and colloquially. Moreover, it is often the benefit of hindsight that allows informants to be recognized as legitimate whistle-blowers, as was the case with Daniel Ellsberg, who released the Pentagon Papers in 1971. In other words, what may be initially reported as an act of treason or subversion may eventually be acknowledged as an act of honour driven by idealism and a selfless commitment to social justice. It is not inconceivable that such a shift will in the future also contribute to a more charitable view of Bradley Manning and his alleged leaking of classified information.

Notes

1. Following the initial Cablegate leaks, several companies – including Amazon, PayPal, Visa, Mastercard, Moneybookers, and Bank of America – either withdrew hosting services or refused to process payments for WikiLeaks. This created a backlash against these organizations, with people sympathetic of WikiLeaks using social media sites to distribute information about how to support or access the website, and also coordinating boycotts of

companies that had withdrawn support for WikiLeaks. In a self-proclaimed act of "payback," the Anonymous group of vigilante hacktivists launched Distributed Denial of Service (DDoS) attacks against service providers that had turned their backs on WikiLeaks.
2. Articles in this context refer to both news reports and opinion columns published on the respective online news sites. No distinction has been made with respect to the articles' relation to the print publications.
3. It should be noted that 60 percent of the articles in this sample contained only a passing mention of Manning – that is, three or fewer paragraphs pertaining to Manning within the article. These have been coded with primary and secondary *framing* of Manning as were the other articles, but primary and secondary *sources* have not been recorded, since these were rarely present or easily identifiable.
4. A number of articles contained two ways of framing Manning – for example, portraying him as a whistle-blower before going on to describe the poor conditions of his custody, effectively also portraying him as a victim. When we were deciding on the classification of such framing as primary or secondary, a number of considerations were made, including: space (measured in paragraphs), prominence or order within article, presence in headline, lead, and conclusion.

References

Beltrone, G. (November 30, 2010). "Mike Huckabee: Leaker should be executed". *Politico*. Retrieved from: http://www.politico.com/news/stories/1110/45757.html
Bollier, D. (2002). *Silent Theft: The Private Plunder of Our Common Wealth*. New York: Routledge
Brenner, M. (1996). The Man Who Knew Too Much, *Vanity Fair*. Retrieved from: http://www.vanityfair.com/magazine/archive/1996/05/wigand199605
Campbell, D. (2011). From the Xerox Machine to WikiLeaks via Ellsberg, Agee and Vanunu, in Mair, J., and Keeble R. L. (eds), *Investigative Journalism: Dead or Alive?* Bury St. Edmunds; Arima, 223–229
Calland, R. and Dehn, G. (2004) Introduction. In: Calland R and Dehn G (eds) *Whistleblowing around the World: Law, Culture and Practice*. Capetown: ODAC and PCAW, 2–20
Davis, M. (1996). "Some paradoxes of whistleblowing". *Business & Professional Ethics Journal*, 15(1), 3–19
De George, R. T. (1990). *Business ethics* (3rd edition). New York: Macmillan
deVreese, C. H. (2005). News framing: Theory and typology. *Information Design Journal + Document Design*. 13 (1), 51–62
Ellsberg, D. (2002). *Secrets: a Memoir of Vietnam and the Pentagon papers*. New York, Penguin
Ellison, S. (2010). The Man Who Spilled the Secrets, *Vanity Fair*. Retrieved from: http://www.vanityfair.com/politics/features/2011/02/the-guardian-201102, February
Elliston, F. A., Keenan, J. P., Lockhart, P., Van Schaick, J. (1985). *Whistleblowing Research: Methodological and Moral Issues*. New York: Praeger
Entman, R. M. (1993). Framing: towards clarification of a fractured paradigm, *Journal of Communication*, 43(4), 51–58

Entman, R. M. (2004). *Projections of Power: Framing News, Public Opinion, and US Foreign Policy*. Chicago, IL: University of Chicago Press

Jaffe, G. and Partlow, J. (July 30, 2010). Joint Chiefs Chairman Mullen: WikiLeaks release endangers troops, Afghans. *The Washington Post*. Retrieved from: http://www.washingtonpost.com/wp-dyn/content/article/2010/07/29/AR2010072904900.html

Johnson, R. A. (2003). *Whistleblowing: when it works- and why*. (Boulder: L. Rienner Publishers)

McCullagh, D. (2010, November 28). "Congressman wants WikiLeaks listed as terrorist group", *cnet News*, Retrieved from: http://news.cnet.com/8301-13578_3-20023941-38.html

Myers, A. (2004). Whistleblowing – the UK experience. In: Calland R and Dehn G (eds) *Whistleblowing around the World: Law, Culture and Practice*. Capetown: ODAC and PCAW, pp. 101–118

Petersen, J. C., and Farrell, D. (1986). *Whistleblowing: Ethical and Legal Issues in Expressing Dissent*. Dubuque, Iowa, Kendall/Hunt

Pilkington, E. (2010, March 12). "Bradley Manning's treatment was cruel and in human, UN torture chief rules". *The Guardian*. Retrieved from: http://www.guardian.co.uk/world/2012/mar/12/bradley-manning-cruel-inhuman-treatment-un

Poulsen, K. and Zetter, K. (June 6, 2010). "U.S. Intelligence Analyst Arrested in Wikileaks Video Probe". *Wired*, Retrieved from: http://www.wired.com/threatlevel/2010/06/leak/

Reese, S. D. (2004). "Militarized journalism: framing dissent in the Gulf Wars", in S. Allan and B Zelizer (eds) *Reporting War: Journalism in Wartime*. London and New York: Routledge

Schmidt, T. S. (January 22, 2007). "A Wiki for Whistle-Blowers". *Time*. Retrieved from: http://www.time.com/time/nation/article/0,8599,1581189,00.html

Sreedharan, C., Thorsen, E. and Allan, S. (2012). "WikiLeaks and the changing forms of information politics in the 'network society'", in Downey, E. and Jones, M. A. (eds) *Public Service, and Web 2.0 Technologies: Future Trends in Social Media*, IGI Global, 167–180

Thomas, S. B. and Quinn, S. (1991). Public Health Then and Now: The Tuskegee Syphilis Study, 1932 to 1972: Implications for HIV Education and AIDS Risk Education Programs in the Black Community. Retrieved from http://minority-health.pitt.edu/393/1/The_Tuskegee_Syphilis_Study_1932_to.pdf

Wahl-Jorgensen, K., and Hunt, J. (2012). "Journalism, accountability and the possibilities for structural critique: A case study of coverage of whistleblowing". *Journalism*, 13(4), 399–416

Zelizer, B. and Allan, S. (2010). *Keywords in News and Journalism Studies*. Maidenhead and New York: Open University Press

7
From the Pentagon Papers to Cablegate: How the Network Society Has Changed Leaking

Patrick McCurdy

On November 28, 2010, WikiLeaks, in partnership with five international media "partners" – the *Guardian* (UK), the *New York Times*, *Der Spiegel* (Germany), *El País* (Spain), and *Le Monde* (France) – began the coordinated public release of a cache of classified diplomatic cables that would become known as Cablegate. It was the largest leak of classified documents in American history.

Although many mainstream news organizations certainly reported on the content of the leaked cables (see Lynch, Chapter 3 of this book), much of the attention focused on sensational headlines and the cult of personality associated with WikiLeaks' enigmatic founder, Julian Assange. While compelling, such content is also distracting. This chapter, in contrast, is interested in how WikiLeaks and its release of a cache of US classified information are representative of changes in the potential and practice of leaking. The transition from an analog age to the network society, this chapter argues, shapes both who can be a leaker and how the practice of leaking is carried out. To make this argument, the case of Daniel Ellsberg and the 1971 leaking of the Pentagon Papers is contrasted with that of Private First Class (PFC) Bradley Manning, the US solider accused of providing WikiLeaks with the Apache helicopter video (*Collateral Murder*), diplomatic cables (Cablegate), and other classified documents. Through examining the similarities and differences between the leakers and the practice of leaking in both cases, this chapter outlines how the rise of the network society has fundamentally altered how information is generated, accessed, controlled, distributed and, ultimately, leaked.

Leaking in the network society

Manuel Castells (1997, 2000, 2007, 2009) describes the current age we live in, which is characterized by the globalization of information and communication technologies, as the network society. In the network society, markets trump hierarchies, and social relationships are extended and reconfigured by dense and overlapping networks of communications. Whereas past communication infrastructures were defined by the dominance of mass communication epitomized by the unidirectional transmission of information to a large audience the network society is defined by "horizontal networks of interactive communication that connect local and global in chosen time" (Castells, 2007, p. 246). Mass communication, of course, still exists, but is now interwoven with horizontal communication networks that simultaneously reconfigure and augment the reach and speed of traditional power holders. Horizontal networks, Castells argues, also pose new risks and challenges to traditional power holders by allowing oppositional networks to harness and exert "counter power" in an effort to alter "power relations institutionalized in society" (Castells, 2007, p. 248). Sreedharan, Thorsen and Allan (2012) explicitly position WikiLeaks within Castells's network society. The authors view WikiLeaks as holding and exerting counter-power through harnessing the communicative capabilities of the interent to produce and distribute its message to a global audience using what Castells terms, "mass-self communication" (Castells 2009, p. 55). Meanwhile, Yochai Benkler, in Chapter 1 of this book, also argues that networked processes have given rise to what he calls "the networked fourth estate," with WikiLeaks cast as an exemplar of the network free press and exactly the kind of challenge to traditional power that Castells's theory of the network society anticipates.

The network society is also defined by digitalized flows of information that can be instantly shared across mass media and horizontal communication networks, with each one having the capacity to set the agenda of the other. Moreover, because digital information can be replicated ad infinitum, it poses significant challenges to traditional tools of information management and control. Indeed, "there is no delete button on the Internet," as the saying goes, which makes complete information control extremely difficult, if not impossible. Arguably, such dynamics give rise to new kinds of challenges to power, based on leaking, disclosing and publicizing information that others struggle to keep out of the public eye and by struggles over representations of contested issues in the media. Such practices, in fact, are the stock and trade of WikiLeaks. As Castells argues, in the network society, the new kind of "power lies in codes of information and in the images of representation around which societies organise their institutions, and people build their lives, and decide their behaviour. The sites of this power are people's minds" (Castells, 1997, p. 359; also see Dahlgren, 2009).

But more than being just power and counter-power, however, digital information and its networked flows are also a source of risk. Indeed, attempts to manage and keep control over massive stocks of information magnify risk. The network society thus in some respects is also a "risk society" (Beck, 1992). WikiLeaks embodies the nature of risk in such societies, where even the most concerted efforts by the most powerful actors in the world – the US military and government, in this case are not able to fully control and manage their own information resources and environments.

Analogue and digital leaks: comparing the Pentagon Papers and Cablegate

Governments and organizations have always been vulnerable to information leaks. Yet the rise of the network society has fundamentally altered how information is generated, accessed, controlled, distributed and, ultimately, leaked. This evolution of the media and communications environment can be illustrated by comparing the 1971 release of what became known as the Pentagon Papers and its leaker Daniel Ellsberg with WikiLeaks' 2010 release of classified US government information that it had allegedly obtained from leaker and whistle-blower Bradley Manning.

The Pentagon Papers: Daniel Ellsberg and analogue leaking

In October 1969, just as the first ever messages were being sent over the ARPANET (Advanced Research Projects Agency Network), then the embryonic backbone of the Internet, two employees at the nonprofit Research and Development Corporation, or RAND Corporation, in Santa Monica, California, Daniel Ellsberg and his colleague Anthony Russo, were just beginning the laborious process of manually photocopying a "Top Secret-Sensitive" US military report, *United States –Vietnam Relations, 1945–1967: A Study Prepared by the Department of Defense.* Spread across 47 volumes and consisting of approximately 7,000 pages, the multivolume report would eventually become collectively known as the Pentagon Papers.

Details of the Pentagon Papers case can be found elsewhere (Ehrlich and Goldsmith, 2009; Ellsberg, 2002; PBS, 2010; Prados and Pratt Porter, 2004; Rudenstine, 1996), but for here a quick sketch of the primary leaker and whistle-blower, Daniel Ellsberg, is in order to compare and contrast that case with the WikiLeaks case today. To begin with, Daniel Ellsberg had an elite education. He earned an undergraduate scholarship to attend the ivy-league Harvard University, obtained his bachelor's in economics in 1952, and subsequently undertook a fellowship at King's College, Cambridge. In 1957 Ellsberg returned to Harvard as a junior fellow in the Society of Fellows and in 1962 received his PhD in economics from Harvard (Ellsberg, 2012). Of note, from 1954–1957, in the period after Ellsberg's time at Cambridge University and before his junior fellowship at Harvard, he served for three years as an officer in the United States Marine Corps. While Ellsberg would return to civilian life, he continued to work on military-related files throughout his career at the RAND Corporation (1958–1964; 1967–1970). He worked one year (1964) as special assistant to the Assistant Secretary of Defense, and for the two years (1965–1967) he was employed as a civilian by the State Department based out of Saigon during the Vietnam War (Ellsberg, 2012).

Ellsberg was trusted early in his career with "top-secret" information. In 1964 he obtained a GS-18 position, the highest civil service super-grade offered by the Defense Department; it was the civilian equivalent of a military rank between lieutenant general and major general (Ellsberg, 2002, p. 36). At RAND, Ellsberg was a high-ranking analyst. RAND security protocol usually meant that top-secret documents had to be read in its Top Secret Control Room and could not be left in one's office unless the person had a top-secret safe, which not many people did. As Ellsberg notes, such a safe was a "status symbol; it could be spotted immediately in someone's office because it was black instead of grey. Most of them were two-drawer. Mine had four drawers, all full" (Ellsberg, 2002, p. 305). Ellsberg, in other words, was the consummate insider.

It was in the autumn of 1969, while working at the RAND Corporation, and after previously having served in Vietnam as a civilian contractor, that Ellsberg developed sentiments against the Vietnam War (Ehrlich and Goldsmith, 2009; Ellsberg, 2002). In "an act of deliberate civil disobedience" (Ellsberg, 2002, p. 441), Ellsberg began photocopying the United States Department of Defense study, with the assistance of his friend Tony Russo, after hours in an advertising agency. Part of the photocopying ritual involved what Ellsberg described as "declassifying" the documents, which meant using scissors to cut off the "Top Secret" stamp from the top and bottom of each page of the first round of photo-copies (Ellsberg, 2002, p. 392). This was done to make it less evident that the papers were classified when they were hauled around in the open.

The copying and cleaning process was methodical and painstaking. During this time, Ellsberg tried to get senior American politicians inter-ested in the Pentagon Papers, with little success. Finally, in early March 1971, Ellsberg told *New York Times* journalist Neil Sheehan about the Pentagon Papers in a private meeting at Sheehan's house in Washington, D.C. Ellsberg was already acquainted with Sheehan, having previously leaked classified documents pertaining to the Vietnam War to him in March 1968 (Ellsberg, 2002, p. 365). By April of 1971, Ellsberg agreed to hand over a set of the meticulously photocopied Pentagon Papers (approximately 7,000 pages) to Sheehan.[1] Unbeknownst to Ellsberg, the *Times* already had obtained a copy, leaked as a result of Ellsberg's addi-tional efforts to distribute the material.

The *Times* began publishing excerpts from the Pentagon Papers on June 13th, but on June 15th, after its third installment, it received a court order to cease publication. At the time of the court order, the *New York Times* had exclusive access to the Pentagon Papers. After initially being hesitant, on Wednesday June 16th, Ellsberg made contact with Ben Bagdikian, a *Washington Post* editor, and made arrangements to hand over a copy of the Pentagon Papers at a covert meeting in a Boston motel room. Upon receiving the files, the *Post* published its first Pentagon Paper story on June 18th and was quickly subject to a publi-cation injunction. Ellsberg, with the help of a still unnamed source referred to only as "Mr. Boston," arranged for subsequent copies of the Pentagon Papers to be sent in a serial fashion to media outlets one at a time across the country, including the *Boston Globe*, the *Chicago Sun-Times*, the *L.A. Times* and the *Christian Science Monitor*. This stag-gered approach was intended to draw the story out, while keeping Ellsberg and the Pentagon Papers in the public eye (Ellsberg, 2002, pp. 407–408). According to Ellsberg, all of the newspapers that he and Mr. Boston approached to participate in the publication of the Pentagon Papers agreed to do so. Interestingly, the three major TV networks at the time, NBC, ABC and CBS, all turned down the opportunity to publish excerpts of the Pentagon Papers (Ellsberg, 2002, p. 399). By June 24th, multiple other American papers had also picked up and published the material.

While some American newspapers continued to publish extracts from the Pentagon Papers, after a series of appeals, the injunction against the *New York Times* and the *Washington Post* reached the US Supreme Court. On June 30th, the Supreme Court announced its verdict in *New York Times Co. v. United States 403 U.S. 713* and, in a 6 to 3 decision, lifted the publication injunction. The Supreme Court ruled that the US government had not adequately proven that the publication of the Pentagon Papers would cause direct harm to the United States.[2] The ruling continues to be seen as a triumph for the First Amendment (Abrams, 2005).

Two days before the Supreme Court ruling, Daniel Ellsberg turned himself in to a Boston courthouse, at which point he, along with Anthony Russo, was indicted by a Los Angeles grand jury. Details of Ellsberg's trials are provided elsewhere (Abrams, 2005; Blanton, 2001; Ellsberg, 2002; Rudenstine, 1996; Salter, 1975; Ungar, 1972), but some context is needed to understand the outcome of the case and how it compares with the case of Bradley Manning. Just under two years after being indicted, and after a mistrial, the judge in the case dismissed all charges against Ellsberg and Russo. The charges were dismissed because of criminal interference by the Nixon Administration, due to the creation of "the Plumbers." The Plumbers were a covert White House Special Investigations Unit assembled by the Nixon Administration to stop leaks of classified information. During Ellsberg's court case it was revealed that the Plumbers had previously broken into the office of Ellsberg's psychoanalyst in an unsuccessful bid to acquire ammunition for an extralegal smear campaign against Daniel Ellsberg.

At the request of President Richard Nixon, the United States Secret Service secretly installed a system to listen in and record the President's White House conversations (Nixon Presidential Library and Museum, 2012). These later came to be known as the White House tapes when their existence was revealed during Watergate senate hearings in 1973. White House tapes released in April 2001 reveal that President Nixon was keen to seek retribution in the Pentagon Papers case. On June 15, 1971 he stated:

> Goddamn it....Somebody has got to go to jail [*pounding desk*]. Somebody's got to go to jail, that's all there is to it. Our people here can't just [*unclear*] anything about the war....You've got to fight it. (Ellsberg, 2002, p. 428)

In another conversation two days later, President Nixon stated that, in pursuing the leaker, part of his goal was to put "the fear of God into other people in this government" (Ellsberg, 2002, p. 428). President Nixon also wanted to go beyond the criminal courts to try Daniel Ellsberg in the media, as the following extract of a conversation between President Nixon, National Security Advisor Henry Kissinger and Attorney General John N. Mitchell, in the wake of Supreme Court hearing lifting the *New York Times* publication ban, makes clear.

> We've got to get him [Ellsberg]. ... Don't worry about his trial. Just get everything out. Try him in the press. Try him in the press. Everything, John, that there is on the investigation, get it out, leak it out. We want to destroy him in the press. Press. Is that clear? (Ellsberg, 2002, p. 432)

Kissinger and Mitchell agreed.

If Daniel Ellsberg were to release the Pentagon Files today as a PDF computer file, they would be no larger than 10 mB file – small enough to send as an e-mail attachment with most free e-mail accounts. That said, on June 13, 2011, 40 years after they were leaked, the Pentagon Papers were declassified and were made freely available on the Internet from the US National Archives.[3] In an interview with Ellsberg in the *Boston Globe*, one of the papers that published the original Pentagon Papers, Ellsberg replied to a question about how he would handle the Pentagon Papers today by saying he "would have just put them on the Internet" (Storin, 2008). Arranging to have classified files placed on the Internet is exactly what Bradley Manning was charged with.

Cablegate: Bradley Manning and digital leaking

Bradley Manning was born in 1987, in Crescent, Oklahoma, at a time when digital technologies were beginning to flourish. Bradley Manning's father was an adept computer programmer and shared these skills with his son (Nakashima, 2011). For Manning, according to his father, computers became "a focal point of his life" (PBS, 2011). And, it would be Bradley Manning's computer-savvy skills that would be put to work by the US Army.

Manning's home life was less than idyllic. His parents divorced when he was 13, at which point Manning relocated with his mother from Oklahoma to Haverfordwest, Wales. He lived there for four years, completing his General Certificate of Secondary Education (GCSE), but, in 2005 he moved to Oklahoma City to live with his father. The period between Manning's return to America and his enlistment saw Manning move from his father's house and across America. He held a number of low-paying jobs, from pizza maker to coffee barista and travelled from

Tulsa, Oklahoma, to Chicago, and eventually ended up at his aunt's in Potomac, Maryland. In October 2007, after being encouraged by his father, Manning enlisted in the army. According to Nicks (2012), PFC Manning found basic training difficult. He was bullied by superiors and alienated by its hypermasculine and homophobic culture, including its now repealed Don't Ask, Don't Tell policy (Hansen, 2011; Nicks, 2012).

In October 2009, two years after enlisting, PFC Manning was deployed to Forward Operating Base (FOB) Hammer, 40 miles east of Baghdad. Prior to deployment, PFC Manning's superiors had raised concerns about his mental health, because of his clashes with superiors. However, these concerns were reportedly overlooked, because of a shortage of intelligence analysts (O'Kane, Madlena and Grandjean, 2010; Zetter, 2011a, 2011b).[4] PFC Manning worked inside FOB Hammer's Sensitive Compartmented Information Facility (SCIF), which was essentially a room that met the US government's standards for handling classified information. As part of the job, PFC Manning had Top Secret – Sensitive Compartmented Information (TS-SCI) clearance, which allowed him to work at a SCIF computer terminal with access to the Secret Internet Protocol Router Network (SIPRNet). SIPRNet is a secret-level "hidden" military computer network, which allows users to share and access database such as the Net Centric Diplomacy database, the source of the Cablegate diplomatic cables (Borger and Leigh, 2010).

The US government had strict operations security (OPSEC) protocols for handling sensitive and classified information. However, although these protocols may have been followed in Washington, D.C., at FOB Hammer in Iraq where Manning was stationed, such protocols were routinely broken with, for example, passwords to access military computers written on paper and stuck to the terminals (O'Kane, Madlena and Grandjean, 2011; Zetter, 2011c). This lack of security is captured well in the following extract from the "Manning-Lamo"[5] instant message logs released by *Wired*:

> bradass87: there was no physical security…it was there, but not really…5 digit cipher lock…but you could knock and the door [would be opened]…
>   bradass87: everyone just sat at their workstations…watching music videos / car chases / buildings exploding…and writing more stuff to CD/DVD…the culture fed opportunities. (Hansen, 2011)

This culture of opportunity, in turn, enabled the gathering of digital information. Arguably the Achilles heel in the mix was the failure to prohibit soldiers at FOB Hammer from installing software and using personal media on the military computers. It is alleged that Bradley Manning installed the open-source, data-mining software Wget on his SIPRNet computer and used computer scripts to download information from the military network onto his workstation (Zetter, 2011c). Information would then be transferred to a rewritable compact disk (CD-RW). This process was described by Bradley Manning (bradass87) as follows:

> bradass87: i would come in with music on a CD-RW ... labelled with something like "Lady Gaga" ... erase the music ... then write a compressed split file ... no-one suspected a thing I lipsyncehd to Lady Gaga's Telephone ... i didnt even have to hide anything (Hansen, 2011)

How WikiLeaks received the classified files has still not been confirmed. As bradass87 acknowledges in the same chat log:

> bradass87: [the] hardest part is arguably internet access ... uploading any sensitive data over the open internet is a bad idea ... since networks are monitored for any insurgent/terrorist/militia/criminal types info@adrianlamo.com: tor?
> bradass87: tor + ssl + sftp

In these passages, bradass87 describes a collection of resources (computer software and networks) which, together with AES-256 bit encryption, could facilitate secure and anonymous Internet browsing, chat and the transfer of digital information to anyone, including someone who bradass87 described as a "crazy white haired aussie who can't seem to stay in one country very long" (Hansen, 2011).

In November 2009, one month after arriving in Iraq, Manning was promoted to Specialist, a rank above Private First Class. However, on May 24, 2010, Manning was demoted back to Private First Class as punishment for assaulting a fellow army officer earlier that month. The brig psychiatrist recommended Manning for discharge and diagnosed him with an "occupational problem and adjustment disorder with mixed disturbance of emotions and conduct" (Nakashima, 2011).[6] These claims, and the emphasis placed on them by government and military sources, must also be viewed as being made within a system of media representation that favours personality politics and sensationalism the framing of which can have can important impact on the public's perception of the case. Yet, it is the anonymity, at least in terms of the source, on the Internet that facilitates leaks and whistle-blowing in the first place, as noted in a 2008 report on WikiLeaks by the US Army Counterintelligence Center:

> Web sites such as Wikileaks.org use trust as a center of gravity by protecting the anonymity and identity of the insiders, leakers, or whistleblowers. The identification, exposure, or termination of employment of or legal actions against current or former insiders, leakers, or whistleblowers could damage or destroy this center of gravity and deter others from using Wikileaks.org to make such information public. (Horvath, 2008, p. 3)

The above strategy can be summarized as follows: If you can't denigrate the message, denigrate the messenger. In this context, focusing on the leaker's identity fits both the logic of media representation in the network society *and* the goal of the US military to deter leakers by exposing and, where possible, alienating and shaming them. This is not to suggest that claims about Manning are untrue, but it does seek to make clear the strategic military and government value in playing up PFC Manning's 'deviancy': to diminish trust in the whistle-blowing message clearly evident in the Manning-Lamo chat logs and to deter others who might be thinking about following a similar course of action (see below).

On May 26, 2010, two days after his demotion, PFC Manning was arrested by the US Army Criminal Investigations Command and promptly transferred to Camp Arifjana, Kuwait. Manning's treatment in detention will be returned to shortly. First, however, it is important to briefly disclose how he came to be arrested. On May 21, 2010, after some failed e-mail attempts, PFC Manning allegedly sought electronic solace from infamous grey-hat hacker Adrian Lamo via instant messenger. For the next 5 days, the two would have sporadic and often asynchronous instant messenger chats. At the outset of the chat, Adrian Lamo typed the following assurance:

> I'm a journalist and a minister. You can pick either, and treat this as a confession or an interview (never to be published) & enjoy a modicum of legal protection. (Hansen, 2011)

However, the same day PFC Manning allegedly reached out to Lamo, Lamo reached out, via intermediaries, to the US Army Criminal Investigation Command (Nicks, 2012). Lamo and Manning were in contact with each other right up until Manning's arrest (Zetter, 2011d). As an "insurance file" for his dealings with the authorities, Lamo provided *Wired* magazine with a copy of the chat logs between himself and bradass87. Select excerpts of the chats were first published on June 22, 2010 (see Zetter and Poulsen, 2010) and, nearly 13 months later, the entire chat was published (see Hansen, 2011). Included in the discussions are disclosures by Bradley Manning that suggest he developed sentiments against the war while serving in Iraq:

> bradass87: i think the thing that got me the most...that made me rethink the world more than anything
> bradass87: was watching 15 detainees taken by the Iraqi Federal Police...for printing "anti-Iraqi literature"...the iraqi federal police wouldn't cooperate with US forces, so i was instructed to investigate the matter, find out who the "bad guys" were, and how significant this was for the FPs...it turned out, they had printed a scholarly critique against PM Maliki...i had an interpreter read it for me...and when i found out that it was a benign political critique titled "Where did the money go?" and following the corruption trail within the PM's cabinet...i immediately took that information and *ran* to the officer to explain what was going on...he didn't want to hear any of it...he told me to shut up and explain how we could assist the FPs in finding *MORE* detainees...
> bradass87: everything started slipping after that...i saw things differently
> bradass87: i had always questioned the things worked, and investigated to find the truth...but that was a point where i was a *part* of something...i was actively involved in something that i was completely against...(Hansen, 2011)

The revelations of bradass87 provided sufficient information for the military to identify and arrest PFC Bradley Manning. Manning was first charged on July 5, 2010 for two offenses under the Uniform Code of Military Justice. However, on March 1, 2011, the army filed 22 new charges against PFC Manning, including theft of public property, computer fraud and violating the Espionage Act, the same act that Daniel Ellsberg and Anthony Russo were charged under (Savage, 2011). After being declared fit for trial and after a military pretrial hearing (Article 32 hearing), which ruled PFC Bradley Manning could be court martialed, *United States v. Bradley Manning* began in April 2012 and, at the time of publication, is ongoing.

Leaking in the age of the "data dump"

This final section examines how the rise of the network society has shaped the landscape of leaking and, in fact, has changed the type of person who can be a leaker. Perhaps the first thing to note is that Daniel Ellsberg was a real insider, a member of the elite with an academic pedigree from some of the world's finest universities and some of the highest security clearance in the US. Moreover, Ellsberg worked close to the seat of power on the very dossier he eventually leaked. Manning, on the other hand, was a low-level security analyst, a node in a vast industry of networked individuals authorized to access SIPRNet. While the US government will not confirm numbers, the BBC has estimated that approximately "2.5 million US military and civilian personnel" can access SIPRNet (BBC, 2010). Consequently, PFC Manning's network access – along with that of at least 2.5 million fellow security-cleared individuals – must not be seen as an exception, but as *typical* of military work in the network society. The normality of this situation, as Nicks (2012) notes, "conspired to give [PFC Manning] unprecedented access to state secrets" (Nicks, 2012, p. 116).

The rise and reach of SIPRNet and the related digitalization and networking of US government and military resources epitomizes Castells's network society. It also accounts for how such a low-level analyst could have access to such a vast trove of information. This ease of access was also magnified in the wake of the September 11, 2001 terrorist attacks, on account of the fact that the 2004 National Commission on Terrorist Attacks Upon the United States (the 9/11 Commission) identi-fied "breakdowns in information sharing and the failure to fuse perti-nent intelligence (i.e., 'connecting the dots') as key factors in the failure to prevent the 9/11 attacks" (Bjelopera, 2011, p. 2). In other words, too little access to information and sharing was the problem, not too much. This finding set into motion a series of government initiatives to tear down information silos and to promote the sharing of information – particularly information pertaining to terrorist threats – across relevant government bodies. It also saw the US government balloon personnel and resources dedicated to generating, gathering and sharing such information (Priest and Arkin, 2011). Expenditures were also massively increased, with the US federal government spending $11 billion in 2011 to protect its classified information, double the amount spent in 2001 (Shane, 2012).

Although Daniel Ellsberg and Bradley Manning differed in status and security levels of their jobs, there is a more significant difference between their two cases: the information environment. In the case of Manning, government and military information-driven initiatives, coupled with existing information systems already in use, gave more people access to digital information than ever. With unprecedented numbers of people having access to the US government's network of classified information, there was a shift from information being concentrated in the hands of insiders to its being shared with a vast, global network of security-cleared personnel. With this, the potential for leaking becomes democratized, open to anyone with network access. While classification and OPSEC systems provide some control (if they are followed), the spread of information across vast networks and sheer volume of digital data generated, spurred on by a culture of endemic overclassification, increases the risk that some information might escape.

Leaking in the digital age

Leaks in the network society can thus be seen as a function of the volume of data available and the ease with which it can be spread around and shared. Throughout much of the media coverage of WikiLeaks, much emphasis has been placed on the volume of data released. Todd Gitlin (2010), for example, criticized WikiLeaks for engaging in a "data dump," a term that implies the wanton release of information with connotations of waste and carelessness. Micha Sifry, on the other hand, argues that the "volume of data" is a key feature of the Information Age (2010, p. 155). As such, we should not always expect leaks to be refined, well researched and neatly photocopied reports, as was the case of the Pentagon Papers.

Instead, they may be large, unwieldy, messy and, likely, digital. Leaks may be raw, like the databases of field reports from Iraq and Afghanistan. Data analysis of the leaked Iraq War logs revealed the deaths of 15,000 civilians, which the US military knew about, but did not publicly disclose (Leigh, 2010). Yet, analysing the Iraq War logs required both journalistic inquisitiveness and a high level of computer aptitude (Leigh and Harding, 2011). Thus, while a leaker may help get the information to the public, specialized digital skills may be required to decipher and/ or emphasize the public value of such information. As Yochai Benkler in Chapter 1 argues, the actual release of Cablegate documents was not a data dump. Instead, it was a selective release of information staggered over time, filtered in a partnership between activists and mainstream media and synched in time. Thus the WikiLeaks case demonstrates the role of trusted intermediaries who are able to offer secure Internet-based platforms on which to submit leaks. Further it emphasizes the role of digitally savvy individuals or teams thereof who are able to unpack, interpret and safely distribute leaked material. Lastly, it captures the importance of data journalists and well-resourced news organizations in helping to make sense of the massive volumes of raw data and package it for popular consumption in the network society.[7]

Whereas the volume of information may have presented an issue in the past – again, think of the time needed to photocopy, "declassify," and collate the 7,000-page Pentagon Papers – digital information can easily be encoded onto multiple media simply and instantly, and shared across computer networks worldwide at minimal cost. To help gain some perspective on this point imagine this: if Cablegate were released as an analogue leak, and assuming each cable is a page or less, it would take 41.8 hours of straight printing at a rate of 100 pages a minute. The print job would use almost 503 reams of paper. Yet, in a digital age, the Cablegate and related files were not printed but were digitally distributed. Each trove was eventually made available on the Internet as a reasonable-sized torrent: Cablegate (1.61 GB), Afghan War Diaries (75.7 MB), Iraq War Logs (354.18 MB), and the *Collateral Murder* video and raw Apache footage (249.19 MB). Given that the average CD-RW holds around 700 MB, these files could fit, likely with room to spare, on 4 CDs or on a single USB flash drive.

Given the portability and replicability of digital information, its control remains a central concern for power holders. This is rooted in a tension between the need to have free information flows across relevant bodies to facilitate the identification and analysis of global risks and, at the same time, the need to effectively manage information to ensure that it stays within the intended networks. Addressing this tension, in October 2011, the Obama administration issued Executive Order 13587, which set about both procedural and structural changes across US government agencies, in an effort to strike a balance between sharing and securing information (Federal Bureau of Investigation, 2011; The White House, 2011). Taking a harsher stance towards alleged leakers, the Obama administration has also charged an unprecedented six people under the Espionage Act; double the number charged by all past presidents combined (Winseck and McCurdy, 2012). The Obama administration's treatment of whistle-blowers, as noted below, has come under international criticism.

Digital leakers and iron bars

PFC Manning's treatment after his arrest, and particularly his time at Marine Corps Base Quantico (MCB Quantico), has been condemned domestically and internationally (Greenwald, 2010). Manning was transferred from Kuwait to MCB Quantico on July 29, 2010, where he was immediately placed in maximum custody and put under Prevention of Injury (POI) watch. In a blog post titled "A Typical Day for PFC Bradley Manning," David E. Coombs, Manning's lawyer, described the pretrial conditions as follows:

> PFC Manning is held in his cell for approximately 23 hours a day...The guards are required to check on PFC Manning every five minutes by asking him if he is okay. PFC Manning is required to respond in some affirmative manner. At night, if the guards cannot see PFC Manning clearly, because he has a blanket over his head or is curled up towards the wall, they will wake him in order to ensure he is okay. He receives each of his meals in his cell. He is not allowed to have a pillow or sheets. However, he is given access to two blankets and has recently been given a new mattress that has a built-in pillow. He is not allowed to have any personal items in his cell. (Coombs, 2010)

In addition to the above restrictions, during some of his pretrial detention at MCB Quantico, Manning was also forced to sleep in the nude and remain naked for his cell inspection. Juan Méndez, the UN Special Rapporteur on torture, investigated Manning's pretrial treatment and condemned it:

> The Special Rapporteur concludes that imposing seriously punitive conditions of detention on someone who has not been found guilty of any crime is a violation of his right to physical and psychological integrity as well as of his presumption of innocence. (Méndez, 2012, p. 75)

Méndez's report was made public at the end of February 2012. In April 2010, the US government transferred Manning to a medium-security pretrial detention facility at Fort Leavenworth, Kansas. Upon his transfer, many of the restrictions were lifted with Manning allowed to mix with other pretrial detainees and keep personal items in his cell. Significantly, on January 7, 2013, military judge Colonel Denise Lind ruled that Bradley Manning was treated unlawfully while at MCB Quantico. As compensation, Manning was awarded 112 days credit towards a future prison sentence.

Theories abound for the cause of PFC Manning's disproportional treatment, at least if our standard for comparison is Daniel Ellsberg. Many argue that the objective has essentially been to beat Manning into coughing up evidence directly implicating Julian Assange with the leak. Yet, Manning's treatment can also be seen as a public display of punishment, the kind that Michael Foucault describes in the opening to *Discipline & Punish,* in his gruesome account of how Robert-François Damiens was drawn and quartered for the attempted regicide of King Louis XV of France in 1757. The public execution, Foucault notes, is an episodic show of power by the King. It is an effort to control. A deterrent. A warning to others and a reassertion of authority.

Similarly, Manning's treatment at MCB Quantico can be seen this way. Given that America is a developed democracy, someone like PFC Manning cannot simply be killed on the basis of leak accusations. Thus it is through public details of Manning's cruel, inhuman and degrading treatment during his pretrial detention and through his stalled and extended prosecution that the harsh lessons about what happens to whistle-blowers and leakers are still broadcast to the public. The price of betraying state secrets is shown to be high and profoundly humiliating, indeed. Moreover, the road to justice is slow; Bradley Manning has been held, since his arrest, in pretrial custody for over 1000 days and counting [as of February 21, 2013], far beyond the legal requirement of 120 days (Coombs, 2012b)[8]. Thus, in the network society, even though the government cannot always control information once released, it can control the body of the accused and, critically, the media representations of him or her too. Leakers and mass media, state power, counter-power and the costs of transgression each have their place in the WikiLeaks saga, an emblematic case of politics and power in the network society. If you can't press a delete button on the Internet, you can endlessly persecute whistle-blowers and leakers, and in this case, that person is Bradley Manning.

The continuation of whistle-blowing

Hell, I wouldn't prosecute the *Times.* My view is to prosecute the goddamn pricks that gave it to 'em. (Richard Nixon, June 14, 1971)

There is a striking similarity between the Pentagon Papers and the WikiLeaks cases, insofar that they both have prominent yet completely different characters at the center of them: Daniel Ellsberg and Bradley Manning, the whistle-blowers. Perhaps with some of the fog of the

Vietnam War having cleared, and with the added benefit of hindsight, history has canonized Daniel Ellsberg. He is seen as a hero, as someone who broke the law, but did so in good faith, intentions that Ellsberg himself has made clear (Ellsberg, 1972; 2002). Manning stands in a different place, to put it mildly.

At the time of publication, PFC Manning had not entered a plea in his court-martial. However, on November 7, 2012, lawyer David Coombs made known Manning's willingness to enter a guilty plea to select charges through a process known as "pleading by exceptions and substitutions" (Coombs 2012c). This revelation by Manning's lawyer gave a boost to a popular movement which has emerged around Manning, framing him as a whistle-blower with legitimate grievances and a right to have taken the stance he did. Manning was also voted by Guardian readers as the 2012 Guardian person of the year in an online poll hosted by the media organisation (News Blog, 2012)[9]. Like all classic whistle-blowers, he exposed wrongdoing to the public. That he saw himself in this way is evident in documents released by WikiLeaks, as well as in the famous *Wired* chat logs:

> bradass87: if you had free reign over classified networks for long periods of time ... say, 8–9 months ... and you saw incredible things, awful things ... things that belonged in the public domain, and not on some server stored in a dark room in Washington DC ... what would you do? ... theres so much ... it affects everybody on earth ... its open diplomacy ... world-wide anarchy in CSV format ... its beautiful, and horrifying ... and ... its important that it gets out ... i feel, for some bizarre reason it might actually change something. (Hansen, 2011)

In June 2012 Manning's lawyer, David Coombs, published a blog post with a statement from Bradley Manning that read, "I am very grateful for your support and humbled by your ongoing efforts" (Coombs, 2012a). Among Bradley Manning's most prominent supporters is Daniel Ellsberg, who has passionately argued in his defense. "I was Bradley / Pentagon Papers 1971" [Figure 7.1], Ellsberg declares on a sign held aloft as part of his support of the Bradley Manning Support Network's "I Am Bradley Manning" campaign. In the text describing the photo, Ellsberg writes:

> I was the Bradley Manning of my day. In 1971 I too faced life (115 years) in prison for exposing classified government lies and crimes. President Obama says "the Ellsberg material was classified on a

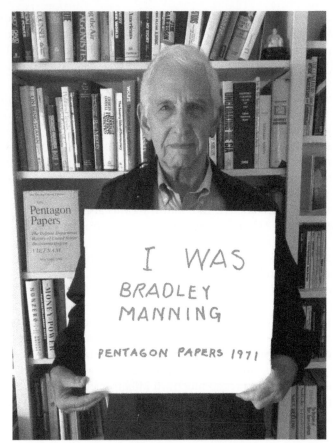

Figure 7.1 Daniel Ellsberg (pictured) as part of the "I am Bradley Manning" campaign

different basis." True. The Pentagon Papers were not Secret like the WikiLeaks revelations, they were all marked Top Secret – Sensitive.

Ultimately all charges in my case were dropped because of criminal governmental misconduct toward me during my proceedings. Exactly the same outcome should occur now, in light of the criminal conditions of Manning's confinement for the last six months.(Iam. BradleyManning.org, 2011)

In contrast to Ellsberg, however, Manning has been detained without trial for over two and a half years (since May 26, 2010) and faces the prospect of life in prison. Although he is one of the most prominent cases, the Manning case must also be seen as symptomatic of the bigger crackdown on unauthorized leaking of information by the Obama administration. Obama's administration has shown very little acceptance of whistle-blowing; Obama's passing comment that PFC Manning "broke the law"(Lee and Phillip 2011) during a campaign fundraiser indicates that he'll be getting no quarter from the White House.

Manning, to be clear, is in a different legal environment from Ellsberg. He faces a military court, where the *Military Judges' Benchbook* is concerned with the act of leaking and not the motivations behind it, or even the harm or lack thereof caused by the leak, as the case may be. And although a military judge will ultimately pass judgment on the charges against Bradley Manning, history will be another judge. While a military court may not deem a whistle-blowing argument as valid or show compassion, history books, with the benefit of hindsight and after the fog of has been lifted, should view Bradley Manning as a legitimate whistle-blower. He will likely be seen as following in the footsteps of all those before him, like Daniel Ellsberg, who disclosed information about public problems for the greater public good. And in that, whether analog and broadcast or digital and networked, stands the risky and radical practice of the leak, a position filled in the body by Manning, but in the broader networked free press by WikiLeaks, the organization that he allegedly reached out to.

Notes

1. For a detailed account of Ellsberg's interactions with the *New York Times,* see Ellsberg (2002), Chapter 26.
2. Of note, just as the "harm" caused by the publication of the Pentagon Papers material played a central role in the *New York Times* Supreme Court case, Bradley Manning's defense lawyer David Coombs has continually sought evidence from the US government as to the "harm" caused by the WikiLeaks releases. Despite this parallel, the *New York Times* as a publisher of leaked material was in a vastly different position to that of Bradley Manning as the (alleged) leaker.
3. Although some versions of the Pentagon Papers online are around 10 megabytes, the official version provided by the National Archives is almost 1.5 gigabytes. It is available here: http://www.archives.gov/research/pentagon-papers/
4. It should be noted that in PFC Manning's Article 32 hearing, the defense has stressed the emotional challenges faced by Manning (Gosztola, 2011).
5. On June 10, 2010, *Wired* published excerpts of Internet chat conversations that they reported to be between Adrian Lamo and Bradley Manning

(Poulson and Zetter, 2010). While the chat log only contained the name "bradass87," Wired replaced the handle with the name "Bradley Manning" and subsequently named him in the release of the full logs (Hansen, 2011). The chat logs have also been subsequently discussed in Manning's Article 32 hearing and were provided as evidence. Consequently, this chapter is based on premise that bradass87 is Bradley Manning.

6. While much attention has been placed on Manning's sexuality, desire for gender reassignment, and fragile mental state both before and after his arrest, this chapter does not dwell on this aspect of PFC Manning's story, although it has loomed large both in the US government's case against him and in Manning's defense team response (Gosztola, 2011; Kuo, 2012). Gender identity issues also arise in the *Wired* chat logs (see Hansen, 2011).

7. For more on the relationship between the future of networked journalism and WikiLeaks see Beckett and Ball (2012).

8. Over the course of ten days between November 27, 2012 and December 11, 2012, a pre-trial hearing was held at Fort Meade, Maryland concerning Bradley Manning's treatment at the Marine brig in Quantico, Virginia. Manning's lawyer, David Coombs, filed a motion calling for the charges against Manning to be dropped in light of his client's degrading treatment. The judge refused to dismiss Manning's charges but did award him 112 days credit towards any future prison sentence. Credit was done on a 1-1 basis for specific incidents identified by the judge. Manning's defence had sought a credit ratio of 10-for-1.

9. This victory was somewhat controversial. While the Guardian did name Bradley Manning as the winner, they also stated that the poll had "fishy voting patterns" (News Blog, 2012). The Guardian linked these to WikiLeak's twitter account (@Wikileaks) asserting WikiLeaks drove traffic to the Guardian's website to deliberately skew poll results.

References

Abrams, F. (2005). *Speaking Freely: Trials of the First Amendment.* New York: Viking

Beck, U. (1992). *Risk Society: Towards a New Modernity.* London: Sage

Beckett, C. and Ball, J. (2012). *WikiLeaks: News in the Networked Era.* Cambridge: Polity

BBC, (2010, November 29). "Siprnet: Where the leaked cables came from". Retrieved from: http://www.bbc.co.uk/news/world-us-canada-11863618

Benkler, Y. (2013). WikiLeaks and the networked fourth estate. In B. Brevini, A. Hintz, and P. McCurdy, (eds), *Beyond WikiLeaks: Implications for the Future of Communications, Journalism, and Society.* Palgrave Macmillan, [our current book]

Bjelopera, J. (2011). Terrorism Information Sharing and the Nationwide Suspicious Activity Report Initiative: Background and Issues for Congress. *Congressional Research Service.* CRS Report R4090.1 Retrieved from: http://fpc.state.gov/documents/organization/166837.pdf

Blanton, T. (ed.). (2001). "The Pentagon Papers: Secrets, Lies and Audio Tapes" National Security Archive Electronic Briefing Book Number 48, June 2001. Retrieved from: http://www.gwu.edu/~nsarchiv/NSAEBB/NSAEBB48/

Borger and Leigh, D. (2010, November 28). "Siprnet: where America stores its secret cables". *Guardian*, Retrieved from: http://www.guardian.co.uk/world/2010/nov/28/siprnet-america-stores-secret-cables

Castells, M. (1997). *The Power of Identity* (Vol. 2). Oxford: Blackwell

Castells, M. (2000). *The Rise of the Network Society*. Oxford: Blackwell

Castells, M. (2007). Communication, Power and Counter-power in the Network Society. *International Journal of Communication*, 1,238–266

Castells, M. (2009). *Communication Power*. Oxford: Oxford

Coombs, D. (2010, December 18). "A Typical Day for PFC Bradley Manning" The Law Offices of David E Coombs [blog post]. Retrieved from http://www.armycourtmartialdefense.info/2010/12/typical-day-for-pfc-bradley-manning.html

Coombs, D. (2012a, June 12). "Supporting Bradley Manning" The Law Offices of David E Coombs [blog post]. Retrieved from: http://www.armycourtmartialdefense.info/2012/06/supporting-bradley-manning.html

Coombs, D. (2012b, September 27). "Defense's Speedy Trial Motion" The Law Offices of David E Coombs [blog post]. Retrieved from: http://www.armycourtmartialdefense.info/2012/09/defenses-speedy-trial-motion.html

Coombs, D. (2012c, November 7). "PFC Manning's Offered Plea and Forum Selection" The Law Offices of David E Coombs [blog post]. Retrieved from: http://www.armycourtmartialdefense.info/2012/11/pfc-mannings-offered-plea-and-forum.html

Dahlgren, P. (2009). *Media and Political Engagement*. New York: Cambridge University Press

Ehrlich, J. and Goldsmith, R. (Producers & Directors). (2009). *The Most Dangerous Man in America: Daniel Ellsberg and the Pentagon Papers* [film documentary]. USA. Retrieved from: http://www.mostdangerousman.org/

Ellsberg, D. (1972). *Papers on the War*. New York: Simon & Schuster

Ellsberg, D. (2002). *Secrets: A Memoir of Vietnam and the Pentagon Papers*. New York: Penguin

Ellsberg, D. (2012). Bio – Daniel Ellsberg. Retrieved from: http://www.ellsberg.net/bio

Federal Bureau of Investigation. (2011). *FBI Information Sharing Report 2011*. Retrieved from: http://www.fbi.gov/stats-services/publications/national-information-sharing-strategy-1/national-information-sharing-strategy

Gitlin, T. (2010, December 7). "Everything Is Data, but Data Isn't Everything", *The New Republic*. Retrieved from: http://www.tnr.com/blog/foreign-policy/79678/data-isnt-everything-wikileaks-julian-assange-daniel-ellsberg

Gosztola, K. (2011, December 18). Bradley Manning Pre-Trial Hearing: Live Blog, Day 3. Blog of Kevin Gosztola. Retrieved from: http://dissenter.firedoglake.com/2011/12/18/bradley-manning-pre-trial-hearing-live-blog-day-3/

Greenwald, G. (2010, December 15). "The inhumane conditions of Bradley Manning's detention" *Salon.com*, Retrieved from http://www.salon.com/2010/12/15/manning_3/

Hansen, E. (2011, July 13). "Manning-Lamo Chat Logs Revealed". Retrieved from: http://www.wired.com/threatlevel/2011/07/manning-lamo-logs

Horvath, M. D. (2008). *Wikileaks.org – An Online Reference to Foreign Intelligence Services, Insurgents, or Terrorist Groups?* Army Counterintellegence Center Special Report. Retrieved from: http://mirror.wikileaks.info/leak/us-intel-wikileaks.pdf

Iam.BradleyManning.Org (2011). "Daniel Ellsberg". Retrieved from http://iam.bradleymanning.org/post/5535584206

Lee, M.J. and Philip, A. (2011, April 22). "Barack Obama on Bradley Manning: 'He broke the law'", *Politico*. Retrevied from: http://www.politico.com/news/stories/0411/53601.html

Leigh, D. (2010, October 22). "Iraq war logs reveal 15,000 previously unlisted civilian deaths", *Guardian*. Retrieved from: http://www.guardian.co.uk/world/2010/oct/22/true-civilian-body-count-iraq?intcmp=239

Leigh, D. and Harding, A. (2011). *WikiLeaks: Inside Julian Assange's War on Secrecy*. London: The Guardian

Kuo, L. (2012, February 23). "WikiLeaks suspect Manning defers plea, court-martial begins". Retrieved from: http://www.reuters.com/article/2012/02/23/us-usa-manning-idUSTRE81M20M20120223

Méndez, J. E. (2012, February 29). Report of the Special Rapporteur on torture and other cruel, inhuman or degrading treatment or punishment, Juan E. Méndez. United Nations General Assembly, Human Rights Council, Nineteenth session. Document ID: A/HRC/19/61/Add.4 Retrieved from: http://www.ohchr.org/Documents/HRBodies/HRCouncil/RegularSession/Session19/A_HRC_19_61_Add.4_EFSonly.pdf

Nakashima, E. (2011, May 4). "Bradley Manning is at the center of the WikiLeaks controversy. But who is he?" *Washington Post*. Retrieved from: http://www.washingtonpost.com/lifestyle/magazine/who-is-wikileaks-suspect-bradley-manning/2011/04/16/AFMwBmrF_print.html

News Blog, (2012). "Guardian person of the year: Voters choose Bradley Manning" News Blog. *Guardian*. Retrieved from: http://www.guardian.co.uk/world/blog/2012/dec/10/bradley-manning-guardian-person-of-the-year-2012

Nicks, D. (2012). *Private: Bradley Manning, WikiLeaks, and the Biggest Exposure of Official Secrets in American History*. Chicago: Chicago Review Press

Nixon Presidential Library and Museum (2012). "History of the White House Tapes". Nixon Presidential Library and Museum. Retreved from: http://nixon.archives.gov/forresearchers/find/tapes/learn/history.php

O'Kane, M., Madlena C. and G. Grandjean (2011, May 27). "WikiLeaks accused Bradley Manning 'should never have been sent to Iraq'" *Guardian*. Retrieved from: http://www.guardian.co.uk/world/2011/may/27/bradley-manning-wikileaks-mentally-fragile

PBS (2010). Point of View, "The Most Dangerous Man in America: Daniel Ellsberg and the Pentagon Papers". Retrieved from: http://www.pbs.org/pov/mostdangerousman/ellsbergs.php

PBS (2010). (2011). "Frontline: Interview with Brian Manning". Retrieved from: http://www.pbs.org/wgbh/pages/frontline/wikileaks/bradley-manning/interviews/brian-manning.html

Prados, J. and Pratt Porter, M. (eds). (2004). *Inside the Pentagon Papers*. (Lawrence: University Press of Kansas).

Priest, D. and Arkin, W. (2011). *Top Secret America The Rise of the New American Security State*. London: Little, Brown and Company

Rudenstine, D. (1996). *The Day the Presses Stopped: A History of the Pentagon Papers Case*. Berkeley: University of California Press

Salter, K. (1975). *The Pentagon Papers Trial*. Berkeley, CA: Editorial Justa Publications

Savage, C. (2011, March 2). "Soldier Faces 22 New WikiLeaks Charges" *New York Times*. Retrieved from: http://www.nytimes.com/2011/03/03/us/03manning.html

Shane, S. (2012, July 3). "Cost to Protect U.S. Secrets Doubles to Over $11 Billion", *New York Times*. Retrieved from: http://www.nytimes.com/2012/07/03/us/politics/cost-to-protect-us-secrets-doubles-in-decade-to-11-billion.html

Sreedharan, C., Thorsen, E. and Allan, S. (2012). "WikiLeaks and the Changing Forms of Information Politics in the "Network Society". In E. Downey and M. Jones (Eds). *Public Service, Governance and Web 2.0 Technologies: Future Trends in Social Media*. Hershey, PA: IGI Global, 167–180

Sifry, M. (2011). *WikiLeaks and the Age of Transparency*. New Haven: Yale

Storin, M. (2008, June 22). A victory for the Globe and the press. *Boston Globe*. Retrieved from: http://www.boston.com/bostonglobe/editorial_opinion/oped/articles/2008/06/22/a_victory_for_the_globe_and_the_press/

Ungar, S. J. (1972). *The Papers & The Papers: An Account of the Legal and Political Battle over the Pentagon Papers*. New York: Dutton

Winseck, D. and McCurdy, P. (2012, May 17). "Twitter-WikiLeaks case a test of press and privacy rights online" *Globe and Mail Online*. Retrieved from: http://www.theglobeandmail.com/technology/digital-culture/twitter-wikileaks-case-a-test-of-press-and-privacy-rights-online/article4184669/?page=all

The White House, Office of the Press Secretary (2011). "Executive Order 13587 – Structural Reforms to Improve the Security of Classified Networks and the Responsible Sharing and Safeguarding of Classified Information [press release]" Retrieved from: http://www.whitehouse.gov/the-press-office/2011/10/07/executive-order-13587-structural-reforms-improve-security-classified-net

Zetter, K. and Poulsen, K. (2010, June 11). 'I Can't Believe What I'm Confessing to You': The Wikileaks Chats. *Wired*. Retrieved from: http://www.wired.com/threatlevel/2010/06/wikileaks-chat/

Zetter, K. and Poulsen, K. (2011a, December 5). Bradley Manning's Defense Attorney Looks to Blame Military for Leaks. *Wired*. Retrieved from: http://www.wired.com/threatlevel/2011/12/psychologist-manning-dangerous/

Zetter, K. and Poulsen, K. (2011b, December 8). Army Disciplined 15 People Over Bradley Manning Failures. *Wired*. Retrieved from: http://www.wired.com/threatlevel/2011/12/army-disciplined-15

Zetter, K. and Poulsen, K. (2011c, December 18). Forensic Expert: Manning's Computer Had 10K Cables, Downloading Scripts. *Wired*. Retrieved from: http://www.wired.com/threatlevel/2011/12/cables-scripts-manning/

Zetter, K. and Poulsen, K. (2011d, December 20). In WikiLeaks Case, Bradley Manning Faces the Hacker Who Turned Him In. *Wired*. Retrieved from: http://www.wired.com/threatlevel/2011/12/adrian-lamo-bradley-manning/

8
Dimensions of Modern Freedom of Expression: WikiLeaks, Policy Hacking, and Digital Freedoms

Arne Hintz

Introduction

The recent history of Internet development can easily be interpreted as a constant expansion of free communication and citizen journalism. From the open-publishing experiments by the global Indymedia network (http://www.indymedia.org), to their emergence as a mass phenomenon through blogging and commercial social networking platforms such as Facebook and Twitter, to the incorporation of user-generated content by established media (e.g., CNN's iReporter), to Wikipedia and similar projects, participating in the production of media messages, information, and knowledge has changed the ways in which understandings and interpretations about the world are created. The "people formerly known as the audience" (Rosen, 2006), i.e., the new generation of netizens, have applied the now-classic Indymedia slogan: "Don't hate the media, be the media!"

Soon the role of social and interactive media in processes of democratization and political change became apparent, from the use of SMS (short text messages sent by cell phone) for protest mobilizations in Spain and in the Philippines in the early 2000s to the use of Twitter and Facebook in Iran, Moldova, and elsewhere at the end of the decade. Uprisings such as the Arab Spring have led to claims of Twitter and Facebook revolutions and overall to great enthusiasm about the democratic potential of technology (Morozov, 2011). As "liberation technology," as scholar Larry Diamond notes, social media and other information and communication technology (ICT) applications enable "citizens to report news, expose wrong-doing, express opinions, mobilize protest, monitor elections, scrutinize government, deepen participation, and expand the horizons of freedom" (Diamond, 2010, p. 70). In Tunisia, Egypt, and elsewhere, social media helped mobilize a critical mass of protesters and generate a social space for developing critical discourses, thus becoming "effective catalysts" (Khamis and Vaughn, 2011, p. 1) of change and amplifiers of social movement activism. Some even claimed that communication platforms constituted the fundamental triggers for revolution. In the words of Egyptian activist (and Google employee) Wael Ghonim: "If you want to free a society, just give them Internet access" (ibid.).

The WikiLeaks project can be placed in the midst of these examples of the use of liberation technology and the various experiences of individuals and movements in advancing free expression, transparency, and social transformation. The leaks platform has bypassed information restrictions, expanded the range of publicly available information, and challenged the leading media players to change their routines and practices.[1] Demonstrating the capacity of technical experts to challenge major powers, WikiLeaks seems to express a broader trend in which the power relations between individuals and institutions are shifting in favour of the former (Grimsson, 2011). In that sense, citizen journalism, the Arab Spring, and WikiLeaks may confirm some of the predictions of cyber-libertarians and techno-utopians, who have long criticized traditional institutions as outdated and have praised the power of individuals in cyberspace (Barlow, 1996).

However, this reading of recent events may be premature. Just as social media have been used by activists to advance political change, they have been used by governments to control and deter such action, for example, by identifying protesters (as in Tunisia, Syria, and Iran). Vital online resources and funding streams have been cut to weaken dissident organizations (as happened to WikiLeaks in December 2010 and ever since). And if social media applications or even the Internet as such become a threat to an existing political order, they can be shut down (as happened in Egypt in 2011). We are witnessing increasing online surveillance and filtering, new forms of censorship, the vulnerability of Internet infrastructure, and the persistence of criminalization and physical violence. A major – and open-ended – struggle around the use of ICTs for political change and free communication has emerged. And WikiLeaks has been very much in the center of the storm.

It is pertinent, then, to take stock of the effects that the current turmoil may have on future practices, challenges, and understandings of free expression, and particularly, to consider the implications of digital environments. While the case of WikiLeaks demonstrates the power of

ICT uses for social change, it also points us to new practices of censorship and other restrictions, and thus to some of the cornerstones for protecting or limiting future freedom of expression.

In this chapter I therefore ask what the WikiLeaks experience can tell us about current contestations in the field of digital freedom of expression. In the first part, I outline an analytical structure for understanding and investigating these dynamics, focusing on the dimensions of information control, access to infrastructure, surveillance, critical resources, and physical violence, and I provide examples for public and private restrictions based on the experiences of the WikiLeaks saga and other recent developments. In the second part, I will explore how civil-society-based campaigns are challenging these restrictions by advocating policy change and developing alternative policy frameworks. Again, WikiLeaks is a useful lens for observing such initiatives, because it has been instrumental in creating one: the Icelandic Modern Media Initiative (IMMI), which has declared its mission as safeguarding "modern freedom of expression."[2] I briefly outline this campaign, as well as further examples, and investigate their agendas and strategies. These practical experiences will provide insights on how digital restrictions are perceived by free-expression advocates, and they can therefore serve to test the model that is presented first.

Together, these dynamics demonstrate some of the key struggles and contestations over freedom of expression in the current digital media environment. They highlight strategic points of intervention and control by different actors (particularly states, businesses, and civil society), and they point us to some of the core requirements for freedom of expression in an online world.[3]

Emerging obstacles to free expression online

In the wake of both the WikiLeaks saga and the Arab Spring, governmental reaction has been partly enthusiastic and partly hostile. With regard to the democratization processes in North Africa and the Middle East, development agencies and foreign affairs ministries in the West and North quickly adopted the liberation discourse and have explored ways to support ICT use for democratic change in developing countries and authoritarian states. As "Net activists are the new democracy fighters" (Gunilla Carlsson, Swedish Minister for International Development Cooperation, quoted in Christensen, 2011, p. 234), the Swedish, US, and other governments have provided aid for online freedom of expression and the use of social media in the service of global democratic change (e.g., Christensen, 2011; Kaplan, 2012). The Internet Freedom Agenda, prominently advanced by the US State Department, underpins these efforts through international norm-building.

At the same time, actual communication policy inside both Eastern and Western countries has moved in a different direction. Observers from civil society and academia have increasingly adopted a more sober, and in some cases even alarmed[4] view of the restrictions to free online communication that are emerging rapidly. Partly those obstacles originate in government policy, partly in business practices, and often we can observe combinations and interactions of the two. As a result, what previously seemed like the borderless and uncontrollable cyberspace is increasingly domesticated and controlled.

In the following, I will outline a more systematic structure for understanding these obstacles. This may help us to develop criteria for free expression in digital environments, as well as policy agendas for its protection.

Information control

The most immediate practice for controlling communication flows is to curtail access to information. WikiLeaks has highlighted this issue by making information public that either governments or businesses have wished to conceal. The state's interest in preventing its citizens from accessing information that is collected about them or in their name has been significant, and even where new laws have been set in place to expand access to information, political pressures quickly emerged to reduce their scope and reintroduce restrictions.[5]

The filtering of Web content has become a particularly common practice across the globe. According to the OpenNet Initiative, 47 percent of the world's Internet users experience online censorship, with 31 percent of all Internet users living in countries that engage in "substantial" or "pervasive" censorship (Open Net Initiative, 2012). While the Chinese "Great Firewall" and filtering practices in other authoritarian countries have been well documented (e.g., Deibert et al., 2008), filtering is also common in Western democracies, often initiated with the rationale of restricting illegal or otherwise unacceptable content such as child pornography, but increasingly expanding to other fields. Access to the WikiLeaks website has been blocked in US government facilities. File-sharing websites such as the Pirate Bay have been blocked, for example in the United Kingdom, because of alleged copyright infringements (BBC, 2012). Intermediaries such as Internet service providers (ISPs) and search engines are increasingly enlisted by governments to control and restrict access to Internet content, and thus they become "proxy censors" (Kreimer 2006, p. 13).[6]

WikiLeaks points us not just to state secrecy and to filtering initiated by public bodies, but also to private forms of censorship. Some of its earlier scoops, such as the publication of documents in 2009 proving illegal toxic waste dumping in Côte d'Ivoire by British company Trafigura, concerned information that had been banned from being published by other media for libel reasons. In countries such as the United Kingdom, where Trafigura had prevented the *Guardian*, the BBC, and others from discussing the case, strict libel and antidefamation laws have become a key tool for businesses (and celebrities) to shut down critical reporting. Further prominent examples that have involved WikiLeaks include the case of the Kaupthing Bank in Iceland, which was granted an injunction against the national public broadcaster RUV in August 2009, just minutes before RUV news was to report extensively on Kaupthing's fraudulent financial dealings, which had contributed to the collapse of the Icelandic economy. The injunction stopped the story from being aired, and instead RUV had to point its audience to the WikiLeaks website, where detailed documents on the case had been posted, thereby making WikiLeaks instantly famous in Iceland.[7]

Access to infrastructure

All information and communication exchange that is not limited to face-to-face speech requires a technological infrastructure that enables this exchange and potentially allows for the storage of relevant data.[8] This may include the radio-frequency spectrum, telecommunications infrastructure (cables and satellites), and Internet servers, but also may include "logical" infrastructure such as codes, protocols, and standards. Points of access to infrastructure are prime points of control where people, media, organizations, and information can be stopped and prevented from participating in communication exchanges.

WikiLeaks has implicitly emphasized the centrality of infrastructure access through its practice of using decentralized server networks and by placing servers in countries with beneficial laws that prevent or reduce the risk of censorship and surveillance. Its successes in keeping its published information open and available attest to the importance of this strategy, and so do its failures. As internal conflicts led to the departure of several members in late 2010, the availability of both technical skills and secure infrastructure was affected, and WikiLeaks' effectiveness was compromised.[9]

Prominent recent examples for restrictions to infrastructure access include the almost complete Internet shutdown in Egypt in January 2011, when the government successfully ordered an international provider (in this case, Vodaphone) first to distribute pro-government SMS messages and later to suspend its services (Webster, 2011). The US debate over an Internet kill-switch, and UK government proposals of temporary blockages of social networking platforms in times of political turmoil, have further demonstrated the willingness of governments to interfere with online communication, and have highlighted the vulnerability of the supposedly borderless cyberspace. As we can see with regard to the other types of restrictions presented in this chapter, government power intersects with corporate power, particularly as services such as ISP or social media services are concentrated in the hands of just one or a few providers, who either complicitly or reluctantly comply with government requests or even advocate for restrictions, as in the case of the Net neutrality debate.

The controversies on Net neutrality – initiated in the United States and increasingly spreading to other jurisdictions – have highlighted the role of network providers as potential gatekeepers who have an interest in favouring the content and applications of some information sources and services over others, and who might block access to disfavoured sites or require a special fee. This form of content discrimination through infrastructure control provides particular challenges for non-commercial content and small businesses, and for oppositional and dissident news sources, but it may affect all media organizations, because network providers may favour particular business partners (Balkin, 2009).

More crudely, governments are increasingly considering physical restrictions of online access for certain users. So-called "three strikes" rules are now widely discussed and have been implemented in countries like France. They restrict people's access to the Internet in cases where they have been found to repeatedly violate, for example, intellectual property law by downloading copyrighted content.[10] In the United States, content owners and Internet service providers have agreed to the Copyright Alert System, a "six-strike" plan that includes sending educational alerts and potentially hijacking browsers and slowing or temporarily blocking the Internet service of users accused of copyright infringement. The mechanism bypasses governmental and judicial oversight, and therefore puts both the definition of and the punishment for copyright infringement in the hands of content owners and Internet service providers or ISPs (Flaim, 2012).

While new sets of restrictions appear online, the more traditional questions of who has and who is denied access to broadcast infrastructure and the radio-frequency spectrum are not necessarily resolved. Frequency allocation in response to political favours remains a widespread phenomenon, and auctioning off frequencies to the highest bidder is common practice, with questionable democratic implications (see, e.g., Waisbord, 2010). Community broadcasting, i.e., participatory and non-profit radio and TV that is self-managed by a civil society association or a citizen group, remains outlawed in many countries, while in others it has to compete for frequencies with commercial broadcasters or is severely limited due to discrimination regarding its reach and funding (Coyer, 2006; Coyer and Hintz, 2010; Hintz, 2011). The transition from analogue to digital broadcasting provides new challenges: While the US digital radio system IBOC discriminates in favour of incumbent license-holders, the European system DAB focuses on standardized national coverage and introduces a new set of private-sector gatekeepers – the multiplex operators – that may be able to make decisions on who is carried on the multiplex and who is excluded (Hallett and Hintz, 2010).

Critical resources and applications

Online publications and services typically require a broad set of resources, such as funding, as well as an infrastructure that allows them to generate, access, and use those resources. Actors that are able to block access to such infrastructure and thus to cut off critical resources constitute important gatekeepers. Their role became particularly apparent in December 2010 when Amazon, Paypal, and others closed the services they had previously provided for WikiLeaks, depriving the leaks platform of its domain name and of access to necessary funds in the middle of a major release that required both. This "denial of service," as Benkler (2011) has put it, propelled the providers of critical services into the spotlight of the debate on WikiLeaks and on freedom of expression. It helped clarify and perhaps revise our understanding of so-called "cloud" services which – despite the beautiful picture of a floating data cloud that is accessible always and everywhere – exert significant power in allowing and disallowing access to information and services, and control the gates that enable Internet users to participate in increasingly cloud-based communication exchanges. Further, the actions by Amazon, Paypal, etc., demonstrated the vulnerability of these services to political interventions, as they coincided with pressure from members of the US political elite, both inside and outside government (Benkler, 2011).

The relative success of the denial of service strategy in the WikiLeaks case will certainly have an influence on the repertoires of control that state actors will apply in the future. Recent policy proposals, such as the Stop Online Piracy Act (SOPA), a bill that was discussed in the United States in early 2012, already included the blocking of access to critical resources as means of punishment. According to the proposed (but eventually unsuccessful) legislation, the main countermeasure against a website that facilitates piracy would have been to cut it off from funding and other private-sector services. Again, this approach demonstrates the increasing trend for Internet intermediaries to be used to police the network and exert punishment, and thus a trend to the privatization of Internet policing (see also the chapter by Brevini and Murdoch in this volume).

App stores have come to occupy positions of similar influence, which have allowed them to censor apps based on, for example, political disagreements or pressures. Again, WikiLeaks provides a key example, as Apple removed the WikiLeaks app in late 2010, following the Cablegate releases (Kiss, 2010). Beyond such specific gatekeeping functions, the increasing role of apps and similar services for accessing online information has been criticized, as they limit what users can do online and therefore may transform the traditionally open cyberspace into a set of "sterile appliances tethered into a network of control" (Zittrain, 2008, p. 3).

Surveillance

With the ubiquity of electronic communication, the "capacity of the state to gather and process information about its citizens and about the resources and activities within its space is growing by orders of magnitude" (Braman, 2006, p. 314). We are witnessing a trend a) to replace the dedicated gathering of specific data with the systematic and ongoing retention of all data, and b) to enable law enforcement to access data without judicial oversight and established notions of due process.

Recent examples, at the time of writing this text, include the European Data Retention Directive, the proposed "lawful access" legislation in Canada, and the proposed Cyber Intelligence Sharing and Protection Act (CISPA) in the United States. CISPA, if adopted, would allow government and businesses to monitor private communication, share users' private information, and effectively suspend any privacy considerations in the name of a vaguely defined notion of "cybersecurity" (Lee, 2012). New surveillance policy discussed in the United Kingdom would require ISPs to install eavesdropping hardware that allows governmental agencies to monitor communication on social media, Skype calls, and e-mail as well as logging every site visited by Internet users (APC, 2012). Typically, not all such policy proposals make it to the stage of legal implementation, but they demonstrate an urge by lawmakers to expand digital surveillance, and they highlight the preferred techniques, particularly the involvement of private intermediaries. Their goal is to facilitate, legalize, and enforce the collection of personal Internet data by private companies, as well as the sharing of that information with the government. CISPA, moreover, would allow for a broad range of "countermeasures," which may include the right to "block online entities such as Wikileaks or sites accused of copyright infringement" (Rodriguez, 2012).

The recent events in the Middle East and North Africa (MENA) have highlighted increasing governmental practices of social media surveillance to generate information on protesters and dissidents. In Tunisia and Iran, authorities have used Facebook to collect user data. Syrian opposition supporters were targeted using Trojans – programs that covertly install spying software onto the infected computer – and phishing attacks, which steal YouTube and Facebook login credentials. In one case, the malware was included in software that would purportedly offer Skype encryption and thereby allow anonymous communication. Instead, it allowed the attacker to capture webcam activity, record keystrokes, and steal passwords (Villeneuve, 2012). The region has thus been a laboratory for developing and testing surveillance concepts and tools. Many of the necessary technical tools and services have been provided by technology companies in the West, as projects such as WikiLeaks' Spyfiles and Bugged Planet have shown.[11]

The WikiLeaks case, too, has problematized the widespread public use of social networking and its increasing integration into surveillance regimes. In their quest to contain the WikiLeaks phenomenon and learn more about its supporters, US authorities turned to social media companies. Twitter was forced to hand over the account data of known WikiLeaks activists and their followers, and one can only speculate which other online services received the same requests and complied quietly (see also the chapter by Winseck in this volume). Google publishes the numbers of requests by state authorities for the disclosure of its user data in its Transparency Report, and it reports that it received 5,950 such requests from the US government in the first six months of 2011 alone (i.e., 1,000 a month or 33 a day), a number that is up 70 percent from 2010. Google has complied in 93 percent of the cases (Google, 2011).

Physical repression

Finally, a much cruder yet persistent threat to free online expression encompasses criminalization, physical violence, imprisonment, and other forms of direct physical repression. The imprisonment of bloggers in the Arab world has repeatedly demonstrated these non-digital and non-mediated restrictions to free speech. In post-Mubarak Egypt, thousands of dissidents continued to be tried in military courts, among them numerous bloggers and social media users (York, 2011).

WikiLeaks has reminded us that practices of repression are not limited to certain regions and "nondemocratic" states. Alleged whistle-blower Bradley Manning has spent (at the time of writing this chapter) two years in solitary confinement, without a trial and under circumstances that the United Nations' special rapporteur on torture has called cruel, inhuman, and degrading (Mendez, 2012). The attempts to charge Julian Assange, and the calls for his assassination by leading US politicians, provide further examples.

Globally, Internet activists who provide communications infrastructure for social movements or publish oppositional content have been subject to police operations such as house raids or have been incriminated through the use of antiterrorism legislation. Servers and other technical infrastructure have been seized, often with questionable justification (Hintz and Milan, 2009).

Power and property

Value systems differ across the globe, and so the backgrounds and reasons for these various types of interventions into free online expression differ, too. In some societies questions of decency, religion, specific historical circumstances, or the respect of eminent personalities require caution and, in some instances, compromises to unrestricted freedom of expression. The most widespread reason for restrictions, though, is the protection of social and political stability, and thus the maintenance of an established social order. In the words of Kuwait's information minister, laws to regulate the use of social networking sites such as Twitter are needed in order to "safeguard the cohesiveness of the population and society" (quoted in Galperin, 2012).

When that order, or "cohesiveness," is threatened by protests and activism, restrictions to free communication are put in place, and dissident behaviour may lead to draconian punishment. The WikiLeaks saga has highlighted these dynamics, both in terms of the extent of interventions into communication processes and the severity of punishment. Similarly, governmental debates and proposals in the wake of the

London riots in the United Kingdom in August 2011 mirrored some of the responses by Arab governments during the Arab Spring. Protesters were identified by the authorities through their use of social media, proposals included the temporary shutdown of social networking during protest situations, and merely communicating about the riots on social media led to severe punishment, including prison sentences (The *Guardian*, 2011).

If the maintenance of stability is a key reason for governmental interventions, intellectual property protection is a close second. The expansion of intellectual property law has, in itself, provided challenges to publishers and disseminators of information, as it restricts access to information. In what has been termed the "second enclosure" (Boyle, 2008), we are witnessing a trend towards the commodification of knowledge and its removal from the public domain. And as we have seen in the previous sections, intellectual property violations have been the rationale for wide-reaching interventions into the uses of both content and infrastructure. Legal initiatives such as SOPA and the international anti-counterfeiting treaty ACTA are attempts to provide a discursive and regulatory framework for such interventions.

As the types and the scale of interventions at both the content and infrastructure level differ significantly across countries, Internet users can access different applications and content in different jurisdictions. As Bambauer (2009, p. 481) notes: "There is no longer one Internet. Technological censorship by countries worldwide means that how the Net appears depends upon where you access it."

Policy initiatives in response to communication restrictions

Free online communication has typically been advanced and enabled by technical development and expertise, and so the prime strategy to deal with the restrictions outlined in the previous section has been to bypass them at the technical level. Internet activists, including members and supporters of WikiLeaks, have applied anonymizing tools such as Tor, have experimented with strategies for secure online communication and have, at times, been supported by research centers, civil society groups, and companies elsewhere.[12] WikiLeaks supporters – for example, those connected with the Anonymous network – have responded with technical direct action such as distributed denial of service (DDoS) attacks to the access restrictions by Paypal, Amazon, and others on WikiLeaks' resources, or to governments in the Middle East (see chapters by Coleman and Milan in this volume).

While these technical strategies make up an important part of civil society responses to the challenges presented here, we can also observe a different approach that focuses on policy, rather than on technology, and aims at changing the legal environment. Such initiatives can tell us something about how the restrictions described in the previous section are perceived by free-expression advocates, and they can therefore serve as test cases for the validity of the dimensions presented above.

The Icelandic Modern Media Initiative

The Icelandic Modern Media Initiative (IMMI) provides an interesting example of a national policy advocacy initiative that addresses some of the challenges and restrictions. IMMI emerged in the context of the financial collapse of the Icelandic economy in late 2008. The initiative was set up to change no less than the development model of the country, which had until then thrived as a safe haven for banks and financial services. Instead of the secrecy and the suppression of information that accompanied the old model,[13] which had become disastrous for Iceland's economy, society, and democracy, IMMI has aimed at transforming Iceland into a transparency haven and a favourable environment for media and investigative journalism. Local social and media activists, supported by international civil society organizations, created a bundle of legal and regulatory proposals to "protect and strengthen modern freedom of expression."[14] WikiLeaks was instrumental in starting the initiative: WikiLeaks activists raised the idea of a transparency haven, provided knowledge on relevant laws in other countries, and developed some of the thematic cornerstones, together with local and international experts.

Not surprisingly, IMMI's understanding of "modern freedom of expression" focuses on the area of information control. At its core is the concern to prevent the suppression of content by both public and private actors. IMMI has initiated the development of a new Freedom of Information Act to enhance access for journalists and the public to government-held information and to end the previous culture of secrecy. It has proposed measures to limit the exploitation of restrictive libel laws and strategic lawsuits that serve to block legitimate information – "legal harassment" of media and publishers, as IMMI puts it. The group also initiated a new law on source protection, making it illegal for media organizations to expose the identity of sources for articles, books, etc., if the source or the author request anonymity. IMMI has developed policy proposals on whistle-blower protection and intermediary protection, and it thus responds to the privatization of media policy, as well as to concerns regarding repression and critical resources. Further, it has made proposals on safeguarding Net neutrality, and IMMI activists have engaged with debates on the European Data Retention Directive and, more broadly, on surveillance (IMMI, 2012).

If implemented, the full IMMI package would provide a legal environment that protects national and international publishers from content restrictions. All information originating from or routed through Iceland would be governed by the new set of laws and would therefore be very difficult to suppress. In a new media environment, this does not necessarily require the physical relocation of publishing houses to Iceland, but merely the posting of content on webservers hosted in the country. Blogs, websites, and all kinds of online publications would thereby fall under Icelandic jurisdiction and would be safe(r) from censorship (Bollier, 2010). IMMI's understanding of freedom of expression is not limited to traditional journalism, but it includes nonprofessional citizen journalists, publishers of blogs, and civil society groups in the remit of information producers, thereby expanding classic notions of journalism.

IMMI's strategies: policy hacking

Beyond its thematic innovation and its interpretation of "modern freedom of expression," IMMI has applied an interesting set of strategies. At its core is what we may call "policy hacking." IMMI cherry-picked laws and regulations from other countries, creating a puzzle of tried-and-tested components. For example, the original IMMI proposal included components from the Belgian source protection law, the Norwegian Freedom of Information Act, Swedish laws on print regulation and electronic commerce, the EU Privacy Directive, the New York Libel Terrorism Act, and the Constitution of Georgia.[15] Quite in line with its WikiLeaks influence, it has assembled, revised, and "upgraded" legal instruments – just as hackers and technical developers would upgrade code – towards a new "legal code." This relation between technical and legal expertise has also been observed in other networks, such as the open-source movement, as "tinkering" with technology and the law requires similar skills and forms of reasoning (Coleman, 2009).

The practice of policy hacking highlights the importance of the international dimension even for a national initiative such as IMMI. References to international norms and other national regulations are at the core of IMMI's approach, and its own policy proposals may serve as models for other countries too.[16] Its networked policy approach displays further similarities to WikiLeaks' efforts to create a decentralized international server structure, utilize a transnational strategy to create immunity for itself, and protect its information from censorship (Beckett, 2012). Apart from the fact that IMMI's efforts may turn Iceland into an important building block in this strategy, as a safe haven for media organizations, they demonstrate crucial components of policy activism in a globalized and networked environment.

The IMMI experience also highlights the existence of a policy window as an important condition for successful policy interventions. Policy windows are temporary openings for affecting policy change, which may emerge when, for example, a crisis in a social, political, economic, or ideological system leads to disunity of political elites and creates a dynamic in which established social orders become receptive to change and new actors can enter the field and advance their agendas (Kingdon, 1984). "Policy monopolies" – stable configurations of policy actors – may be weakened or even broken up as political constellations change and the balance of power shifts (Meyer, 2005). In Iceland, a crisis led to a window of opportunity: As the economic breakdown affected large parts of the population and the secrecy of banks was widely debated and criticized, a significant section of the public was in favour of a radically new model. Parts of the old political class were delegitimized, new social actors were swept into politics, and thus traditional policy monopolies were broken.

Further cases: advocacy on infrastructure, surveillance, intellectual property

A brief overview of select initiatives cannot do justice to the variety of policy advocacy that exists on a wide range of issues. Here I will just point to a few examples that demonstrate engagement with the issue areas proposed above. On the theme of access to infrastructure, a prominent dynamic has been the struggle on Net neutrality in North America. Groups such as Free Press (United States) and Open Media (Canada) have campaigned for the protection of Net neutrality, against powerful and well-resourced adversaries, such as network operators and telcos (Blevins and Shade, 2010).

Campaigns for the legalization of community broadcasting have helped to open up the radio-frequency spectrum to citizens and civil society, most recently in countries such as India, Nigeria, the United Kingdom, the United States, and across Latin America. In Argentina, for example, a civil society coalition developed guidelines for a new national media law, and a coalition member was charged to draft the law, incorporating international norms and other legal precedents, and thus applying similar strategies to IMMI's. Following numerous open hearings and the inclusion of further civil society comments, a demonstration of 20,000 people brought the final text to Parliament, where it was adopted in 2009 (Loreti, 2011). The new law not only legalizes community and non-profit media, but reserves for it one third of the radio-frequency spectrum. According to the World Association of Community Broadcasters (AMARC), the law has "transformed Argentina into one of the best references of regulatory frameworks to curtail media concentration and promote and guarantee diversity and pluralism" (AMARC, 2010, p. 10).

Mass protests against the Data Retention Directive in the European Union have addressed the problem of data gathering and surveillance. Mobilized by Internet activists, privacy advocates, and civil liberties groups, numerous campaigns and initiatives emerged across Europe after the directive was adopted in 2006. They have benefited from strong national campaigns, such as the German AK Vorrat, which have inspired activists in other countries, and from international nongovernmental organizations (NGOs), such as European Digital Rights (EDRI), which have raised awareness across the region.[17] Demonstrations and protests have brought tens of thousands of people to the streets, including over 50,000 in Berlin alone in September 2009 and 2010. Constitutional complaints have challenged data retention law in several countries – for example, over 30,000 people signed a legal challenge before the German Constitutional Court, making it the largest constitutional complaint in German history.

In the field of intellectual property, the anti-counterfeiting trade agreement ACTA, a multinational treaty that was negotiated between 2006 and 2011, has drawn criticism from civil society groups (such as the French La Quadrature du Net). As the adoption of the agreement became imminent in early 2012, protests erupted and stopped its ratification.[18] At the same time, campaigns against the SOPA bill in the United States were successful in stopping its adoption. Earlier, campaigns by European Net activists against the introduction of software patents had led to widespread online and offline protests in 2005.[19]

Conclusion

Beyond its many scoops and revelations, WikiLeaks can provide us with a lens for observing current trends in Internet policy. Both its actions and strategies, and the challenges that it has been facing, highlight strategic points of intervention and control by different actors, but also point us to core requirements for freedom of expression in an online world.

In this chapter I proposed five areas in which these contestations currently take place: information control, access to infrastructure, critical resources and applications, surveillance, and physical repression. In all these areas, governments and businesses have erected restrictions and controls that hinder the free information and communication exchange and serve as attempts to tame the previously open and borderless cyberspace. In the words of Google's Sergey Brin: "I thought there was no way to put the genie back in the bottle, but now it seems in certain areas the genie has been put back in the bottle" (quoted in Katz, 2012). Private-sector intermediaries, such as Google, ISPs, and telecommunications operators, are increasingly included in control strategies and comply – sometimes reluctantly, sometimes complicitly.

However, WikiLeaks also provides us with a starting point to look at the other side of the struggle, i.e., to creative practices of challenging the new restrictions through civil-society-based policy initiatives. These campaigns and networks have addressed several of the dimensions highlighted above, with some focusing on specific areas such as surveillance or infrastructure, and others developing broader agendas. IMMI, particularly, presents us with the conceptual framework of "modern freedom of expression," and with innovative strategies such as "policy hacking," which connect legal advocacy with the technological approach applied by WikiLeaks. A catalogue of demands and policy goals emerges from these initiatives. These include, among others, access to information; protection of information sources and whistle-blowers; limits to the use of libel laws and other forms of private censorship; infrastructure demands including Net neutrality and access to the airwaves; the reduction, rather than expansion, of filtering, online surveillance, and data retention; limits to intellectual property protection; and the protection and independence of intermediaries and providers of critical resources.

Together, the recent restrictions to digital freedoms and the demands by policy campaigns can help us identify key components of the current struggles and contestations regarding freedom of expression in a digital media environment. WikiLeaks thus provides us with an understanding of both the challenges and the opportunities that we will likely encounter in upcoming conflicts around "modern freedom of expression."

Notes

1. Several examples are highlighted in the introduction to this book.
2. See http://www.immi.is, and the foreword to this book by Birgitta Jónsdóttir.
3. Research for this article is based on document analysis, investigations of social media sources, and in-depth interviews with members of policy initiatives. It partly draws from research conducted within the international collaborative project Mapping Global Media Policy, which was developed together with Marc Raboy and Claudia Padovani, and from collaborative work with Stefania Milan.
4. See, for example, the series on the "Battle for the internet" in the *Guardian* in April 2012 (http://www.guardian.co.uk/technology/series/battle-for-the-internet).
5. For example, in South Africa, where a progressive freedom of information law has been in place since the 1990s, a Protection of Information bill was passed in 2011, which grants the government broad powers to classify documents for reasons ranging from national security to protection of state possessions (Le Pelley, 2011). Also see the chapter by Banisar and Fanucci in this volume.
6. Prior to the Pirate Bay decision, agreements between the government and ISPs in the United Kingdom had already led to the automatic and mandatory filtering of all online pornography in the country. Internet users are still allowed to contact their ISPs, though, and request that pornography sites be enabled for their Internet connection.
7. Even more than large media organizations, grassroots alternative and citizen media have been vulnerable to mere threats of legal action as they typically lack the resources to defend themselves in court. Such threats regularly lead to self-censorship (Hintz and Milan, 2009).
8. Arguably, face-to-face speech requires such infrastructure, too, as it takes place in a physical space where access and behaviour can be controlled and restricted by public or private owners (for example, in a shopping mall).
9. Anecdotes can be found, for example, in Domscheit-Berg (2011), although their validity has been questioned by Julian Assange.
10. See http://www.laquadrature.net. In 2006, as part of a chapter entitled "How governments rule the net," Goldsmith and Wu noted: "There may soon come a time when abusing your privileges as a member of the Internet could lead to expulsion from the club" (Goldsmith and Wu, 2006, p. 79). It appears this time has come.
11. http://www.spyfiles.org, http://www.buggedplanet.info
12. For example, Facebook has helped activists in Tunisia use their website anonymously, and research centers such as the Citizen Lab at University of Toronto have developed programs such as Psiphon, which are used for secure communication.
13. See the anecdote mentioned above on RUV's failed reporting on financial corruption.
14. For all quotes from the IMMI proposal, see http://immi.is/Icelandic_Modern_Media_Initiative
15. http://immi.is/Reference_Material#Law_references_from_IMMI_proposal
16. IMMI activists have discussed and advocated their initiative at a wide range of international meetings, from activist gatherings to the European Commission.

17. See http://www.vorratsdatenspeicherung.de and http://www.edri.org
18. Among them Poland and Germany, where an estimated 100,000 people took to the streets in February 2012.
19. See http://www.stoppt-softwarepatente.de

References

AMARC (World Association of Community Broadcasters, 2010). "AMARC Deplores Suspension of New Communications Law in Argentina". *AMARC Link* 13(1), January-March 2010. Retrieved from http://www.amarc.org/amarclink/amarc_link_AVRIL_2010_EN_final.pdf

APC (Association for Progressive Communications, 2012). "The big snoop: The UK's temptation to become a big brother and what it means for the rest of us", April 20, 2012. Retrieved from http://www.apc.org/en/news/big-snoop-uk039 s-temptation-become-big-brother-and

Balkin, J. M. (2009). "The Future of Free Expression in a Digital Age". *Pepperdine Law Review* 36(2), 427–444.

Bambauer, D. E. (2009). "Cybersieves". *Duke Law Journal* 59(3), 377–446.

Barlow, J. P. (2006). "A declaration of the independence of cyberspace". Retrieved from http://homes.eff.org/~barlow/Declaration-Final.html

BBC (2012). "The Pirate Bay must be blocked by UK ISPs, court rules". April 30, 2012. Retrieved from http://www.bbc.com/news/technology-17894176

Beckett, C. (2012). "Wikileaks: Lessons for Media and Regulation". *LSE Media Policy Blog*, March 5, 2012. Retrieved from http://blogs.lse.ac.uk/polis/2012/03/05/wikileaks-lessons-for-press-policy-regulation/

Benkler, Y. (2011). "A Free Irresponsible Press: WikiLeaks and the Battle over the Soul of the Networked Fourth Estate". Working draft. Retrieved from http://www.benkler.org/Benkler_Wikileaks_current.pdf

Berners-Lee, T. (2012). "Analysis: 'Cybersecurity' bill endangers privacy rights", *ars technica*, April 18, 2012. Retrieved from, http://arstechnica.com/tech-policy/news/2012/04/analysis-cybersecurity-bill-endangers-privacy-rights.ars

Blevins, J. L., and Shade L. R. (2010). "International Perspectives on Network Neutrality: Exploring the Politics of Internet Traffic Management and Policy Implications for Canada and the U.S.". *Global Media Journal – Canadian Edition* 3(1), 1–8

Bollier, D. (2010). "A New Global Landmark for Free Speech". June 16, 2010. Retrieved from http://www.bollier.org/new-global-landmark-free-speech

Boyle, J. (2008). *The Public Domain: Enclosing the Commons of the Mind*. New Haven: Yale University Press

Braman, S. (2006). *Change of State: Information, Policy, and Power*. Cambridge: MIT Press

Christensen, C. (2011). "Discourses of Technology and Liberation: State Aid to Net Activists in an Era of 'Twitter Revolutions'". *The Communication Review* 14(3), 233–253

Coleman, G. (2009). "Code is Speech: Legal Tinkering, Expertise, and Protest Among Free and Open Source Software Developers". *Cultural Anthropology* 24(3), 420–454

Coyer, K. (2006). "Community Radio Licensing and Policy: An Overview". *Global Media and Communication* 2(1), 129–134

Coyer, K., and Hintz, A. (2010). "Developing the 'third sector': Community media policies in Europe". In Beata Klimkiewicz (ed.). *Media Freedom and Pluralism: Media Policy Challenges in the Enlarged Europe*. Budapest: CEU Press

Deibert, R. J., Palfrey, J. G. , Rohozinski, R. and Zittrain, J. (2008). *Access Denied: The Practice and Policy of Global Internet Filtering*. Cambridge: MIT Press

Domscheit-Berg, D. (2011). *Inside WikiLeaks: My Time with Julian Assange at the World's Most Dangerous Website*. London: Random House

Downing, J. D. H. (2001). *Radical Media: Rebellious Communication and Social Movements*. London: Sage

Diamond, L. (2010). "Liberation Technology". *Journal of Democracy* 21(3), 69–83

Flaim, S. M. (2012). "Op-ed: Imminent 'six strikes' Copyright Alert System needs antitrust scrutiny". *ars technica*, March 19, 2012. Retrieved from http://arstechnica.com/tech-policy/news/2012/03/op-ed-imminent-six-strikes-copyright-alert-system-needs-antitrust-scrutiny.ars

Galperin, E. (2012). "Kuwait Prepares to Crack Down on Social Media". *Deeplinks*, May 2, 2012. Retrieved from https://www.eff.org/deeplinks/2012/05/kuwait-prepares-crack-down-social-media

Goldsmith, J., and Wu, T. (2006). *Who Controls the Internet? Illusions of a Borderless World*. Oxford: Oxford University Press

Google (2011). Transparency Report 2011. Retrieved from http://www.google.com/transparencyreport/governmentrequests/US/?p=2011-06

Grimsson, O. R. (2011). Keynote address to the conference of the European Consortium for Political Research (ECPR), Reykjavik, August 25, 2011

Hallett, L., and Hintz, A. (2010). "Digital Broadcasting – Challenges and Opportunities for European Community Radio Broadcasters". *Telematics and Informatics* 27(2), 151–161

Hintz, A. (2011). "From Media Niche to Policy Spotlight: Mapping Community Media Policy in Latin America". *Canadian Journal of Communication* 36(1), 147–159

Hintz, A., and Milan, S. (2009). "At the Margins of Internet Governance: Grassroots Tech Groups and Communication Policy". *International Journal of Media & Cultural Politics* 5(1), 23–38

IMMI (2012). *IMMI Status Report*. April 9, 2012. Retrieved from http://immi.is/images/8/8c/2012-04-15_IMMI_status_report.pdf

Kaplan, D. (2012). *Empowering Independent Media: U.S. Efforts to Foster a Free Press and an Open Internet Around the World – Second Edition: 2012*. Washington, D.C.: Center for International Media Assistance

Katz, I. (2012). "Web freedom faces greatest threat ever, warns Google's Sergey Brin". *The Guardian*. April 15, 2012. Retrieved from http://www.guardian.co.uk/technology/2012/apr/15/web-freedom-threat-google-brin

Khamis, S., and Vaughn, K. (2011). "Cyberactivism in the Egyptian Revolution: How Civic Engagement and Citizen Journalism Tilted the Balance". *Arab Media & Society* (13)

Kingdon, J. W. (1984). *Agendas, Alternatives, and Public Policy*. Boston: Little Brown

Kiss, J. (2010). "Apple pulls Wikileaks app, but Android apps remain". *The Guardian: PDA – The Digital Content Blog*, December 21, 2010. Retrieved from http://www.guardian.co.uk/media/pda/2010/dec/21/apple-wikileaks-app

Kreimer, S. F. (2006). "Censorship by Proxy: The First Amendment, Internet Intermediaries, and the Problem of the Weakest Link". *University of Pennsylvania Law Review*, 155(11)

LePelley, M. (2011). Das Jahrzehnt der Informationsfreiheit in Afrika? *FES Perspektive, Dezember 2011*, Friedrich Ebert Stiftung. Retrieved from http://library.fes.de/pdf-files/iez/08818–20120110.pdf

Loreti, D. (2011). Research interview by Arne Hintz. Montreal, February 11, 2011

Mendez, J. E. (2012). *Report of the Special Rapporteur on torture and other cruel, inhuman or degrading treatment or punishment, Addendum: Observations on communications transmitted to Governments and replies received.* Report to the United Nations General Assembly, February 29, 2012. A/HRC/19/61/Add.4

Meyer, D. S. (2005). "Social Movements and Public Policy: Eggs, Chicken, and Theory". In David S. Meyer, Valerie Jenness and Helen Ingram (eds). *Routing the Opposition. Social Movements, Public Policy, and Democracy.* Minneapolis: University of Minnesota Press

Morozov, E. (2011). *The Net Delusion: The Dark Side of Internet Freedom.* New York: Public Affairs

Open Net Initiative (2012). "Global Internet Filtering in 2012 at a Glance". Blog post, April 3, 2012. Retrieved from http://opennet.net/blog/2012/04/global-internet-filtering-2012-glance

Rodriguez, K. (2012). "The Impending Cybersecurity Power Grab – It's not just for the United States". *Deeplinks*, April 18, 2012. Retrieved from https://www.eff.org/deeplinks/2012/04/impending-cybersecurity-power-grab-its-not-just-united-states

Rosen, J. (2006). "The People Formerly Known as the Audience". *PressThink.* Retrieved from http://journalism.nyu.edu/pubzone/weblogs/pressthink/2006/06/27/ppl_frmr.html

The Guardian (2011). "Facebook riot calls earn men four-year jail terms amid sentencing outcry". August 16, 2011. Retrieved from http://www.guardian.co.uk/uk/2011/aug/16/facebook-riot-calls-men-jailed

Villeneuve, N. (2012). "Fake Skype Encryption Service Cloaks DarkComet Trojan". *TrendLabs Malware Blog,* April 20, 2012. Retrieved from http://blog.trendmicro.com/fake-skype-encryption-software-cloaks-darkcomet-trojan/

Waisbord, S. (2010). "The pragmatic politics of media reform: Media movements and coalition-building in Latin America". *Global Media and Communication* 6(2), 133–153

Webster, S. C. (2011). "Vodaphone confirms role in Egypt's cellular, Internet blackout". *The Raw Story,* January 28, 2011. Retrieved from http://www.rawstory.com/rs/2011/01/28/vodafone-confirms-role-egypts-cellular-internet-blackout/

York, J. (2011). "2011 in Review: Internet Freedom in the Wake of the Arab Spring". *Deeplinks.* December 31, 2011. Retrieved from https://www.eff.org/deeplinks/2011/12/2011-review-internet-freedom-wake-arab-spring

Zittrain, J. (2008). *The Future of the Internet – And How to Stop It.* New Haven: Yale University Press

9
Weak Links and WikiLeaks: How Control of Critical Internet Resources and Social Media Companies' Business Models Undermine the Networked Free Press

Dwayne Winseck

In his seminal piece on WikiLeaks, Yochai Benkler (2011; also see Benkler's chapter in this volume) makes a compelling case for why WikiLeaks is a vital element of the networked fourth estate and why we should view its harsh treatment by the US government as a threat to the free press. As he says, the case embodies a struggle for the soul of the Internet, a battle that is being waged through both legal and extralegal means, with major corporate actors – Apple, Amazon, eBay (Paypal), Bank of America (Visa), Mastercard, etc. – using their control over critical Internet resources to lean in heavily on the side of the state and against WikiLeaks.

This chapter builds on Benkler's case for seeing WikiLeaks as a crucial element of the networked free press by presenting an important new element to the story: the role that Twitter, the social media site, has played in what I will call the Twitter–WikiLeaks cases. In contrast to the pliant commercial interests that Benkler discusses, Twitter fought hard in a series of legal cases from December 14, 2010 until November 11, 2011 to avoid having to turn over subscriber account information for several people of interest to the US Department of Justice's (DoJ) ongoing WikiLeaks investigation: Birgitta Jónsdóttir, an Icelandic MP and co-producer of the *Collateral Murder* video whose distribution over the Internet by WikiLeaks put it, and her, on a collision course with the United States; WikiLeaks' volunteer and Tor developer, Jacob Applebaum;

and the Dutch hacktivist Rop Gongrijp. The DoJ's "secret orders" raise urgent questions about state secrets and transparency, the rule of law, Internet users' communication rights, and the role of commercial entities that control critical Internet resources. The Twitter–WikiLeaks cases also cut to the heart of journalism in light of how journalists routinely use social media such as Twitter and Facebook, but also search engines and Internet access services, to access sources, share information, and generally to create and circulate the news.

WikiLeaks and the emergence of next-generation Internet controls

Information filtering, blocking, and censorship have been the hallmark of China's model of the Internet since the 1990s. Now, however, we are at critical juncture in the evolution of the Internet, with the United States government's anti-WikiLeaks campaign showcasing how such methods are being augmented by a wide range of legal and extralegal methods in capitalist democracies. Among other things, the WikiLeaks case shows how mechanisms of Internet filtering and blocking are being outsourced, with commercial businesses seeming to be all too willing to serve the state on bended knees (Deibert and Rohozinski, 2011) – albeit with some important exceptions to the rule as the Twitter–WikiLeaks cases discussed in this chapter illustrate.

Three intertwined tendencies are stoking the shift to a more controlled and regulable Internet. First, the concentration of ownership and control over critical Internet resources is increasing: incumbent cable and telecom firms' dominate Internet access, while a few Internet giants do the same with respect to search (Google), social media platforms (Facebook, Twitter), over-the-top services (Apple, Netflix), web hosting and data storage sites (Amazon), and payment services (Visa, Master Card, PayPal), among others. Simply put, more concentrated media are more easily regulable than many players operating in a more heterogeneous environment. Second, the media and entertainment industries have scored victories in Australia, the United Kingdom, New Zealand, the United States, Taiwan, South Korea, France, and a handful of other countries for three-strikes rules that require Internet Service Providers (ISPs) to cut off Internet users who repeatedly run afoul of copyright laws. A 2011 UN report condemned these measures as disproportionate and at odds with the Internet's status under the right to communication set out in Article 19 of the Universal Declaration of Human Rights (1948), but they remain operative nonetheless (La Rue, 2011). Lastly, the

Internet is being steadily integrated into national security and military doctrines, with 30 or so countries, notably the United States, Russia, and China, leading the push (US Congressional Research Service, 2004). The US Department of Defense's revised "information operations" doctrine in 2003, for instance, defines the Internet (cyberspace) as the fifth frontier of warfare, after land, sea, air, and space (United States, Department of Defense, 2003). National security and law enforcement interests are also central in new laws currently being considered in the United States (CISPA, the Cyber Intelligence Sharing and Protection Act), Canada (Bill C-30) and the United Kingdom (Communications Data Bill).

These trends are increasing the pressure to turn Internet service providers (ISPs) and digital intermediaries into gatekeepers working on behalf of other interests, whether those of the copyright industries or of law enforcement and national security. Such trends are not new, but they are becoming more firmly entrenched in authoritarian countries and liberal capitalist democracies alike. This is the big context within which the anti-WikiLeaks campaign led by the US government has unfolded. (On trends in Internet controls and challenges to freedom of expression, also see Hintz's chapter in this volume.)

WikiLeaks and the networked free press

The rise of WikiLeaks in the heart of the networked free press presents a countercurrent to this trend. While it is common to bemoan the crisis of journalism, Benkler (2011) strikes a cautiously optimistic note, laying the blame for the ongoing turmoil among traditional news outlets on their own self-inflicted wounds that have festered since the 1980s. The rise of the Internet and the changing technological and economic basis of the media magnifies these problems, he argues, but the Internet is not responsible for them. In fact, nascent forms of non-profit, crowd-sourced, and investigative journalism may be improving the quality of journalism.

WikiLeaks is part and parcel of these trends. In the events that put it on a collision course with the US government, the whistle-blowing site burnished its journalistic credentials by working hand in glove with the *Guardian,* the *New York Times, Der Spiegel, Le Monde,* and *El País* to select, edit, and publish the Afghan and Iraq war logs and embassy cables. In other words, WikiLeaks material was selected, edited, and published according to professional news values. For its efforts, WikiLeaks chalked up a bevy of awards for its significant contributions to access to information, transparency, and journalism, adding to a long list of honours that it had already won from press and human rights organizations, including from British-based Index on Censorship, Amnesty International, and *Time* magazine, among many others, since its inception (see WikiLeaks Press, n.d.).

That the interjection of WikiLeaks into the journalistic process led to outcomes that are probably better than the "good ole days" of the traditional press is underscored by the fact that while the *New York Times* consulted with the Obama Administration *before* publishing the war logs and the diplomatic cables, it did not withhold the material for a year, as it did in 2005 at the behest of the Bush Administration when two of the paper's reporters, James Risen and Eric Lichtblau (2006), blew the whistle on the massive use of unauthorized and secret wiretaps by the National Security Agency in cooperation with AT&T, Verizon, and almost all of the other major telecom-ISPs in the United States (Calame, 2006). Because of WikiLeaks' role in these events, the war logs and embassy cables stories likely became headline news in 2010 faster than would otherwise have been the case.

WikiLeaks is emblematic of a broader set of changes that, once the dust settles, will likely stabilize around a new model of the networked fourth estate, an assemblage of elements consisting of (1) traditional media companies; (2) small commercial media (Huffington Post, the Tyee, Drudge Report, Global Journalist, etc.), (3) non-profit media (WikiLeaks, Wikipedia), (4) partisan media outlets (Rabble.ca, Daily Kos, TalkingPointsMemo), (5) hybrids that mix features of all the others and (6) networked individuals (Benkler, 2009). The fact that WikiLeaks is so central to these developments, and so solidly at one with journalistic and free-press traditions, helps to explain why neither it nor any of the newspaper organizations it partnered with have faced direct efforts by the United States to suppress the publication of WikiLeaks' documents (Benkler, 2011).

Using ownership and control of critical internet resources to cripple WikiLeaks

The problem, however, as Benkler (2011) states, is that what the United States was not able to obtain by legal measures it gained with remarkable ease from private corporations and market forces. Thus, buckling under the slightest of pressure, Amazon banished WikiLeaks' content from its servers the same day (December 1, 2010) that Senator and Senate Committee on Homeland Security and Governmental Affairs Chair Joe Lieberman (2010) called on any "company or organization that is hosting WikiLeaks to immediately terminate its relationship with them." WikiLeaks quickly found a new home at webserver firm OVH in France, but lost access to those facilities after the French Industry Minister warned companies on December 4 that there would be "consequences" for helping keep WikiLeaks online. A day later, the Swedish-based Pirate Party stepped in to host the "Cablegate" directory after they were taken off line in France and the US.

WikiLeaks' troubles didn't end there, because just a day before it was kicked out of France, the US company everyDNS delisted it from its domain name registry. As a result, Internet users who typed WikiLeaks. org into their browser or clicked on links pointing to that domain came up with a page indicating that the site was no longer available (Benkler, 2011; Arthur, 2011). The Swedish DNS (Domain Name Service) provider Switch faced similar pressure, but refused to buckle. It continues to maintain the WikiLeaks.ch address that Internet users still use to access the site, but has faced a barrage of Distributed Denial of Service (DDoS) attacks for doing so.

As Amazon, OVD, and everyDNS took out part of WikiLeaks' technical infrastructure, several other companies moved in to disable is financial underpinnings. Over the course of four days, Paypal (eBay; December 4), MasterCard, and the Swiss Postal Office's PostFinance (December 6), and Visa (December 7) suspended payment services for donors to the site. Two weeks later, Apple removed a WikiLeaks app from the iTunes store (Apple removes WikiLeaks, 2010). Thus, within a remarkably short period of time, a range of private actors cut off WikiLeaks' access to critical Internet resources. The actions did not kill the organization, but they did contribute mightily to the fact that WikiLeaks' funding plummeted by an estimated 90 percent (WikiLeaks, 2011).

Privacy rights online and Internet companies' business models

One important entity has stood outside this state-corporate tryst on the outskirts of the law: Twitter. Indeed, it has stood alone among big American corporate Internet media brands in refusing to assist the United States' anti-WikiLeaks campaign. Faced with a court order to secretly disclose subscriber information for three of its users, it said no.

In December 2010, at the same time as WikiLeaks was being cut off from critical Internet resources, the US Department of Justice demanded that Twitter turn over subscriber account information for Birgitta Jónsdóttir, Jacob Applebaum, and Rop Gongrijp as part of its ongoing WikiLeaks investigation. The information sought was not innocuous and general, but intimate and extensive: i.e,. subscriber registration pages, connection records, length of service, Internet device identification number, source and destination Internet protocol addresses, and more (United States, 2011a). Twitter was also told not to disclose the request to the people concerned, and to stay quiet about the whole thing. It did none of this.

Instead, the company mounted a serious legal challenge to the Department of Justice "secret orders" and pushed the envelope in interpreting what it could do to protect its subscribers' information (McCullagh, 2011). In Twitter–WikiLeaks Case #1, the social media site won a small victory by gaining the right to at least tell Jónsdóttir, Applebaum, and Gongrijp that the DoJ was seeking information about their accounts (United States, 2010). They were given 10 days to respond before Twitter was compelled to comply with the DoJ order. It also took the extra step of recommending that Jónsdóttir, Applebaum, and Gongrijp seek legal help from the Electronic Frontier Foundation (EFF), a public interest law watchdog on all matters digital and about Internet/cyberspace governance (a copy of Twitter's letter to Gongrijp is available at Gongrijp, 2011).

The EFF has represented Jónsdóttir on the matter since, while Twitter's lead counsel, Alex MacGillvray, has stood for the company. Interestingly, Iceland has also weighed in by strongly criticizing the United States over Jónsdóttir, while a group of 85 European Union parliamentarians condemned the United States' pursuit of WikiLeaks. They were especially critical about how the United States was harnessing Internet giants to its campaign. They "failed to see" how, among other things, the Twitter Order could be squared with Article 19 of the *Universal Declaration of Human Rights*. More to the point, they worried that the United States' actions were contributing to the rise of a "national and international legal framework concerning the use of ... social media ... [that] does not appear to provide sufficient ... respect for freedom of expression, access to information and the right to privacy" (Intra-Parliamentary Union, 2011).

The first Twitter–WikiLeaks case, or "Twitter Order," was a shallow victory as it did not prevent the actual disclosure. Yet it looks positive in comparison to how easily Amazon, Apple, eBay (Paypal), MasterCard, Bank of America (Visa), everyDNS, etc., enlisted in the United States' campaign against WikiLeaks. Twitter staked out a decidedly different position that insisted upon the rule of law, speaking out in public, and going beyond what was necessary to help its subscribers ensure that their rights and personal information are respected.

Jónsdóttir, Applebaum, and Gongrijp appealed part of the first case to overturn, and thus prevent, the requirement that Twitter hand over their account details to the DoJ, leading to Twitter–WikiLeaks Case #2 (United States, 2011a). The US District Court's decision in the case in November 2011 had direct results and some potentially far-sweeping implications. The court required Twitter to hand over Jónsdóttir, Applebaum, and Gongrijp's subscriber information and decided they have no right to know whether the DoJ has approached Facebook, Google, or other Internet companies with secret orders, and if so, for what kinds of information, and with what results. The court seems to believe that neither the people directly concerned nor the public in general have the right to know the answers to these questions. For their part, Google, Facebook, and Microsoft (Skype) have stayed silent on the affair, despite their frequent pontificating about Internet freedom in a generic sense and mostly in relation to "axis of Internet evil" countries, such as Saudi Arabia, China, Russia, and Iran, among a rotating cast of others.

More sweeping implications flow from two other directions. The first is the poor analogy the court draws between the Internet and banks to ground its decision as to why companies of the former type must hand over subscribers' information just as much as the latter type do after being served with a court order. There is a lot of potential discussion on this point alone, but for now it suffices to say that thinking about social media in terms of banking, insurance, and clients is a long way from comprehending the Internet as a public communications space.

Of more interest here is the claim that Internet users forfeit any expectation of privacy – and hence, privacy rights – once they click to accept Internet companies' terms of service policy. As the court put it, Jónsdóttir, Applebaum, and Gongrijp "voluntarily relinquished *any* reasonable expectation of privacy" as soon as they clicked on Twitter's terms of service (United States, 2011a, p. 28). Thus, instead of constitutional values, law, or social norms governing the situation, the court ruled that privacy rights are creatures of social media companies' business models.

However this assumption runs counter to the business models of advertising-driven media, as Twitter, Facebook and Google's terms of service policies are about *maximizing* the collection, retention, use and commodification of personal data, not privacy. It is as if the ruling is intentionally out of whack with the political economy of the Internet so as to give the state *carte blanche* to do with digital intermediaries as it pleases. Christopher Soghoian (2011) captures the crux of the issue in relation to Google, but his comments apply to Internet companies in general:

> Google's services are not secure by default, and, because the company's business model depends upon the monetization of user data, the company keeps as much data as possible about the activities of its users. These detailed records are not just useful to Google's engineers and advertising teams, but are also a juicy target for law enforcement agencies.

Conclusions and implications: the networked fourth estate and the Internet on imperilled ground

Things don't have to be this way. The idea that privacy rights turn on the terms of service policies of commercial Internet companies rests upon a peculiarly squint-eyed view and leverages the mass production and storage of personal data enabled by Twitter, Facebook, Google, and so forth for the advantage of the state. But even if we took corporate behaviour as our moral compass, Twitter has occasionally distinguished itself, as it did during the London riots/uprising in August 2011, by refusing to comply with the UK government's requests to shut down its service and hand over users' information, while Facebook complied.

Concentrated Internet markets and small details

Changing the business model of Internet companies to *minimize* the collection, retention, and disclosure of personal information, as the EFF recommends and as some non-commercial sites such as IndyMedia sources do would be helpful. Sonet.net, a small ISP with 45,000 Internet subscribers in the San Francisco area, and which is also implicated in the WikiLeaks case because Jacob Applebaum, a key figure in the Twitter–WikiLeaks case, as we saw above, has been one of its subscribers, does just this. Most ISPs, in contrast, take the opposite view, as a cursory review of the terms of service policies from AT&T, Comcast, Verizon., and Time Warner – the big four ISPs in the United States that account for just over 60 percent of Internet access revenues (Noam, 2012) – illustrates. While Sonet.net may offer a model of a free and open Internet that maximizes its users' privacy by *minimizing* data collection and retention, the fact of the matter is that with less than. 05 percent of the US Internet subscriber base, it is easily ignored.

Ultimately, the relevant measuring rod of communication rights is *not* corporate behaviour or the market, but legal and international norms.

In addition, social norms govern how we disclose personal information in complex negotiated and contingent ways, as well (Nissenbaum, 2011). Internet companies' terms of service policies and the Twitter–WikiLeaks cases largely ignore these realities. These issues as well as the fact that the vast majority of people do not even read online terms of service policies – and those who do more often than not do not fully understand them – were brought to the court's attention, but brushed aside. The decision at least makes it clear that the hypercommercialized "free lunch" model of the Internet comes with a steep price: our privacy rights and an entire industrial arrangement poised to serve as handmaiden to the national security state.

The virtues and vices of Twitter

It is against this backdrop that the significance of what Twitter has done is clear. It has not flouted the law, but has been hoisted upon its own petard on account of its "business model." Nonetheless, Twitter went beyond just complying with the law to afford as much respect for users' rights as circumstances allowed. We might also ask if Twitter's recent adoption of a "transparency report" chronicling government requests for user information and requests to take down certain content reflect lessons learned by the company in the midst of the anti-WikiLeaks campaign.

Deepening national security imperatives

The US government's campaign against WikiLeaks further entrenches the post 9/11 securitization of the telecom-Internet infrastructure, in the United States and globally, given the reach of the most well-known US telecom and Internet giants (Risen and Lichtblau, 2006; Calame, 2006). Some courts have condemned expansive claims of state secrets and unbound executive powers when it comes to national security matters, but others seem to grant the state a blank cheque (United States, 2006; United States, 2011b). When the law has not proved serviceable, as the earlier discussion suggests, important US government figures have tiptoed around its edges, compliant private companies in tow, to get what they want. Congress has also stepped in occasionally to make legal what before was not, as in the passage of the much revised and expanded Foreign Intelligence Services Act (FISA) in 2008, which is up for renewal again and set to pass with little opposition in Congress in latter half of 2012 (United States, 2008).

The global dimension

The campaign against WikiLeaks cannot be kept to narrow confines and readily spills over into wide-ranging areas, including diplomatic and global Internet policy angles. Nation-states, and the United States in particular, are flexing their muscles and attempting to assert their sovereignty over cyberspace. Struggles over the Internet Corporation for the Assignment of Names and Numbers (ICANN), the rift between Google and China, and the United States' campaign against WikiLeaks expose the supposed immunity of cyberspace as a fallacy. Criticism of US dominance of critical Internet resources has been a staple of global debates on Internet politics, both at the International Telecommunication Union (ITU), the World Summit on the Information Society (WSIS) in 2003 and in 2005, and since the creation of the Internet Governance Forum (2006) (Mueller, 2010). The WikiLeaks case offers a rational basis for such concerns. The *Guardian* newspaper in the United Kingdom underlined this point by choosing Jónsdóttir, Assange, Applebaum, and Twitter's chief legal counsel Alex MacGillvray for its list of 20 "champions of the open Internet" in April 2012 (Ball, 2012). Many of the awards bestowed upon WikiLeaks by respectable human rights and free-press organizations before and after the organization's *Collateral Murder* video, war logs, and Embassy Cables trilogy in 2010 are of a similar kind.

The Twitter–WikiLeaks rulings may serve the US government's bid to drive WikiLeaks out of business well, but they have also lit a fire in the belly of hacktivist groups like Anonymous and LulzSec, for whom such things are their *raison d'être*. It may not be too much to suggest that the whiff of the anti-WikiLeaks campaign fresh in the air helped to bring about the demise of recent attempts to strengthen national and international copyright laws – e.g., SOPA (the proposed Stop Online Piracy Act), PIPA (the proposed Preventing Real Online Threats to Economic Creativity and Theft of Intellectual Property Act) and ACTA (Anti-Counterfeiting Trade Agreement) – given that, like the campaign against WikiLeaks, each sought to leverage critical Internet resources to control content and further restrict what people can do with their Internet connections. If that, in fact, is the case, perhaps the battering of WikiLeaks may have unintentionally served a noble cause.

Perhaps we can take solace in that and in the fact that the distributed nature of the Internet means complete copies of WikiLeaks files have been scattered across the planet, beyond the reach of any single state, no matter how powerful: the ultimate free speech trump card. Yet, the fact that WikiLeaks is now floundering, one of its founding figures on the lam, and its funding down to a tenth of what it once was means that we ought not be so sanguine in our views. Happy stories about digital democracy should not deter us from the harsh reality that important open-media principles have already been badly compromised, and more are at stake yet. Indeed, the deep ecology of the Internet is at stake, and so too is how we will conduct our lives in this highly contested place.

References

Apple removes iPhone WikiLeaks app from iTunes. BBC, December 22, 2010. Available at: http://www.bbc.com/news/technology-12059577 (last visited, July 12, 2012)

Arthur, C. (January 8, 2011). WikiLeaks Under Attack: Definitive Timeline. *The Guardian,*. http://www.guardian.co.uk/media/2010/dec/07/WikiLeaks-under-attack-definitive-timeline (last visited, July 12, 2012)

Ball, J. (April 20, 2012). Battle for the Internet: The Guardian's Open 20 – Fighters for Internet Freedom. *The Guardian.* Available at: http://www.guardian.co.uk/technology/2012/apr/20/twenty-fighters-open-internet (last visited, July 12, 2012)

Benkler, Y. (2011). A Free Irresponsible Press: WikiLeaks and the Battle over the Soul of the Networked Fourth Estate. *Harvard Civil Rights-Civil Liberties Law Review.* http://benkler.org/Benkler_WikiLeaks_current.pdf (last visited, July 12, 2012)

Benkler, Y. (March 4, 2009). Correspondence: A new era of corruption? *The New Republic.* http://www.tnr.com/article/correspondence-new-era-corruption (last visited, July 12, 2012)

Calame, B. (January 1, 2006). Behind the eavesdropping story, a loud silence. *New York Times,* www.nytimes.com/2006/01/01/opinion/o1publiceditor.html (last visited, July 12, 2012)

Deibert, R. and Rohozinski, R. (2010). Beyond Denial: Introducing Next-Generation Information Access Controls. In R. J. Deibert, J. G. Palfrey, R. Rohozinski and J. Zittrain (eds) *Access Controlled.* Cambridge: MIT Press, pp. 1–14

Gongrijp, R. (January 8, 2011). US DOJ wants my twitter account info. Available at: http://rop.gonggri.jp/?p=442 (last visited, July 12, 2012)

Intra-Parliamentary Union (October 19, 2011). Case No. IS/O1 – Birgitta Jónsdóttir: *Resolution adopted unanimously by the IPU Governing Council at its 189th session*http://www.ipu.org/hr-e/189/Is01.htm (last visited, July 12, 2012)

La Rue, F. (2011) Report of the Special Rapporteur on the promotion and protection of the right to freedom of opinion and expression. United Nations Human Rights Council, Seventeenth session Agenda item 3, A/HRC/17/27 of 17 May 2011. Available at http://www2.ohchr.org/english/bodies/hrcouncil/docs/17session/A.HRC.17.27_en.pdf (last visited, July 12, 2012)

Lieberman, Senator J. (2010). Amazon Severs Ties with WikiLeaks. Press Release. http://lieberman.senate.gov/index.cfm/news-events/news/2010/12/amazon-severs-ties-with-WikiLeaks (last visited, July 12, 2012)

McCullagh, D. (Jan. 11, 2011). European politicos protest DOJ WikiLeaks-Twitter probe. *Wired.* Available at: http://news.cnet.com/8301-31921_3-20028239-281.html?tag=nl.e703 (last visited, July 12, 2012)

Mueller, M. (2010). *Networks and States.* Cambridge, MA: MIT

Nissenbaum, H. (2011). A Contextual Approach to Privacy Online. *Daedalus*, 140(4), 32–48. http://www.amacad.org/publications/daedalus/11_fall_nissenbaum.pdf (last visited, July 12, 2012)

Noam, E. (2012). International Media Concentration – United States. *International Media Concentration Research Project*, Columbia University, New York. Available at: http://internationalmedia.pbwiki.com/ (last visited, July 12, 2012)

Risen, J. and Lichtblau, E. (December 16, 2005). Bush lets US Spy on Callers Without Courts. *New York Times*. Available at: http://www.nytimes.com/2005/12/16/politics/16program.html?pagewanted=all (last visited, July 12, 2012)

Soghoian, C. (November 2, 2011). Two honest Google employees: our products don't protect your privacy. *Slight Paranoia*. http://paranoia.dubfire.net/2011/11/two-honest-google-employees-our.html (last visited, July 12, 2012)

United States (2008). Foreign Intelligence Security Act of 1978 Amendment Act of 2008. Available at: http://intelligence.senate.gov/laws/pl110261.pdf (last visited, July 12, 2012)

United States, Congressional Research Service (2004). *Information Warfare and Cyberwarfare: Capabilities and Related Policy Issues*. Washington, D.C.: Congressional Research Service. Available at http://www.dtic.mil/cgi-bin/GetTRDoc?AD=ADA477185 (last visited, July 12, 2012)

United States, Department of Defense (2003). *Information Operations Roadmap*. Washington, D.C. Available at: http://www.gwu.edu/~nsarchiv/NSAEBB/NSAEBB177/info_ops_roadmap.pdf (last visited, July 12, 2012)

United States, District Court of Eastern Virginia (2011a). In re. Application of the United States of America for an Order pursuant to 18 U.S.C §2703(d): Memorandum and Opinion. Available at: http://t.co/ZdzGQiIQ (last visited, July 12, 2012)

United States Court of Appeals for the Second Circuit (2011b). Amnesty International et. al. vs. James P. Clapper, Director, National Intelligence, et. al. Available at: http://dwmw.files.wordpress.com/2011/03/aclu-v-clapper.pdf (last visited, July 12, 2012)

United States, District Court of Eastern Virginia (December 14, 2010). In re. Application of the United States of America for an Order pursuant to 18 U.S.C §2703(d): Order. Available at: https://www.eff.org/sites/default/files/filenode/dorders_twitter/34%20USA%20Position%20Re%20Unsealing%20Records%20as%20to%20Appelbaum%20et%20al.pdf (last visited, July 12, 2012)

United States, District Court of Eastern District of Michigan (August 17, 2006). American Civil Liberties Union, et. al. v. National Security Agency, et. al. (2006). *Memorandum Opinion*. Case No. 06-CV-10204. Available at: http://cryptome.org/aclu-nsa-2.pdf (last visited, July 12, 2012)

WikiLeaks (October 24, 2011). WikiLeaks: Banking Blockade and Donations Campaign. Available at: http://WikiLeaks.org/IMG/pdf/WikiLeaks-Banking-Blockade-Information-Pack.pdf (last visited, July 12, 2012)

WikiLeaks Press (n.d.). Accolades. http://WikiLeaks-press.org/category/latest-news/accolades/ (last visited, July 12, 2012)

10
Wikileaks, Secrecy, and Freedom of Information: The Case of the United Kingdom

David Banisar and Francesca Fanucci

Introduction

The bulk releases of internal information about US military and foreign affairs by WikiLeaks were a shock to American officials in their scope and scale. However, so far, despite the public anger showed by the US government and immediate action against the lone alleged leaker, no new legislation restricting free expression rights has been adopted by Congress and signed by the president.

Clearly, the WikiLeaks saga has triggered a vigorous debate far beyond the borders of the United States. In the United Kingdom, where Julian Assange has been very active – given his collaboration with UK-based news outlets and his participation in numerous public discussions – WikiLeaks has renewed the debate on the balance between secrecy and openness and the prospects for reform.

Because the United Kingdom presents a significantly different appreciation of openness and freedom of speech when compared to the United States, we decided to explore what would happen if a similar release of information were to occur in the United Kingdom. Hence, this chapter sets out to explore the comprehensive system of secrecy engrained in the British government, the legislative framework that characterizes it, and the past and current efforts made to promote a culture of openness.

The UK culture of secrecy

It is a cliché to say that the United Kingdom has a "culture of secrecy." But while there has been substantial progress in the past few years, the UK government still has a seemingly instinctive need for secrecy. This is supported by a legal framework that has not fully embraced society's demand for openness.

Up until a little more than 20 years ago, the secrecy of government information was the extreme default. Virtually every bit of information that government created, collected, or held was considered off limits to the public unless the government decided to release it. Government phone directories, cups of tea consumed at government commissaries, and new carpets in ministers' offices were all official secrets, protected from public disclosure by threat of imprisonment. Even public buildings such as the BT Tower, obvious to everyone in the city of London, were not on maps.[1] The intelligence agencies were not formally legally created and publicly recognized until the 1990s, even though they were widely known and their activities were regularly published in the papers.[2]

Under this regime, many cases were brought against journalists and whistle-blowers for the revealing of "sensitive" security information. Newspapers were gagged from publishing stories. The cases against the journalists were generally unsuccessful, but many whistle-blowers were successfully prosecuted.

Things have improved markedly since then, but freedom of information is a fairly recent visitor to the United Kingdom. The United Kingdom was one of the last major countries in Europe to adopt legislation on access to government files, and there is still wide resentment among officials that they are forced to act somewhat in the open (Hazell et al., 2010). There is a regular drumbeat among them that freedom of information is a burden and needs to be limited (Holehouse, 2011). Even former prime minister Tony Blair, who introduced the UK Freedom of Information Act (albeit reluctantly and ensuring that it was delayed long enough so he was out of office before it was fully in place), recently described it in his autobiography as his biggest mistake in government (Blair, 2011).

Furthermore, freedom of information has barely touched the national security state. As described below, the primary access law, the Freedom of Information Act 2000, has been hobbled by broad exceptions for national security-related information. At the same time, the courts have for the most part been highly deferential and supportive of efforts to ban publication of secret information. The secrets laws, while modified, are still in force and have not lost their bite.

Secrets everywhere

The cornerstone of the UK secrecy system is the Official Secrets Act (OSA). The first OSA was adopted in 1889 as a measure to limit disclosures by officials.[3] It was then hastily replaced with more far-reaching legislation in 1911, following a scare over German spies.[4] At the time it was adopted, it was promised that the Act would only be used against leaking officials and not against journalists. The Act was subsequently amended in 1920[5] and 1939[6] and, most substantially, in 1989.[7]

Section 1 of the OSA makes it a crime punishable up to 14 years in prison to "obtain, collect, record, or communicate to any person any information that might be or is intended to be useful to an enemy," which has also been broadly interpreted to apply to cases of public disclosure by officials. Section 2 of the 1911 OSA classified the release of virtually any bit of information held by a government body, no matter how trivial or non-sensitive it was, or conversely how important to the public it might be. A Parliamentary Committee in 1972 described the broad scope of the Act at the time:

> It catches all official documents and information. It makes no distinction of kind, and no distinction of degree. All information which a crown servant learns in the course of his duty is "official" for the purposes of Section 2, whatever its nature, whatever its importance, whatever its original source. A blanket is thrown over everything. Nothing escapes. (Departmental Committee, 1972, p 14)

The 1920 amendments further expanded criminal offenses to unauthorized retention of access to official documents and introduced a new crime of incitement or abetment to a violation of the OSA, an obligation to turn in documents to a police constable, and a duty to provide information to police about violations of the Act, including confidential sources.

In 1989, following a number of embarrassing public trials, Parliament amended the OSA, repealing some of the most notorious aspects of Section 2 and replacing it with a somewhat more specific regime of documents protected by the law. Section 2 now applies to six broad areas, mostly but not exclusively relating to national security.[8] However, when adopting the 1989 OSA, Parliament declined to reform Section 1 of the 1911 Act and other provisions from the 1920 Act, which remain largely as they were originally. It also failed to introduce any mechanisms for public access such as a Freedom of Information Act, as proposed by previous governments.[9]

The 1989 OSA broadly applies to all civil servants and government contractors if damage can be shown or alleged to be likely to occur in any of the six areas covered. It is an absolute offense for intelligence and security services officials to disclose any information that they learned in the course of their employment.

Furthermore, there is no specific public interest defence for officials who leak information. The House of Lords ruled in 2002 that leaking officials can not claim a defence in the name of the public interest under the OSA.[10] However, the Lords did indicate that there could be a defence of "necessity," which would be used in cases where information was released to avoid an imminent peril of danger to life or serious injury. This was raised in a subsequent case of a whistle-blower who revealed spying at the UN, but the case was dropped before trial (BBC News, 2004).

Attempts to introduce a public-interest test in the OSA have also been rejected.[11] Furthermore, the primary legislation on whistle-blowing, the Public Interest Disclosure Act, adopted in 1998, exempts violations of the OSA.[12]

However, the defence of public interest for disclosure of classified information has more recently been the subject of a decision of the European Court of Human Rights (ECHR), which may eventually affect UK practices. In 2008, the Court ruled in the *Guja v. Moldova* case that Article 10 of the ECHR on freedom of expression protects government whistle-blowers for a variety of disclosures.[13] In the case, the Court found a violation of Article 10 when a public employee who released to the media a classified document revealing political manipulation of the justice system was dismissed. The Court noted that even secret information could be released when there is illegal conduct or wrongdoing and there is a strong public interest in the release.

In the meanwhile, the OSA is still being used against officials who reveal information of public interest. In 2007, for example, a civil servant and a parliamentary aide were convicted and jailed for short periods under the OSA for disclosing to an MP the minutes of a meeting between UK Prime Minister Tony Blair and US President George Bush at the White House that revealed that Bush wanted to bomb broadcaster Al Jazeera (BBC News, 2007). In the same year, charges were brought against Foreign Office official Derek Pasquill for leaking information about CIA rendition flights and official dealings with domestic Muslim groups with radical ties (O'Neill, 2008). In 2009, Army Lt. Colonel Owen McNally was arrested for allegedly providing statistical information about civil casualties in Afghanistan to a researcher from Human Rights Watch, following a critical report issued by the organization (Rayner et al., 2009). The OSA was even cited to threaten private parties dealing with non-national-security-related information, such as medical staff

(Malik and Gentleman, 2012) and visitors to prisons (Farquharson, 2005).

It is important to highlight that a journalist or any other person who receives information from a government employee can be charged under the OSA if he or she discloses the information. There has not been a successful prosecution of any journalist under the OSA in over 50 years. However, that does not mean that they are not open to prosecution under other legislation as well. As noted by the Crown Prosecution Service,

> Although the provisions of the OSA 1989 are primarily aimed at specific individuals who are subject to it and at Crown servants, they may be relevant when prosecutors are considering cases involving journalists or those who interact with them, because sections 44 to 46 of the *Serious Crime Act* 2007 create offences of intentionally encouraging or assisting an offence; encouraging or assisting an offence believing it will be committed; and encouraging or assisting offences believing one or more will be committed. (Crown Prosecution Service, 2012)

Even in the absence of successful prosecutions, the OSA and related laws have been used frequently to threaten journalists and attempt to stop stories from being published. In 2011, the Metropolitan Police cited the OSA in an application for a court order to obtain information on the sources of *Guardian* reporter Amelia Hill after she published a series of stories based on whistle-blowers' information revealing that the police had failed to investigate the *News of the World* phone-hacking scandal (Bowcott, 2011).The order was withdrawn and the Deputy Assistant Police Commissioner apologized after the attempt was widely criticized by Members of Parliament and the media. Other cases where the OSA was used to arrest or threaten journalists include the publication of the Blair/Bush memo noted above (Norton-Taylor and White, 2005), the revelation that the police had lied to cover up the mistaken shooting of a Brazilian plumber (Keane, 2008), and the arrest of Shadow Immigration Minister Damien Green after he received a series of leaks regarding immigration policy (PA Committee, 2009).

Shhhh – Gagging public discussion

In addition to the criminal penalties set out in legislation, the UK secrecy system also provides for other limits to the publication of materials by the media. These limits are enacted both informally through cooperation with the media, and formally through court orders.

The courts have strong powers to formally block publication of information relating to national security and to prohibit newspapers from publishing excerpts and even from discussing the ban. In the *Spycatcher* case, the House of Lords initially barred publication of materials from a book published in the United States by a former director of MI5 that alleged spying on public officials.[14] However, the Lords later rejected a permanent injunction because the information was widely available.[15] The bans can be issued following a closed hearing over the telephone at the last minute (Laville, 2009), and information that has been already been made publicly available can also be banned in some cases. The ban can also be based on the Law of Confidence.[16]

There are also powers under the OSA and the Contempt of Court Act to ban discussion of public trials. The Act allows judges to exclude the public from trials if "publication of the evidence to be given would be prejudicial to the national safety."[17] In the prosecution of the two officials for releasing the Bush-Blair memo, the trial judge issued an order partially closing the trial and prohibiting the media from reporting what was said in open court about the case. Most of the ban was overturned by the Court of Appeal.[18]

The government can also use a Public Interest Immunity (PII) certificate to prevent disclosure of information in national-security-related trials (Scott Report, 1996). Under it, ministers can issue a certificate that information should be withheld if its disclosure "would cause a real risk of serious prejudice to an important public interest and the relevant Agency's Minister believes properly ought to be withheld" (ibid).The most infamous case – Matrix Churchill – was used by the government to suppress key evidence of government misconduct relating to arms sales to Iraq.[19] It was also used for cases where there was no apparent national security interest, such as a 2008 murder trial (Johnson, 2008). However, in a recent case on extraordinary rendition, the Court of Appeal stated that the imposition of PII cannot be considered as definitive and must be balanced against principles of open justice (Justice and Security Green Paper, 2011).

The UK government has recently proposed a bill that would extend secrecy to civil cases. The government claims that it "has received clear signals that if we are unable to safeguard material shared by foreign partners, then we can expect the depth and breadth of sensitive material shared with us to reduce significantly ... there is already evidence that the flow of sensitive material has been affected" (Justice and Security Green Paper, 2011).

In addition to the formal system of restrictions set out in law, there are also informal mechanisms that encourage censorship. In 1912, the government set up the so-called "Defence Notice (D-Notice) System – now named Defence Advisory Notice (DA-Notice) – a voluntary code of conduct between media editors and the military on certain subjects that are considered sensitive and should not be published without consultation from the government (Defence, Press and Broadcasting Advisory Committee, 2011). Although the system is not established by law, it is considered highly influential to the point of nearly being mandatory. The DA-Notice system is overseen by the Defence, Press and Broadcasting Advisory Committee (DPBAC), made up of government officials as well as media representatives including the BBC, the Press Association, and Google.[20] The DPBAC receives around 7–10 inquiries each week regarding stories and books, and it issues advisory letters on how to report specific subjects in the news. Currently, there are five categories of information covered by DA-Notices: 1) Military operations, plans and capabilities, 2) nuclear and non-nuclear weapons and equipment, 3) ciphers and secure communications, 4) sensitive installations and home addresses, 5) United Kingdom security and intelligence services and special services.

Each of these categories has guidance on the types of information that should not be published. The guidelines are not mandatory and, as the DPBAC notes, "Compliance with the DA-Notice system does not relieve the editor of responsibilities under the Official Secrets Act" (Defence, Press and Broadcasting Advisory Committee, 2011). The committee issues advisory letters in certain public controversies. In particular, in November 2010, when WikiLeaks was about to release a bulk of diplomatic files, a letter was sent asking editors to seek advice before publishing any of the materials, especially relating to categories 1 and 5 (Wintour, 2010).

A tiny breath of fresh air: the Freedom of Information Act, 2000

The secrecy of the state has undergone a semi-revolution in the past decade. In addition to the reform of the infamous Section 2 of the OSA, after 30 years of advocacy, Parliament acted again in 2000 to promote government openness in adopting the Freedom of Information Act (FOIA), 2000. The Act, in force since 2005, acknowledges a general right of access to information held by public authorities.[21] The public authorities are also generally required to confirm or deny whether they hold the requested information, regardless of the final decision to disclose it or not.[22] However, the principle of general access to public information is limited by a series of exemptions set out in the Act.[23] Nine of these exemptions are absolute, i.e., when they apply, the information requested can be denied by the competent authority without consideration of the public interest in its disclosure.[24] One absolute exemption from disclosure, for example, includes information "directly or indirectly supplied by, or relating to" bodies dealing with security matters," which is indeed the type of information often disclosed by organizations like WikiLeaks.[25] This very broad class of information, according to the interpretation of the Information Tribunal, includes "not just the content of information handled by a specified body but the fact that it handled it."[26]

The other exemptions listed in the FOIA are qualified, so when they are engaged, the competent public authorities must apply the so-called "public interest test," i.e., they must consider whether the public interest in disclosure outweighs the public interest in maintaining the exemption before deciding whether to release the information or not.[27] Some of the qualified exemptions apply to information whose disclosure would be likely to prejudice the "safeguarding of national security,"[28] the defence of the country,[29] international relations between the United Kingdom and any other State, international organizations, or courts,[30] or else, if "in the reasonable opinion of a qualified person," its disclosure would be likely to inhibit "the free and frank provision of advice or ... exchange of views for the purposes of deliberation" between civil servants and politicians.[31]

Furthermore, in many cases where an absolute or qualified exemption applies, the requested public authority is not even obliged to confirm or deny whether it holds the information, if the reply itself would trigger the exemption.[32]

The FOIA also sets out another significant limit, i.e., the possibility for the relevant government department to "veto" the release of the requested information even when the disclosure has been ordered by the information commissioner or the Information Tribunal.[33] Given the serious implications of the use of this power, the government has issued a policy statement that sets out the "exceptional cases" in which a veto can be used by the Ministry of Justice (2012). Interestingly, the first time the veto was issued was in response to a decision of the Information Tribunal that ordered the disclosure of the minutes of a Cabinet meeting discussing going to war in Iraq (IC, 2009).

Finally, the FOIA originally established that after 30 years since its creation, a record becomes "historical and is transferred to the National Archives."[34] Subsequently, the 30-year period has been reduced to 20 years.[35] However, this does not entail that the record becomes automatically available to the public. The exemptions that can be applied to its disclosure are reduced, but a significant number can still apply and include, *inter alia*, the exemptions seen above regarding information supplied by security bodies or information likely to harm national security, defence, or international relations.[36] In *Campaign Against Arms Trade (CAAT) v. Information Commissioner and Ministry of Defence*, it was acknowledged that the full disclosure of documents relating to sales of arms between the United Kingdom and Saudi Arabia in 1971/72 could still have prejudiced international relations between the two countries.[37] However, in a similar case, the tribunal stated that, "in addition to the general public interest in transparency and accountability," if the requested documents point out the possible involvement of United Kingdom officials in corrupt activities ("payment of commissions or agency fees in connection with arms sales"), then the public interest in disclosure outweighs the potential harm to bilateral relations between the countries.[38]

Prospects for reform

Currently, there is little prospect for legislative reform and indeed the trend is mostly negative. The government is holding a consultation on the FOIA which would further limit access by creating a class exemption for all documents broadly described as "Cabinet documents," as well as modifying the fee structure to place administrative barriers on requesters (Ministry of Justice, 2011; Campaign for Freedom of Information, 2012). The creation of a new National Crime Agency was announced in the Queen's Speech; it is likely to be exempt from the FOIA like its predecessor, the Serious and Organised Crime Agency (SOCA). The Parliament Home Affairs Committee requested that the government ensure that the new agency be subject to the FOIA, but did not receive any assurance from it on this point (Home Affairs Committee, 2011). Furthermore, the government has also proposed placing a new substantial limitation on the 1998 Public Interest Disclosure Act by requiring that all persons filing complaints must show that there is a public interest in the application.[39] In none of these bills or consultations was there any consideration of increasing public transparency of security bodies or limiting national security exemptions to public disclosure.

On the positive side, there is a nascent movement by some campaign groups to place a public interest test for journalists in a wide variety of criminal legislation, including the 1989 OSA, but the campaign is still in the early stages (Cathcart, 2012). However, given the lack of success in previous efforts to amend the law, it remains to be seen if it will get the requisite public support. Like most other reform initiatives, including the FOIA, the Public Interest Disclosure Act, and even the 1989 OSA, reform is going to require both a sustained effort by civil society in the media and tangible evidence that reform is necessary, most likely through public scandals that secrecy was deliberately covering up. At the moment, this perfect storm has yet to form and the few civil society groups are focusing their efforts on preventing further damage to existing legislation by secrecy-oriented officials.

Notes

1. HL Hansard, 19 February 1993, Col. 634.
2. Intelligence Services Act, 1994 (c. 13), legally creating the Secret Intelligence Service (MI6) and the Government Communications Headquarters (GCHQ); Security Service Act 1989 (MI5).
3. Official Secrets Act 1889 (52 & 53 Vict. c. 52).
4. Official Secrets Act 1911 (1 & 2 Geo 5 c28).
5. Official Secrets Act 1920 c. 75 (Regnal. 10 and 11 Geo 5)
6. Official Secrets Act 1939 c. 121 (Regnal. 2_and_3_Geo_6)
7. Official Secrets Act 1989 (c. 6)
8. The six areas covered by the OSA are: 1) Security and intelligence; 2. defence; 3) international relations; 4) crime and special investigation powers; 5) information resulting from unauthorized disclosures or entrusted in confidence; 6) information entrusted in confidence to other States or international organisations.
9. See Campaign for Freedom of Information, The Official Secrets Bill, 1988. http://www.cfoi.org.uk/osareform.html
10. *R v Shayler* [2002] UKHL 11.
11. In 1988, Parliament defeated a private members bill to put a public interest test into the law. It also defeated two efforts in 1995 to introduce a bill on the subject: see Don Touhig, private members bill and Tony Wright, *Whistleblower Protection Bill*.
12. Public Interest Disclosure Act 1998, c. 23, §1 states "A disclosure of information is not a qualifying disclosure if the person making the disclosure commits an offence by making it."
13. Guja v. Moldova, Application No. 14277/04, 12 February 2008.
14. Attorney-General v. Guardian Newspapers Ltd (No.1) [1987] 1 WLR 1248.
15. Attorney-General v. Guardian Newspapers Ltd (No.2) [1988] 3 WLR 776.
16. Lord Advocate v. Scotsman Publications [1989] UKHL 7 (06 July 1989).
17. R v Yam [2008] EWCA Crim 269.

18. Times Newspapers Ltd and Others. [2007] EWCA Crim 1925 (mostly overturning ban).
19. Report of the Inquiry into the Export of Defence Equipment and Dual-Use Goods to Iraq and Related Prosecutions (Scott Report), HMSO London, 1996.
20. See Committee Membership, http://www.dnotice.org.uk/committee.htm
21. Freedom of Information Act 2000 (FOIA), 2000 Chapter 36, 30th November 2000, entered in force on 1st January 2005.
22. FOIA, Section 1(1).
23. FOIA, Part II, Sections 21–44.
24. The absolute exemptions are set out in FOIA Sections 21, 23, 32, 34, 36 (so far relating to information held by the House of Commons or the House of Lords), section 37(1) (a),(b) and subsection (2), section 40(1) and (2), sections 41 and 44.
25. FOIA, Section 23. The list of bodies dealing with security matters include, among others, the Security Service, the Secret Intelligence Service and the Government Communications Headquarters.
26. First-tier Tribunal (Information Rights), *The Commissioner of Police of the Metropolis v Information Commissioner*, EA/2010/0008, par. 15.
27. FOIA, Section 2(b).
28. FOIA, Section 24. Neither the FOIA nor any other statutes provide a definition of "national security." In *Baker v Information Commissioner and the Cabinet Office*, EA/2006/0045, par. 26, the First-tier Tribunal (Information Rights) refers to a House of Lords decision that states that: (i) "national security" means "the security of the United Kingdom and its people"; (ii) the interests of national security are not limited to action by an individual which can be said to be "targeted at" the UK, its system of government or its people; (iii) the protection of democracy and the legal and constitutional systems of the state is a part of national security as well as military defence; (iv) "action against a foreign state may be capable indirectly of affecting the security of the United Kingdom" (v) "reciprocal co-operation between the United Kingdom and other states in combating international terrorism is capable of promoting the United Kingdom's national security."
29. FOIA, Section 26.
30. FOIA, Section 27.
31. FOIA, Section 36(2)
32. FOIA, Section 2(1) and (2). See, e.g., First-tier Tribunal (Information Rights), *All Party Parliamentary Group on Extraordinary Rendition ("APPGER") v Information Commissioner and the Foreign and Commonwealth Office*, EA/2011/0049–0051.
33. FOIA, Section 53.
34. FOIA, Part VI and Public Records Act 1958, as amended by the FOIA.
35. Constitutional Reform and Governance Act 2010, Schedule 7, par. 4. The new 20-year-period rule is bound to enter into force after a transitional period of 10 years.
36. FOIA, Sections 65–66.
37. First-tier Information Tribunal (Information Rights), *Campaign Against Arms Trade (CAAT) v. Information Commissioner and Ministry of Defence*, EA/2011/0109.

38. First-tier Information Tribunal (Information Rights), *Gilby v Information Commissioner and Foreign and Commonwealth Office*, EA/2007/0071, 0078 and 0079, par. 55.
39. Enterprise and Regulatory Reform Bill, §14.

References

BBC News (2004) GCHQ translator cleared over leak, *BBC News*, Retrieved from http://news.bbc.co.uk/1/hi/uk/3485072.stm
BBC News (2007). Pair jailed over Bush memo leak, *BBC News*, May 10, 2007 Retrieved from http://news.bbc.co.uk/1/hi/england/northamptonshire/6641983.stm
Blair, T. (2011) *A Journey*. Deckle Edge: London
Bowcott, O. (2011). Met criticised by Keith Vaz for Official Secrets Act threat to the Guardian, *The Guardian*, Retrieved from http://www.guardian.co.uk/media/2011/sep/23/met-keith-vaz-secrets-guardian
Cathcart, B. (2012). Journalism and the public interest: a Hacked Off initiative, *Inform Blog*, Retrieved from http://inforrm.wordpress.com/2012/05/30/journalism-and-the-public-interest-a-hacked-off-initiative-brian-cathcart/
Campaign for Freedom of Information (2012). Supplementary submission to the Justice Select Committee, May 21, 2012. Retrieved From http://www.cfoi.org.uk/pdf/foipostlegscrutiny_cfoI_supplementary.pdf
Crown Prosecution Service, (2012). Interim guidelines for prosecutors on assessing the public interest in cases affecting the media, April 2012. Retrieved from http://www.cps.gov.uk/consultations/mg_consultation.pdf
Defence, Press and Broadcasting Advisory Committee, (2011). History of the DA-Notice System Retrieved from http://www.dnotice.org.uk/history.htm
Departmental Committee (1972). Departmental Committee on Section 2 of the Official Secrets Act 1911, Volume 1: Report of the Committee, September 1972
Farquharson, H. (2005). Cell visitors silenced, *Richmond and Twickenham Times* Retrieved from http://www.richmondandtwickenhamtimes.co.uk/news/659513.cell_visitors_silenced/
Hazell, R. Worthy, B. and Glover, M. (2010). *The Impact of the Freedom of Information Act on Central Government in the UK Does FOI Work?* Palgrave Macmillan: London, UK
Home Affairs Committee (2011). Fourteenth Report – New Landscape of Policing, 15 September 2011, § 91–94. Retrieved from http://www.publications.parliament.uk/pa/cm201012/cmselect/cmhaff/939/93902.htm
House of Commons Library Report (2008). House of Commons Library Report, Official Secrecy, SN/PC/02023, December 30, 2008
Holehouse, M. (2011). "Change the law to keep Cabinet secret, urges Sir Gus O'Donnell", *The Telegraph*, Retrieved from http://www.telegraph.co.uk/news/politics/8962828/Change-the-law-to-keep-Cabinet-secret-urges-Sir-Gus-ODonnell.html
IC (2009). Information Commissioner's Office, *Freedom of Information Act 2000 Ministerial Veto on Disclosure of Cabinet Minutes Concerning Military Action against Iraq*, Information Commissioner's Report to Parliament, June 10, 2009

Johnson, A. (2008). The extraordinary case of Britain's most secret murder trial, *The Independent,* Retrieved from http://www.independent.co.uk/news/uk/crime/the-extraordinary-case-of-britains-most-secret-murder-trial-774661.html

Justice and Security Green Paper, 2011 CM 8194, October 2011

Keane, F. (2008). Menezes: The Woman who leaked the story, *BBC News* Retrieved from http://news.bbc.co.uk/1/hi/uk/7795289.stm

Laville, S. (2009). Government bans former anti-terror chief's tell-all book, *The Guardian* Retrieved from http://www.guardian.co.uk/uk/2009/jul/02/andy-hayman-terrorist-hunters-banned

Malik, S. and Gentleman, A. (2012). Private sector medical staff assessing benefit claimants told to sign Official Secrets Act, *The Guardian,* Retrieved from http://www.guardian.co.uk/society/2012/apr/12/atos-doctors-sign-official-secrets-act

Ministry of Justice (2011). Memorandum to the Justice Select Committee Post-Legislative Assessment of the Freedom of Information Act 2000, December 2011. Retrieved from http://www.justice.gov.uk/downloads/publications/policy/moj/post-legislative-assessment-of-the-foi-act.pdf

Ministry of Justice (2012). Statement of HMG Policy, Use of the executive override under the Freedom of Information Act 2000 as it relates to information falling within the scope of Section 35(1)

Norton-Taylor, R. and White, M. (2005). Secrecy gag prompted by fear of new Blair-Bush revelations, The Guardian, Retrieved from http://www.guardian.co.uk/media/2005/nov/24/pressandpublishing.usnews

O'Neill, S. (2008). Whistle-blower cleared over Islamist leaks, *The Times,* January 10, 2008

PA Committee, (2009). Public Administration Committee – Tenth Report: Leaks and Whistleblowing in Whitehall July 16, 2009

Rayner, G., Gammell, C. and Simpson, A. (2009). Army Colonel arrested over alleged leaks to human rights researcher, *The Telegraph*. Retrieved from http://www.telegraph.co.uk/news/uknews/defence/4513991/Army-Colonel-arrested-over-alleged-leaks-to-human-rights-researcher.html

Scott Report (1996). Report of the Inquiry into the Export of Defence Equipment and Dual-Use Goods to Iraq and Related Prosecutions (Scott Report), HMSO London, 1996. Retrieved from http://www.cps.gov.uk/legal/d_to_g/disclosure_manual/disclosure_manual_chapter_34/

Wintour, P. (2010). Expected WikiLeaks disclosures prompts warning for editors *The Guardian,* Retrieved from http://www.guardian.co.uk/media/2010/nov/26/wikileaks-documents-downing-street-editors

11
WikiLeaks, Anonymous, and the Exercise of Individuality: Protesting in the Cloud

Stefania Milan

When WikiLeaks released the *Collateral Murder* video in spring 2010, featuring a US army helicopter shooting Iraqi civilians, cyberactivism was not a hot topic in the mainstream media. However, thanks to the ability to leverage the potential of the Internet to influence political debate, WikiLeaks quickly imposed itself as a headline-grabbing organization. The mass media fell in love with WikiLeaks, not least because of its enigmatic nature, its organizational model based on individuality, and the juicy revelations about its frontman Julian Assange. In the wake of WikiLeaks' major releases that year, the amorphous online network known as Anonymous also came under the spotlight, notably for its pro-WikiLeaks cyberattacks. In February 2011, a CNN journalist wrote, "Perhaps the most controversial incarnation of the WikiLeaks model comes from Anonymous" (CNN, 2011).

Both WikiLeaks and Anonymous point to something new in the realm of organized collective action. They have changed our perception of cyberactivism and of its role in the cyberpower game, but especially they have challenged our understanding of collective action in the time of the Internet.

WikiLeaks and Anonymous are instances of cyberactivism. By cyberactivism I mean collective action in cyberspace that addresses network infrastructure or exploits the infrastructure's technical and ontological features for political or social change.[1] Examples of cyberactivism include electronic disturbance tactics and online civil disobedience, self-organization and autonomous creation of infrastructure, software and hardware hacking, and hacktivism.[2] Leaking can be seen as another example, as it takes advantage of the distribution capacity of the Internet.

Generally speaking, cyberactivists are part of the organized civil society.[3] However, they dispute some of our fundamental interpretations of said civil society. They challenge the increasing professionalization of transnational activist networks by erratically involving non-professional activists, and point to the disembodiment of activism by decoupling resistance and physical presence (Wong and Brown, 2012).

This chapter introduces the concept of cloud protesting as a theoretical artifact to understand the activism of Anonymous and WikiLeaks, as well as that of other contemporary outbreaks of protest, such as the Occupy mobilizations of 2011. It focuses on the changes brought by the Internet to organized collective action. I move from the empirical case of Anonymous, seen as a proxy for current cyberactivism, to discuss the rise of a new way of political organizing that has individuals at its core. WikiLeaks serves as both an example of some of the features of cloud protesting and as the springboard that gave an unprecedented visibility to much of this activism. I investigate what is new in the organizational as well as collective identity pattern, exploring the role of communication technology, and the Internet in particular, in enabling cloud protesting. What is distinctive in these relatively new instances of online collective action? What can we learn from them that can illuminate the most innovative aspects of contemporary activism? Do Anonymous and WikiLeaks point to new forms of collective organizing, or even to a new wave of social mobilization?

Anonymous and the explosion of cyberactivism

Anonymous is a moniker for an online community whose self-identified members engage in disruptive activities using electronic civil disobedience techniques in support of freedom of speech on the Web. Membership in the group is informal and fluctuating: among its members are techno-savvy activists, but also digital natives and netizens who believe in the potential of the Internet for collective action. Anonymous originated in online chat rooms that focused on politically incorrect pranks. The group later mutated into a politically engaged collective of hacktivists, but maintained an orientation to the "lulz" – a neologism that derives from LOL, "laughing out loud" – which indicates the fun associated with pranks (Gorenstein Massa, 2010; Coleman 2010, and Chapter 12 in this book). Earlier actions included online and offline mobilization and nuisance campaigns against the Church of Scientology, accused of censoring its members' opinions; the International Federation of the Phonographic Industry, for its pro-copyright battles; and child pornography sites. But it was with their support to WikiLeaks that Anonymous came under the global spotlight.

In the eyes of Anonymous, WikiLeaks represented more than just an online drop-box amassing leaked classified documents. As soon as WikiLeaks came under pressure internationally, it became the fetish of online free speech and the mainspring of a cyber-crusade. The pressures enacted on the whistle-blower website spurred the mobilization of hundreds of people not directly linked to its core group. These people provided technical support to the WikiLeaks cyber-infrastructure. They mirrored the site when it was taken offline, contributing to the spread and visibility of WikiLeaks content, and they mobilized in support of the organization, for example by attacking (i.e., taking down, defacing, making temporarily unavailable) the websites of companies that had taken action against the whistle-blower website. Most of this kind of activism existed long before WikiLeaks started making the news in 2010. Electronic disturbance and electronic civic disobedience had been theorized and practiced already in the 1990s by groups like the Critical Art Ensemble, an art and technology collective (Critical Art Ensemble, 1993 and 1996). Tactical media, too, have been extensively explored as hit-and-run media interventions into society (Garcia and Lovink, 1997). But the WikiLeaks saga changed the scale of things, as well as the visibility and ambitions of cyberactivists.

This type of cyberactivism is called "hacktivism." Hacktivism indicates the politically motivated use of technical expertise like coding: activists seek to fix society through software and online action. In other words, it is "activism gone electronic" (Jordan and Taylor, 2004, p. 1). The hacker collective known as Cult of the Dead Cow (currently Hacktivismo) claims to have invented the term, a portmanteau of "hacking" and "activism," in 1998 (Delio, 2004). Hacktivism is a highly contested concept, and different groups of people associate different objectives and tactics under its umbrella, not all of which are compatible. For example, while some hacktivists like the Anonymous may not hesitate to deface websites or launch distributed denial of service attacks (DDoS), others, such as the aforementioned Hacktivismo, consider these tactics a fundamental breach of freedom of speech that are counter to the aims of hacktivism.[4] With this contention in mind, I outline a few sociological characteristics of contemporary hacktivism, which, as we will see, apply also to other groups engaged in Internet-based activism. I focus on the features of groupings, decision-making practices, tactics, and relations with societal norms. It is worth looking at Anonymous as a case study, as it brings together in a rather visible, efficient, and

condensed way many of the features of similar contemporary forms of
activism rooted in cyberspace.

Hacktivist groups, like other direct action networks, tend to "reflect
the *convergence* of the people who act through them, as opposed to
being the 'organized expression' of a group, class or community"
(McDonald, 2004, p. 115; emphasis added).[5] They embody traits of
both subcultural communities and identity-oriented countercultural
movements. Like any other subcultural community (albeit one with
loose and permeable boundaries), hacktivists share a set of core values
and defining behaviours that set members apart from the dominant
culture. In particular, they embody an oppositional and pro-openness
ethos, which explains their frequent actions against government
and security companies' websites. Means and ends of hacktivists are
blurred, as often happens among identity-oriented countercultural
groups. Members define themselves through the confrontational
interaction with other groups; repression typically strengthens their
identity and cohesion (Kriesi et al., 1995). In this respect, hacktivism
is characterized by an impulse towards the transgression of existing
states of affairs, and "a sense of solidarity in pursuit of [said] transgression" (Jordan, 2002, p. 12).

When it comes to action, Anonymous functions as an affinity group
(McDonald, 2002; Jordan, 2002; Finnegan, 2003). An affinity group is
made of individuals gathering around a given objective, usually direct
action (e.g., a roadblock or a virtual sit-in). They are temporary aggre-
gates regulated by trust, loyalty, and personal care, and they are typically dissolved at the conclusion of the action. Affinity is grounded
on shared values (often tacit, and usually existing prior to action) and
common interests – in the case of hacktivists, technical skills or the willingness to engage in Internet-rooted disruptive action. New members
are recruited over time, according to the same affinity principle.

Individuals are at the core of hacktivism, for two main reasons.
First, individual skills (i.e., technical expertise) are highly valued, as
they make action possible. Second, cultural and ideological references
of hacktivists (the hacker and Do-It-Yourself or "maker" culture, for
example) tend to emphasize the individual component and subcultural
elements such as lifestyle. Organization principles, too, tend to afford
the individual a total autonomy of judgment (c.f., Lichterman, 1996),
which results in the typical refusal of formal delegation and representation mechanisms. In this respect, internal decision-making is normally
characterized by horizontality and decentralization. However, the
weight activists attribute to action may result in the potential distortion of collective decision-making processes – what a tech activist once

called the "dictatorship of action," by which the urgency of taking action may result in decision-making cliques (Milan, 2013) or situations of "miniconsensus" (Gastil, 1993).

As a result of the centrality of taking action, which has an expressive and performative function, the group becomes virtually invisible. Invisibility is obtained through the recourse to anonymity (for example, via the use of a nickname and encryption software), and the circumvention of clues that could smooth the identification process by third parties. This is partially justified by the Web environment, which enables invisibility, but also by the fear of repression that networks like Anonymous have suffered since their inception, and by the partially illegal nature of some of their activism. However, on the symbolic level, invisibility is explained by the relevance of the action (and its outcome) compared to that of the acting individual. It is the action that is visible, simply because the action is the very quintessence of the group and the primary justification for its existence. The group (the "we") identifies itself with its action.

Owing partially to cyberlibertarian thought[6] and partially to the subcultural nature of this type of collective action, hacktivists tend to see cyberspace as a secluded free space where rules and norms of "real" life do not apply (Milan, 2012). Cyberspace functions as a cultural laboratory as well as a place where to have fun by one's own rules and regardless of whether fun implies politically incorrect or law-breaking behaviours. But the Internet also offers a platform for identification with peers, where one can experience a sense of safety and solidarity, as can be observed within subcultural communities. In this sense, groups like Anonymous tend to enjoy a certain degree of autonomy from the political context in which they are embedded (Kriesi, 2004).

Finally, hacktivists take action against companies, governments, and individuals in retaliation for behaviours that are a threat to their norms and values. Such threats include attacks on openness and on the uncensored Internet. Threats act as "moral shocks" fostering reaction, as activists find themselves at odds with norms that conflict with their own. In reacting to threats, they adopt both transgressive and defensive tactics. Transgressive tactics include the infamous DDoS (distributed denial of service) attacks, often aimed at disclosing the cyber-weakness of their enemies, but also include trickery and nuisance cyber-campaigns (as well as offline actions) intended to ridicule and destabilize targets. Occasionally hacktivists step out of cyberspace: for example, since 2008 Anonymous members have periodically taken to the streets in different locations wearing Guy Fawkes masks; the same masks appeared at Occupy Wall Street protest sites around the world.

Anonymous highlights and condenses many features that I believe are typical of contemporary forms of collective action – namely, the centrality of the Internet and its tools as platforms for and arenas of collective action, the crucial role played by individuals, the move towards networked collective action at the expense of more traditional organizational forms, the centrality of the private and subjective experiences of individual activists, and the expressive and performative valence of action. In what follows I investigate these changes in the context of an exploration of the notion of cloud protesting, using Anonymous and also WikiLeaks and the Occupy Wall Street mobilizations as empirical examples.

Centrality of individuals and changing organizational patterns

As exemplified by nebulous networks such as Anonymous and even more so by the WikiLeaks project, individuals have come to constitute central nodes in contemporary activism networks.

Several authors have emphasized the growing role of individuality in contemporary societies. Castells (1996) argued that, in the network logic that characterizes the post-industrial society, the personal experience of individuals replaces groups and pre-existing social categories. In his own words, "Our societies are increasingly structured around the bipolar opposition of the Net and the Self," where the Net indicates the network organizations that constitute the dominant form of contemporary social organization (Castells, 1996, p. 3). Melucci (2000), too, observed the growing importance of individuality, as opposed to generality, as the guiding principle of increasingly complex societies. Negri and Hardt (2004) maintained that the "multitude" has replaced the depersonalized "mass" as the organizing paradigm of the postmodern society. The multitude is composed of individuals who are bearers of unique needs, interests, and emotions. It embeds both dynamics of sociality and individuality, of uniqueness and commonality, but is by no means fragmented, as the singularities share some classlike grievances and have the ability to act together (Negri and Hardt, 2004, pp. 127–129).

Social movements, too, have not been immune to individualism.[7] McDonald (2004) identified such tendencies in the anti-globalization protests of the 1990–2000s. In his view, those streams of activism were characterized by a break in the structures of representation and delegation, whereby social actors did not seek to manifest a group identity through action. McDonald went as far as to speak of an "experience movement" to indicate those movements that cannot be explained in terms of the relation of the individual with the collective, but where the individual experience per se takes central stage. Such movements are no longer characterized by "the power to represent," but involve "other grammars of action: healing, touching, hearing, feeling, seeing, moving"...in other words, "grammars of embodiment" (McDonald, 2006, p. 37), both in cyberspace and in real life.

No doubt these changes are reflected in the movements' organizational patterns. If we look at the evolution of the types of organizations that have characterized organized collective action in the West from the 1960s onwards, we can identify three main phases, the last of which is represented by what I have termed "cloud protesting."[8]

The first phase is characterized by the so-called *social movement organizations*. During the mass protests of the 1960s, people took the streets under the aegis of students groups, antiwar organizations, identity-based groups, and church groups – all of them characterized by a strong sense of belonging and by clear-cut membership (c.f. Tilly, 2009). Social movement organizations[9] steered the crowds, managing crucial resources[10] like funding. Championing a joint narrative, they monopolized the cultural and normative production of the movements, a crucial step towards norm change that is the ultimate goal of all movements. Serving as access points for journalists and news media, they were the voice of social movements; providing collective identity and leadership, they performed the role of social movement entrepreneurs. In short, formal groupings had organizational control over the movement.

Starting from the second half of the 1990s, *informal networks and affinity groups* took central stage. These new configurations were in part inspired by the diffusion of the Internet, which became the backbone and metaphor of new ways of organizing (Bennett, 2003), while helping social movements to externalize costs (Tarrow, 1994). Informal groups and networks characterized by multiple and flexible identities, temporary nodes, and horizontal leadership staged noisy protests and disruptive actions against global summits and multilateral institutions (della Porta and Tarrow, 2005). Easily mobilized and connected across borders, thanks to the Internet, the composite movement(s) struggling for global justice became transnational. What was new was the informal character of most of the actions, still however anchored to (informal) groups and collectives. At the grassroots level, affinity groups became the main organizing principle. The cultural and normative production of the movement(s) was no longer monopolized by resource-rich large-scale organizations; the different nodes would voice their claims and build their narratives in a number of scattered websites and in online self-organized platforms, bypassing mainstream media (Langlois and Dubois, 2005).

After a period of relative quiescence, a new wave of protests spread across the world in 2010, inaugurating the phase of *networked individuals*. We have already seen how Anonymous is composed of individuals acting on their own capacity in the context of a loosely connected network. Outside cyberspace, 2010 saw mass uprisings in the Middle East and North Africa, which resulted in regime change in, for example, Egypt and Tunisia. In early 2011, the Spanish movement of the *Indignados* (literally, "the outraged") staged a series of protest camps and street demonstrations and demanded radical change in Spanish politics. In fall 2011, protesters in several Western countries went back to the streets to protest against the greedy Western banking system and to demand financial equality. It all started in September 17, 2011, when a group of activists staged an occupation of New York City's Wall Street financial district. The protest spread rapidly across the world, as activists, inspired by the *Indignados*, started camping in city parks and public squares. At first the "Occupy" protests seemed to address merely financial inequality and express disaffection towards institutions; observers, however, suggested they represent a quest for recognition and citizen participation (Tarrow, 2011) and for "real democracy" (Hardt and Negri, 2011). Although protesters were not entirely the new kids on the block and most of their organizing innovations were already visible in embryonic form, in the horizontal and autonomous politics of portions of the global justice movement, they seemed to privilege a way of coming together that focused on and highly valued individual needs and contributions.[11] I suggest calling this (relatively) new approach to collective action "cloud protesting," to indicate a type of social organizing for collective action with individuals and their needs, preferences, bodies, and individualities at its core.

The cloud as organizational form may be best understood by looking, for example, at a typical general assembly, the governing body of Occupy camps. General assemblies follow similar patterns in most camps across the world, in which activists implement a technique known as the "human microphone." Apparently just a low-tech solution to delivering a speech in busy meetings, the human microphone involves the unison repetition by the people near a speaker of what the speaker says. With each speaker having (supposedly) an equal standing within the assembly, the human microphone ensures that everyone will be reached, while it promises focused participation and involvement of the whole assembly. The assembly unfolds similarly to *a conversation in a social networking platform or Internet-relay chat*, with self-contained individuals rather than pre-existing groups as protagonists. Pre-existing membership-based groups and non-governmental organizations (NGOs) have moved to the background or have vanished, as activists appear to reject pre-packaged non-negotiable identities and organizations.[12] Many of the nodes in the mobilized networks are individuals, something we have already observed within Anonymous.

The cloud is a metaphor for individualization and for specific ways for creating meaningful connections among individuals, but it is also a reference to the technology that has become the metaphor and organizing principle of collective action (Bennett, 2003; Bennett and Segerberg, 2011 and 2012). In what follows, I explore the features of cloud protesting by looking at the communication technology that supports and enables it, namely the Internet and its tools. Focusing on communication technology involves looking at specific technological platforms and specific ways of interactions on such platforms. In this context, communication technology is to be interpreted as both a metaphor and an enabler force. It also functions as a sort of mirror of the tendencies towards individualization triggered in contemporary societies by a number of combined socioeconomic (and non-technological) factors.

Core features of cloud protesting

In computing, the "cloud" indicates the delivery of services such as storage space and software over a network – typically, the Internet. Rather than being stored on dedicated servers managed and owned by individual organizations, services are kept "in the cloud." Organizations can reach their resources stored remotely through a friendly Web interface that does not require the end user to have any specialized knowledge of the system. Services can be customized to the needs of single organizations, and the sharing of products and infrastructure results in an overall reduction of costs for the end user. In short, the cloud enables organizations to have a lighter structure and enjoy a more diffuse and flexible access to resources fundamental to their operation.

Applying the computing metaphor to collective action, the cloud takes on two meanings: it is a metaphor for a specific way of connecting individuals in an instance of collective action, but it is also an *imagined space*, partially hosted in cyberspace, where *soft* resources crucial to collective action are stored and enjoyed by participants. In this respect, contemporary protest is best described as a cloud where a set of ingredients enabling mobilization coexist – namely, identities, narratives, meanings, and know-how. They are negotiated both offline and online, but are brought to life, exchanged and stored "in the cloud" composed of blogs, social networking and microblogging platforms, and other tools such as digital storytelling websites. Such imagined space is to be intended in the guise of a *symbolic place between* technology devices and platforms, similar to Bruce Sterling's definition of cyberspace as "the 'place' place" where a telephone conversation appears to occur. Not inside your actual phone, the plastic device on your desk. Not inside the other person's phone, in some other city. The place between the phones" (Sterling, 1992).

As in cloud computing, within a social movement the cloud reduces the costs of mobilization by offering resources that can be accessed and enjoyed independently by individual activists: joint meanings, but also solidarity networks; a relaxed affiliation working on an individual basis; the option to reclaim and reinvent a collective space (both virtual and real); an occasion for self-expression; and the possibility of customizing one's own participation and narrative.

The cloud gives a presence and a multifaceted shape to immaterial resources like identities, narratives, and meanings, in an array of digital objects such as tweets, links, photographs, and videos that render meanings "tangible." These embodiments are to a large extent immanent to cyberspace, as they do not exist *in the same form* outside the cloud. The cloud (as the symbolic "place between") becomes the platform where the cultural and symbolic production of the movement takes place through the contribution of a variety of individual actors acting on their own account. Services like social media or Internet-relay chat become the means through which activists can shape in the first person the meanings attached to collective action. There is no need for (and no means of) organizational monopolistic control over the collective narrative of the protest, because the cloud, as the metaphor for a new form of collective actor, "votes" and collectively determines what fits and what does not. In this respect, the cloud leaves little room for classical social movement organizations like NGOs. The very same symbolic space identified by the cloud becomes the group: it provides a perhaps loose sense of belonging, but requires far less responsibility towards fellow activists.

Finally, resources are in the cloud to be enjoyed by participants in a pick-and-choose fashion, rather than being managed by social movement organizations. Each individual participant can pick what fits best to her identity, preferences, and emotions. She can join when it is more convenient and bring along her own identity, cultural and political background, grievances, and claims. In other words, the cloud allows each individual to *tailor* her participation.

In the cloud: collective identity and the performative role of action

Collective identity is defined as the process that allows social actors to give meaning to their own experiences and to develop emotional attachment to their fellows (Polletta and Jasper, 2001). Identity contributes to keeping together a movement by ensuring a sort of correspondence between individual activists and the collective "we": the individual is functional in the group she is part of, and the group attributes meaning to the individual. McDonald (2004) criticized this instrumental conception of collective identity that holds the "we" as an exclusive point of reference of collective action while dismissing the role of the individual. In cloud protesting, too, individuals occupy a central position. In this section, I reflect on patterns of collective identity formation and on the performative role of action in cloud protesting, returning to the example of Anonymous.

Within Anonymous, collective identity is the result of specific dynamics rooted in the individual. In fact, hacktivism is characterized by the hegemony of hands-on technical expertise, which is owned at the individual level. Although taking action such as launching a DDoS attack gains symbolic meaning (and effectiveness in practice) in interaction with the community of peers and in the reputation system that regulates tech and hacker communities, it relies on individual activities where the subject interacts with the machine. The dimension of the private and subjective experience is at the core of what is collective, insofar as it is the *experience of the action* (and not the actual action, as it would be in a street demonstration, for example) that is shared within the group. The collective identity is therefore realized in the experience of difference and affinity in the encounter between a self-contained "I" with another "I," rather than in the collapsing of the "I" into the "we" acting together. In other words, it is a matter of "stories of 'I' encountering others" (McDonald, 2004, p. 589). The collective "we" does not cease to exist, as this would undermine the very same nature and notion of collective action. But individual action assumes a performative valence of the "I," making the representative function of the "we" almost irrelevant. The resulting collective identity is visible in the set of shared meanings that have survived the filter of the exercise of pooling together individual experiences.

A similar process is at play in other instances of cloud protesting. Within WikiLeaks, for example, individual whistle-blowers and the crowd-sourced pool of individual analysts, with their respective personal grievances and values, pulled their skills together to offer an innovative online platform for the release to the public of classified documents.[13] Within the Occupy mobilizations, protesters actively participated in building a collective identity by partaking in action through, among other means, social media. When he or she takes part in the protests and makes them visible via, for example, the microblogging platforms Twitter or Thumblr, each individual becomes the hero of the story. Each participant defines herself, and by extension the mobilization, by means of posts, Tweets, links, pictures, and short videos. She selects other similar material posted on the Web by fellow protesters and passes on (e.g., re-Tweets) what she believes is exciting, interesting, and appropriate to the collective representation of "who we are." The resulting collective identity is particularly flexible and can virtually fit anyone, since it is built on malleable minimum common denominators and ephemeral 140-character slogans, rather than on ideological strongholds impermeable to individual interpretations.

Further, the relevance of the subjective experience of the individual is translated online into a *politics of visibility* typical of the Internet. WikiLeaks, for example, combined the publication of leaks with a well-staged media strategy. Although it did not fully work as planned, it was oriented to give visibility not only to the leaked documents but also to the organization itself, and to its frontman in particular. Anonymous, in turn, framed their demonstrative actions in a way that raised awareness of free expression and openness issues while at the same time contributing to build a sort of myth around the group and its members. To some extent the Occupy protests were about "being there" and becoming visible over the Internet, through video streaming and a myriad of online platforms.[14] Occupy protest events and actions unfold on these same online platforms as much as they take place in real life. Further, protest actions are reproduced, played out, and discussed beyond the actual occurrence, stretching the duration and life cycle of a demonstration or a camp. The cloud, as an imagined space where meanings are created and reproduced, allows everyone to participate in building the collective plot. It gives voice and visibility to personalized yet universal narratives: this hashtag-style[15] collective narrative is flexible, real-time, and crowd-controlled. It connects individual stories into a broader context that gives them meaning. Following McDonald, "the grammar of action is one where the actor is an other for another, leading to an ethic and forms of action underlining *presence* rather than mediated relationships" (McDonald, 2004, p. 590; emphasis added).

Conclusions: A new wave of social mobilizations?

In this chapter, I explored WikiLeaks, Anonymous, and some aspects of the Occupy mobilizations as examples of cloud protesting, a relatively new way of social organizing, which puts individuals (and their individualized digital media platforms, as well as their preferences, desires, and personalities) at the centre of action and symbolic production. To different degrees, these three examples pinpoint the features of cloud protesting – namely, the power of networked individuals over more traditional groups, the role of the Internet as platform for and arena of collective action, the relevance of individual activists' subjective practices and stories, and the expressive value of action. In this section I reflect on the present and immediate future of Internet-based collective action, arguing that we are in presence of a new wave of social mobilizations rooted in cyberspace.

The WikiLeaks saga has served as a catalyst for emerging networks of hacktivists like Anonymous. By giving them visibility and fame, it encouraged people to take part in online collective action, spurring an unprecedented wave of cyberactivism. Cyberspace has imposed itself as a central arena for civic engagement. WikiLeaks and Anonymous proved how activism that originates and lives in cyberspace is possible and worth it. Compared to other activism tactics such as campaigning or street demonstrations, cyberdisruption and electronic disturbance have an intense and real-time impact, even with limited deployment of resources. Similarly, the Occupy tactic of camping jointly with the Internet-enabled politics of visibility proved to be sufficient to make the news and enter public discourse – at least in the short run.

What we have seen in action with WikiLeaks and Anonymous is the manifestation of a wave of movement activity that is virtual, distributed, and individualized. In the three examples, the Internet is no longer just a tool for networking and mobilizing, but has become one of the main platforms for action, recruitment, and identification. Decentralized individuals come together as a cloud, where the cloud is both the metaphor for unmediated interaction among individuals and the *ensemble* of the Internet-based platforms that enable individuals to participate without the mediation of formal organizations. Cloud protesting challenges many of the notions on which social movement research is grounded. It calls for the reversal of the very definition of collective identity, no longer based on a preponderance of the "we," but on the centrality of the private experience of individuals.

Contrary to scholarly expectations, these online "experience movements" do generate strong networks, a solid sense of belonging, and a strong collective identity rooted in the uniqueness of individuals and in the performative valence of action. This is true for four main reasons. First, the generation of newly recruited hacktivists are socialized into interacting with friends and peers through the mediation of the Internet, which makes face-to-face interactions redundant. Second, threats to the activists' values and activities (for example, closure of the Internet to Anonymous and WikiLeaks, or the eviction for Occupy camps) strengthen the perception of being part of a group. Third, the awareness of being engaged in a global struggle, be it an "information war" or a mobilization against financial inequality, has the potential to foster transnational solidarity. Finally, the immediacy of outcomes and the intensity of effects of activist interventions contribute to create a sense of empowerment that cements activist networks.

To conclude, I believe that projects like WikiLeaks and Anonymous represent the nucleus of an embryonic social-movement wave that puts individuals and their individualized digital media at the centre. Activism is not completely moving online, but, as the WikiLeaks-spurred upsurge of hacktivism showed, it can no longer do without a strong online component – where the Internet is not only a platform for networking and exchange of information or a mirror of offline actions, but the very same locus of activism where new narratives of participation and empowerment, as well as new identities, are created and reproduced.

Notes

1. Cyberspace encompasses the realm of digital electronic communication, including, but not limited to, the Internet.
2. Vegh (2003) arranges cyberactivism tactics into three categories: awareness/advocacy (e.g., carrying out action), organization/mobilization (e.g., calling for action), and action/reaction (e.g., hacktivism). In this chapter, the focus is on collective actors such as networks and activist groups acting in a

collective capacity –, Individuals, such as bloggers writing solely in their own capacity, will not be considered.

3. By organized civil society I mean the realm of nonstate and nonbusiness actors, organized in formal groupings (non-governmental organizations) or informal groupings (social movements, loose networks).

4. The Cult of the Dead Cow assumes as an ethical reference the Universal Declaration of Human Rights – in particular, article 19. The Cult's notion of what is a legitimate tactic reflects its adhesion to the so-called hacker ethics. The hacker ethic is a set of tacit values shared within the hacker community, such as freedom of speech, access to information, world improvement, and non-interference with the system's functionality. These values are summarized in the injunctions to "leave no damage" and "leave things as you found them [or better]" (Levy, 1984). Typically hackers are apolitical and emphasize a "do not harm" approach that is alien to groups like Anonymous.

5. McDonald's analysis refers to the UK's direct action network known as Reclaim the Streets!

6. Cyberlibertarianism revolves around ideas of self-organization, informal experimental practices, openness, and bottom-up processes. The so-called Declaration of Independence of Cyberspace (Barlow, 1996), considered the founding document of cyberlibertarianism, states the right of the individual to explore all information in cyberspace – unimpeded and uncensored – and to contribute and share knowledge (Jordan, 1999).

7. However, social movement scholars, with the exception of resource mobilization theorists (who highlighted material incentives and resource availability as factors that encourage people to take action; c.f. Edwards and McCarthy, 2004) have traditionally emphasized the group dimension, at the expense of a much-needed analysis of the role of individuals and their motives within collective action.

8. What I outline here is an overly simplified version that does not take into account the complexity of movements, the life cycle of individual organizations, or the actual coexistence of different types of organizations in the same period, but attempts at identifying macro-trends within a long period of time in our complex recent history.

9. Although different notions coexist in the literature, traditionally in social movement studies social movement organizations have been equated with complex and formal organizations seeking to implement a movement's goals (McCharty and Zald, 1977).

10. In the short history of social movement studies as a discipline, the notion of resources has occupied a central spot, in particular in the framework of the theoretical current known as "resource mobilization." Since the 1970s, American sociologists like Tilly (1978) and McCharty and Zald (1977) have focused their attention on the role of resources in the emergence of collective action. Movements and movement organizations were seen as rational actors calculating the costs and benefits and being heavily influenced by the presence (or lack) of resources. Resources, both material (e.g., services and funding) and immaterial (e.g., social relationships, authority), determined tactical choices of social actors. In this chapter, however, I rely on a definition of resources that 1) emphasizes immaterial and symbolic resources

such as knowledge, meaning and narratives, while virtually ignoring material resources, and 2) focuses on the interaction between said resources and social actors, both collective and individuals.

11. However, this supposed lack of formal affinity groups within the Occupy camps might be explained by the fact that activists did not have to go out on direct actions. Certainly people quickly learned to work together, creating a number of thematic working groups to address the different challenges of running a camp.

12. This is only partially true; the picture is more nuanced. WikiLeaks, Anonymous, and Occupy share an emphasis on "structureless" organizational forms geared towards participation, project ownership, and transparency *towards members*. However, to profane eyes they might appear to be characterized rather by "opacity...by design" (Barnett, 2010). Further, structure is likely to matter more than activists like to think. Actions and organizational forms risk being ephemeral; impact and effectiveness might be hindered by the lack of sustained structure.

13. However, insider accounts of WikiLeaks show that, in reality, the ethos of cloud protesting did not fully work for the organization, given the dominant role of one individual in WikiLeaks.

14. In this respect, the cloud has the potential of influencing not only the nature of civic engagement, but also the tactics adopted by activists. It fits resource-poor activists, who would otherwise lack the resources to organize a grand street protest. This is the case also with Anonymous actions: as dedicated software and botnets become increasingly available online, launching large-scale disruptive actions becomes easier.

15. A hashtag is a metadata tag, in other words a keyword assigned to a piece of information to make sense of it by assigning it to categories.

References

Barlow, J. P. (1996). "A Declaration of Independence of Cyberspace". https://projects.eff.org/~barlow/Declaration-Final.html

Barnett, J. (2010). "WikiLeaks and a Failure of Transparency", *Nieman Journalism Lab*, 29 July. www.niemanlab.org/2010/07/wikileaks-and-a-failure-of-transparency/

Bennett, W. L. (2003). "Communicating global activism: strengths and vulnerabilities of networked politics", *Information, Communication & Society*, 6(2), pp. 143–168

Bennett, L. W. and A. Segerberg (2012). "The logic of connective action", *Information, Communication & Society*, 15(5), pp. 739–768

Bennett, W. L. and Segerberg, A. (2011). "Digital media and the personalization of collective action: social technology and the organization of protests against the global economic crisis", *Information, Communication & Society*, 14, pp. 770–799

Castells, M. (1996). *The Rise of the Network Society*. Cambridge, MA and Oxford: Blackwell

CNN World (2011). "Anonymous vows to take leaking to the next level", 23 February. Available online: http://articles.cnn.com/2011-02-23/world/

wikileaks.anonymous_1_wikileaks-world-s-most-dangerous-website-daniel-d omscheit-berg?_s=PM:WORLD (retrieved May 16, 2012)

Coleman, G. (2010). "What It's Like to Participate in Anonymous' Actions", *The Atlantic*, 10 December, http://www.theatlantic.com/technology/ archive/2010/12/what-its-like-to-participate-in-anonymous-actions/67860/

Critical Art Ensemble (1993). *The Electronic Disturbance*. New York: Autonomedia

Critical Art Ensemble (1996). *Electronic Civil Disobidience*. New York: Autonomedia

Delio, M. (2004). "Hacktivism and How It Got Here", *Wired*, 14 July, http://www. wired.com/techbiz/it/news/2004/07/64193?currentPage=all

della Porta, D. and Tarrow, S. (2005). *Transnational Protest and Global Activism*. Lanham, MD: Rowman & Littlefield

Edwards, B. and McCarthy, J. D. (2004). "Resources and Social Movement Mobilization", in Snow, D. A., S. A. Soule and H. Kriesi, (eds), *The Blackwell Companion to Social Movements*. Oxford: Blackwell, pp. 116–152

Finnegan, W. (2003). "Affinity Group and the Movement Against Corporate Globalization", in Goodwin, Jeffrey and James M. Jasper, eds., *The Social Movements Reader*. Oxford, Blackwell, pp. 210–218

Gastil, J. (1993). *Democracy in small groups. Participation, Decision Making & Communication*. Philadelphia, PA, and Gabriola Island, BC: New Society Publishers

Garcia, D. and G. Lovink (1997). "The ABC of Tactical Media". http://project. waag.org/tmn/frabc.html

Gorenstein Massa, F. (2010). "Out of Bounds: The Anonymous Online Community's Transition to Collective Action". Unpublished manuscript, Boston College

Hardt, M. and A. Negri (2011). "The Fight for 'Real Democracy' at the Heart of Occupy Wall Street", *Foreign Affairs*, 11 October: http://www. foreignaffairs.com/articles/136399/michael-hardt-and-antonio-negri/ the-fight-for-real-democracy-at-the-heart-of-occupy-wall-street

Langlois, A. and F. Dubois, (eds.) (2005). *Autonomous Media: Activating Resistance & Dissent*. Montréal: Cumulus Press

Levy, S. (1984). *Hackers: Heroes of the Computer Revolution*. New York: Dell/ Doubleday

Lichterman, P. (1996). *The Search for Political Community. American Activists Reinventing Commitment*. Cambridge: Cambridge University Press

Kriesi, H. (2004). "Political Context and Opportunity", in D. A. Snow, S. A. Soule and H. Kriesi, (eds), *The Blackwell Companion to Social Movements*. Oxford: Blackwell, pp. 67–90

Kriesi, H., Koopmans, R. WillemDuyvendak, J. and Giugni, M. M. (1995). "Social Movements Types and Policy Domains", in Kriesi H., R. Koopmans, W. Duyvendak, J. W. Duyvendak and M.M. Giugni, (eds), *New Social Movements in Western Europe. a Comparative Analysis*. Minneapolis: University of Minnesota, pp. 82–110

Jordan, T. (1999). *Cyberpower: The Culture and Politics of Cyberspace and the Internet*. London: Routledge

Jordan, T. (2002). *Activism! Direct Action, Hacktivism and the Future of Society*. London: Reaktion Books

208   *Stefania Milan*

Jordan. T. and Taylor, P. A. (2004). *Hacktivism and Cyberwars: Rebels with a Cause?* London: Routledge

McCharty, J. D. and Zald, M. N. (1977). "Resource Mobilization and Social Movements: A Partial Theory", *American Journal of Sociology*, 82, pp. 1212–1241

McDonald, K. (2002). "From Solidarity to Fluidarity: Social Movements Beyond 'Collective Identity' – the Case of Globalization Conflicts", *Social Movement Studies*, 1, pp. 109–128

McDonald, K. (2004). "One as Another: From Social Movement to Experience Movement", *Current Sociology*, 52(4), pp. 575–593

McDonald, K. (2006). *Global Movements: Action and Culture*. Malden, MA: Blackwell

Milan, S. (2012). "When Politics and Activism Speak the Same Language: Stewardship in Cyberspace According to Cyberactivists". Cyberdialogues Paper Series, Toronto: Canada Center for Global Security Studies

Milan, S. (2013). *Wiring Social Movements: Building Autonomous Communication Infrastructure Through Emancipatory Practices* (provisional title). Forthcoming, Palgrave Macmillan

Negri, T. and Hardt, M. (2004). *Moltitudine: Guerra e democrazia nel nuovo ordine imperiale*. Bologna: Rizzoli

Polletta, F. and Jasper, J. (2001). "Collective Identity and Social Movements", *Annual Review of Sociology*, 27, pp. 283–305

Snow D.A. and McAdam, D. (2000). "Identity Work Processes in the Context of Social Movements: Clarifying the Identity/Movement Nexus", in Striker, S., Owens T. J. and White, R., (eds), *Self, Identity and Social Movements*, Minneapolis: University of Minneapolis Press, pp. 41–67

Sterling, B. (1992). "Introduction". *The Hacker Crackdown*. New York: Bantam House. http://cyber.eserver.org/sterling/crackdwn.txt

Tarrow, S. (1994). *Power in Movement: Social Movements, Collective Action and Politics*. New York and Cambridge: Cambridge University Press

Tarrow, S. (2011). "Why Occupy Wall Street is Not the Tea Party of the Left. The United States' Long History of Protest", *Foreign Affairs*, 11 October, http://www.foreignaffairs.com/articles/136401/sidney-tarrow/why-occupy-wall-street-is-not-the-tea-party-of-the-left

Tilly, C. (1978). *From Mobilization to Revolution*. Reading, MA: Addison-Wesley

Tilly, C. and L. Wood (2009). *Social Movements, 1768–2008*, 2nd edition. New York: Paradigm Publishers

Vegh, S. (2003). "Classifying Forms of Online Activism: The Case of Cyberprotests against the World Bank", in Martha McCaughey and Michael D. Ayers, (eds), *Cyberactivism: Online Activism in Theory and Practice*, New York: Routledge, pp. 72–73

Wong, W. and Brown, P. A. (2012). "Nobody from Everywhere: IR and the Politics of Wikileaks and Anonymous". Paper for the BSIA conference, University of Waterloo, 17 April

12
Anonymous and the Politics of Leaking

Gabriella Coleman

Once used exclusively to refer to people who staged fearsome Internet pranks, today the name "Anonymous" belongs to many individuals and groups engaging in diverse genres of collective action, ranging from online stunts and political campaigns to expediting in-person protests. Their interventions have included protesting the Church of Scientology, hacking into servers to scour for politically worthwhile information to leak, and providing technological support for citizens in Tunisia, Egypt, and Libya during the 2011 Arab Spring revolutions.

Anonymous, despite its broad array of tactics, is often described by a rather narrow band of words: hackers, hacking, and hacktivism. But in contrast to other political groups associated with such activities, such as WikiLeaks, Anonymous is in fact more open and participatory, the name free to all and accommodating those with or without technical skills (Coleman, 2011; 2012). Nevertheless, by the summer of 2011, smaller, more exclusive groups of hackers became prominent fixtures within the Anonymous landscape and thanks to media obsessed with hackers (Thomas, 2003), these groups were catapulted into the limelight. Whether individual participants liked it or not, Anonymous became synonymous with hacktivism, hackers, and hacks.

Among Anonymous participants (commonly referred to as "Anons"), these hacker crews and individuals provoked considerable controversy and anxieties. They were encouraged or at minimum tolerated, often in the hopes they could provide politically significant leaks in much the same way as WikiLeaks. But as members of these groups such as Topiary and Sabu built prominent and extensive public profiles on Twitter and elsewhere, a notable number of Anons were disappointed, some even outraged, with what they saw as their personal self-promotion. The cultivation of fame clashed with a robust anticelebrity sentiment so central to Anonymous.

This chapter considers the tension between the anticelebrity ethic common to Anonymous and the growing visibility of their politics of hacking and leaking. "WikiLeaks," media scholar Finn Burton (2011) perceptively insists, "commands attention now, but, if it is to be truly successful, it will be the first word rather than the last, the advent of a method rather than the founding of a lone institution." Anonymous – although organizationally and ethically distinct from WikiLeaks – carried forward the *experiment* with leaking. Unlike WikiLeaks, a life project built over many years, the leaking within Anonymous arose organically over the course of mere months due to accidental discoveries and took a distinct course from WikiLeaks, which distributed leaks sourced from others. Hacker groups within Anonymous tended to seek materials themselves, rather than calling for whistle-blowers to pass data on to them. Unlike Wikileaks, whose founders were adamant that it was a legitimate media organization, Anonymous was not seeking to construct its actions as a journalistic endeavour.[1] Anonymous-led hacking and leaking, which received more consistent media coverage than other Anonymous campaigns, were still made possible with what WikiLeaks had set into motion and also were limited and shaped by Anonymous-bred ethical imperatives.

The lulzy birth of Anonymous

If one term embodies the seemingly paradoxical and contradictory character of Anonymous it is *lulz* (a corruption and pluralization of "lol," or "laugh out loud"). Lulz is Internet slang for something done "for the laughs." Lulz activities stretch from "safe for work" jokes and memes such as adorable LOLcats to sordid NSFW ("not safe for work" and thus potentially offensive or obscene) content to the most fearsome of trolling attacks, from invading other online forums with memes and spam, to ordering hundreds of pizzas, taxis, and possibly SWAT teams to the houses of any number of random unfortunates considered to be fun targets for the proponents of lulz.

Before 2008, the name Anonymous was used almost exclusively on the image board 4chan.org to deliver pranks – to "troll," in Internet parlance, targeting people and organizations, desecrating reputations, and revealing humiliating information, and it was done in the name of the lulz (Knuttila, 2011). Modelled on the Japanese image board Futaba Channel, 4chan is composed of over fifty topic-based forums, ranging from anime to health and fitness, and has long been perceived to be one of the most offensive quarters of the Internet. The "random" forum, /b/, teems with pornography, racial slurs, and lulzy humour derived from defilement and an anything-goes attitude.

Anonymous was so well known for its trolling that in 2007 Fox News dubbed Anonymous and 4chan as the "Internet hate machine" populated by "hackers on steroids." Anons, pleased with the attention, released a video, a grim parody that took cues from Hollywood-style slasher flicks, proclaiming Anonymous "the face of chaos," laughing "in the face of tragedy."[2] It was meant as an ironic, snide jest, but it also captured trolling's terrifying potential, especially for those not in on the joke. It was hard to imagine that six months after this video's release, others would seize the ethic of anonymity and concomitant iconography – headless men and women in black suits – to coordinate strident and earnest forms of protest.

The activism began soon after Anonymous started trolling the Church of Scientology in January 2008, impelled by Scientology's threats to sue websites that refused to take down an internal recruitment video of Tom Cruise praising the church's efforts to "create new and better realities."[3] The video was supposed to be serious and persuasive and use Cruise's celebrity to legitimate Scientology, but Internet geeks (and most others) saw it as a hilarious (and lulzy) attempt to bestow credibility on pseudoscience. The video promptly went viral.

It was clear that Anonymous's willingness to wreak havoc in pursuit of lulz was also, at least incipiently, done in defence of free speech and in opposition to the deceptions of Scientology. Statements such as the following, taken from an Anonymous IRC (IRC is a type of online chat room), crystallized the revolutionary, activist spirit beginning to take shape:

<Su> The ultimate scenario: Anonymous prank call + DDoS [Distributed Denial of Service attack, a method of pooling the resources of many computers in order to flood websites with traffic and temporarily render them inoperable], US and French Government renew fraud charges, tax evasions, and illegal activities charges, local Church pastors telling their congregation the evils of Scientology, former members and families interviewed on TV about experience, activist groups holding licensed rallies and protests, and the news covering all of the above with independent...

<Su> Keep in mind this is war of attrition. We can not bankrupt Scientology directly – this is about getting media attention, informing the public, wearing down their members, pissing off their IT/phone services, counter-brainwash their potential recruits, and for lulz

Soon after these distributed denial of service (DDoS) attacks and pranks, Anonymous shifted from (as one participating Anon explained to my class) purely delivered "ultra-coordinated motherfuckary" to dissemination of incriminating facts about Scientology and forging bonds with an older generation of dissidents highlighting the church's use of censorship and abuse of human rights. Trolling had thus given birth to an earnest activist endeavour, as if Anonymous had emerged from its online sanctuary and set out to improve the world.

Ironically, Anonymous's political awakening was aided by the distribution of "Message to Scientology,"[4] a video made for the lulz alone that lampoons Scientology and calls for a "systematic" dismantling of the church for "our own enjoyment." The video, one of many urging people to take action against the church, provoked a lengthy discussion among Anons in IRC rooms about whether they should protest in earnest or remain faithful to their deviant roots; they decided to hold street demonstrations. And so on February 10, 2008, an estimated 7,000 Anons and supporters hit the streets in over 127 cities around the world for a day of action against Scientology, events straddling the line between serious political protest and carnivalesque shenanigans. Although the protests were exceedingly well organized – websites were brimming with detailed organizational information and dozens of beautifully designed flyers to download, and IRC channels teeming with life as participants coordinated the global day of protests – many arrived lacking substantial knowledge about the Church and its abuses, much less any intention of becoming activists. After collectively staging a successful demonstration and arming themselves with relevant knowledge, many returned for subsequent protests.

This decision to continue to protest the Church, however, was not only a matter of individual desire and personal dispositions. The formation of a political will was sparked, in part by the success of the street demonstrations and especially the media coverage they received, a dynamic repeated many times in the history of Anonymous (Phillips, 2012). That evening, women and men in Guy Fawkes masks and black suits with signs announcing "We Are the Internet" could be seen on cable news shows around the world. Hundreds of photos and dozens of homemade videos from local protests were shared on Facebook, Internet Relay Chat, and Twitter. For many Anons, the campaign – and especially the reports circulating through both the backwaters of the Internet and the mainstream media – validated what came to be known as Project Chanology.

Protests against Scientology's crackdown on its critics, especially those who dared to disclose or circulate internal documents (which the church refers to as "secret scriptures") continued. Other Anons, satisfied with a lulzy day of action, simply returned from whence they came, the Internet; many of them now contest Anonymous's current political sensibility, deriding their peers as "moralfags" on 4chan, preferring to troll and trade in pornography. But the seeds of irreverence and deviance had been sown in Anonymous, and ever since, some degree of lulz, pranking, and tricksterism have still marked the operations of politically minded "moralfags."

So, over the course of a few months, the denizens of one of the Internet's seediest corners unexpectedly engendered a political movement. Many Anons started to self-identify as bona fide activists, albeit with an irreverent flair. Unrelated nodes would emerge, thus the name 'Anonymous' became an example of what media scholars define as an improper name: "The adoption of the same alias by organized collectives, affinity groups, and individual authors" (2012, p. 141). Over the course of a few years, the concept of Anonymous was mobilized by various political networks, and activists spearheaded dozens upon dozens of operations that would bring the attention of governments and media outlets the world over.

Botnets for justice and the revenge of the Lulz

<biella> i dont know how deep to ask about botnets
<g> it's an integral part of irc hacker culture
<biella> yea it is
<g> which is what we grew out of
<g> mixed with strong dose of 4chan (Conversation on AnonOps IRC)

Anonymous is distinctive for its organic political evolution, along with its feral, lulzy tricksterism and expert online organizing. The entity's organizing principles – anonymity (technically pseudo-anonymity), and the existence of multiple and often unrelated nodes of communication, make it difficult to assess how many people are involved. Participation is fluid. Anonymous includes hackers who break into systems, and others who stage denial of service attacks upon websites. These attacks are commonly augmented by the use of botnets. A botnet is a large collection of compromised computers, connected to a central command and control server from which the botnet owner can use the bandwidth and resources of all the compromised machines simultaneously to release crippling DDoS attacks on other servers. But hackers are only a subset of Anonymous. Many more people contribute in other ways, by editing videos, penning manifestos, or publicizing actions on any number of social networking platforms. Lacking an overarching vision and strategy, Anonymous usually operates reactively and tactically, along the lines proposed by Michel de Certeau. "It is always on the watch for opportunities that must be seized 'on the wing,'" he writes in *The Practice of Everyday Life* (1980, p. xix). "Whatever it wins, it does not keep. It must constantly manipulate events in order to turn them into 'opportunities.' The weak must continually turn to their own ends forces alien to them" (ibid.). This approach could otherwise potentially devolve into unfocused operations that dissipate the group's collective strength.

It is unsurprising, then, that nearly every commentator or journalist – including myself in my earlier writings – describes Anonymous as inaccessible, inchoate, and spectral, identifying its defining attribute as the provocative spirit of the lulz. To be sure, no single group or individual can monopolize the name and iconography, much less claim legal ownership over them, and its next steps are difficult to predict. But Anonymous is made possible due to a stable foundation of labour and friendships, skills and capacities, and technologies and infrastructure, including servers, botnets, and Internet Relay Chat platforms. Operations may be tactical, but they do not simply spring out of the ether and can often be easily linked to a particular network, such as AnonOps, AnonNet, or VoxAnon, to take three of the most important at the time of writing. At minimum, these networks usually will lay claim to, or deny that they are the source of, an operation.

One of the largest, most stable, and especially most prolific networks of the last year is AnonOps. Founded in autumn 2010, that December it earned the spotlight for mobilizing thousands to protest the actions of PayPal and MasterCard. Anons targeted these corporate pay portals after it appeared that they had bowed to governmental pressure to stop processing donations to WikiLeaks, which had become (in)famous for Cablegate, the release of scores of hitherto secret diplomatic cables. After someone announced the operation on a blog, news spread on 4chan and Twitter, and once officially reported by established media outlets, it attracted at first hundreds, and then thousands of participants, spectators, researchers, journalists, and, most likely, government agents. One Anon told me they too were taken aback at the multitude that had arrived at their shores.

Such large numbers could participate since AnonOps operates in a more open manner than WikiLeaks. Technical elites maintain a platform, notably IRC servers, that is an apt example of what sociologists of social movements define as a "free space" – a place where alternative identities can be forged, skills are developed, and associative ties are nurtured, all of which, under the right circumstances, might be mobilized for collective action (Polletta, 1999). AnonOps encouraged the use of a tool, Low Orbit Ion Cannon (LOIC), which individuals could use to contribute to the DDoS campaign. This openness does not necessarily entail transparency. As with most Anon-based DDoS operations, botnets are the real ammunition – a fact not exactly publicized. One participant put it in no uncertain terms: "The heavy lifting was done by a few people in the background [with botnets], using the masses with LOIC basically as cover for their activities."

Although the technical work of bringing down websites was coordinated by a select number of participants using botnets, a huge cohort of individuals also joined in the attack with LOIC. When used in December 2011, LOIC lacked privacy protections, so unless users took extra measures, it also put them at legal risk – something they were not informed of consistently. But participants were also able to feel collectively empowered by attacking the front-end websites of large corporations (back-end transaction processing infrastructure usually remained unaffected) and this mass participation rendered visible the level and extent of deep disenchantment with the corporate acts of censorship of WikiLeaks. This spontaneous gathering was one of the first large demonstrations conducted on the Internet; Anonymous provided the key infrastructure and a political vocabulary to channel and render visible the discontent over PayPal's and MasterCard's actions.

Even if DDoS attacks lean heavily on individuals with technical skills and capacities, these individuals are not vested with the power to commandeer every single operation. On IRC, where many operations are coordinated and discussed, users are generally afforded the freedom to initiate their own operations and channels. While the network founders and staff can and do ban individuals or a channel, or discourage an operation from flourishing, most IRC networks have a long tradition – and this is no different with Anonymous – of a laissez faire, hands off approach to the creation of new chat rooms by the users. Those who manage and control technical resources do wield extra power (admins can and do ban users with some frequency and will do so for violating explicit rules, informal norms, and over petty personal disagreements), but there is no one group with the authority to control and command the dozens of operations.

Still, when it comes to single operations, there usually are, as one Anon put it, "ad hoc leaders" who, if they stick around and continue to work, become prominent and trusted figures. Every operation has its own history and organizational culture, and of course the technologically naive rely on participants with technical skills. But individuals with fewer technical skills can and do become prominent operators and ad hoc leaders. One of the initiators of a key operation in the Middle East that provided technology assistance to revolutionary activists seeking to topple a dictatorial regime in January 2011 was neither a skilled systems administrator nor a hacker, but started the campaign, which he explained as follows during an IRC conversation:

> \<biella\>   but i am trying to figure out how it is that people come to start working with others and trusting each other
> \<biella\>   you seemed like a good person to ask as you have been around for a long time, know lots of folks, etc etc. it is just is so enigmatic and perhaps that is what it is
> \<a\>   well i think either doing something that gains you respect and in the process gets you 'friends'
> \<a\>   also if people help me i feel inclined to help in return
> \<biella\>   so what is an example of something you did that gained that respect (ofc keep it legal :-))
> \<biella\>   and also can you elaborate on the 'friends' bit
> \<a\>   well i founded and coordinated op ##
> \<biella\>   ok, yep, i can see why that would gain respect ;-)
> \<biella\>   i did not know that
> \<a\>   so i worked very hard for a while 4hrs sleep a night online 20hrs a day
> \<a\>   for 2ish weeks
> \<biella\>   and people started contributing and you all felt prolly close as a result
> \<a\>   yeah so up popped some individuals – who are now 'famous' and said can we help and i worked with them
> \<biella\>   like hacker types you mean?
> \<a\>   yeah ;)

Prompted by the Tunisian government's blocking of WikiLeaks, Anonymous announced OpTunisia on January 2, 2011. Anonymous leaned on a technical elite who could attack government websites and jam programs used by the dictatorial regime to spy on their citizens. They soon began acting more like a human rights advocacy group, enabling citizens to circumvent censors and evade electronic surveillance and sending care packages – created by the activist organization Telecomix – with advice and security tools.

This operation helped catalyze the string of Anonymous-led interventions in the Middle East, dubbed the Freedom Ops. By the end of January 2011, AnonOps seemed to be devoting itself entirely to activist campaigns, and some Anons lamented the waning of the lulz. Though many Anons were invigorated by contributing to the historic toppling of dictatorial regimes in the Middle East, for others there could be no clearer evidence that, in Anonymous, the "moralfags" were now in the ascendant.

Then came Operation HBGary, which replenished the lulz and laid the groundwork for future hacking and leaking. In February, Aaron Barr, CEO of the HBGary Federal security firm, claimed to have "pwned" (compromised) Anonymous, discovering the real identities of top operatives. It was reported in the *Financial Times,* he was ready to hand these over to the FBI. In response, Anons commandeered Barr's Twitter account and used it to spew 140-character racial slurs while following the accounts of Justin Bieber, Gay Pride, and Hitler. They hacked HBGary servers and downloaded 70,000 e-mails and deleted files, purportedly wiped out Barr's iPhone and iPad, and then published the company's data alongside Barr's private communications. Anonymous unearthed a document entitled "The WikiLeaks Threat," which outlined how HBGary, in conjunction with the U.S. Chamber of Commerce, Bank of America, and other security companies, might undermine WikiLeaks by submitting fake documents to the site. There was also evidence of plans to ruin the careers of WikiLeaks supporters, among them Salon. com writer Glenn Greenwald.

What started with retaliatory trolling ended up exposing what seemed to be a conspiracy so damning that members of Congress called for an investigative committee. Given that these were private firms, the evidence obtained by hackers could never have been procured through legal channels such as a Freedom of Information Act request.

The necessarily clandestine nature of such hacks was also criticized by those who saw it as counter to the ethos of transparency. At the time, however, most Anons were thrilled. After the hack, hundreds of Anonymous onlookers watched and discussed the flurry of trolling events on IRC, describing it as a "triumph":

<A5>   NPR asked me who did HBGary
<A5>   I told them "a team of Anonymous ninjas."
<A17>   HAHA
<A17>   yes!
<AF>   LOL

    <A6>   lol nice
    <A28>   lmfao
    <A17>   This is a triumph

The message to Anonymous participants and onlookers was clear: Anonymous had not become Human Rights Watch; the pursuit of a more "mature" agenda did not mean parting way with the lulz. This celebrated hack inspired technological elites to continue in this style, first with a breakaway group, LulzSec, and subsequently with Operation Antisec. This mode of hacking – publicly breaking into servers to expose security flaws and access politically sensitive information – had been uncommon to AnonOps, though other techniques, such as web defacing, were occurring (though covertly). Operation HBGary's success helped launch wings of Anonymous composed of smaller, more exclusive hacker crews dedicated to exposing security vulnerabilities and generating disclosures of e-mails and documents, further aligning the hackers with the goals of WikiLeaks. As one Anon put it, quite succinctly: "Operation HBGary was so explosive that there was a serious thirst for more."

These groups received an extraordinary amount of media coverage, particularly due to a remarkable 50-day hacking spree by the first of these groups, LulzSec, which was only loosely associated with Anonymous. Many Anons watched with glee as LulzSec unabashedly humiliated corporate giants and governments; their targets ranged from security contractors like Infragard, to PBS, the CIA, Sony Pictures, and the United States Department of Justice. The mood eventually soured after LulzSec retired and a new group, Antisec (composed of many of the same individuals) arose and rejoined Anonymous. They were tolerated for their potential political yields, such as leaks, but eventually, as we will see below, they were disliked by some for how they put the collective's ethical principles at risk through their cultivation of individual fame and status and their seemingly scattershot choice of targets to attack.

Ethics: e pluribus unum

[The] bottom line should be whether he tries to front [him]self off as a "leader" or "official" spokesperson, or "just" another anon supporter/volunteer. If he claims, or implies, some "special" status in group, without consensus of the group, that is definitely fucked up. [On the other hand], he seems very prolific and assertive, so by sheer dint of exposure, could become "known" as a "spokesperson", whether he claims this is "official" or not. (Excerpt from a collaborative document assessing the role of Barrett Brown, an Anon who frequently appeared on the news on behalf of Anonymous and was seen to become a media personality.)

When individuals collaborate, they invariably craft ethical principles – both informal and explicit values guiding action and interaction. Even if Anonymous resists formalizing ethical mandates, mores still take hold. Among Anons the revelation of self and especially the accumulation of individual public prestige is taboo (Coleman, 2012; Wesch, 2011). They replace attainment of individual recognition or fame with the attainment of it for the group as a whole – credit goes to Anonymous, not to any individual. Violations of this principle are often met with harsh public criticism and even banning from particular IRC networks. Anonymous may be politically a multitude – its name free to be taken by anyone, but ethically it is configured as *e pluribus unum*: Out of many, one.

For Anons, anonymity is sometimes an abstraction; at other moments they instantiate it via action. In preparing an op-ed, dozens of Anons contributed their thoughts about the power and limits of anonymity. Here is just one of more than a dozen musings on anonymity within a collaboratively produced digital document:

> What is important here is that the singular individual and his actions become subordinate to the "larger" yet anonymous result of the collective process that is the production of knowledge. It is the nameless collective and the procedures by which it is governed which in the end prevail over the necessarily biased and single-minded individual. Yet, at the same time, the individual's ability to contribute to this communal process of the production of knowledge has never been greater before.[5]

I witnessed this ethic in practice dozens of times, once when I shared an article from a well-known national newspaper on the reporter IRC channel. Many participants on AnonOps were indignant that the featured Anon had revealed details about his personal life to the reporter, an infraction made worse by the fact that he had not substantially contributed to the recent DDoS operations. One of the Anon IRC operators assessed the situation as follows: "Attempting to use all the work that so many have done for your personal promotion is something i will not tolerate." A number of Anons then called this person into a different channel, asked him to justify his actions. Unsatisfied with his answers, they kicked him off by z-lining (banning) him on this particular network.

Even if this anticelebrity stance is a living ethos, it alone cannot prevent concentrations of power, and some Anons certainly think that power had pooled to an intolerable degree, even if they are not forthcoming on this subject to the media. If much of the labor in Anonymous is political, there is also considerable internal soul searching. This spring 2011 critique targeted the administrators who run AnonOps:[6]

- If there are no leaders, then who is there to wrest control from?
- If there's no leaders, why couldn't everyone read PMs [private messages] in realtime?
- If there's no leaders, why couldn't everyone set the target for the LOIC hivemind?
- If there's no leaders, why do opers [network staff] have to be respected, and why can I be kicked/banned for mentioning __ name too many times? Why can I be banned for making a joke that ___ doesn't like?

This list concludes, "The statement that AnonOps was a leaderless command structure is the most dishearteningly effortless lie I've ever had to read from an Anon."

This discontent at the perceived concentration of power in AnonOps continued, with groups of Anons agitating against the network, and this frustration grew over the course of 2011 with AnonOps' promotion and support for elements such as the hacker group AntiSec (more on which below). In February 2012, some Anons, disillusioned with the current Anonymous IRCs, founded the new network VoxAnon. The founders released a Constitution stating the network's purpose and the role of its technical guardians. Quoting a small section offers a rather precise sense not only of how these participants strove for a moral commonweal, but their awareness of the ways that technological capacities, realities, and skills constrain ethical realities:[7]

1. This Network upholds a policy of unconditional free speech, unless that speech poses a direct threat to the network. Such a threat must be proven.
2. Network Administrators must not/are not allowed to interfere in channel management unless required to do so in order to prevent

a direct threat to the network, or if the channel owner explicitly requests for a network administrator to do so.

3. You have the right to privacy in private channels. No oper may join a private channel unless invited, or to prevent a direct threat to the existence of the network.

At the time of this writing it is too early to predict how VoxAnon will fare, especially in comparison to other networks that favour implicit and tacit norms rather than explicit statements. But ethical life within Anonymous is everywhere predicated not only on ideals that run deep but also on experimentation, though with greater or lesser success and often in reaction to the rise of new patterns and possibilities.

The summer of endless hacks

"If we can get that level of information then we really are the private CIA lol." – Greg Hoglund, Chief chief Technology technology Officer officer of government cybersecurity contractor HBGary Federal (comment shortly before being mercilessly hacked by Anonymous in February).[8]

As one of only a handful of outsiders in daily contact with Anonymous, I became an important conduit for information about their activities and history. Over the winter and spring of 2011, I gave over 70 interviews to journalists, students, and filmmakers, during which I routinely sought to stamp out misconceptions, especially those concerning hacking. I explained repeatedly that hacking is only one weapon of many that are employed by Anonymous, and some ops vehemently oppose hacking and even DDoSing. Anonymous, I insisted, also engages in other work: writing stirring press releases and manifestos, designing propaganda posters, and making videos. After a certain point, however, no one was listening, and understandably. Beginning in May, but peaking in June, barely a day passed without major media outlet reporting a hack, defacement, or security leak. It became the summer of endless hacks. On Twitter, the hacker organization and publication 2600, whose website had been momentarily toppled by LulzSec, captured the mood in a mere 140 characters: "Hacked websites, corporate infiltration/scandal, IRC wars, new hackers groups making global headlines – the 1990s are back!"[9]

Hacking had been a tactic central to the AnonOps network, but it largely existed as an underground affair, coordinated in any number of invite-only IRC chat rooms. One particularly important private IRC chat room, #internetfeds, operated like a secret bunker of hackers, administrators who ran core infrastructure, and those with access to botnets. Though they contributed essential technical work, these hackers remained hidden. This all changed when some of the hackers involved in Internet Feds went on to form LulzSec, the first breakaway group to fuse hacking exploits with witty, often taunting, Twitter messages and entertaining videos featuring Internet memes such as Nyan cats and pirates. LulzSec distanced itself from Anonymous, partly due to the unfavourable reaction prompted by its infamous Sony PlayStation Network hack, controversial among Anons for targeting "innocent customers," as one Anon explained it to me:

> They split initially because they wanted to do things which they knew would upset other Anons, that's why LulzSec became LulzSec. After the Sony hack, they realized that such tactics would meet with a lot of irritation from Anons ... They wanted to continue with their "sledgehammer" approach, that being, attacking innocent customers as a way of totally destroying a company. [T]hey had to deal with the fallout of that hack and a lot of anger from Anons, it caused infighting and civil war, a LOT of drama. Would seem at that point that x just said "Look, this is going to happen every time we hack like this in the name of Anon so let's relabel it and avoid clashing.

Although some LulzSec participants were motivated by political causes – in fact, they conceptualized their work as following the WikiLeaks mold – they also felt constrained by AnonOps' informal codes of conduct, such as the mandate to never attack the press (Olson, 2012). By breaking away from Anonymous, they could hack as they pleased, for whatever reason, without provoking disparaging rants from Anonymous: for the lulz, to make a political point, to expose the weak state of Internet security, or for all these reasons at once.

On May 7, 2011, LulzSec initiated a 50-day hacking spree, first by targeting Fox News, then everything under the sun, from government agencies to television broadcasters. With constant coverage on TV news and newspaper front pages, hackers and hacking groups became the public (and notorious) face of Anonymous, even if other operations were ongoing and LulzSec had, for the time being, proclaimed its independence from Anonymous. On May 13, 2011, LulzSec declared on Twitter: "Must say again: we're not AnonOps, Anonymous, a splinter group of Anonymous, or even an affiliate of Anonymous. We are #Lulzsec :D"[10] Although LulzSec and Anonymous shared a kindred spirit, culture, and even some personnel, there was enough ideological distance between the two that many Anons, along with security professionals, geeks, activists, and hundreds of thousands of Twitter followers, either seemed to genuinely enjoy their antics and supported them, or at least were compelled enough to watch the wild show LulzSec put on.

This small crew of hackers, embroiled in their own dramas, eventually retired on June 25, 2011, but many of the same individuals subsequently banded under "Antisec." Now, unlike what they had done with LulzSec, they branded themselves loud and proud as an Anonymous operation. While not forsaking deviant humour, the tone became more militant. Governments, law enforcement agencies, and private security firms were targeted in the name of political causes.

As weeks turned into months, criticism mounted of Antisec's defacements and hacks, even in the context of continued support. Antisec was seen as acting recklessly, and many were suspicious of its motives. Eventually, rumours swirled that Antisec might even be a false flag operation – that is, external saboteurs were using it to discredit and destabilize Anonymous. Antisec became gnarled in controversy among Anons with what was seen to be its cultivation of fame, individuals inside it building prominent public profiles. This sentiment is captured in the following "tale" relayed on IRC in September 2011 by one active Anon, right before quitting:

<ha> wtf happened to #antisec
<ha> let me tell you a story
<ha> gather round kids
<ha> Once upon a time there was a team of status fag hackers, most of which where okay as people, we all have our flaws. They came to be known as lulzsec
<ha> These hackers decided it would be a good idea to use there [sic] status fag powers to gather anons against the infosec industry.
<ha> It was then someone decided to give monkies machine guns and taught them the weakness of sql tables[11] [a database system commonly used in websites]. These monkies decided they wanted to look good for lulzsec and hacked every possible thing they could, releasing all the information they plundered reguardless[sic] to such things as consequence and public realtions[sic].
<ha> Private data leaked faster then WikiLeaks brand condom.
<ha> They continued hacking away hoping to gain a pat on the back from Sabu.
<ha> Then the summer vacation ended.

<ha> They found themselves unable to continue there [sic] hackery as more pressing matters became apparent, such as who do i sit with during lunch and whats a cooler elective to take, french or band.
<ha> Thus ends the saga of #antisec

Some Anons, like ha, slammed this status-seeking behaviour. However, others, even some of those critical of what they called "fame whoring" still stood by the crews' actions, hoping Antisec would find (worthwhile) political leaks, or classified or secret information impossible to procure legally.

It is rather unsurprising that Antisec was simultaneously respected, tolerated, and vilified. The name Anonymous is difficult to police, and many of these hackers had been an essential part of the Anonymous/AnonOps constellation. They became significant just when WikiLeaks seemed to be fading or crumbling from internal frictions and legal troubles. Antisec, it was hoped, could more directly challenge the power of corporations or governments, not simply by producing momentary spectacles as is the case with DDoS attacks, but by finding and releasing hard evidence of corporate or government malfeasance (although the act of hacking, like the DDoS, certainly also worked as spectacle). Some Anonymous participants had hopes that breakaway hacker groups such as Antisec would acquire and release data that would shed light on the shadowy world of the intelligence and cybersecurity industry, especially the "private CIA," that is, corporations with government contracts to supply surveillance, data mining, and propaganda services to Western governments.

This outsourcing is not entirely new. Pinkerton Government Services, to take one of the most famous examples, is an American security company that was established in 1850. Its operatives were routinely hired by the US government (and corporations) to break up unions. What is new is the extent of the industry *and* the lack of credible information about its operations. The intelligence contracting industry may now be at the centre of government security and intelligence work. So posits Tim Shorrock, one of the few investigative journalists to research this topic extensively. Yet information is scarce, as he explains:

Outsourcing has become so pervasive that the Director of National Intelligence decided to study the phenomenon last year. But when the report was finally completed in April 2007, the results were apparently so stunning that the DNI vetoed the idea of putting out a report and instead told reporters that disclosure of the figures would damage national security.[12]

Although Antisec targeted many different organizations and engaged in other activities unrelated to leaking, they were one of the few groups prepared to tackle the murky world of government defence contractors. For better or worse, their activities were also magnified and amplified by constant media coverage. Among Anons, they commanded, if not exactly admiration, a hope or expectation of unveiling the inner workings of a world seemingly beyond democratic oversight: The three-letter-agencies, with their opaque budget allocations and their privatized and semi-privatized spin-offs and subsidiaries.

After a year of hacking, news broke on March 6, 2012 that Sabu, the most famous of the LulzSec and Antisec hackers, was, subsequent to his arrest and at least since the late summer of 2011, working as an FBI informant. It confirmed the long-standing suspicion that informants had infiltrated Anonymous and that Antisec had been at least partly manipulated by government interests. Mistrust, always hanging over the Anonymous networks, thus started to give way to a bleaker, ominous paranoia.

With many of its core members arrested, Antisec has, for now, taken a back seat. Other, smaller groups of hackers, LulzSec Reborn and the Ateam continue to deface, hack, and leak. A new leaking platform, Par: AnoiA (Potentially Alarming Research: Anonymous Intelligence Agency), with some participants from Antisec are now publishing leaks. Those currently involved are doing their work a little more quietly, leaving named individuals, even if pseudonymous, out of the equation.

Conclusion

In an age of atomization, when individuals seek profit or, at minimum, recognition for every expression and creation, Anonymous has captivated the public's imagination precisely because it provides a provocative antithesis to the contemporary cult of celebrity. Nevertheless, Anonymous does not signal the reappearance of the mass political subject united by one program or aspiration. It is not a united front, but a multitude, a rhizome, a "hive mind" in the parlance of those participating, comprising numerous different networks and working groups that are often at odds with one another and displaying evidence of hierarchies, power bases among individuals, as well as cliques and elite groups. This is one reason Anonymous spawns new groups and networks, like VoxAnon and Antisec, and why new operations appear seemingly out of the blue: in one month, June 2012, interventions appeared in Quebec, India, and Japan.

Every new network cultivates a distinct political culture. But Anonymous still shares some unifying ideals, such as the brazen spirit of lulz and its anticelebrity ethic, whereby the accumulation of individual public power and prestige is cast in a negative light; it is one of the core reasons that hacker groups who became so famous over the last year internally received so much flak. Anonymous thus is not just an array of political groups, a series of IRC servers, a collective of tricksters, hackers, and activists, and an Internet subculture. It represents a mindset, an adherence to a humourous aesthetic and a moral sensibility that binds participants the world over into one entity: Anonymous can, more than anything else, be described as an idea, and as was said by Topiary of LulzSec prior to his arrest: "You cannot arrest an idea."[13]

Anonymous nevertheless manifests only through its diverse, often contradictory practices and tactics, from releasing videos and manifestos to forging alliances with other activists, as was the case when Anonymous became a prominent public relations mouthpiece for the Occupy movement. For well over a year, hacker groups part of, or affiliated with, Anonymous experimented with the activist tactic of hacking to leak, with many successes and failures. The most significant threat to their survival has been government crackdowns. Scores of hackers around the world have been arrested and face decades in jail. And while there have been some politically significant revelations released by the hacker groups over the years, the rising tide of leaks that many Anons and others had hoped for was never quite realized – in terms of high-impact leaks, they delivered more of a trickle than a flood.

Their actions also shed light on constraints brought by media presence and status. For these hacker groups, spectacle was also essential for gaining attention, but perhaps media attention and column inches became an end in itself. With this came the constant need to outdo themselves, to surpass what had already been staged to prevent a fickle media turning its eye elsewhere. Antisec became trapped, needing to produce a dramatic show and at times exaggerating the importance of their leaks. On top of it, the media gave less attention to some Anonymous operations in favour of playing up others. In a frank moment of journalistic self-criticism, Quinn Norton (2012) reflects thoughtfully on myopias in the last year of Anonymous media coverage:

> Antisec, and LulzSec before it, enjoyed huge media attention from people like Olson and myself, to the point where they marginalized more effective anon ops around the Arab Spring and political

resistance to anti-internet laws like ACTA – even when sometimes these ops were done by the same people ... We should have seen Antisec as one phenomenon among many, not as a group we could finally treat like rock stars, a group that made our job easy.

Surely these hacker groups felt pressure to not disappoint, to not leave their audience waiting, and to make each new performance, each leak, more spectacular than the last. This might also explain why the choice of targets became more scattershot with time, the pressure to satisfy expectations an ever-growing factor. Though media presence is essential, it can become counterproductive to political movement building in general (Anderson 2011, Gitlin 2003) and in specific for effective hacking, where choosing targets carefully and painstakingly gathering information that is worth leaking to the public becomes a harder or secondary task to sating the press and public hunger for more spectacle.

Notes

I would like to thank the editors of this volume, Danielle Citron, Whitney Phillips, and various Anonymous participants for their generous feedback. Small portions in the first two sections have previously appeared in E. G. Coleman (2012) "Our Weirdness Is Free, The logic of Anonymous – online army, agent of chaos, and seeker of justice," *Triple Canopy*, http://canopy-canopycanopy.com/15/our_weirdness_is_free

1. While Antisec members always claimed responsibility for the hacks, there were rumours that some key hacks were sourced from other hacker crews.
2. https://www.youtube.com/watch?v=RFjU8bZR19A, accessed May 24, 2012.
3. http://www.youtube.com/watch?v=UFBZ_uAbxS0, accessed June 12, 2012.
4. http://www.youtube.com/watch?v=JCbKv9yiLiQ, accessed June 25, 2012.
5. Document on file with the author.
6. Document on file with the author.
7. http://wiki.voxanon.org/wiki/Constitution_of_Voxanon, accessed July 5, 2012.
8. http://pastebin.com/raw.php?i=u4mtivNN, accessed July 2, 2012. HB Gary took it upon themselves to place suspected hackers under surveillance.
9. https://twitter.com/2600/status/76931363755925504, accessed July 10, 2012.
10. https://twitter.com/LulzSec/status/69051330660007936
11. This refers to SQL injection, a very common technique used by hackers to break into websites. This type of attack is noteworthy in that it takes little technical skill or knowledge to perform and was one of the most common methods used by Antisec to perform their hacks.
12. http://timshorrock.com/?page_id=141, accessed July 10, 2012.
13. https://twitter.com/atopiary/status/94225773896015872, accessed June 21, 2012.

228   *Gabriella Coleman*

References

Anderson, C. (2011). "Spotlights and Shadows Revisted: The Case of Julian Assange", *The New Everyday*/Cluster Politics in the Age of Secrecy and Transparency http://mediacommons.futureofthebook.org/tne/pieces/spotlig hts-and-shadows-revisited-case-julian-assange

Brunton, F. (2011). "After Wikileaks, Us", *The New Everyday*/Cluster Politics in the Age of Secrecy and Transparency, http://mediacommons.futureofthebook. org/tne/pieces/after-wikileaks-us

Coleman, E. G. (2011). "Hacker Politics and Publics", *Public Culture*, 23(3), 511–516

Coleman, E. G. (2012). "Our Weirdness Is Free, The logic of Anonymous – online army, agent of chaos, and seeker of justice", *Triple Canopy*, 15, http://canopy-canopycanopy.com/15/our_weirdness_is_free

DeCerteau, M. (1980). *The Practice of Everyday Life* Berkeley: University of California Press

Deseriis, M. (2012). "Improper names: Collective pseudonyms and multiple-use names as minor processes of subjectivation", *Subjectivity*, 5(2), 140–160

Gitlin, T. (2003). *The Whole World is Watching: Mass Media in the Making and Unmaking of the New Left*. Berkeley: University of California Press

Knuttila L. (2011). "User Unknown: 4chan, *Anonymity and* Contingency", *First Monday*, 16(10), http://firstmonday.org/htbin/cgiwrap/bin/ojs/index.php/fm/article/view/3665/3055

Norton, Q. (2012). "In Flawed, Epic Anonymous Book, the Abyss Gazes Back", Wired/Threat Level, http://www.wired.com/threatlevel/2012/06/anonymous-parmy-olson-review/all/

Olson, P. (2012). *We Are Anonymous: Inside the Hacker World of LulzSec, Anonymous, and the Global Cyber Insurgency*. New York: Little Brown

Phillips, W. (forthcoming). "The House That Fox Built: Anonymous, Spectacle and Cycles of Amplification", *Television and New Media*, http://tvn.sagepub.com/content/early/2012/08/27/1527476412452799.abstract?rss=1

Polletta, F. (1999). "Free Spaces in Collective Action". *Theory and Society*, 28, 1–38

Thomas, D. (2003). *Hacker Culture*. Minnesota: University of Minnesota Press

Wesch, M. (2011). "Anonymous, Anonymity, and the End(s) of Identity and Groups Online: Lessons from 'the First internet-Based Superconsciousness'", in Whitehead, N and Wesch, M. (eds), *Human No More: Digital Subjectivities, Unhuman Subjects, and the End of Anthropology*. Boulder: University of Colorado Press

13
The Internet and Transparency Beyond WikiLeaks

Jillian C. York

Not two months after WikiLeaks began to release the cache of diplomatic cables allegedly leaked by Pvt. Bradley Manning, Al Jazeera entered into a leaking experiment of its own. Though it was quickly overshadowed by growing uprisings in Tunisia and Egypt, "The Palestine Papers"[1] – a release of more than 1,600 documents from a decade of internal Israeli-Palestinian negotiations – marked an important milestone for Arab media. It was the first time a major Arab publication had been involved in notable whistle-blowing since 1986, when Lebanese paper *Al-Shiraa* exposed the Iran-Contra Affair.

Though their access to the documents may have predated WikiLeaks' release of the cables, it was clear that Al Jazeera was inspired by the whistle-blowing site, which had been making waves in the region for months already, since the release of the video *Collateral Murder*. Tunisia in particular was impacted by the cables, which – as Tunisian activist Sami Ben Gharbia would later claim – "helped tip the balance."

Though, as Tunisian activists would later attest, many citizens were aware of the corruption of the Ben Ali regime, the widespread sharing of that information in Tunisia, made possible by WikiLeaks' release, provided what academic Zeynep Tufekci has called "a mechanism that allowed everyone to overcome [pluralistic ignorance]" (Sims 2011).

The release of the cables in Tunisia was unique: WikiLeaks partnered with Nawaat.org – a longtime activist media site – giving exclusive rights of numerous Tunisia-related cables to Nawaat, to be published and translated on a special site called TuniLeaks. Gharbia, a co-founder of Nawaat who worked on TuniLeaks, told Al Jazeera that his team read the documents, published them with context, and translated them into French to allow Tunisian readers to understand them. The first posts on

TuniLeaks went live less than an hour after WikiLeaks published the diplomatic cables on its own site on November 28, 2010 (Ryan 2011). Demonstrating the effect of the cables on the Tunisian populace, Nawaat's editor stated on the day of the release that "it is striking to note the United States' preoccupation with human rights" (see: Nawaat 2010). In the conclusion to the post, the editor added: "What is certain in any case, is that transparency will always be a good thing."

In contrast, Egyptian activists stated WikiLeaks' influence on their uprising as minimal, yet the release of the cables – which exposed the brutality of the Egyptian government – created a shift in how US media covered the revolution, providing rich details on Mubarak's regime. In some cases, this stood in sharp contrast to the actions of the US government. Take, for example, the fact that the Department of State proposed Egypt's VP Omar Suleiman as Mubarak's successor (Cooper and Landler 2011). The media quickly reported his personal role in the CIA's extraordinary rendition program and torture, laid out in the WikiLeaks cables (Cole and Wali, 2011), and they were credited with quickly scuttling his chances of stepping in as Egypt's leader (Youssef, 2012).

By the time WikiLeaks was ready to release another round of US diplomatic cables, more Arab publications had stepped forward. *Al Akhbar*, an independent Lebanese paper, somehow obtained cables that had not previously been published on WikiLeaks' own site and posted the 183 cables in their original English on its website, promising to translate them into Arabic. (See also Lisa Lynch's chapter in this volume.)

A Moroccan version of TuniLeaks – aptly titled MoroLeaks – also later cropped up to publish and translate cables related to Morocco. The importance of this project increased as the government sought to ban publications highlighting the cables focusing on Moroccan government corruption. One such publication was the daily *Al Quds Al Arabi*, which published a piece entitled "Moroccans discover the 'truth' about their officials because of 'WikiLeaks': A weak and naïve image, with many faces" (Maarouf 2010).

But while MoroLeaks provided access to the cables for Moroccans, they were not necessarily surprised by the contents. As one blogger wrote: "sensational stuff, but nothing we did not know before, and no immediate threat to the stability of the incumbent regime" (Zouhair 2010). Nonetheless, for some the release was inspiring; "For me, the leaked documents have transformed the notions of sovereignty and borders," wrote journalist Hind Subaï Idrissi (2010).

As companies reacted to WikiLeaks by cutting off payment mechanisms and cutting the site off from hosting services, the Anonymous movement also began to gain traction, and the zeitgeist in the Arab world began to bend toward transparency. As, by and large, Arab governments tried to censor WikiLeaks (Black 2010), a poll conducted by the Doha Debates found that support for WikiLeaks across the Arab world was widespread, with 60 percent of those polled stating belief that "the world is better off with WikiLeaks," and nearly 75 percent of respondents stated a desire to see WikiLeaks publish more on the Arab world (see: The Qatar Peninsula 2011).

It would appear that, although WikiLeaks was no more or less a catalyst of the Arab Spring than Facebook, it has shifted attitudes toward government transparency, perhaps shaping the trajectory of future uprisings. As *Egypt Independent* columnist Ahmed El-Sawi asked, "imagine what a hypothetical 'Arab WikiLeaks' would reveal about our regimes?" (2010).

An age of transparency

In the time that has passed since Tunisians made their first bold foray onto the streets of Sidi Bouzid, there has indeed been a greater push for transparency in the Arab world, made apparent by ongoing activism in the countries touched by the Arab Spring, as well as in others.

In Egypt, for example, where activists stormed the state security offices just weeks after Hosni Mubarak stepped down as president, civil society groups submitted a draft Freedom of Information Act to the People's Assembly – Egypt's lower House of Parliament – with the goal of creating the position of an independent Information Commissioner to arbitrate requests (Egyptian Initiative for Personal Rights, 2012). The draft act states that it is responsibility of governmental and private agencies to "routinely and periodically publish essential data, and to facilitate their information officials in making information available."

Similarly, in January 2012, Tunisia's post-revolution Constituent Assembly voted 149–3 in favour of including a clause in the new constitution that would guarantee transparency and open government (Keskes 2012). The clause, Article 62, reads: "Public information is the rule, secrecy is the exception," and leaves room for exceptions to be determined by committee. A group called OpenGovTN,[2] whose aim is the inclusion of Tunisian citizens in the government's decision-making processes, proposed the clause.

Amidst the unending conflict in Syria, activists have taken matters into their own hands, hacking into and leaking information from the accounts of government officials, including President Bashar al-Assad.

These "hacktivists" – some of whom claim affiliation with the amorphous Anonymous, others with the hacking collective Telecomix – are acting counter to the designs of the government, which has utilized sophisticated surveillance technology to spy on activists and citizen journalists.

Of course, it is important to note that over the past decade, young tech-savvy activists have been pushing for greater transparency through various initiatives, many of which make use of widely available online tools. For example, years before Egyptians stormed the state security apparatus, they had created Piggipedia, a Flickr directory of police involved in torture or brutality.[3] Years before thousands poured into Tahrir Square, bloggers used video to cover protests that journalists ignored; as blogger Wael Abbas wrote about the Kifaya movement in an op-ed in 2007, "[We] bloggers decided to take matters into our own hands. We believed in the people's right to know" (Abbas 2007).

In Morocco – four years before the Feb20 movement made international headlines, the "Targuist sniper" had bravely set up his camera on a hilltop in the southern town of Targuist to record police taking bribes, sparking an investigation of police forces (Abdo, 2007). And in Jordan, where King Abdullah recently promised reforms, including greater government transparency (Halaby 2011), bloggers have long been asking for the same thing. But as prominent blogger Naseem Tarawnah (2011) writes: "[Until] the state decides to embrace transparency and establish it as a first step towards serious reform in Jordan, one can only utter these five words with some relief: Thank God for the Internet."

While these initiatives indicate an evolving and growing trend, it is the climate that has formed in the wake of the Arab Spring and the rise of WikiLeaks that has allowed for greater collective action toward the common goal of transparency. What the vast majority of these initiatives – both those that predate and those that come after the Arab Spring – have in common is the Internet. And, tellingly, the openness of the Internet is increasingly under threat from both repressive and democratic governments.

As Micah L. Sifry asserts in his book, *WikiLeaks and the Age of Transparency*, the "battle over WikiLeaks" has "delivered a wake-up call to everyone who thought the free and open Internet was already a fact ... [While] the Internet has drastically lowered the barriers to entry into the public sphere, it has not eliminated them" (Sifry, 2011, p. 175).

Indeed, both the battle over WikiLeaks and the fights against online censorship that have taken place in Egypt, Tunisia, Syria and elsewhere exemplify this. Egyptian observers compared the telecommunications shutdown perpetrated by San Francisco's public transit police to their government's earlier version of the same (see Henry, 2011); in the same vein, China has justified its "Great Internet Firewall" by the censorious actions of Western governments (see: State Council Information Office of the People's Republic of China, 2010). And when the Obama Administration remains behind a wall of secrecy not unlike that of a less democratic government, it becomes easier for citizens of different nations to come together in the fight for transparency (see Timm, 2012).

The desire for transparency and freedom is an effect of repression, not of the Internet, yet the Internet remains the unique factor in this epoch. Its ability to connect us, both within a country and globally is, as Tufekci stated (Sims 2011), the mechanism that allows us to overcome our pluralistic ignorance; once we realize a common goal, we are more easily able to organize around it. And if that common goal is government transparency, then an online platform allows for a multitude of actors to contribute information to the cause.

In light of the controversy surrounding WikiLeaks founder Julian Assange, it is unlikely that the platform will carry global transparency efforts forward, but rather that will be done by one of its many successors. Ideally, a robust landscape of whistle-blower platforms would exist, taking away the risk of personality cult that undoubtedly occurred with Assange. To that end, there is GlobaLeaks – a leaking platform that will be available to a variety of clients, such as news sites or government agencies – as well as numerous other alternatives, like OpenLeaks, Cryptome, and proprietary sites like a forthcoming effort from press watchdog Reporters Without Borders.[4] It is also likely that local efforts such as those undertaken by TuniLeaks or MoroLeaks will continue to crop up when the time is right.

The future of the transparency movement beyond WikiLeaks is undoubtedly global and will certainly find its home online. The only question that remains, then, is if it can outrun the greater powers that seek to silence it. That concern is indeed an argument in favour of a diverse landscape beyond WikiLeaks; a mere replacement will not stave off the myriad threats that plagued WikiLeaks, from denial of service from webhosts and payment providers to the threats from governments facing Assange. Ensuring that transparency activism is the domain of many rather than few not only ensures that whistle-blowing will not become a partisan affair, but also that it will be able to thrive in censorious environments.

As the famous saying attributed to writer Stewart Brand goes, "Information wants to be free" – but as Cory Doctorow (2010) has argued, it is not information, but people, that wish to be free. Information is the catalyst, and the Internet the vessel that will allow transparency activism, beyond WikiLeaks, to thrive.

Notes

1. Al Jazeera's "The Palestine Papers" may be accessed at: http://www.aljazeera.com/palestinepapers/
2. OpenGovTN's website is available at: http://opengovtn.info.
3. The *Piggipedia* can be seen at http://www.flickr.com/groups/piggipedia/pool/
4. See: http://wefightcensorship.org/en.html.

References

Abbas, W. (May 27, 2007). Help Our Fight for Real Democracy. *Washington Post*. Retrieved from: http://www.washingtonpost.com/wp-dyn/content/article/2007/05/25/AR2007052502024.html

Abdo, L. (November 12, 2007). Morocco's "video sniper" sparks a new trend. *Menassat*. Retrieved from http://www.menassat.com/?q=en/news-articles/2107-moroccos-video-sniper-sparks-new-trend

Black, I. (December 17, 2010). How Arab governments tried to silence WikiLeaks. *The Guardian*. Retrieved from http://www.guardian.co.uk/world/2010/dec/17/arab-governments-silenced-wikileaks

Cole, M. and Wali, S. O. (February 1, 2011). New Egyptian V.P. Ran Mubarak's Security Team, Oversaw Torture. *ABC Nightline News*. Retrieved from http://abcnews.go.com/Blotter/egypt-crisis-omar-suleiman-cia-rendition/story?id=12812445#.UAhx2zH-98t

Cooper, H. and Landler, M. (February 3, 2011). White House and Egypt Discuss Plan for Mubarak's Exit. *New York Times*. Retrieved from http://www.nytimes.com/2011/02/04/world/middleeast/04diplomacy.html

Doctorow, C. (May 18, 2010). Saying information wants to be free does more harm than good. *The Guardian*. Retrieved from: http://www.guardian.co.uk/technology/2010/may/18/information-wants-to-be-free

Egyptian Initiative for Personal Rights (2012). Civil Society Presents Draft Freedom of Information Act: Freedom of Information Promotes Investment, Ensures Social Justice and Protects National Security ... Act Creates the Position of Information Commissioner Whilst Ensuring its Independence. *Press Release*. Retrieved from http://eipr.org/en/pressrelease/2012/03/01/1396

El-Sawi, A. (October 25, 2010). An Arab WikiLeaks? *Egypt Independent*. Retrieved from http://www.egyptindependent.com/opinion/arab-wikileaks

Halaby, J. (January 28, 2011). Unrest in Arab World Puts Pressure on Jordan's U.S.-Friendly King. AP. Retrieved from http://cnsnews.com/news/article/unrest-arab-world-puts-pressure-jordans-us-friendly-king

Henry, D. (August 16, 2011). #MuBARTek. *Media in Egypt* blog. Retrieved from http://www.mediainegypt.com/2011/08/mubartek-in-solidarity-with-egyptian.html

Keskes, H. (January 7, 2012). Constituent Assembly Members Vote in Favor of Transparency. *Tunisia Live.* Retrieved from http://www. tunisia-live.net/2012/01/07/constituent-assembly-members-vote-in-favor-of-transparency/

Maarouf, M. (December 6, 2010). Moroccans discover the "truth" about their officials because of "WikiLeaks" A weak and naïve image, with many faces. *Al Quds Al Arabi.* Retrieved from http://www.alquds.co.uk/index.asp?fname=today%5C06qpt90.5.htm&arc=data%5C2010%5C12%5C12-06%5C06qpt90.5.htm

Nawaat (November 28, 2010). TuniLeaks, les documents dévoilés par Wikileaks concernant la Tunisie : Quelques réactions à chaud. Nawaat.org. Retrieved from http://nawaat.org/portail/2010/11/28/tunileaks-les-documents-devoiles-par-wikileaks-concernant-la-tunisie-quelques-reactions-a-chaud/

The Qatar Peninsula (February 16, 2011). Majority in Arab World backs WikiLeaks. Retrieved from http://www.thepeninsulaqatar.com/qatar/142783-majority-in-arab-world-backs-wikileaks.html

Ryan, Y. (October 6, 2011). Breaking Through the Information Monopoly. *Al Jazeera English.* Retrieved from http://www.aljazeera.com/indepth/features/20 11/10/2011104115312389414.html

Sifry, M. (2011). *WikiLeaks and the Age of Transparency.* Berkeley: Counterpoint

Sims, J. (October 25, 2011). Zeynep Tufekci: Tech tools can overcome "pluralistic ignorance". *Events Archive of the Harvard University Kennedy School's Joan Shorenstein Center on the Press, Politics and Public Policy.* Retrieved from http://shorensteincenter.org/2011/10/zeynep-tufekci-tech-tools-can-overcome-pluralistic-ignorance/

State Council Information Office of the People's Republic of China. (2010). Australia Proposed Network Safety Inspectors to Combat Pornography. Retrieved from http://www.scio.gov.cn/wlcb/yjdt/201003/t555682.htm

Subaï Idrissi, H. (December 28, 2010). WikiLeaks or the New Frontline. *Talk Morocco.* Retrieved from http://www.talkmorocco.net/articles/2010/12/wikileaks-or-the-new-frontline/

Tarawnah, N. (January 24, 2011). Why Transparency May Be The First Step For Serious Reform in Jordan. *The Black Iris* Blog. Retrieved from http://www.black-iris.com/2011/01/24/why-transparency-may-be-the-first-step-for-serious-reform-in-jordan/

Timm, T. (January 26, 2012). Under Obama, the Freedom of Information Act is Still in Shackles. *DeepLinks* Blog of the Electronic Frontier Foundation. Retrieved from https://www.eff.org/deeplinks/2012/01/under-obama-administration-freedom-information-act-still-shackles

Youssef, N. (2012). Omar Suleiman, Egypt's longtime spy chief, dies in U.S. McClatchy. Retrieved from http://www.mcclatchydc.com/2012/07/19/156795/omar-suleiman-egypts-longtime.html

Zouhair (December 28, 2010). Moroccan WikiLeaks. *Talk Morocco.* Retrieved from http://www.talkmorocco.net/articles/2010/12/moroccan-wikileaks/

14
WikiLeaks and the Arab Spring: The Twists and Turns of Media, Culture, and Power

Ibrahim Saleh[1]

Introduction

In 2011, global audiences followed the uprisings across the Middle East and North Africa (MENA) with inspiration, fascination, and astonishment. The use of media technologies and social media platforms became a focal point of discourse and spurred debates between *techno-utopians* and *techno-dystopians* as to the role new technology played in what came to be referred to as the "Arab Spring." This chapter engages with the question of whether WikiLeaks' releases of material related to the Middle East and North Africa (MENA) contributed to the sudden explosion of angry protests, and it argues that such a connection exists, even though it has to be considered in the context of the broader media landscape and the political environment of the region. Further, the chapter places WikiLeaks in the context of emerging communication platforms, such as Facebook, Twitter, and YouTube, which provided a human narrative on the activities and effects of oppressive regimes in the MENA region and served as important tools in the fight for freedom and democracy. Social media helped dissidents to organize protests and voice anger, and their social and cultural effects concerned conceptions of the individual vis-à-vis established authorities, destabilized societal attitudes toward authority and established hierarchies, and highlighted their own role in the construction of knowledge.

The account provided here is based on hands-on experience in the region, as well as an understanding of the Arabic language and of the role of local cultures. The chapter opens with a brief outline of political and media-related contexts; then it discusses the role of WikiLeaks, and finally it broadens its perspective towards the uses of new media for political change.

WikiLeaks cables and the Arab Spring

The self-immolation by Mohammed Bouazizi – a desperate young fruit-seller – in Tunisia in December 2010 may have provided the spark for the revolution, which successively moved towards other countries of the region and soon came to be known as the Arab Spring. However the widely available proof of government corruption and hypocrisy based on an unstoppable flow of leaks was significant in fanning the flames of anger and agitation among citizens throughout the region.

On the eve of the revolutions, many countries in the MENA region were suffering from high rates of unemployment, widespread poverty, and a dysfunctional and propagandist media system that primarily served the interests of ruling elites. Dictatorships held a tight grip on social and political life in most countries, and civil society advocates and activists regularly faced harassment and punishment. Governments exerted strong control over all media through licensing, legal action, and the provision and withdrawal of financial resources (Saleh, 2011). The political culture in MENA was typically described as authoritarian and patriarchal in nature, and it enabled leaders to remain in office for long periods without significant challenges to their rule.

The Arab Spring changed the political climate as it uncovered the previously hidden (or rather, suppressed) conflict between authoritarian rulers and those who promote political change. At its basis was the transformation of social spaces into political spaces where deliberation on the problems of society emerged and quickly started to spread to different social sectors and locations. New information sources and communication tools were vital for this process. As a whistle-blower platform, WikiLeaks could play a significant role as a new window for unveiling the hidden ills of society, for naming and shaming individuals, and for establishing the issues that served as triggers for mobilization. WikiLeaks cables thus helped expose the "hot tin roof" of widespread discontent and helped to reveal the secrets behind closed iron walls (Bachrach, 2011, Chabaan, 2009).

To start off, WikiLeaks' release of the Cablegate documents offered a detailed account of corruption taking place in top levels of government in MENA. For example, several cables describe the lavish lifestyles led by former Tunisian President Zine al-Abidine Ben Ali and his extended family and linked them with cases of corruption to the extent of describing them as "the nexus of Tunisian corruption" (Crethi Plethi, 2011). As the revolutions unfolded, three further topics appeared in WikiLeaks cables and led to widespread public debate. The first concerns the diplomatic positions of Arab leaders toward Iran and Israel; second, the leaks highlighted the US backing of dictators in the region; and third, and particularly in Egypt, the WikiLeaks cables focused heavily on abuses of civil liberties. The following section will discuss these topics in more detail.

Cables demonstrated that Arab leaders were overwhelmed with fear of Iran, and they therefore encouraged other governments to take a hard-line stance. For example, the Saudi ambassador in Washington reminded the senior Americans that when it comes to Iran, King Abdullah told them "to cut off the head of the snake" (Bowen, 2010). Other cables showed that the Israeli-Palestinian dispute was not a priority on Arab leaders' agendas – very much in contrast to those leaders' public statements – and thus exposed the hypocrisy of the official Arab narrative that supported the Palestinian cause. As stated by Noah Pollak, the executive director of the Emergency Committee for Israel: "In private, we now know that the Arabs barely ever mention Palestine" (Duss, 2010). The Hudson Institute supported this argument and added that Arab leaders are far more concerned with shoring up, and directing attention from, their own dictatorships than they are with some notion of their acclaimed "justice" for the Palestinians (Duss, 2010).

The WikiLeaks cables not only exposed secrets about Arab leaders, but also demonstrated the US role in supporting dictatorships in the region, while expanding US interests in the region at a time when aging rulers were slowly losing their grip on power (Smith, 2010). Arab leaders were framed in cables as subservient to the interests of the United States, rather than to the interests of their own people (Richburg and Fadel, 2010). A cable from March 2010 emphasized Egypt's fears about the possibility of its neighbour Sudan splitting into two countries. In the cable, the foreign ministry official urged the United States to help postpone a referendum on independence for Southern Sudan, by stating that it will mean the creation of "a non-viable state" that could threaten Egypt's access to the River Nile (Ross, 2010). This disclosure contrasted with the official narrative that warmly welcomed the referendum.

Civil liberties were among the key topics exposed in the documents – in particular the brutal attacks by the Mubarak regime against journalists, bloggers, and artists. Cables discussed in detail a number of cases, for example the case of an amateur poet who was imprisoned for three months for allegedly "defaming" Mubarak, and the case of a blogger who was held at an airport for 13 hours and had his laptop confiscated by authorities (Alvarez, 2011). In December 2010, the *Guardian* (UK) published the US Embassy Cables stating: "They tolerate no advice or criticism, whether domestic or international. Increasingly, they rely on the police for control and focus on preserving power. And, corruption in the inner circle is growing. Even average Tunisians are now keenly aware of it, and the chorus of complaints is rising" (The Guardian, 2010).

Other dispatches were made public in January 2011 concerning the Mubarak regime that drew attention to concerns about Egyptian officials' treatment of jailed dissidents and bloggers and kept tabs on reports of torture by the police. For instance, a cable dated March 2009 discussed a Facebook-based group of young Egyptians that started the April 6 Movement, stimulating lively political debate and mobilizing significant protests that swept across Egypt. The cable described how group leaders were jailed and tortured by the police (Landler and Lehren, 2011).

Using social media for political change

Media in the Middle East and North Africa (MENA) have long been strictly controlled, particularly by a unified legal framework that was finalized in 1981 through multilateral cooperation within the League of Arab States (Saleh, 2003). Within this centralized media system, attempts to tame public outrage have included authoritative control over social media discourse, exercised by limiting Internet access, posting statements of support for the regime, and systematically spreading misinformation – for example, falsely announcing that protests had been cancelled in an attempt to limit their impact (Preston, et al., 2011). Not surprisingly, the state television headquarters in Egypt was the first site secured by the Supreme Council of Armed Forces (SCAF) during the protests in spring 2011, and the Minister of Information directed the content of TV programming to focus on the lawlessness caused by the protests (Fahim, 2011). The mainstream media narrative projected public anger as "foreign and violent," which helped the former regime to retain control in the early days of the protests. MENA governments attempted different tactics to marginalize the reporting of protests through the implementation of a series of restrictive practices, including censoring any information or documents by WikiLeaks related to the Arab Spring and the issues mentioned above.

However, these strategies proved largely unsuccessful over time. Protestors developed innovative communications techniques to overcome them, thereby mobilizing public support for the revolutions (Wagner, 2011). As established news sources were banned by governments, cables were spread around in other forms, and were also translated. Facebook was a popular tool used to pass crucial information during the uprisings. Research by Samir Garbaya (2011) on Facebook posts during the revolution and on the time spans between an event and its posting and commenting indicated an exponential decrease from four days in November 2010 to less than three minutes when the former president Ben Ali fled the country. Young activists also embraced YouTube, using videos to create a new political language. This breakthrough of former traditional limitations enabled the previously silenced voices to move beyond activists' personal ties and to connect with larger networks of groups and individuals. These new networks enabled groups to connect and articulate their shared discontent within the new street public in MENA (Wall and El-Zahed, 2011). News was co-constructed by bloggers and activists alongside journalists to support the distribution of information through avenues such as Twitter, in particular in times of major news events (Sutton, Palen and Shklovski, 2008); tools like Wikipedia were used to build collective memory[2] and to advance diverging positions.

Over the course of the protests, it became clear that the centralized regulatory systems in MENA could not stop the development and expansion of a grassroots movement, bolstered by the gradual decentralization of media and communications (Russell, 2011). In this context, one has to emphasize the role played by grassroots organizations such as Takriz in Tunisia, and April 6 in Egypt in circulating information released in the cables and sharing logistical information for mass protests (Pollock, 2011). Furthermore, government tactics to interrupt media backfired and accelerated the revolutionary mobilization by thwarting government attempts to control venues for organization (Hassanpour, 2011). Even within the realm of traditional media, opposition newspapers, such as *Al Akbar* in Arabic from Lebanon, and *Al-Masry al-Youm* in Egypt began publishing WikiLeaks documents. For instance, in a bold move, *Al-Masry al-Youm* published a number of critical cables that came out about the Tunisian regime, and about Ben Ali (Assange, 2011).

Yet the wide success of grassroots movements in harnessing media and communications in a restrictive media environment was hampered by several factors. First, government restrictions of online information through measures such as blocking and filtering, while not cutting off communication streams, compromised them significantly (Saleh, 2010). Secondly, economic factors undermined the engagement and participation of poor, uneducated, and unemployed citizens in MENA. The financial burden of using the Internet has prohibited access for many Arabs, even if they have the necessary motivation and skills. The use of tools such as Facebook, Twitter, and YouTube has largely been limited to the privileged elite, because of issues surrounding information literacy and accessibility. In 2009, according to a Gallup survey, less than 9 percent of Egyptians had Internet access at home, and only 3 percent had it in Yemen, even though the number is higher in other countries, climbing to 21 percent in Tunisia and 80 percent in Bahrain (Gallup 2009). Most social groups still rely primarily on the use of face-to-face interaction and organizational membership as the main channels of communication (Zhuo, Wellman and Yu, 2011). Furthermore, there is a strong generational gap between Internet-savvy and politically-interested younger populations, and older age groups (Iskander, 2011).

However, the Arab Spring has perhaps been most significant in overcoming these limits by generating spaces where collective dissent could be articulated through the dialectical relationship between online and offline political action. In many ways, one could say that the political *knowledge* derived from embodied experiences was combined with a pragmatic understanding of both the online and offline balance of power. It was this mixed effort of a new online space and of street-level organizations that spent hours talking with and persuading locals, posting fliers, and testing protest routes that made the Arab spring move from the online domain into the offline and real-life resolution in MENA.

Concluding remarks

The WikiLeaks releases played an influential role in fuelling public anger in the region and in shaping global audiences' understanding of the causes of what became known as the Arab Spring. By exposing hidden secrets, double standards, and hypocrisy by Arab leaders, they provided new perspectives on Arab politics, as well as confirming widespread suspicions, and thus put angry publics in direct confrontation with autocratic governments. WikiLeaks offered critical information, contributed to the mass mediatization of events both locally and internationally, and helped formulate and clarify both the critique of the existing political situation and democratic alternatives. It thereby constituted an important component of the revolutionary momentum that swept the region in 2011.

This chapter discussed the role of the WikiLeaks releases in the broader context of the effects of new communication technologies for social change. Recent events in the Arab region and elsewhere have demonstrated how technology, and particularly social media platforms, can be used to enhance protest mobilizations and democratic debate. Despite the problems of limited Internet access and social inequality, social media offered a space for participation and complemented the role of traditional media and face-to-face communication for information exchange. Particularly for younger and more affluent sectors of the population, the availability of social media offered new ways to voice their grievances to the outside world. Even though WikiLeaks cables were not given prime attention in the established media, alternative communication networks and connections emerged during the revolution that allowed advocates of democratic change to transmit and exchange information, despite governments' attempts to control and censor.

What happened in MENA is the amplification of political communication via participatory media with a new intensity that pushed individual voices beyond activists' personal ties to larger networks of other, perhaps previously unconnected groups and individuals, many of whom decided to articulate their discontent on the streets. The overall result of complimentary online and real-world actions could be considered a loosely synchronized enactment of a new form of Arab and Middle Eastern citizenship, based on a belief in the power of the ordinary and previously marginalized "third sector" to construct reality.

The lasting effect of the Arab Spring on media in the region is difficult to assess, but the WikiLeaks releases uncovered a struggle between the ideals of freedom and democracy, on the one side, and the narrow self-interests of regional rulers, as well as the ruthless demands of foreign interests, on the other. The chapter suggests that media stoked the flames of revolt by providing alternative, accessible information.

Notes

1. Arne Hintz and Heather Gilberds provided contributions to this chapter.
2. Collective memory plays a therapeutic function for community members, who actively participate in a sense-making process, interpreting and elaborating the past through the creation of different narratives and other memory representations. This negotiation of a crystallized shared experience allows the community to symbolize the trauma and provides better opportunities for coping and healing (Wang, 2008)

References

AFP (2011). Assange hails WikiLeaks role in Middle East revolt. *Agence France Press (AFP)*, (February 13, 2011). Available at http://www.google.com/hostednews/

afp/article/ALeqM5gNJhV-MEAbPHUuZ_WzQXzeXOrwAQ?docId=CNG.
e6210a294125e6051fab15d1b9c3fb5a.621

Alvarez, A. (2011). WikiLeaks' Cables Reveal Important Background on Egyptian Uprising. *Mediaite, LLC,* (January 28, 2011). Available at http://www.mediaite. com/online/recently-released-wikileaks-cables-reveal-important-background-on-egyptian-uprising/

Assange, J. (2011). WikiLeaks Role in Arab Spring. *Towards Freedom, Democracy Now,* (July 6, 2011). Available at http://www.towardfreedom.com/global-news /2455-wikileaks-role-in-arab-spring

Bachrach, J. (2011). Did WikiLeaks Spur Arab Spring? *World Affairs Journal,* (August 26, 2011). Available at http://www.realclearworld.com/2011/08/25/ did_wikileaks_spur_arab_spring_126995.html

Bowen, J. (2010). WikiLeaks opens window on the Middle East thinking. *BBC News,* (November 30, 2010). Available at http://www.bbc.co.uk/news/ world-us-canada-11874082

Chabaan, J. (2009). Youth and development in the Arab countries: the need for a different approach. *Middle Eastern Studies,* 45(1), 33–55

Duss, M. (2010). Linkage and its discontents: What WikiLeaks reveals about Israel-Palestine. *The Middle East channel,* (December 12, 2010) Available at http://mideast.foreignpolicy.com/posts/2010/12/16/ linkage_and_its_discontents_what_wikileaks_reveals_about_israel_palestine

Fahim, K. (2011). State TV in Egypt offers murky window into power shift. *New York Times,* (31 January, 2011). Available at http://www.nytimes. com/2011/02/01/world/middleeast/01statetv.html

Gallup Survey (2009). *Cell Phones Outpace Internet Access in Middle East.* Retrieved from http://www.gallup.com/poll/121652/cell-phones-outpace-internet-acces s-middle-east.aspx on July 10, 2012

Garbaya, S. (2011). *The other dimension of the virtual space in the revolution of freedom in Tunisia: from Facebook to Streetbook.* The North African Journal, March, 2011. Retrieved from http://www.north africa.com/social_polics/secu-rity_politics/446.html on July 10, 2012

Godec, R. F. (2009). US embassy cables: Tunisia – a US foreign policy conundrum. *The Guardian,* (July 17, 2009). Available at http://www.guardian.co.uk/ world/us-embassy-cables-documents/217138

Godec, R. F. (2011). WikiLeaks: U.S. Embassy Cables Deeply Unflattering about Tunisia: Cable Gate. *Crethi Plethi,* (July 17, 2009). Available http://www.crethip-lethi.com/wikileaks-u-s-embassy-cables-deeply-unflattering-about-tunisia/ usa/2011

Hassanpour, N. (2011). Media Disruption Exacerbates Revolutionary Unrest: Evidence from Mubarak's Natural Experiment, *APSA 2011 Annual Meeting Paper.* Available at http://papers.ssrn.com/sol3/papers. cfm?abstract_id=1903351&download=yes

Helfont, T. (2011). E-Notes: Middle East Media Monitor: WikiLeaks in the Arab Press. *Foreign Policy Research Institute,* (February 2011). Available at http://www. fpri.org/enotes/201102.helfont.wikileaks.html

Iskander, E. (2011). Connecting the National and the Virtual: Can Facebook Activism Remain Relevant After Egypt's January 25 Uprising? *International Journal of Communication* 5 (1), 1225–1237

Landler, A. and Lehren, W. A. (2011). Cables Show Delicate U.S. Dealings with Egypt's Leaders. *New York Times*, (January 28, 2011). Available at http://www.nytimes.com/2011/01/28/world/middleeast/28diplo.html?_r=1&pagewanted=all

Pollock, J. (2011). How Egyptian and Tunisian youth hacked the Arab Spring. *Streetbook Technology Review, MIT. Available at:* http://www.technologyreview.com/featured-story/425137/streetbook/

Preston, J., Kirkpatrick, D., Fahim, K. and Shadid, A. (2011). Movement began with outrage and a Facebook page that gave it an outlet. *New York Times*, (6 February). Available at http://www.nytimes.com/2011/02/06/world/middleeast/06face.html

Richburg, K. B. and Fadel, L. (2010). Media in China, Arab Middle East suppressing WikiLeaks coverage. *Washington Post*, (December 1, 2010). Available at http://www.washingtonpost.com/wp   dyn/content/article/2010/12/01/AR2010120106809.html

Ross, W. (2010). WikiLeaks memo reveals Egypt's Nile fears over Sudan. *BBC News Africa*, (December 3, 2011). Available at http://www.bbc.co.uk/news/world-africa-11913940

Russel, A. (2011). Extra-National Information Flows, Social Media, and the 2011 Egyptian Uprising. *International Journal of Communication* 5 (1), 1238–1247

Saleh, I. (2003). *Unveiling the Truth About Middle Eastern Media. Privatization in Egypt: Hope or Dope?* Cairo: Cairo Media Centre

Saleh, I. (2011). The challenges of media education in coercive societies: A case study of Middle East & North Africa (MENA). In Cheung, C.-K. (ed.), *Research in Media Education*, Nova Science Publishers, Inc., USA, 63–82

Smith, L. (2010). WikiLeaks Revelations: More Good than Bad? *Middle East Forum*, (December 28, 2010).Available at http://www.meforum.org/2815/wikileaks-revelations

Sutton, J., Palen, L., and Shklovski, I. (2008). Back-channels on the front lines: Emerging uses of social media in the 2007 Southern California wildfires. *Proceedings of the 5th International ISCRAM Conference – Washington, DC, USA, May 2008* Available at http://www.cs.colorado.edu/~palen/Papers/iscram08/BackchannelsISCRAM08.pdf

Wagner, B. (2011). "I Have Understood You": The Co-evolution of Expression and Control on the Internet, Television and Mobile Phones During the Jasmine Revolution in Tunisia. *International Journal of Communication*, 5 (1), 1295–1302

Wall, M. and El-Zahed, S. (2011). "I'll Be Waiting for You Guys": A YouTube Call to Action in the Egyptian Revolution, *International Journal of Communication*, 5(1), 1333–1343

Zhuo, X., Wellman, B. and Yu, J. (2011). "Egypt: The First Internet Revolt?" *Peace Magazine*. Available at: http://homes.chass.utoronto.ca/~wellman/publications/egypt/PMag-1107-Egypt-offprint.pdf

15
Twelve Theses on WikiLeaks[1]

Geert Lovink and Patrice Riemens

Thesis 0

"What do I think of WikiLeaks? I think it would be a good idea!" (after Mahatma Gandhi's famous quip on "Western Civilization")

Thesis 1

Disclosures and leaks have been a feature of all eras, however never before has a non-state or non-corporate affiliated group done anything on the scale of what WikiLeaks has managed to do, first with the *Collateral Murder* video, then with the Afghan War Logs, and most recently with Cablegate. It looks like we have now reached the moment that the quantitative leap is morphing into a qualitative one. When WikiLeaks hit the mainstream early in 2010, this was not yet the case. In a sense, the "colossal" WikiLeaks disclosures can be explained as the consequence of the dramatic spread of IT use, together with the dramatic drop in its costs, including costs for the storage of millions of documents. Another contributing factor is the fact that safekeeping state and corporate secrets – never mind private ones – has become difficult in an age of instant reproducibility and dissemination. WikiLeaks becomes symbolic for a transformation in the "information society" at large, holding up a mirror of things to come. So while one can look at WikiLeaks as a (political) project and criticize it for its modus operandi, it can also be seen as the "pilot" phase in an evolution towards a far more generalized culture of anarchic exposure, beyond the traditional politics of openness and transparency.

Thesis 2

For better or for worse, WikiLeaks has skyrocketed itself into the realm of high-level international politics. Out of the blue, WikiLeaks has become a full-blown player both on the world scene and in the national spheres of some countries. Small player as it is, WikiLeaks, by virtue of its disclosures, it appears to be on a par with governments or big corporations (its next target), at least in the domain of information gathering and publication. At same time, it is unclear whether this is a permanent feature or a temporary, hype-induced phenomenon. WikiLeaks appears to believe the former, and that looks more and more likely to be the case. Despite being a puny non-state and non-corporate actor, in its fight against the US government WikiLeaks does not believe it is punching above its weight – and it is starting to behave accordingly. One might call this the "Talibanization" stage of the postmodern "Flat World" theory, where scales, times, and places are declared largely irrelevant. What counts is celebrity momentum and the intense accumulation of media attention. WikiLeaks manages to capture that attention by way of spectacular information hacks, where other parties, especially civil society groups and human rights organizations, are desperately struggling to get their message across. While the latter tend to play by the rules and seek legitimacy from dominant institutions, WikiLeaks' strategy is populist insofar as it taps into public disaffection with mainstream politics. For WikiLeaks, political legitimacy is no longer something graciously bestowed by the powers that be. WikiLeaks bypasses this Old World structure of power and instead goes to the source of political legitimacy in today's info society: the rapturous banality of the spectacle. WikiLeaks brilliantly puts to use the "escape velocity" of IT, using IT to leave IT behind and rudely disrupt the realm of real-world politics.

Thesis 3

In the ongoing saga called "The Decline of the US Empire," WikiLeaks enters the stage as the slayer of a soft target. It would be difficult to imagine it being able to inflict quite the same damage to the Russian or Chinese governments, or even to the Singaporean – not to mention their "corporate" affiliates. In Russia or China, huge cultural and linguistic barriers are at work, not to speak of purely power-related ones, which would need to be surmounted. Vastly different constituencies are also factors there, even if we are speaking about the narrower (and allegedly more global) cultures and agendas of hackers, info-activists, and investigative journalists. In that sense, WikiLeaks in its present manifestation remains a typically "Western" product and cannot claim to be a truly universal or global undertaking.

Thesis 4

One of the main difficulties with explaining WikiLeaks arises from the fact that it is unclear (even to the WikiLeaks people themselves) whether it sees itself and operates as a content provider or as a simple conduit for leaked data (the impression is that it sees itself as either/or, depending on context and circumstances). This, by the way, has been a common problem ever since media went online en masse and publishing and communications became a service rather than a product. Julian Assange cringes every time he is portrayed as the editor-in-chief of WikiLeaks, yet WikiLeaks says it edits material before publication and claims it checks documents for authenticity with the help of hundreds of volunteer analysts. Content vs. carrier debates of this kind have been going on for decades among media activists, with no clear outcome. Instead of trying to resolve the inconsistency, it might be better to look for fresh approaches and develop new critical concepts for what has become a hybrid publishing practice involving actors far beyond the traditional domain of the professional news media. This might be why Assange and his collaborators refuse to be labelled in terms of "old categories" (journalists, hackers, etc.) and claim to represent a new *Gestalt* on the world information stage.

Thesis 5

The steady decline of investigative journalism caused by diminishing funding is an undeniable fact. Journalism these days amounts to little more than outsourced PR remixing. The continuous acceleration and overcrowding of the so-called attention economy ensures there is no longer enough room for complicated stories. The corporate owners of mass circulation media are increasingly disinclined to see the workings and the politics of the global neoliberal economy discussed at length. The shift from information to infotainment has been embraced by journalists themselves, making it difficult to publish complex stories. WikiLeaks enters this state of affairs as an outsider, enveloped by the steamy ambiance of "citizen journalism," DIY news reporting in the blogosphere, and even faster social media like Twitter. What

WikiLeaks anticipates, but so far has been unable to organize, is the "crowd sourcing" of the interpretation of its leaked documents. That work, oddly, is left to the few remaining staff journalists of selected "quality" news media. Later, academics pick up the scraps and spin the stories behind the closed gates of publishing stables. But where is the networked critical commentariat? WikiLeaks generates its capacity to inspire irritation at the big end of town precisely because of the transversal and symbiotic relation it holds with establishment media institutions. There's a lesson here for the multitudes – get out of the ghetto and connect with the Oedipal other. Therein lies the conflictual terrain of the political.

Traditional investigative journalism used to consist of three phases: unearthing facts, cross-checking these, and backgrounding them into an understandable discourse. WikiLeaks does the first, claims to do the second, but omits the third completely. This is symptomatic of a particular brand of open-access ideology, where content production itself is externalized to unknown entities "out there." The crisis in investigative journalism is neither understood nor recognized. How productive entities are supposed to sustain themselves materially is left in the dark: it is simply presumed that analysis and interpretation will be taken up by the traditional news media. But this is not happening automatically. The saga of the Afghan War Logs and Cablegate demonstrate that WikiLeaks has to approach and negotiate with well-established traditional media to secure sufficient credibility. At the same time, these media outlets prove unable to fully process the material, inevitably filtering the documents according to their own editorial policies.

Thesis 6

WikiLeaks is a typical SPO (Single Person Organization) or UPO (Unique Personality Organization). This means that the initiative taking, decision making, and execution are largely concentrated in the hands of a single individual. Like small and medium-sized businesses, the founder cannot be voted out, and, unlike many collectives, leadership does not rotate. This is not an uncommon feature within organizations, irrespective of whether they operate in the realm of politics, culture, or the "civil society" sector. SPOs are recognizable, exciting, inspiring, and easy to feature in the media. Their sustainability, however, is largely dependent on the actions of their charismatic leader, and their functioning is difficult to reconcile with democratic values. This is also why they are difficult to replicate and do not scale up easily. Sovereign hacker Julian Assange is the identifying figurehead of WikiLeaks, and the organization's notoriety and reputation merge with Assange's own. What WikiLeaks does and stands for becomes difficult to distinguish from Assange's rather agitated private life and his somewhat unpolished political opinions.

Thesis 7

WikiLeaks raises the question as to what hackers have in common with secret services, since an elective affinity between the two is unmistakable. The love-hate relationship goes back to the very beginning of computing. One does not have to be a fan of German media theorist Friedrich Kittler or, for that matter, conspiracy theories, to acknowledge that the computer was born out of the military-industrial complex. From Alan Turing's deciphering of the Nazi Enigma code up to the role played by the first computers in the invention of the atomic bomb, from the cybernetics movement up to the Pentagon's involvement in the creation of the Internet – the articulation between computational information and the military-industrial complex is well established. Computer scientists and programmers have shaped the information revolution and the culture of openness; but at the same time they have also developed encryption ("crypto"), closing access to data for the non-initiated. What some see as "citizen journalism" others call "info war."

WikiLeaks is also an organization deeply shaped by 1980s hacker culture, combined with the political values of techno-libertarianism that emerged in the 1990s. The fact that WikiLeaks was founded – and to a large extent is still run – by hard-core geeks is essential to understanding its values and moves. Unfortunately, this comes together with a good dose of the less savoury aspects of hacker culture. Not that idealism, the desire to contribute to making the world a better place, could be denied to WikiLeaks: on the contrary. But this brand of idealism (or, if you prefer, anarchism) is paired with a preference for conspiracies, an elitist attitude, and a cult of secrecy (never mind condescension). This is not conducive to collaboration with like-minded people and groups, who are relegated to being the simple consumers of WikiLeaks output. The missionary zeal to enlighten the idiotic masses and "expose" the lies of government, the military, and corporations is reminiscent of the well-known (or infamous) media-culture paradigm from the 1950s.

Thesis 8

Lack of commonality with congenial, "another world is possible" movements drives WikiLeaks to seek public attention by way of increasingly spectacular and risky disclosures, thereby gathering a constituency of often wildly enthusiastic but generally passive supporters. Assange himself has stated that WikiLeaks has deliberately moved away from the "egocentric" blogosphere and assorted social media and nowadays collaborates only with professional journalists and human rights activists. Yet following the nature and quantity of WikiLeaks exposures from its inception up to the present day is eerily reminiscent of watching a fireworks display, and that includes a "grand finale" in the form of the doomsday-machine-pitched, yet-to-be-unleashed "insurance" document (".aes256"). This raises serious doubts about the long-term sustainability of WikiLeaks itself, and possibly also of the WikiLeaks model. WikiLeaks operates with ridiculously small staff; probably no more than a dozen of people form the core of its operation. While the extent and savviness of WikiLeaks' tech support is proved by its very existence, WikiLeaks' claim to several hundreds of volunteer analysts and experts is unverifiable and, to be frank, barely credible. This is clearly WikiLeaks' Achilles' heel, not only from a risk and/or sustainability standpoint, but politically as well, which is what matters to us here.

Thesis 9

WikiLeaks displays a stunning lack of transparency in its internal organization. Its excuse that "WikiLeaks needs to be completely opaque in order to force others to be totally transparent" amounts, in our opinion, to little more than *Mad* magazine's famous Spy vs. Spy cartoons. You beat the opposition but in a way that makes you indistinguishable from it. Claiming the moral high ground afterwards is not helpful. Tony Blair too excelled in that exercise. As WikiLeaks is neither a political collective nor an nongovernmental organization in the legal sense, and not, for that matter, a company or part of social movement, we need to discuss what type of organization it is that we are dealing with. Is WikiLeaks a virtual project? After all, it does exist as a (hosted) website with a domain name, which is the bottom line. But does it have a goal beyond the personal ambition of its founder(s)? Is WikiLeaks reproducible? Will we see the rise of national or local chapters that keep the name? What rules of the game will they observe? Should we rather see it as a concept that travels from context to context and that, like a meme, transforms itself in time and space?

Thesis 10

Maybe WikiLeaks will organize itself around its own version of the Internet Engineering Task Force's slogan, "Rough consensus and running code." Projects like Wikipedia and Indymedia have both resolved this issue in their own way, but not without crises, conflicts, and splits. A critique such as the one voiced here is not intended to force WikiLeaks into a traditional format; on the contrary, it is to explore whether WikiLeaks (and its future clones, associates, avatars, and congenial family members) might stand as a model for new forms of organization and collaboration. The term "organized network" has been coined as a possible term for these formats. Another term has been "tactical media." Still others have used the generic term "internet activism." Perhaps WikiLeaks has other ideas about the direction it wants to take. But where? It is up to WikiLeaks to decide for itself. Up to now, however, we have seen very little by way of an answer, leaving others to raise questions, for example about the legality of WikiLeaks' financial arrangements (*Wall Street Journal*).

We cannot flee the challenge of experimenting with post-representational networks. As ur-blogger Dave Winer wrote about the Apple developers, "it's not that they're ill-intentioned, they're just ill-prepared. More than their users, they live in a Reality Distortion Field, and the people who make the Computer For the Rest of Us have no clue who the rest of us are and what we are doing. But that's okay, there's a solution. Do some research, ask some questions, and listen."

Thesis 11

The widely shared critique of the self-inflicted celebrity cult of Julian Assange invites the formulation of alternatives. Wouldn't it be better to run WikiLeaks as an anonymous collective or "organized network"? Some have expressed the wish to see many websites doing the same work. One group around Daniel Domscheit-Berg, who parted company with Assange in September 2010, is already known to be working on a WikiLeaks clone. What is overlooked in this call for a proliferation of WikiLeaks is the amount of expert knowledge required to run a leak site successfully. Where is the ABC toolkit of WikiLeaks? There is, perhaps paradoxically, much secrecy involved in this way of making-things-public. Simply downloading a WikiLeaks software kit and getting going is not a realistic option. WikiLeaks is not a plug 'n' play blog application like Wordpress, and the word "Wiki" in its name is really misleading, as Wikipedia's Jimmy Wales has been at pains to stress. Contrary to the collaboration philosophy of Wikipedia, WikiLeaks is a closed shop run with the help of an unknown number of faceless volunteers. One is forced to acknowledge that the know-how necessary to run a facility like WikiLeaks is pretty arcane. Documents not only need to be received anonymously, but also to be further anonymized before they are released online. They also need to be "edited" before being dispatched to the servers of international news organizations and trusted, influential "papers of record."

WikiLeaks has built up a lot of trust and confidence over the years. Newcomers will need to go through that same time-consuming process. The principle of WikiLeaks is not to "hack" (into state or corporate networks) but to facilitate insiders based in these large organizations to copy sensitive, confidential data and pass it on to the public domain, while remaining anonymous. If you are aspiring to become a leak node, you'd better start to get acquainted with processes like OPSEC or operations security, a step-by-step plan that "identifies critical information to determine if friendly actions can be observed by adversary intelligence systems, determines if information obtained by adversaries could be interpreted to be useful to them, and then executes selected measures that eliminate or reduce adversary exploitation of friendly critical information" (Wikipedia). The WikiLeaks slogan says: "Courage is contagious." According to experts, people who intend to run a WikiLeaks-type operation need nerves of steel. So before we call for one, ten, many WikiLeaks, let's be clear that those involved run risks. Whistle-blower protection is paramount. Another issue is the protection of people mentioned in the leaks. The Afghan War Logs showed that leaks can also cause "collateral damage." Editing (and eliding) is crucial. Not only OPSEC, also OPETHICS. If publishing is not carried out in a way that is absolutely secure for all concerned, there is a definite risk that the "revolution in journalism" – and politics – unleashed by WikiLeaks will be stopped in its tracks.

Thesis 12

We do not think that taking a stand for or against WikiLeaks is what matters most. WikiLeaks is here to stay, until it either scuttles itself or is destroyed by opposing forces. Our point is rather to (try to) assess and ascertain what WikiLeaks can, could, and maybe even should do, and to help formulate how "we" could relate to and interact with WikiLeaks. Despite all its drawbacks, and against all odds, WikiLeaks has rendered a sterling service to the cause of transparency, democracy, and openness. As the French would say, if something like it did not exist, it would have to be invented. The quantitative – and what looks soon to become the qualitative – turn of information overload is a fact of contemporary life. The glut of disclosable information can only be expected to continue grow, and exponentially so. To organize and interpret this Himalaya of data is a collective challenge that is clearly out there, whether we give it the name "WikiLeaks" or not.

Author's note: This is an extended version of an article first published on the nettime mailing list and elsewhere in August 2010.

Note

1. First published by the authors on December 7, 2010

16
Amy Goodman in conversation with Julian Assange and Slavoj Žižek

The following is a shortened and edited transcript of a conversation between Julian Assange, editor-in-chief of WikiLeaks, and Slavoj Žižek, Slovenian philosopher and cultural theorist. The conversation was moderated by journalist Amy Goodman from the TV news show *Democracy Now!* and sponsored by the Frontline Club. It took place in front of a live audience on July 2, 2011 at the Troxy, London, England.

Amy Goodman: The *National Review* calls Slovenian philosopher Slavoj Žižek "the most dangerous political philosopher in the West," and the *New York Times* says he's "the Elvis of cultural theory." Slavoj Žižek has written over 50 books on philosophy, psychoanalysis, theology, history, and political theory. His latest book, is *Living in the End Times*. We're joined by another man who has published perhaps more than anyone in the world. He wrote a book on the underground computer information age called *Underground: Tales of Hacking, Madness, and Obsession on the Electronic Frontier,* but with the Iraq War Logs, the Afghanistan War Logs, the U.S. government cables, I would say that Julian Assange is perhaps the most widely published person on earth.

I'd like to ask Julian to begin by going back to that moment in 2007, as we talk about the Iraq War Logs, and talk about the significance of them for you and why you've chosen to release this information.

Julian Assange: We make a promise to sources that if they give us material of diplomatic, critical, ethical or historical significance, that is not published and under some sort of threat, we will publish it. And that actually is enough.

Of course, we have a goal with publishing material in general. But it has been my long-term belief that what advances us as a civilization is the entirety of our intellectual record and the entirety of our understanding about what we are going through, what human institutions are actually like and how they actually behave. And if we are to make rational policy decisions, insofar as any decision can be rational, then we have to have information that is drawn from the real world. At the moment, we are severely lacking in the information from the interior of big secretive organizations that have such a role in shaping how civilization evolves and how we all live.

The Iraq War Logs and the historical record

Julian Assange: Getting down into Iraq, that was 400,000 documents, each one written in military speak; each one having a geographic coordinate down often to 10 meters, a death count of civilians, U.S. military troops, Iraqi troops and suspected insurgents. It was the largest and most detailed significant history of a war to have ever been published, probably at all, but definitely during the course of a war. It provided a picture of the everyday squalor of war, from children being killed at roadside blocks to over a thousand people being handed over to the Iraqi police for torture, to the reality of close-air support and how modern military combat is done, linking up with other information such as this video that we discovered of the men surrendering, being attacked.

As an archive of human history, this is a beautiful and horrifying thing, both at the same time. It is the history of the nation of Iraq during its most significant development in the past 20 years. And while we always see newspaper stories revealing and personalizing some individual event or some individual family dying, this provides the broad scope of the entire war and all the individual events, the details of over 104,000 deaths.

We worked together to statistically analyze this with various groups around the world, such as Iraq Body Count, who became a specialist in this area, and lawyers here in the U.K. who represented Iraqi refugees, to pull out the stories of 15,000 Iraqis, labelled as civilians by the U.S. military, who were killed, who were never before reported in the Iraqi, U.S. or world press, even in aggregate saying, "Today a thousand people died." And you just think about that: 15,000 people whose deaths were recorded by the U.S. military but were completely unknown to the rest of the world. That's a very significant thing. And compare that to the 3,000 people who died on 9/11. Imagine the significance for Iraqis.

That is something that we specialize in and that I like to do not just by abstraction or by analogy, but actually by encompassing all of it together, the individual relationship plus the state relationship plus the relationship that has to do with civilization as a whole.

Ideology and denial

Amy Goodman: Slavoj Žižek, what's the importance of WikiLeaks today in the world?

Slavoj Žižek: Let me begin with the significance of the *Collateral Murder* video released by WikiLeaks in spring 2010. You know why this is important? Because of the way ideology functions today. It's not so much that people didn't know about it, but the way those in power manipulate it. We all know dirty things are being done, but you are being informed about this obliquely, in such a way that basically you are able to ignore it.

The same thing happened about two years ago in Serbia. People rationally accept that we did horrible things in Srebrenica, but it was just abstract knowledge. Then, by chance, all the honour to Serb media who published this, they got hold of a video effectively showing a group of Serbs pushing to an edge and shooting a couple of Bosnian prisoners. And the effect was total national shock, although, again, strictly seeing, nobody learned anything new.

So here we should see the significance of WikiLeaks. Many of my friends who are sceptical about it are telling me, "So, what did we really learn? Isn't it clear that every power, in order to function, (generates) collateral damage? You have to have a certain discretion – what you say, what you don't say." Of course, I'm not a utopian. Neither me nor Julian believes in this kind of a pseudo-radical openness – everything should be clear and so on. But, what are we dealing with here?

Of course we all know they are not telling the entire truth, but that is the trick of ideology. Even if they don't lie directly, the implications, the unsaid, is a lie. And you bring this out. You are not so much catching them, as they put it, with their pants down, lying on behalf of what they explicitly say, but precisely on behalf of what they are implying. And I think this is an absolutely crucial mechanism in ideology. It doesn't only matter what you say; it matters what you imply to say.

Are we aware at what an important moment we are living today? On the one hand, as you said, information is crucial, even economically. I claim that one of maybe the main reasons capitalism will get into crisis is intellectual property. In the long term, it simply cannot deal with it. Just take the phenomenon that media are trying to get us enthusiastic (about) clouds like computers getting smaller and smaller, and all is done for you up there in a cloud. But the problem is that clouds are not up there in clouds. They are controlled. This is the danger today. It's no longer this clear distinction: private space/public space. The public space itself gets privatized in a whole series of invisible ways, like the model of it being clouds, which is why this involves new modes of censorship.

(So) you shouldn't be tricked when you say, "But what really did we learn new?" Maybe we learned nothing new, but it's the same as in that beautiful old fairytale, "The Emperor's New Clothes." We may all know that the emperor is naked, but the moment somebody publicly says, "The emperor is naked," everything changes. This is why, even if we learned nothing new – we did learn many new things – but even if nothing is learned, the forum matters. So, don't confuse Julian and his gang with this usual bourgeois heroism, the fight for investigative journalism, free flow and so on. You are doing something much more radical. You are – that's why it aroused such an explosion of resentment – not only violating the rules, disclosing secrets. Let me call it in the old Marxist way: The bourgeois press today has its own way to be transgressive. Its ideology not only controls what one says, but even how one can violate what one is allowed to say. So you are not just violating the rules. You are changing the very rules how we were allowed to violate the rules. This is maybe the most important thing you can do.

Media Collaborations

Amy Goodman: And yet, Julian, even as you were releasing information in all different ways, you then turn to the very gatekeepers who, in some cases, had kept back this information, and you worked with the mainstream media throughout the world in releasing various documents. Talk about that experience and that level of cooperation and what has happened after that.

Julian Assange: If you want to have an impact and you're an organization which is very small, you have to co-opt or leverage the rest of the mainstream press. Under our model of how you make an impact and how you get people to do things that you wouldn't have been otherwise able to do, unless you have an army that can physically go someplace, the only way that you can easily make an impact is push information about the world to many people across the world. The mainstream press has developed expertise on how to do that. It is competition for people's attention. If we had had several billion dollars to spend on advertising across the world and we can get our ads placed, we wouldn't easily be able to have made the same impact that we did. And we don't have that kind of money. Instead, we entered into relationships with now over 80 media organizations across the world, including some very good ones, to increase the impact and translate and push our material into now over 50 different countries endemically. And that has been subverting the filters of the mainstream press.

An interesting phenomenon has developed amongst the journalists who work in these very large organizations that are close to power and negotiate with power at the highest levels. Having read our material and having been forced to go through it to pull out stories, they have become educated and radicalized. And that is an ideological penetration of the truth into all these mainstream media organizations, (which), to some degree, may be one of the lasting legacies over the past year.

Even Fox News, which is much disparaged, is an organization that wants viewers. It cannot do anything without viewers. It will try and push news content. So, for example, with *Collateral Murder*, CNN showed only the first few seconds, and they blanked out all the bullets going to the street and said that they did so out of respect for the families of the people who were killed. Well, there was no blood, there was no gore but they cut out all the most politically salient points. And the families had come forward and said it was very important for us to know that they had already seen it. Fox actually displayed the first killing scene in full. And so, Fox, motivated to grab as great an audience share as possible, took this content and gave it to more people. Afterwards they put in their commentators to talk against it, but I think the truth that we got out of Fox was often stronger than the truth that we got out of CNN, and similarly for many institutions in the media that we think of as liberal.

Slavoj Žižek: With all the respect I have for honest liberals who really believe people should be informed, there are limits in the very mode of how they function. Let me add another example from a totally different domain, but from fiction, cinema, TV series, which I think reproduces the same duality. We have the usual Hollywood left. Thrillers like *The Pelican Brief*, *All the President's Men*, which may appear very critical, you know, like, "Oh, my god, the president himself is corrupted, connected to certain corporations and so on." But nonetheless, this is ideology. Why? Because why do you exit the movie theatre in such high spirits after seeing, *All the President's Men*? Because the message is nonetheless: "Look what a great country we are! An ordinary guy can topple the mightiest men in the world" and so on and so on.

The two faces of censorship

Amy Goodman: Newt Gingrich, the former Speaker of the House in the United States, said, "Julian Assange is engaged in warfare. Information terrorism, which leads to people getting killed, is terrorism. And Julian Assange is engaged in terrorism. He should be treated as an enemy combatant, and WikiLeaks should be closed down permanently and decisively."

Judith Miller, who often wrote or co-wrote articles that appeared on the front page of the *New York Times* alleging weapons of mass destruction without named sources, said, "Julian Assange isn't a good journalist," "didn't care at all about attempting to verify the information [that] he was putting out, or determine whether or not it would hurt anyone."

Joe Biden, the Vice President of the United States, said, "Julian Assange is a high-tech terrorist."

Not to just focus on the U.S., Tom Flanagan, a former aide to the Canadian prime minister, has called for Assange's assassination.

Can you respond to these charges?

Julian Assange: Obviously, the calls are wrong and outrageous. But the social and political event in which they occurred was fascinating. Within a few months, we saw a new McCarthyist hysteria arise within the United States in December last year and January this year (2011). It is quite worrying that a new McCarthyism can come up so quickly.

(However) we should see censorship as a positive sign, and the attempts toward censorship as a sign that the society is not yet completely sewn up, not yet completely fiscalized, but still has some political dimension to it – i.e., what people believe and think and feel and the words that they listen to actually matters. And in the United States most of the time, it doesn't matter what you say. (But) we managed to speak and give information at such volume and of such intensity that people actually were forced to respond, something which is rare. This is one of the first positive symptoms I've seen from the United States in a while, that if you speak at this level, the cage can be rattled a bit, and people can be forced to respond.

In China, the censorship is much more aggressive, which, to me, is a hopeful symptom. At the moment, the Chinese government and public security bureau are actually scared of what people think.

Slavoj Žižek: About two or three months ago, a Chinese government agency passed a law, which formally prohibits in public media all stories which deal with time travel or alternate realities. Literally. I checked it up with my friends in China. The official justification was that history is a great matter. It shouldn't be left to such trifling games and so on. But, of course, it's clear what they really are afraid of: for people to even imagine alternate realities, other possibilities. And to repeat your point, I think this is a good sign. They at least need the prohibition.

Now, (let me) make a more important point to the terrorism (issue). You are a terrorist in the sense that Gandhi was a terrorist. He effectively tried to stop, interrupt the normal functioning of the British state in India. And, of course, you are trying to interrupt the normal, oppressive, functioning of the information circulation.

What is your, under quotation marks, "terrorism" compared to the terrorism which we simply accept, which has to go on day by day so that just things remain the way they are? That's where ideology helps us. When we talk about violent terrorism, we always think about acts which interrupt the normal run of things. But what about violence which has to be here in order for things to function the way they are? So I think, the term "terrorism," is strictly a reaction to a much stronger terrorism which is here. If you are a terrorist, my god, what are then they who accuse you of terrorism?

Bradley Manning, torture and extra-legal spaces

Amy Goodman: I wanted to ask Julian about Bradley Manning. Mike Huckabee, who was a presidential candidate and governor of Arkansas, said that the person who leaked the information to Julian Assange should be tried for treason and executed. He said, "Whoever in our government leaked that information is guilty of treason, and I think anything less than execution is too kind a penalty." Bradley Manning is a young U.S. soldier who was in Iraq, has been held for more than a year, much of that time in solitary confinement in Quantico in Virginia. It was exposed that his treatment was tantamount to torture. P.J. Crowley, the State Department spokesperson, spoke to a group of bloggers at MIT and said his treatment is stupid. For that, he was forced out of the State Department. Bradley Manning was then moved to Fort Leavenworth because of the outcry, but he remains in prison. He remains not tried. What are your comments on him?

Julian Assange: Thanks for asking this question. It is difficult for me to speak in detail about that case, but I can speak about why it is difficult for me to speak about it. Bradley Manning is an alleged source of WikiLeaks who was detained in Baghdad, and then shipped off to Kuwait, where he was held in an extrajudicial circumstance, in a similar manner to which detainees are held in Guantánamo Bay. Eventually, through some creative legal methods, he was brought back to the United States, and he's been in prison now for over a year. He was being kept in Quantico for eight months under extremely adverse conditions. Quantico is not meant for long-term prisoners. People that have been visiting Bradley

Manning say that they were applying those conditions to him because they wanted him to confess that he was involved in a conspiracy to commit espionage against the United States with me. That pressure on Manning appears to have backfired. By all reports, this is a young man of high moral character. And when people of high moral character are pressured in a way that is illegitimate, they become stronger and not weaker. And that seems to have been the case with Bradley Manning, and he has told U.S. authorities, as far as we know, nothing about his involvement.

Now, there has concurrently been a secret grand jury taking place six kilometres from the centre of Washington. That grand jury involves 19 to 23 people selected from that area which has the highest density of government employees anywhere in the United States. There is no judge, there is no defence counsel, and there are four prosecutors. A grand jury combines the executive and the judiciary. They have coercive powers. They can force people to testify.

Slavoj Žižek: I would like to say that the terms that you mentioned, (such as) "extralegal space," "unlawful combatants" and so on are crucial. The paradox is that I think we should read these terms as strictly connected to universal human rights. I have nothing against universal human rights. What I'm opposed to is how the reference to universal human rights is *de facto* used in today's ideological struggles, that in order to sustain support within the space of ruling ideology, you have to construct a space which is no longer the space of the enemy – in the sense, enemy to whom the rules apply by the Geneva Convention – but you have to create what the great American thinker and politician Dick Cheney referred to as the "grey zone." You know, like, we have to do something discretely; don't ask us about it.

What I find really terrifying is that concepts like "unlawful combatants" are becoming legal categories. I'm not a utopian here. I can well imagine a situation where I cannot promise you in advance that I wouldn't torture someone. Let's imagine this ridiculous situation where a bad guy has my young daughter, and then I have in my hands a guy, and I know that that guy knows where my daughter is. Maybe out of despair I would have tortured him. What I am absolutely opposed to is to legalize this. If I do something like this out of despair, it should remain something unacceptable. What I'm afraid of is that this system gets institutionalized.

I had just an exchange in *New York Times* with Alan Dershowitz, who wants legalization of torture. And I read one of his proposals. It's an obscenity. You will have doctors who investigate you and determine you can torture him to that degree. For me, what's horrible and even more obscene, is this normalization of torture, which is why, more than you [Assange] Manning is, for me, the hero, because you have a certain moment of glory. That poor guy did something extraordinary. You know how difficult these decisions are that simple, elementary morality prevails over legal considerations.

If there is a person who deserves the Nobel Peace Prize today, it's Manning, or people like that. I'm not bluffing here. Simple, ordinary people – and I'm not even idealizing him. There are many examples that I know of ordinary people who are not anything special, they are not saints. But all of a sudden, they see something, like probably he, if he is the one, saw all these documents and something told him, "Sorry, I will not be pushed more. I have to do something here."

We, the left, should rehabilitate this – I know it doesn't sound very postmodern or cynical – this idea that there are out there quite ordinary guys who all of a sudden, as if in a miracle, do something wonderful. That's almost, I would say, our only hope today.

Public space and the right to communicate

Amy Goodman: Let's talk about the beginning of WikiLeaks. Tell us about how you founded it, named it, and what your hopes were at the time, and if at this point you have been disappointed by what you've been able to accomplish or amazed by it.

Julian Assange: I am amazed by it, of course. It's an extraordinary time that I have lived through, and to see many of your dreams and ideals come into practice.

That said, I think we're only about a hundredth of the way there, in terms of what we have to release and discover and collect and put into people's heads and solidify in the historical record. And once we start getting that sort of volume and concretize and protect the rights of everyone to communicate with one another, which, to me, is the basic ingredient of civilized life – it is not the right to speak. What does it mean to have the right to speak if you're on the moon and there's no one around? It doesn't mean anything. Rather, the right to speak comes from our right to know. And the two of us together, someone's right to speak and someone's right to know, produce a right to communicate, and so that is the grounding structure for all that we treasure about civilized life. And by "civilized," I don't mean industrialized. I mean people collaborating to not do the dumb thing, to instead learn from previous experiences and learn from each other to pull with each other together in order to get through the life that we live in a less adverse way.

That quest to protect the historical record and enable everyone to be a contributor to the historical record is something that I have been involved in for about 20 years, in one way or another. So that means protecting people who contribute to our shared intellectual record, and it also means protecting publishers and encouraging distribution of historical records to everyone who needs to know about it.

I thought I was pretty cynical and worldly five years ago, and of course I was simply a very young and naive fool. From being inside the centre of the storm, I've learned not just about the structure of government, not just about how power flows in many countries around the world that we've dealt with, but rather how history is shaped and distorted by the media. And I think the distortion by the media of history, of all the things that we should know so we can collaborate together as a civilization, is the worst thing. It is our single greatest impediment to advancement. But it's changing. We are routing around media that is close to power in all sorts of ways. What makes it this time so interesting is that we can wrest the Internet and we can wrest the various communication mechanisms we have with each other into the values of the new generation that has been educated by the Internet, outside of that mainstream media distortion. And all those young people are becoming important within institutions.

I do want to talk about what it means when the most powerful institutions, from the CIA to News Corporation, are all organized using computer programmers, using system administrators, using technical young people. What does that mean when all those technical young people adopt a certain value system, and that they are in an institution where they do not agree with the value system, and yet actually their hands are on the machinery? And it is those technical young people who are the most Internet-educated and have the greatest ability to receive the new values that are being spread and the new information and facts about reality that are being spread outside mainstream media distortions.

Slavoj Žižek: I feel now like that Stalinist commentator. The leader has spoken; I provide the deeper meaning. I would really like to begin with what you said. I have a philosophical term for it. When you moved from the right to speak, right to know, communication and so on, I think that in the history of modern thought, the first one to formulate this was Immanuel Kant in his wonderful distinction between private and public use of reason. This distinction is so wonderful because, for Kant, private use of reason is not that I gather with my friends in the kitchen of my apartment or a pub. No, private use of reason is, for Kant, theological faculty, legal faculty, political sciences, where what you are thinking, debating, developing serves a goal set up in advance by a power structure or ideological structure. For Kant, at a distance from this hierarchic political space – in the sense of establishing power structure – we are the public use of reason.

And why is this so important? I see WikiLeaks as part of a global struggle which doesn't concern only in the narrow sense this domain of (the) right to know and right to information, but even education. You know, – by "you" I mean (the) U.K. citizens here – what horrors are being made now in the U.K. university reform (with) new privatizations and so on. This is (a) concerted attack on the public use of reason. It goes on all around Europe. The name is (the) so-called Bologna education reform (Bologna Process), and the goal is very clear. They say it. It's to make universities more responsive to social life, to social problems. It sounds nice. What it really means is that we should all become experts. As a French minister explained to me in a debate in Paris, for example, cars are burning in Paris suburbs. What we need is psychologists who will tell us how to control the crowd, urbanists who will tell us how to restructure the streets so that the crowd is easy to break up. Like, we should be here as a kind of an ideological or specialist serviceman to resolve problems formulated by others. I think this is the end of intellectual life as we know it.

(And in response to) all those right-wing, anti-immigrant, bullshitters: The greatest asset of Judeo-Christian civilization, which you can even detect in notions of the holy spirit as the community of believers outside established structures, is precisely this independent space of public reason. So I'm saying that if there is something really to defend of the so-called Judeo-Christian legacy, (it is) this idea of democracy not only as this masturbatory right to cast a vote totally isolated, but as public space of debate (and) communication. That should be our answer to all those populist, anti-immigrant politicians.

This is, for me, part of a much larger struggle, especially with the problems today, ecological problems, for example. In China, (recently), even the government admitted the catastrophic ecological consequences of the Three Gorges Dam. You know, it's the greatest artificial lake in the world for 250 miles, 400 kilometres long. Now the government admitted that the problem is this one: that lake is above some subterranean faults, which move when there is an earthquake. So they admitted that the big earthquake three years ago was, if not triggered, definitely rendered much stronger because of this. (Further,) because of this collection of water there, the effects of drought are now much stronger. Because the water is too low, the traffic on the Yellow River, which is the main transportation line venue in China, has practically stopped. All this is the end of public reason.

Truth

Just one more thing. This is not a critical point toward you, but a point to clarify what WikiLeaks can do. We should not fetishize truth as such. We live in times of incredible ideological investments, of times when ideology is very strong precisely because it's not even experienced as ideology.

Let me tell you a story from Israel. Some years ago, one of their historians wrote a more truthful account of how in the independence war in 1948, the Israeli army did burn some Palestinian villages. And first, all the leftist critics had a kind of intellectual orgasm. "Oh, wonderful". And then they got a shock of lifetime, when this guy said, "No, no, no. What I meant, that was necessary to do. We should have done it even more." The line of this guy was: "We should have thrown all the Palestinians from the West Bank, and we wouldn't have any problems today."

What I'm trying to say is that I disagree not with you, but, for example, with another person for whom I have respect: Noam Chomsky. A friend of mine told me that Chomsky told him recently that today all the obscenities are so clear that we don't need any critique of ideology, we just need to tell to people the truth. No, truth must be contextualized in the sense of what it justifies, what it says, what it denies.

So, to conclude, this would have been my point about WikiLeaks: You are not just simply telling the truth. You are telling the truth in a very precise way of confronting explicit lines of justification and rationalization – the public discourse with its implicit presuppositions. It's not just about telling the truth.

If you have listened to someone like (the) American defence minister Donald Rumsfeld: his cynical line about Iraq, when it was discovered that there were no weapons of mass destruction, was, "OK, we were lying, but we were lying in a truthful way with a good intention. We manipulated you, but this was part of a larger strategy." This is maybe the most intelligent, tricky and effective, cynical defence of a liar, when he said, "OK, I'm lying, but so what? I openly confess that I was lying, so, in a way, I'm truthful."

Here we should repeat what the Marx Brothers were saying, and this is what you *de facto* are doing. You know that wonderful phrase from Groucho Marx when he's playing a lawyer defending his client, and he says, "This guy looks as an idiot and acts as an idiot. This shouldn't deceive you. This guy is an idiot." We should say to Donald Rumsfeld, "OK, you admit you act as a liar. But this will not deceive us. You effectively are a cheater and a liar." We should not allow them this space of selling their lies in a cynical way as a deeper truth. This is how ideology today functions.

The Arab Spring

Amy Goodman: Julian Assange, I wanted to ask you about the Arab Spring and about what you see as WikiLeaks' role in what started in Tunisia, on to Egypt, and what we're seeing in Bahrain, Yemen, Syria, Libya. What role did WikiLeaks play?

Julian Assange: I lived in Egypt during 2007, so I'm familiar with the Mubarak regime and the tensions within the Egyptian environment. At that time, you didn't feel, in most areas of Cairo, the presence of the dictatorship. But there were around 20,000 political prisoners of different types in Egypt. Those prisoners could gain no traction in the Western press. And yet others, such as in Iran, we hear about all the time. It's very interesting that Egypt was perceived to be a strong ally of Israel and strong ally of the United States in that region, and so all the human rights abuses and political abuses that were occurring every day in Egypt simply did not get traction.

When we worked on Cablegate, we selected a French partner, *Le Monde*, in order to get the cables into French, because we knew that they would have an effect in Francophone Africa. Also, cables were published in early December by *Al Akhbar* in Arabic from Lebanon, and also *Al-Masry Al-Youm* in Egypt, although material that was published in Egypt back in December, under Mubarak, was pretty soft, because of the threats that that newspaper was under. But *Al-Masry Al-Youm* pushed hard, and a number of critical cables came out about the Tunisian regime and about Ben Ali.

Now, of course, the argument that has often been used is you just tell the people what's going on, and then they'll be angry about it, and they'll oppose it. Actually, the real situation is much more rich and interesting than that. Yes, the demos knows, the population starts to know, and they start to know in a way that's undeniable, and they also start to know that the United States knows, and the United States can't deny what was going on inside Tunisia. And then the elites within the country also know what is going on and know they can't deny it. So, a situation developed where it was impossible for the United States to support the Ben Ali regime. Similarly, it was not possible for France to support Ben Ali or other partners in the same way that they might have been able to.

Our survival strategy for Cablegate was to overwhelm. For example, we have Saudi Arabia propping up a number of states in the Middle East, and in fact invading Bahrain even to do this. But when these states have problems and political crises of their own to deal with, they turn inwards, and they can't be involved in this prop-up. So, Cablegate, as a whole, caused these elites that prop each other up within the Arab-speaking countries, and between Europe and these countries and between the United States and these countries, to have to deal with their own political crises and not spend time giving intelligence briefings on activists or sending in the SAS (Special Air Service) or other support. And activists within Tunisia saw this as an opportunity very quickly.

And that information, a number of WikiLeaks sites, were then immediately banned by the Tunisian government. *Al Akhbar* was banned by the Tunisian government. A hacker attack was launched on *Al Akhbar*. What I believe to be state-based computer hackers came in and wiped out all of *Al Akhbar*'s cable publishing efforts.

The cables about Tunisia were then spread around online, in other forms, translated by a little internet group called Tunileaks, and so presented a number of different facets that no one could deny, that the Ben Ali regime was fundamentally corrupt. It's not that the people there didn't know it before, but it became undeniable to everyone, including the United States. So that gave activists and the army a belief that they could possibly pull it off.

So, all that was making a difference and was stirring things up in Tunisia. And then you had this action by 26-year-old Mohamed Bouazizi who self-immolated on December 16 last year and died on January 4th, (2011). And that taking a sort of intellectual frustration and irritation and hunger for change and undeniability to an emotional, physical act on the street is then what changed the equation.

But there's a more systemic issue that was gradually breeding up, which is you had aging rulers in the Middle East whose regimes, to that extent, were becoming weaker, and that the intellectual management of them was decreasing. You also had the rise of satellite TV and the decision by *Al Jazeera* staff to film and broadcast protest scenes in the street.

Most revolutions kick off in a crowd situation like this one. All the time the regime is saying, "This voice is an outcast voice. This is a minority. This is not popular opinion." And what the media does is censor those voices and prevent people from understanding that actually what the state is (claiming to be) the minority is (actually) the majority. And once people realize that their view is in the majority, they understand they physically have the numbers. And there's no better way to do that than in some kind of public square, which is why Tahrir Square in Egypt was so important, because everyone could see that they had the numbers.

Just before the Berlin Wall fell, everyone thought that it was impossible. It wasn't that people suddenly received a lot of new information. Rather, the information that they received was that a large majority of people had the same beliefs that they had, and people became sure of that, and then you have a sudden switch, a sudden state change, and then you have a revolution. So, people becoming aware of what their beliefs are, what each other's beliefs are, is something that introduces that truly democratic shift.

I've often lambasted bloggers as people who just want to demonstrate peer value conformity and who don't actually do any original news or work. Often we find that all these left-wing bloggers do not descend on a fresh cable from Panama, revealing, as it did today, that the United States has declared the right to board one-third of all ships in the world without any justification. Rather, they read the front page of the *New York Times* and go, "I disagree" or "I agree" or "I agree in my categories." And that is something that has sort of angered me – that hypocrisy of saying that you care about a situation, but not actually doing the work.

Amy Goodman: I wanted to ask, since you talked about what you released today, you also have just sued MasterCard and Visa. Can you explain why you did that?

Julian Assange: On December 6th last year (2010), Visa, MasterCard, PayPal, the Bank of America, Western Union all ganged up together to engage in an economic blockade against WikiLeaks, and that economic blockade has continued since that point. So, it's over six months now we have been suffering from an extrajudicial economic blockade that has occurred without any process whatsoever. In fact, there were two formal investigations into this. One was on January 13 (2011) by Timothy C. Geithner, the Secretary of the Treasury, who found that there was no lawful excuse to conduct an economic blockade against WikiLeaks, and the other was by a Visa subsidiary, who was handling our European payments, Teller, who found that we were not in breach of any of Visa's bylines or regulations. And yet, the blockade continues. It's an extraordinary thing, that we have seen that Visa, MasterCard, Western Union, and so on, are instruments of U.S. foreign policy, not as in a state operating under laws' foreign policy but rather instruments of Washington's patronage network policy. So there was no due process at all.

Over the past few months, we have built up the case against Visa and MasterCard, under European law. Visa and MasterCard together own about 95 percent of the credit card payment industry in Europe, and therefore they have a sort of market dominance, and that means, under European law, they cannot engage in certain actions to unfairly remove people from the market.

Julian Assange's extradition case

Amy Goodman: Speaking of other legal cases, I just wanted to ask you about the extradition case.

Julian Assange : The situation – what has happened to Europe and what has happened to Sweden – is fascinating. I mean, it's something that I have come to learn because I've been embroiled in it. So, we see that the European Union introduced an arrest warrant system in response to 9/11 to have fast extradition of terrorists. And it introduced this concept, or rather recycled a European Union concept of mutual recognition. This is a feel-good phrase, (meaning) that one state in the E.U. mutually recognizes another state in the E.U., and that (has) sunk down into mutual recognition between one court in the E.U. to another court in the E.U. But actually, what it seems to be talking about, if you think about it, given the reality that three people a day are extradited from this country to the rest of Europe, is a mutual recognition of the elite in each country in the E.U. It is a method of being at peace and to not complain about (each other's) behaviour.

The European arrest warrant talks about the mutual recognition of judicial authorities – so, courts – but it has permitted each country to define what they call a judicial authority. And Sweden has chosen to call policemen and prosecutors judicial authorities. The basis of this term being used, in the original introduction of the European arrest warrant, was that you would keep the executive separated from the judicial system, and it was meant to be a natural and neutral party who would request extradition. But it's not.

So, there are many things like this that are going on in that case. I haven't been charged. Is it right to extradite someone to a state where they do not speak the language, where they do not have family, they do not know the lawyers, they do not know the legal system? If you don't even have enough evidence to charge them, you won't even come over, as we have offered many times, to speak to the people concerned?

Previous complaints about these sort of problems have led to some inquires in Sweden. For instance, the biggest Swedish law magazine had a survey on this, and one-third of the lawyers responding said that these (aspects of) the Swedish judicial system truly are a problem. On the other hand, it has also engendered a situation where the Swedish prime minister and the Swedish justice minister have personally attacked me and said that I had been charged, to the Swedish public, when I hadn't been.

So it's one thing to be considerate of differences in the way various justice systems are administered, but it is another to tolerate any difference. And I don't think any difference should be tolerated in the E.U.

The only sustainable approach to scrutinizing the justice systems of the E.U. is the extradition process. It is extradition lawyers and defendants who have the highest motivation to scrutinize the quality of justice in the state that they are being extradited to. And that's a healthy system that permits outside scrutiny. But the European arrest warrant system removes that possibility. It's not open to us to look at any of the facts in the case in the extradition at all. That is completely removed. All we're arguing about is whether the two-page request that was filled out, which literally has a box ticked "rape," is a valid document.

Amy Goodman: We'll end with Slavoj Žižek.

Slavoj Žižek: It's a Kafkaesque paradox to be extradited without even being charged.

Very briefly on the *Palestinian Papers*: I've read them, (and) what made me so depressive is that my liberal Israeli friends were telling me all the time, "Listen, we admit it. We are doing bad thing on the West Bank. But you cannot negotiate if they bomb you." And if you examine Gaza, or the West Bank, there was practically total peace the last five, six, even more years. The image you get from these papers is that there was an incredible compromising spirit from the Palestinian side, offering them practically the entire Jerusalem and so on. And it was clear that it's Israel which is not interested in peace.

Second point, I think it's important that they could no longer deny it. We are in a situation in which we all know, but we can still play the cynical game "Let's act as if we don't know." The function of WikiLeaks, I claim, in concrete ideological, political situations, is to push us to this point where you can (no longer) pretend not to know.

Even if you ignore WikiLeaks, it's changed the entire field. It's, again, even at the level of publishing, spreading informations, you pushed things in a very formal way to a point of undeniability. Nobody can pretend that WikiLeaks didn't happen. The point is not to allow to be renormalized, (but) to remain faithful to it.

Amy Goodman: I wanted to end with this question. Julian, tomorrow, July 3rd, you turn 40 years old. What are you hopes for the future?

Julian Assange: Well, there's the big future one can long for. So that is a future where we are all able to freely communicate our hopes and dreams, factual information about the world with each other, and the historical record is an item that is completely sacrosanct, that would never be changed, never be modified, never be deleted, and that we will steer a course away from Orwell's dictum of "he who controls the present controls the past." So that is something that is my life-long quest to do. And from that, justice flows, because most of us have an instinct for justice, and most of us are reasonably intelligent, and if we can communicate with each other, not be oppressed, and know what's going on, then pretty much the rest falls out. So, that is my big hope. In the short term, it is that my staff stops hassling me to tell me to go.

GUESTS

Julian Assange, editor-in-chief of WikiLeaks.org.
Slavoj Žižek, Slovenian philosopher, psychoanalyst and cultural theorist. He is author of dozens of books, his latest is called *Living in the End Times*.
A recording of the full conversation can be watched at http://www.democracynow.org/blog/2011/7/5/watch_full_video_of_wikileaks_julian_assange_philosopher_slavoj_iek_with_amy_goodman

Index